Praise Israel for Wisdom and Instruction

Supplements

to the

Journal for the Study
of Judaism

Editor

John J. Collins
The Divinity School, Yale University

Associate Editors

Florentino García Martínez
Qumran Institute, University of Groningen

Hindy Najman
Department of Near and Middle Eastern Civilizations, University of Toronto

Advisory Board

J. DUHAIME – A. HILHORST – P.W. VAN DER HORST
A. KLOSTERGAARD PETERSEN – M.A. KNIBB
J.T.A.G.M. VAN RUITEN – J. SIEVERS – G. STEMBERGER
E.J.C. TIGCHELAAR – J. TROMP

VOLUME 131

Praise Israel for Wisdom and Instruction

Essays on Ben Sira and Wisdom, the Letter of Aristeas and the Septuagint

by

Benjamin G. Wright III

BRILL

LEIDEN • BOSTON
2008

This book is printed on acid-free paper.

Library of Congress Cataloging-in-Publication Data

Wright, Benjamin G. (Benjamin Givens)
  Praise Israel for wisdom and instruction : essays on Ben Sira and Wisdom, the Letter of Aristeas and the Septuagint / by Benjamin G. Wright III.
    p. cm. — (Supplements to the Journal for the study of Judaism ; v. 131)
  Includes index.
  ISBN 978-90-04-16908-1 (hardback : alk. paper)
  1. Bible. O.T. Apocrypha. Ecclesiasticus—Criticism, interpretation, etc. 2. Wisdom literature—Criticism, interpretation, etc. 3. Bible. O.T. Greek—Versions—Septuagint. 4. Letter of Aristeas. I. Title. II. Series.

  BS1765.52.W75 2008
  229'.306—dc22

                                                                      2008035030

ISSN 1384-2161
ISBN 978 90 04 16908 1

Copyright 2008 by Koninklijke Brill NV, Leiden, The Netherlands.
Koninklijke Brill NV incorporates the imprints Brill, Hotei Publishing, IDC Publishers, Martinus Nijhoff Publishers and VSP.

PRINTED IN THE NETHERLANDS

CONTENTS

PART TWO

THE *LETTER OF ARISTEAS* AND THE SEPTUAGINT

ACKNOWLEDGMENTS

"Wisdom and Women at Qumran." *DSD* 11 (2004) 240–61. Copyright Koninklijke Brill NV, Leiden, The Netherlands. Used by Permission.

"From Generation to Generation: The Sage as Father in Early Jewish Literature." *Biblical Traditions in Transmission: Essays in Honour of Michael Knibb*. Charlotte Hempel and Judith M. Lieu, eds. JSJSup 111. Leiden: Brill, 2006, 309–32. Copyright Koninklijke Brill NV, Leiden, The Netherlands. Used by Permission.

"The Categories of Rich and Poor in the Qumran Sapiential Literature." *Sapiential Perspectives: Wisdom Literature in Light of the Dead Sea Scrolls*. John J. Collins, Gregory R. Sterling, and Ruth A. Clements, eds. *STDJ* 51. Leiden: Brill, 2004, 101–23. Copyright Koninklijke Brill NV, Leiden, The Netherlands. Used by Permission.

"'Who Has Been Tested by Gold and Found Perfect?' Ben Sira's Discourse of Riches and Poverty." With Claudia V. Camp. *Henoch* 23 (2001) 153–74. Copyright Silvio Zamorani. Used by Permission.

"'Fear the Lord and Honor the Priest': Ben Sira as Defender of the Jerusalem Priesthood." *The Book of Ben Sira in Modern Research*. P.C. Beentjes, ed. BZAW 255. Berlin: Walter de Gruyter, 1997, 189–222. Copyright Walter de Gruyter & Co., Berlin. Used by Permission.

"'Put the Nations in Fear of You': Ben Sira and the Problem of Foreign Rule." First published in *Seminar Papers: Society of Biblical Literature Annual Meeting 1999*. Atlanta: Scholars Press, 77–93.

"Wisdom, Instruction and Social Location in Ben Sira and *1 Enoch*." *Things Revealed: Studies in Early Jewish and Christian Literature in Honor of Michael E. Stone*. Esther G. Chazon, David Satran, and Ruth A. Clements, eds. JSJSup 89. Leiden: Brill, 2004, 105–21. Copyright Koninklijke Brill NV, Leiden, The Netherlands. Used by Permission.

"B. Sanhedrin 100b and Rabbinic Knowledge of Ben Sira." *Treasures of Wisdom. Studies in Ben Sira and the Book of Wisdom. Festschrift M. Gilbert.* N. Calduch-Benages and J. Vermeylen, eds. BETL 143. Leuven: Peeters, 1999, 41–50. Copyright Peeters, Bondgenotenlaan 153, B-3000 Leuven, Belgium. Used by Permission.

"The Jewish Scriptures in Greek: The Septuagint in the Context of Ancient Translation Activity." *Biblical Translation in Context.* Frederick W. Knobloch, ed. Studies and Texts in Jewish History and Culture X. Bethesda, MD: University Press of Maryland, 2002, 3–18. Copyright University Press of Maryland. Used by Permission.

"'*Ebd/Doulos*: Terms and Social Status in the Meeting of Hebrew-Biblical and Hellenistic Roman Culture." *Slavery in Text and Interpretation.* Richard Horsley, Allen Callahan, and Abraham Smith, eds. *Semeia* 83/84. Atlanta: Society of Biblical Literature, 2001, 83–111. Copyright Society of Biblical Literature. Used by permission.

"Access to the Source: Cicero, Ben Sira, The Septuagint and Their Audiences." *JSJ* 34 (2003) 1–27. Copyright Koninklijke Brill NV, Leiden, The Netherlands. Used by Permission.

"The *Letter of Aristeas* and the Reception History of the Septuagint." *BIOSCS* 39 (2006) 47–67. Copyright The International Organization for Septuagint and Cognate Studies. Used by Permission.

"Translation as Scripture: The Septuagint in *Aristeas* and Philo." *Septuagint Research: Issues and Challenges in the Study of the Greek Jewish Scriptures.* Wolfgang Kraus and R. Glenn Wooden, eds. SBLSCS 53. Atlanta: Society of Biblical Literature, 2006, 47–61. Copyright Society of Biblical Literature. Used by permission.

"Three Jewish Ritual Practices in *Aristeas* §§158–160." *Heavenly Tablets: Interpretation, Identity, and Tradition in Ancient Judaism* [FS Betsy Halpern-Amaru]. Lynn LiDonnici and Andrea Lieber, eds. JSJSup 119. Leiden: Brill, 2007, 12–29. Copyright Koninklijke Brill NV, Leiden, The Netherlands. Used by Permission.

INTRODUCTION

In the twenty years since I completed my Ph.D. dissertation, the study of Early Judaism has changed dramatically.[1] Among the most important changes that I have experienced is the breaking down of many traditional scholarly categories and boundaries that had long been taken for granted. Of course, despite the increasing fluidity of these boundaries scholars still specialize—and specialize in ever more narrow and detailed subjects—but it has become increasingly difficult to study the Dead Sea Scrolls, the wisdom literature of ancient Israel, or the Septuagint, for instance, in isolation from the remainder of early Jewish literature and history and without viewing all of these texts through a variety of methodological lenses. In my work thus far, I would like to think that I have crossed over some of those conflicted categories and boundaries and that I have made some modest contribution to the exciting new directions in which the study of Early Judaism is moving. As I looked through my earlier work in order to select the articles for this volume, three general themes stood out around which they coalesce: Translation, Social Location and the Transmission of Tradition. Although I have separated the articles published here into two broad groupings—Ben Sira and Early Jewish Wisdom and the *Letter of Aristeas* and the Septuagint—articles from both groupings fit well into one or more of these themes, representing a little more boundary crossing.

Translation

My earliest scholarly work was a rather technical study of some of the translation techniques used by Jesus Ben Sira's grandson, who translated his book from Hebrew into Greek. While work on the minutiae of translation in the Septuagint/Old Greek corpus has generated important insights into the nature, form and development of the biblical text in antiquity, the study of translation literature from multiple methodological perspectives allows scholars alternative avenues into these texts and

---

[1] The dissertation appeared as *No Small Difference: Sirach's Relationship to Its Hebrew Parent Text* (SBLSCS 26; Atlanta: Scholars Press, 1989).

their worlds. One scholarly field, Translation Studies, has much to offer methodologically to those of us who study early Jewish translations, but has not been much utilized as yet by scholars in our field. In three articles I have explored several of the ways that engaging Translation Studies provides insight into the agendas and work of some ancient translators. In "Access to the Source: Cicero, Ben Sira, The Septuagint and Their Audiences" (chap. 12) I look at the way that the intended audience shaped the type of translation that was produced in each case. With respect to the perplexing problem of the origins of the Septuagint, in "The *Letter of Aristeas* and the Reception History of the Septuagint" (chap. 13), I have tried to show that the relationship between a translation's intended position, its textual-linguistic makeup and the strategies employed by a translator enables us to see why the author of *Aristeas* constructs his story the way he does. "Translation as Scripture: The Septuagint in *Aristeas* and Philo" (chap. 14) covers some of the same ground for *Aristeas*, but I also include the myth of the Septuagint as Philo reports it in order to see how and why the story changes between these two Alexandrian authors.

Translations are also executed in particular social contexts; they do not happen in social or cultural vacuums. The translators of the Septuagint, for example, must have had some models for their undertaking—either to follow or to react against—and their translations, like all translations, are not the simple representation of words in one language by words in another. They have encoded within them the social and cultural biases and assumptions of those who do the work. In that light, "The Jewish Scriptures in Greek: The Septuagint in the Context of Ancient Translation Activity" (chap. 10) takes up what possible models might have existed for the translators of the Pentateuch, who themselves served as exemplars for later biblical translators.[2] In "עבד/ΔΟΥΛΟΣ: Terms and Social Status in the Meeting of Hebrew-Biblical and Hellenistic Roman Culture" (chap. 11), I propose that those who produced the Septuagint/Old Greek translations generally used terms for slaves with the same meanings as they had in the Greco-Roman world in which they lived.

The potential payoff for investigating questions such as these is reflected in some of the scholarly debates taking place today. So, to take

---

[2] On the use of earlier translation by later translators, see E. Tov, "The Impact of the LXX Translation of the Pentateuch on the Translation of the Other Books," *Mélanges Dominique Bathélemy* (P. Cassetti, O. Keel, and A. Schenker, eds.; OBO 38; Freiburg–Göttingen: Editions Universitaires–Vandenhoeck & Ruprecht, 1981) 577–92.

just one example, in contemporary Septuagint scholarship much has been written about the extent to which we can talk about exegesis in the Septuagint and whether we can speak of a theology of the Septuagint. How one thinks about these questions has everything to do with how one assesses the purpose, function and techniques of the translations. If the translators intended their product to be an independent scriptural corpus—as the *Letter of Aristeas* claims about the Septuagint—then one can easily construe those who produced the Septuagint as theologians as much as translators. If, however, one argues, as I do in Chapter 13, that the translators were not intending to produce a stand-alone replacement for the Hebrew texts that they translated, then how one identifies exegesis and thereby theology, in the source text becomes quite a different matter.

Social Location

A second theme, which has taken on increased visibility in scholarship over the last several years, is the desire to locate texts in their social worlds or in the social landscape of Second Temple Judaism. In some cases, such as the sectarian texts from the Dead Sea Scrolls, scholars are lucky enough to have some information about who the producers of a text or texts might have been, but identifying a person or group who composed a text is not the same as trying to *locate* texts in their social worlds.

To locate a text in the social landscape means to find the possible social contexts or institutions in which a text might have originated. So, for example, texts identified as either sapiential or apocalyptic have often been thought to come from very different social and cultural places in ancient Judaism. More and more, however, scholars have identified a host of common interests and concerns in these literatures that draw them closer than has been thought previously.[3] If we view the matter in the light of texts like 4QInstruction from Qumran and the Epistle of James in the New Testament, that incorporate both sapiential and apocalyptic perspectives, the difficulties of sustaining clear boundaries between these kinds of texts are put into relief. So, for more than a decade the Wisdom and Apocalypticism in Early Judaism and Early Christianity

---

[3] See, for example, the work of M.E. Stone, J.Z. Smith, and G.W.E. Nickelsburg.

Group of the SBL has been working to break down the categories of wisdom and apocalypticism and to propose new ways of looking at these texts and their social contexts by using their commonalities as a starting point.[4] As part of this larger conversation, I argue in "'Fear the Lord and Honor the Priest': Ben Sira as Defender of the Jerusalem Priesthood" (chap. 5) that the Wisdom of Ben Sira, on the one side, and *Aramaic Levi* together with sections of *1 Enoch*, on the other, use similar authorizing mechanisms for their respective wisdoms, display priestly interests, and were employed by people who knew each other and were perhaps in conflict with one another. In "Wisdom, Instruction and Social Location in Ben Sira and *1 Enoch*" (chap. 7), I conclude that these works have an instructional character and probably come out of a "school" context. Certainly traditional wisdom qualifies as what we might call instructional or didactic literature. Yet certain material in an apocalyptic text like the *Astronomical Book* (*1 Enoch* 72–82), which sets out extensive calendrical data in fine detail, is hard to describe as anything but instructional, even if the purpose of the teaching in the *Astronomical Book* might be different from the objectives that Ben Sira has for his wisdom instruction.

Texts also reveal clues to their worlds in the ways that they construct social relations and political structures, and in several articles I have tried to make some suggestions about the relationship between what might be generally called ideology—that is, an author's commitments and beliefs about political, social and religious matters—and social location or position. In this volume, "Wisdom and Women at Qumran" (chap. 1) asks about the extent to which the wisdom texts from Qumran help us to learn anything about whether women were present at Qumran or not. In this case, as happens perhaps more often that we might like, we learn less about the social reality behind the texts than about their ideological commitments. The language of riches and poverty constitutes another example of the way that we might gain insight into where some ancient Jewish texts belong as "The Categories of Rich and Poor in the Qumran Sapiential Literature" (chap. 3) and "'Who Has Been Tested by Gold and Found Perfect?' Ben Sira's Discourse of Riches and Poverty" (chap. 4) demonstrate. "'Put the Nations in Fear of You': Ben Sira and

---

[4] For some of the results of the group's work, see B.G. Wright and L.M. Wills, eds., *Conflicted Boundaries in Wisdom and Apocalypticism* (SBLSymS; Atlanta: Society of Biblical Literature, 2005).

the Problem of Foreign Rule" (chap. 6) treats Ben Sira's political ideology, and "Three Jewish Ritual Practices in *Aristeas* §§158–160" (chap. 15) takes up the use of *tefillin* and *mezuzot* as described in the high priest Eleazar's *apologia* for the Jewish Law.

Transmission of Tradition

"Tradition" is a frequently occurring word in scholarly discourse, and since most of our evidence from antiquity is textual, "traditions" stand at the heart of what we study. In a way, every article in this volume deals somehow with the transmission of traditions, whether with the construction and practice of ritual as in Chapter 15 or with the form in which a work might have circulated as in "B. Sanhedrin 100b and Rabbinic Knowledge of Ben Sira" (chap. 9). Of course, in scholarly study a great deal of attention gets paid to how "biblical" tradition gets passed down and interpreted from text to text, but the more we study the way that texts use traditions that they have inherited, the more we find how variegated and fluid they really are.

We can also think about traditions via the ways that ancient authors deployed them to represent and to inculcate their values, beliefs and practices. In this sense, questions of a text's discourse(s) and the belief systems and the behaviors that they authorize can be equally fruitful to examine. At the level of discourse, we might ask how these texts employ rhetorical and discursive strategies to inculcate their values and to legitimate themselves and their ideas. Where do these authors position themselves in the stream of tradition, and how do they receive and treat what they inherit? How do Second Temple authors interpret and put into practice what traditional material has come down to them? Several articles in this collection have such questions as part of their concerns, but two specifically focus on discursive strategies and how early Jewish texts, with particular emphasis on the Wisdom of Ben Sira, employ them. In "From Generation to Generation: The Sage as Father in Early Jewish Literature" (chap. 2), I look at one rhetorical feature of wisdom texts, the wisdom teacher's use of "my son" or "my children," and I argue that rather than an innocent or endearing way of referring to students, this rhetorical device and its various manifestations create a fictive parent-child relationship deliberately invoked by the wisdom teacher to coerce the student into accepting his values. "Ben Sira on the Sage as Exemplar" (chap. 8) treats the way that Ben Sira employs the first person in order to construct an ideal sage who functions as an exemplar for his students to emulate. Both of these rhetorical strategies work to make certain that the traditions contained in these works get transferred effectively from one generation to the other.

As scholars continue to investigate the broad range of questions that the themes of translation, social location and transmission raise, we also find that they also are interrelated, that *their* boundaries are fluid. So, although I have created two broad groupings of articles in this book and have identified three discreet themes, I trust that the reader will find that they inherently bear on one another in central rather than in peripheral ways.

The articles in this collection represent the major thrusts of my work over the last decade or so. All but one have been published previously, and I thank the publishers for their permission to republish them here. Of the previously published articles, the only changes made for this volume have been to make the formatting consistent, to correct any obvious errors from the published versions, and in some cases to update bibliographical items in footnotes that were unpublished at the time of the writing but which have since appeared in print. I have also changed footnote references to the articles published here to make them internal to this book. The one previously published work to which I have made revisions is "'Put the Nations in Fear of You': Ben Sira and the Problem of Foreign Rule" (chap. 6), which originally appeared in the 1999 SBL *Seminar Papers* volume. "Ben Sira on the Sage as Exemplar" (chap. 8) is the only piece that has not been published. It was presented to the Hellenistic Judaism Section at the SBL Annual Meetings in San Diego in 2007, and it has been extensively revised for publication. All abbreviations follow the *SBL Handbook of Style*.[5]

Finally, I have many thanks to express. I cannot name every one of them here, but I owe an enormous debt to all my scholarly colleagues who have engaged my work over the years, in both formal and informal contexts. Some have agreed with me and others have not, but all have contributed to making this work better than it was before my interactions with them. I express my sincerest gratitude to John Collins, Florentino

---

[5] Patrick H. Alexander et al., eds., *SBL Handbook of Style: For Ancient Near Eastern, Biblical, and Early Christian Studies* (Peabody, MA: Hendrickson, 1999) [or go to www.sbl-site.org/publications/publishingwithsbl.aspx].

García Martínez and Hindy Najman for accepting this volume into JSJSup and for facilitating its appearance. The seeds of an idea for the book came in a restaurant conversation with John Collins, and I am glad that he did not let the initial idea disappear into the ether. Hindy Najman has encouraged this project from the start, and it would not have gotten off the ground without her friendly nudging. Thanks to Eva Mroczek at the University of Toronto for proofreading the entire manuscript. I am happy to say thank-you to my colleagues in the Religion Studies Department at Lehigh University who have encouraged my work and particularly to Marian Gaumer, our department coordinator, who has taken many a burden off of me as department chair so that I could do my "real" work. And finally, to my family—my spouse, Mary, and my children, Rachel, Nathan and Kate—who have never known a time when some project (or more likely projects) was not on my desk begging for attention, thanks, however deep and heartfelt, can neither replace the time nor repay the debt of love and support.

PART ONE

BEN SIRA AND EARLY JEWISH WISDOM

CHAPTER ONE

WISDOM AND WOMEN AT QUMRAN

Israelite and Jewish wisdom texts form a tributary of a larger stream of ancient wisdom that flowed through the Near East. The primary concerns of these traditions were with interpersonal relationships, with how to live a good life, with humankind's place in the created order and with the way that the created order works (what we in the modern world leave predominantly to scientists). Furthermore, the wisdom traditions particular to ancient Israel and later to early Judaism drew heavily on the larger common stock of ancient Near Eastern wisdom. Thus, much of the content of Israelite and Jewish wisdom is conventional wisdom instruction that cannot be understood as reflecting any specific social situation or political concern at a particular time. For anyone interested in using these texts to assist in reconstructing the social or political realities of early Judaism, the wisdom texts look potentially fruitful, but they present difficult obstacles.[1] Such problems certainly attend any attempt to use these works to shed some light on the possible presence of women in the Qumran community and the roles envisioned for them there. Can the Qumran wisdom texts tell us anything about whether women were present at the community along the shores of the Dead Sea, and if they were, were they members of the sect? Do they provide any evidence for the attitudes of this particular community toward women?

Wisdom Texts at Qumran

Several kinds of wisdom texts came to light among the scrolls from Qumran.[2] There were, of course, biblical wisdom texts (Proverbs,

---

[1] For examples of some of the problems and payoffs using one particular wisdom text, the Wisdom of Ben Sira, see Chapter 4 "'Who Has Been Tested by Gold and Found Perfect?' Ben Sira's Discourse of Riches and Poverty," Chapter 5, "'Fear the Lord and Honor the Priest': Ben Sira as Defender of the Jerusalem Priesthood," and Chapter 6, "'Put the Nations in Fear of You': Ben Sira and the Problem of Foreign Rule."

[2] For a general discussion of wisdom at Qumran and the manuscripts identified as such, see A. Lange, "Die Weisheit aus Qumran," *The Wisdom Texts from Qumran*

Qohelet, Job and targumim to Job, biblical Psalms), along with a number of apocryphal wisdom texts. The Cave 11 Psalms scroll, for example, contained Hebrew versions of apocryphal Psalms 151, 154, 155, known previously only in Syriac, and the poem on wisdom from Sirach 51. Finally, scholars have identified a number of wisdom texts unknown before the discovery of the scrolls. For texts in this latter group, one of the important problems that affects any discussion of women is whether these works were composed at Qumran or brought there from outside.[3]

The Cave 11 Psalms Scroll (11Q5): Of the eight apocryphal compositions in 11Q5, two display characteristics of our topic that appear quite regularly in Jewish wisdom material and that we will see in other Qumran wisdom texts.[4] In Psalm 154 (11Q5 xviii 1–16) wisdom is personified as a woman. How far the idea of personification can be pushed in this psalm is not clear, however, since the grammatical gender of the noun חכמה is feminine, and therefore feminine pronouns are used when referring to wisdom. In many cases, if one translates the feminine pronoun by English "it" rather than "she," there is no substantial difference in the meaning of the text. In lines 10–11, at least some personification seems intended in the references to "her voice" and to "her song."

Such personification is much more clearly intended in Sir 51:13–19, 30 preserved in 11Q5 xxi 11–17, xxii 1 as an independent poem.[5] This text relates the reciprocal longing and search of a young man and

---

and the Development of Sapiential Thought (C. Hempel, A. Lange, H. Lichtenberger, eds.; BETL 159; Leuven: Leuven University Press/Peeters, 2002) 3–30, especially 5–9 where he discusses a number of texts whose wisdom character is not clear due to the considerably damaged nature of the manuscripts.

[3] See the discussion by C. Newsom in " 'Sectually Explicit' Literature from Qumran," *The Hebrew Bible and Its Interpreters* (W. Propp et al., eds.; Winona Lake, IN: Eisenbrauns, 1990) 167–87. A good general introduction to the more comprehensive issue of wisdom at Qumran can be found in D.J. Harrington, *Wisdom Texts from Qumran* (London and New York: Routledge, 1996). Of those texts categorized as "wisdom" at Qumran, one very fragmentary cave 4 text, 4Q426, that looks to be sapiential may have personified wisdom as a woman. Frag. 1 ii 6 contains the phrase "upright, and he will possess her." There is little to make of this text, however, and I will not discuss it below.

[4] These texts were published in J.A. Sanders, *The Psalms Scroll of Qumran Cave 11* (DJD 4; Oxford: Clarendon Press, 1965).

[5] It is clear that the scroll originally contained the entire wisdom poem from Sirach 51 (not including, of course, the later addition found in Ms A from the Cairo Geniza). Verses 13–19 and verse 30 are the only verses preserved in the manuscript.

wisdom for each other. Although scholars have differing estimations of how erotic the language of this poem really is, there seems no doubt that some eroticism is intended.[6] The beginning sets the tone for the remainder: "When I was a young man before I traveled, I sought her. She came to me in her beauty, and unto the end I will search for her."[7]

Proverbs and Sirach: Both of these important wisdom books share the common personification of wisdom as a woman (see, for example, Prov 1:20–33; 8; Sir 4:11–19; 14:20–15:8; 24). Folly also appears in Proverbs (but not in Ben Sira) in the form of the "strange" woman.[8] Besides these personifications both Proverbs and Ben Sira offer extensive advice on the practicalities of relationships with women. In keeping with one of the key purposes of wisdom literature, to live a good and satisfying life, they contain numerous maxims about how to behave toward women in what appear to be potentially real-life situations. Prov 5:18–19 says about one's wife, "Let your fountain be blessed, and rejoice in the wife of your youth, a lovely deer, a graceful doe. May her breasts satisfy you at all times; may you be intoxicated always by her love. Why should you be intoxicated, my son, by another woman and embrace the bosom of an adulteress?" Ben Sira cautions against unbridled libido when he says, "Do not look intently at a virgin, or you may stumble and incur penalties for her. Do not give yourself to prostitutes, or you may lose your inheritance" (9:5–6). Of course, these works intend this advice to be more than just practical; they also construct the ideal woman/ wife who is to be sought and the loose/"strange" woman who is to be avoided. Passages like Prov 31:10–31 and Sir 26:13–18 offer both practical advice—this is the kind of woman one should seek as a wife—and an ideal construct—this is how "good" women ought to be. I will comment below on the extent to which I think that the Qumran wisdom literature reveals the community's adherence to such ideals.

---

[6] Sanders thought the language to be very erotic. Others, like T. Muraoka ("Sir. 51:13–30: An Erotic Hymn to Wisdom?" *JSJ* 10 [1979] 166–78) and Harrington (*Wisdom Texts*, 29), have seen it less so.

[7] Translation from Harrington, *Wisdom Texts*, 29.

[8] See C. Camp, *The Strange Woman and the Making of the Bible* (JSOTSup 320; Sheffield: Sheffield Academic Press, 2000).

4Q184 and 185:[9] J. Allegro in a 1964 article gave 4Q184 the title "Wiles of the Wicked Woman," a name that has stuck ever since.[10] The text relies heavily on the sections in Proverbs 1–9 that describe Woman Folly, whose intention is to seduce the "simple" and "senseless" (cf. Prov 7:4–27 and 9:13–18).[11] The woman figure personified in 4Q184 represents the anti-type of Woman Wisdom. Where Wisdom is to be sought, the righteous man must clearly shun this woman. Although the language that describes the woman of 4Q184 depends on biblical Proverbs, this woman is not simply a foolish or "strange" woman out to pervert the way of some oblivious man. In this text she has a more sinister character.

S.W. Crawford remarks that the woman of 4Q184 "appears to be more cosmic in scope than the simple 'loose woman' of Proverbs 1–9."[12] She further observes that the descriptions of this woman recall ancient Near Eastern beings associated with death, especially the night demon Lilith.[13] Like these ancient death demons, the woman of 4Q184 is associated with the netherworld where she will lead the unsuspecting (see, for example, 4Q184 10–11, 17). In Crawford's words, "Dame Folly has ceased to be simply human and has become demonic."[14]

M. Aubin construes the "sexually voracious, street-walking, brainwashing seductress" of 4Q184 not as a demonic figure, but as an "othering device" that serves to connect femininity with theological error. The author of the text employs this figure, borrowed from the biblical Proverbs, as the vehicle for making the connection.[15] The woman's

---

[9] Both of these texts were edited by J. Allegro in *Qumran Cave 4.I* (DJD 5; Oxford: Clarendon Press, 1968) 82–7, but his work should not be used separately from the supplements and corrections offered by J. Strugnell in "Notes en marge du volume V des 'Discoveries in the Judaean Desert of Jordan,'" *RevQ* 7 (1970) 163–276.

[10] "The Wiles of the Wicked Woman, a Sapiential Work from Qumran's Fourth Cave," *PEQ* 96 (1964) 53–5.

[11] Although these two chapters contain the major speeches of Folly, those passages that speak of the strange woman are also relevant. See Prov. 2:16–19 and 5:3–14. Also Camp, *The Strange Woman*.

[12] S.W. Crawford, "Lady Wisdom and Dame Folly at Qumran," *DSD* 5 (1998) 360.

[13] Crawford, "Lady Wisdom," 360. See also J. M. Baumgarten, "On the Nature of the Seductress in 4Q184," *RevQ* 15 (1991) 136–43.

[14] Crawford, "Lady Wisdom," 361.

[15] "'She is the beginning of all ways of perversity': Femininity and Metaphor in 4Q184," *Women in Judaism: A Multidisciplinary Journal* 2:2 (2001) 22 [www.utoronto.ca/wjudaism/index.html]. Aubin calls the poet of 4Q184 "orthodox." While the poet almost certainly would have thought of himself as "orthodox," Aubin's use of the term seems anachronistic in this context.

dangerous and deviant sexuality expresses a powerful symbol of the theologically pernicious other against which the male poet/author warns his unsuspecting charge. Such voracious error can engulf the simple and upright before they become aware of what is happening.[16]

The elevation, so to speak, of Woman Folly from the human seductress of Proverbs to the demonic figure (Crawford) or perverse heretic (Aubin) of 4Q184 suggests a cosmic dualism between good (in the form of Woman Wisdom?) and evil or a theological/social dualism between the theologically correct "us" and the error-laden other, both important notions in Qumran sectarian writings. But is the text sectarian? R.D. Moore enumerates a number of parallels between 4Q184 and the doctrine of the Two Spirits (1QS 3–4). While he recognizes the similarities between the two texts, he stops short of claiming that 4Q184 is sectarian; he rather seems to assume that it is. His comments about 4Q184 12 are typical of his approach: "Even though a *concrete relationship* [between 1QS and 4Q184] *is not certain*, we are reminded once again of the *conceptual kinship* [emphases mine] between our poem and 'The Two Spirits.'"[17]

One might also point to the character of the seductress's victims as an indication of the sectarian origin of this work. Whereas in Proverbs Folly accosts the "simple" and "senseless," the siren of 4Q184 singles out a "just" man, a "noble" man, the "upright" (ישר) and the "righteous chosen ones" (line 14). She also lures "those who walk uprightly" (הולכי ישר, line 15) and "the humble" (line 16). All these men are clearly following God's path, unlike the intended victims of Proverbs who are regarded as foolish, likely to be taken in by Folly, and who serve as negative examples for the righteous.

Why the difference in the character of the victims? One answer might be that if the text is sectarian, all these adjectives describe the Qumran community.[18] Perhaps, however, the author of 4Q184 has

---

[16] Aubin, "Femininity and Metaphor," 22.

[17] R.D. Moore, "Personification of the Seduction of Evil: 'The Wiles of the Wicked Woman,'" *RevQ* 10 (1979–81) 517.

[18] J.C.R. de Roo argues precisely this way, criticizing Harrington for overlooking the nature of the victims ("Is 4Q525 a Qumran Sectarian Document?" *The Scrolls and the Scriptures: Qumran Fifty Years After* [S.E. Porter and C.A. Evans, eds.; Roehampton Institute London Papers 3; JSPSup 26; Sheffield: Sheffield Academic Press, 1997] 352–53). She claims, "It is typical for Qumran only to instruct, warn, and reprove those who belong to the righteous ones, that is, to the people of their community." What she has overlooked is that 4Q184 may well be more inclusive as I will attempt to show.

read the "simple" and "senseless," those sought by Folly in Prov. 7:7 and 9:16, not as synonyms, but as antonyms. His exegesis of Proverbs understands the "simple" to be those treading God's path, not those who are fools.[19] Certainly the context of 9:14–16 allows such a reading. Speaking of Folly, the sage of Proverbs says, "She sits at the door of her house, on a seat at the high places of the town, calling to those who pass by, who are going straight (המישרים) on their way, 'You who are simple, turn in here!' And to those without sense she says...." Those "who are going straight" or perhaps "walking uprightly" (cf. 4Q184 15) are identified by the author of 4Q184 with the "simple," while the "senseless" are another group altogether. So 4Q184 understands Folly as indiscriminate in her call; she is after everyone. That same approach may, in fact, be found in 4Q184 at the end of the poem where the seductress's victims are the inclusive "sons of men." Apparently, even for 4Q184, all can fall prey to Folly's wiles.

One could marshal two further parallels with Qumran sectarian texts. In line 2 the term יחד appears, a common denotation of the Qumran group in sectarian literature. Here, however, as Moore rightly notes, the word seems to be used as an adverb.[20] In most cases, however, when the word refers to the Qumran community in sectarian literature it has the definite article attached (see, for example, 1QS 1:1, 16; 5:3, 7, 16; 6:3, 10, 14; 1QSa i 27; ii 11). The second parallel is the use of the word חלקות (line 17), usually translated "smooth words" (García Martínez) or "flatteries" (Harrington).[21] This word, as is well known, often designates in sectarian literature one of the groups that the Qumran community saw as an opponent, "the seekers after smooth things," commonly identified with the Pharisees. In 4Q184, though, the word indicates the speech that the seductress uses to seduce people. Prov 2:16 and 7:5 also use the term in the same context as 4Q184 to describe what the "strange" woman says to lure the unwitting.

These arguments, however, even when demonstrating a similarity between 4Q184 and some sectarian texts, do not constitute unequivocal indicators of a Qumran origin for the text. These same similarities have

---

[19] Although the Hebrew word פתאים does not occur in 4Q184 to refer to the righteous, it does apparently in 4Q185 1–2 i 13–14: "And now please hear me, my people (עמי)! Pay attention, simple ones (פתאים)!"

[20] Moore, "Personification," 511–12. But he still understands the word as a self-reference by the Qumran sect.

[21] F. García Martínez, *The Dead Sea Scrolls Translated* (2nd ed.; Leiden/Grand Rapids, MI: Brill/Eerdmans, 1996) 380; Harrington, *Wisdom Texts*, 32.

prompted Harrington to write, "If this text is not clearly 'sectarian,' at least its content and terminology would have appealed to and have been readily appropriated by the Qumran sectarians."[22] We probably have to be satisfied with that characterization.

Some have seen in this text, behind the demonic/heretical figure of Dame Folly, an allegorical reflection of group polemics. J. Maier, in his *Encyclopedia of the Dead Sea Scrolls* article on this text,[23] maintains that the references in 1:1–2 about "words" and "nonsense" and the misleading advice of 1:14–15 indicate controversy between the group represented by the text and some adversarial group. Much depends on whether one understands the references to the "righteous chosen ones" (line 14) and "the humble" (line 16) as indicating a specific community rather than the more universal "sons of men" mentioned in line 17. I do not think, however, that the text unequivocally supports such an interpretation. I agree with Harrington that other interpretations of the text that allegorically represent Woman Folly as Rome or Simon Maccabeus have "no textual foundation at all."[24] Aubin gets it essentially right, I think, when she says, "When this text is read in its full potential as an heir to Jewish wisdom traditions, the question of a concrete historical referent for the Seductress is eclipsed by others concerning the complexity of the poem's structure, its relationship to Proverbs, and its rewriting of Folly as a figure uniting themes of apostasy and adultery."[25]

4Q185 1 and 2 preserve two fragmentary columns of a previously unknown sapiential work.[26] In it a sage both warns and admonishes his "sons," who are also called "simple."[27] The first column contains warnings about God's judgment and the frailty of human existence. 1–2 i 14 preserves the sage's admonition to "Draw wisdom from the power of God," which he connects to God's mighty acts during the

---

[22] *Wisdom Texts*, 34. Aubin ("Femininity and Metaphor," 3, 10) makes the same point.

[23] "Wiles of the Wicked Woman," *Encyclopedia of the Dead Sea Scrolls* (L.H. Schiffman and J.C. VanderKam, eds.; 2 vols.; New York: Oxford, 2000) 2.976.

[24] Harrington, *Wisdom Texts*, 33.

[25] Aubin, "Femininity and Metaphor," 11.

[26] Allegro published this text in DJD 5. As with 4Q184, one must consult Strugnell, "Notes en marge." In addition see H. Lichtenberger, "Eine weisheitliche Lahnrede in den Qumranfunden (4Q185)," *Qumrân: Sa piété, sa théologie et son milieu* (M. Delcor, ed.; BETL 46; Paris: Duculot, 1978) 151–62.

[27] It is also notable that this text also uses the inclusive (at least male-intended inclusive) "sons of man" (בני אדם) in line 9.

Exodus. In column ii 11–14, we find what looks to be the language
of the personification of wisdom much like that of Proverbs and Ben
Sira. The main difference between 4Q185 and these other two wisdom
texts, as T. Tobin observes, is that the extant portion of the Qumran
text preserves no speeches of wisdom like those that we find in both
Proverbs and Ben Sira.[28] Furthermore, the feminine wisdom of this
column does not actively seek out human beings, but God gives her to
human beings as a possession.[29] Column ii also makes reference to "the
path which he decreed to Isaac," and it may have contained a reference
to commandments.[30] Such language suggests that this work may have
equated Wisdom with Torah.

4Q185 is probably not a Qumran composition. A. Lange concludes
that the text's use of the tetragrammaton and אלהים offers the most
compelling reason. "Der freie Gebrauch des Tetragramms in 1–2 II₃
und die für essenische Texte untypische Verwendung von אלהים in
1–2 I₁₄; III₁₃ zeigen, daß es sich um ein mindestens vor 150 v. Chr.
anzusetzendes nichtessenisches Werk handelt."[31] Tobin proposes that
the personification of חכמה as a woman probably indicates a non-
sectarian origin for the text as well, since "[i]n the sectarian texts,
'wisdom' most often refers to the providence with which God created
and sustains the world (e.g., 1QH 1:7, 14–15, 19–20; 9:17; 10:2) or is
connected with the mysteries revealed to the Qumran sectarians (e.g.,
1QS 4:3, 18, 22)."[32] Tobin also notes, however, that two particular ideas
found in 4Q185 would have resonated with the Qumran community

---

[28] T.H. Tobin, "4Q185 and Jewish Wisdom Literature," *Of Scribes and Scrolls: Studies on the Hebrew Bible, Intertestamental Judaism, and Christian Origins* (H.W. Attridge, J.J. Collins, T.H. Tobin, S.J., eds.; Resources in Religion 5; Lanham/New York/London: University Press of America, 1990) 148.

[29] Crawford compares wisdom in this column to the "non-personified wisdom figure of Job 28, where Wisdom is described as established by God, but is not active" ("Lady Wisdom," 363).

[30] "The way that he commanded to Jacob" is reconstructed in the parallel clause by F. García Martínez and E.J.C. Tigchelaar in *The Dead Sea Scrolls Study Edition* (2 vols.; Leiden; Brill, 1997) 1.379.

[31] Lange, "Weisheit," 11. Tobin argues that the use of the tetragrammaton points to the text's non-sectarian origin ("4Q185," 148).

[32] Tobin, "4Q185," 149. Tobin also offers a third reason, which I do not find as convincing. He argues that 4Q370, "An Admonition of the Flood," which was probably not composed at Qumran, displays the closest parallels with 4Q185. C. Newsom has argued for a literary relationship between the two texts, although the precise nature of that relationship is not certain ("4Q370: An Admonition Based on the Flood," *RevQ* 13 [1988] 23–43). Tobin concludes (149–50), "Because the Qumran text to which 4Q185 has the closest affinities was probably not composed at Qumran, this is an additional

and may account for its presence in the Qumran collection. The first is the use of גבורה in the sense of "mighty wisdom," which is found in 1QS and 1QH (1QS 4.3; 10:16; 1QH 12:13) with this meaning, but not in the biblical wisdom books. The second is the role that 4Q185 gives to angels in the judgment of human beings. This theme is, of course, not found in either Proverbs or Ben Sira.[33]

4Q525: This wisdom text from Qumran is best known primarily for its list of five beatitudes or, more properly, macarisms, in frag. 2 ii.[34] In fact, it is a text of 50 fragments, several of which are extensive enough to give a good sense of the content of the work. The extant portions of 4Q525 begin in the third person and then later shift to the second person singular, a usual form of address in other sapiential works. The text consists primarily of admonitions, especially on seeking wisdom, which is portrayed here, as elsewhere, as a woman. In many ways it looks a lot like other traditional Jewish wisdom books. For example, frag. 14 treats, among other things, the proper use of speech, especially care in speaking (cf. Sir 19.4–17). Harrington is almost certainly correct when he argues that the shift in person and the inclusion of standard wisdom fare indicate that at least these parts of the text were intended for the training of young sages.[35] Unlike Proverbs and Ben Sira, however, 4Q525 might display an interest in future (eschatological?) reward and punishment. Unfortunately, the smaller fragments where these ideas might appear are far from clear, but future rewards seem to be enumerated for those who follow Wisdom and punishments for those who abandon her. In frag 24 ii 4–5 "my house is a house of […] 5 […] my house dwells in […] 6 forever" may indicate some future recompense (perhaps based on an exegesis of Psalm 23). References to "eternal curse," the "flames of death" (frag. 15) and "the pit" (frag. 23), for instance, may indicate

---

indication that 4Q185 too was not composed at Qumran." The literary connection would only be decisive if 4Q370 were dependent on 4Q185, however.

[33] Tobin, "4Q185," 150.

[34] É. Puech published the text in *Qumrân Grotte 4.XVIII* (DJD 25; Oxford: Clarendon Press, 1998) 115–78. The extant text only contains four occurrences of אשרי; the first is reconstructed by Puech. On the beatitudes in 4Q525, see Puech, "4Q525 et les péricopes des béatitudes en Ben Sira et Matthieu," *RB* 98 (1991) 80–106 and "The Collection of Beatitudes in Hebrew and in Greek (4Q525 and Mt 5,3–12)," *Early Christianity in Context. Monuments and Documents* (F. Manns and E. Alliata, eds.; Studium Biblicum Franciscanum, Collectio Maior 38; Jerusalem: Franciscan Printing Press, 1993) 353–68.

[35] Harrington, *Wisdom Texts*, 68.

some punishment awaiting the wicked. At the very least, they suggest similarities with a work like 4Q184.[36]

The personification of Wisdom as a woman in this document may reflect the close association of Wisdom and the Law in some Jewish literature (cf. Sirach 24). In fact, since the Hebrew word תורה, like חכמה, is feminine in gender, the feminine pronouns may actually refer to both wisdom and the law in this work. For instance, the macarism beginning at frag 2 ii 3 says, "Blessed is the person who attains wisdom and walks in the law of the Most High (בתורת עליון), and sets his heart to her ways, and is constrained by her discipline and always delights in her admonishments" (lines 3–4). The latter part of the passage is consistent with what other sapiential texts say about one's attitude toward Wisdom (cf. for example, Sir 4:17–19; 6:23–31). Thus, I understand the pronouns as referring primarily to Wisdom, who is more valuable than any precious metal or stone (frag. 2 iii).

Without doubt 4Q525 transmits traditional and rather conventional wisdom material, but could it be a sectarian composition? J.C.R. de Roo has argued that, despite what she calls "a striking resemblance between 4Q525 and traditional Jewish wisdom books such as Proverbs and Ben Sira," 4Q525 is a sectarian text.[37] In support of her case she cites an impressive array of vocabulary and thematic parallels between 4Q525 and several sectarian works. What she fails to treat, however, is the date of the work, and the possibility that 4Q525 has influenced these sectarian texts.

É. Puech, the text's editor, also recognizes similarities between 4Q525 and sectarian literature, especially a tantalizing text in fragments 11–12, but he does not believe 4Q525 to be a sectarian document. It is more likely that 4Q525 has influenced those sectarian works. In that vein, he notes that frags. 11–12 1–2 parallel 1QS iv 7–8, which he thinks has most probably taken the material from 4Q525. He says about these lines, "En effet les frgs 11–12 1–2 semblent avoir des prolongements en 1QS iv 7–8 qui paraissent reprendre ces lignes en les développant."[38] Concerning the date of the work he says, "Si, comme il semble, ce texte de sagesse (4Q525) a pu servir de creuset où ont puisé les différentes *Règles* de la communauté essénienne, il faudrait envisager une composition vers

---

[36] For eschatology in 4Q525, see G.J. Brooke, "The Wisdom of Matthew's Beatitudes (4QBeat and Mt. 5:3–12)," *ScrB* 19 (1988–89) 35–41.

[37] de Roo, "Is 4Q525 a Qumran Sectarian Document?" 345.

[38] Puech, DJD 25, 119.

le milieu du IIe siècle avant J.-C., soit grosso modo entre 160 et 140."[39] If Puech is correct, 4Q525 influenced the Qumran authors, and it is most likely non-Qumranic.

4QInstruction (4Q415, 416, 417, 418, 423): Edited by J. Strugnell and D.J. Harrington in DJD 34, 4QInstruction or מוסר למבין (another copy is found in 1Q26) is the most extensive sapiential text found at Qumran. Eight copies were found in Caves 1 and 4.[40] Despite the fact that the remains of all the copies are very fragmentary, Strugnell and Harrington conclude that 4Q418 "was probably quite as long as the longest Qumran manuscripts." They further argue that the large number of copies indicates that this text "was treated as important, authoritative, perhaps even 'canonical', among the Qumran community."[41]

This work, formerly known as Sapiential Work A, takes the form of instruction from an older sage to a younger one, who is called מבין, which Strugnell and Harrington render "the maven." The large margin before the text in 4Q416 1 may indicate that this column began the work. 4QInstruction thus started with a rather extensive section dealing with cosmology and eschatology, especially with matters of God's judgment of the wicked. This section is characterized by use of the third person without any of the second person instruction found later. In fact, the instruction given to the maven should probably be understood as providing the guidelines for avoiding the impending judgment.

Furthermore, 4QInstruction refers repeatedly to "the mystery that is to come" (רז נהיה), a phrase that also occurs in 1QS 11:3–4 and the Book of the Mysteries (1Q27, 4Q299, 300).[42] Although the text does not reveal its content, the mystery has an esoteric quality about it.

---

[39] Ibid.

[40] *Qumran Cave 4.XXIV* (DJD 34; Oxford: Clarendon Press, 1999). On the number of copies, overlaps between the manuscripts, and other codicological matters, see pp. 1–40. A number of studies of 4QInstruction antedate the appearance of Strugnell and Harrington's DJD edition. Although I will refer to several of them in the course of my discussion of this text, I take the new DJD volume as the most definitive yet on this text. Strugnell and Harrington list the most important of these earlier studies in DJD 34, 37–40. See more recently, however, E.J.C. Tigchelaar, *To Increase Learning for the Understanding Ones: Reading and Reconstructing the Fragmentary Early Jewish Sapiential Text 4QInstruction* (STDJ 44; Leiden: Brill, 2001).

[41] Strugnell and Harrington, DJD 34, 2.

[42] Strugnell and Harrington note that the Book of the Mysteries, although certainly a separate document from 4QInstruction, has a lexicon "quite close to that of 4Q415ff.—indeed, it is appropriate to ask whether 4Q415ff. knew the Book of Mysteries or was known to it" (ibid.).

The maven is to "study" it, "gaze upon" it, "understand" it, and these activities will bring reward to the maven. Harrington concludes on the basis of the noun phrases that parallel the phrase "mystery that is to come" in 4QInstruction that the mystery concerns creation, ethics and eschatology.[43]

4QInstruction's emphasis on mystery and eschatological judgment sets it apart from a work like Ben Sira, whose emphasis is on the practicalities of life, creation, Torah and the history of Israel.[44] That is not to say, however, that 4QInstruction is not practical. In fact, the paranesis given to the maven is eminently practical and much like that of Ben Sira. A good portion of the text offers advice on various family relationships and financial affairs, which frequently depends on the traditions found in the Torah. In this sense 4QInstruction is like most other wisdom literature. The advice given to the maven assumes that he is immersed in the realities of daily life—providing surety for loans, honoring parents, getting married and having a family. The maven is not one who has withdrawn from social life and relationships, and he is certainly not a member of a celibate, indeed isolationist, communal society like the one so often pictured for Qumran.

Both the assumption of the work that the maven participates in the larger social world, on the one hand, and the language of 4QInstruction, on the other, raise the question of its origins. The work contains some language found in other Qumran works, and

> it contains also many eschatological and cosmological passages anticipatory of what we find in normative Qumran texts such as *Serekh ha-Yahad* and the *Hodayot*...Moreover, considered sociologically 4Q415ff. does not reflect a specific sect or closed community like that of Qumran, nor an earlier quasi-sectarian group. Indeed, it is dubious whether one should

---

[43] D.J. Harrington, "Two Early Jewish Approaches to Wisdom: Sirach and Qumran Sapiential Work A," *SBL 1996 Seminar Papers* (Atlanta: SBL, 1996) 130. See also on the "mystery that is to come" and its content, T. Elgvin, "Wisdom, Revelation, and Eschatology in an Early Essene Writing," *SBL Seminar Papers 1995* (E.H. Lovering, ed.; Atlanta: Scholars Press, 1995) 440–63; idem, "Early Essene Eschatology: Judgment and Salvation according to *Sapiential Work A*," *Current Research and Technological Developments* (D.W. Parry and S.D. Ricks, eds.; STDJ 20; Leiden: E.J. Brill, 1996) 126–65; idem, "The Mystery to Come: Early Essene Theology of Revelation," *Qumran Between the Old and New Testaments* (F.H. Cryer and T.L. Thompson, eds.; JSOTSup 290; Sheffield: Sheffield Academic Press, 1998) 113–50; D.J. Harrington, "The *Raz Nihyeh* in a Qumran Wisdom Text (1Q26, 4Q415–418, 4Q423)," *Hommage à Józef T. Milik, RevQ* 17 (1996) 549–53; idem, *Wisdom Texts from Qumran*, chap. 6.

[44] Harrington, "Two Early Jewish Approaches," 130.

talk of communities or groups at all in looking for the background of
this work.

The work is addressed, then, not to any closed community like that at
Qumran, nor to any earlier and theologically cognate population, but to
a typical junior sage (מבין) who receives advice appropriate for his needs
in every stage of his life (e.g. the priesthood, administration, marriage)
and in various professions.[45]

Unlike the other Qumran wisdom texts that I have sketched above,
4QInstruction does not, at least in any of its extant fragments, personify
wisdom or folly as a woman. Whatever material it contains about
women falls into the category of practical advice.

Quite a number of the fragments in 4Q415–418, 423 refer or allude
to women. Much of the advice is based on biblical texts. 4Q416 2 iii
20–iv 6, for example, derives from a transparent exegesis of Gen 2:24
and 3:16.

> And if you are poor as […] 20 without statute. You have taken a wife in
> your poverty; take her offspring in your lowly estate […] 21 from the mys-
> tery that is to be/come while you keep company together. Walk together
> with the helpmeet of your flesh […] iv 1 his father and his mother […]
> 2 you He has set in authority over her […] her father 3 He has not set
> in authority over her; from her mother He has separated her and toward
> you shall be [her desire and she will become] 4 for you one flesh. Your
> daughter to another he will separate and your sons […] 5 And you will
> be made into a unity with the wife of your bosom for she is flesh of your
> nakedness; 6 and the one who claims authority over her apart from you
> has displaced the boundary of his life.[46]

4Q416 2 iv 8–10 takes up the matter of a man's right to annul the vow
of his wife or daughter as authorized in Num 30:3–15, a biblical text that
receives attention in other Qumran texts (see also Temple Scroll [11Q19]
53:16–54:3 and Damascus Document [CD] 16:10-12). One matter of
note here is that 4QInstruction appears to take a dim view of women
making vows and grants the husband/father an absolute right to annul
a woman's vow. The Damascus Document, on the other hand, qualifies
such annulment by the addition of "if it violates the covenant."

In one remarkable passage, 4Q415 2 ii, the sage of 4QInstruction
addresses a woman. Harrington characterizes this fragment as "highly

---

[45] Strugnell and Harrington, DJD 34, 36.
[46] Harrington, *Wisdom Texts*, 44.

unusual,"[47] which seems a bit of an understatement, since I know of no other Jewish wisdom text in which the addressee is a woman. Unfortunately the fragment is not well preserved and only phrases remain, but the extant text indicates that the advice to the woman was pretty conventional. The column begins with "honor him like your father," presumably a reference to the woman's father-in-law.[48] Line 3 is evidently the end of some kind of warning to the woman, but unfortunately the text of the actual warning does not survive. The remaining text reads, "lest you neglect [his?] holy covenant"—a possible reference to the marriage bond. Lines 5 and 7 contain two feminine possessives, "your soul" and "your covenant." The phrase "praise [in the m]outh of all men" (תהלה] [פי כ׳ל אנשים) in line 8 most likely indicates the results of the woman's appropriate behavior. Perhaps Proverbs 31 forms one of the bases of the entire section. Strugnell and Harrington suggest that the phrases used in this fragment most likely address the wife of the maven.[49] Another possibility, however, might be to imagine the presence of wise women or even women sages in Israel during this period, as C. Camp has done for the Persian period (see below).

Overall, the man-woman relationship in 4QInstruction, whether it be with a wife or daughter, is hierarchically conceived and essentially based on those biblical texts that can be read in that fashion. The husband has authority over his wife and the father over his daughter. Yet one can observe two interesting features of this text. First, within the context of such a hierarchy, 4QInstruction teaches that the husband should treat his wife with honor and respect. The sage enjoins the maven to "walk with the helpmeet of your flesh" (4Q416 2 iii 21); he further advises the husband not to "treat with contempt the vessel (כלי) of your bosom" (4Q416 2 ii 21). Strugnell and Harrington remark that this latter passage represents the sage's attempt to extend the honoring of one's father and mother to one's wife.[50] Second, there are apparently no "bad" women talked about in 4QInstruction like those in Proverbs and Ben Sira. While the sage admonishes the maven to hold his spouse in high regard and he encourages the woman addressee of 4Q415 2 ii to act properly, the extant fragments do not seem to preserve warnings

---

[47] Ibid., 57.
[48] Strugnell and Harrington, DJD 34, 48.
[49] Ibid.
[50] Ibid., 109. This text also bears on the interpretation of difficult use of σκεῦος in 1 Thess 4:4. See the Excursus, 109–10.

against loose or "strange" women. This absence could simply be the accident of what has survived or it could be that the work contained no such warnings. If it is the latter, what should we make of it?[51]

WISDOM AND WOMEN AT QUMRAN

As E. Schuller has noted, despite the rather dramatic rise in the number of books and articles on women in ancient Judaism and Christianity, "the one area for which there is still virtually no bibliography is study about women in the type(s) of Judaism which produced the Dead Sea Scrolls."[52] Yet, perhaps as a recognition of the inherent difficulty of trying to tease social realities out of wisdom literature, the article in which Schuller made the above remark contains almost no treatment of the sapiential texts discovered at Qumran—only a brief mention of Sir 51:13–30 and 4Q184. In a second article on women in the scrolls, Schuller devotes a bit more attention to the wisdom texts, but here, too, she makes little of them. The following paragraph seems to encapsulate her approach to these texts.

> While these manuscripts are of great interest in and of themselves and as evidence of the ongoing productive wisdom tradition, it is less clear how relevant they are to a reconstruction of the role of women in associations that produced the rules and legal materials we examined earlier (that is, those from Qumran). Even the main large work, "Instruction A," does not display any knowledge of the organization of the *yaḥad*, its particular piety concerns, or sectarian vocabulary and theology; in fact, this composition seems to predate the Qumran community. Although the presence of six copies (1Q26, 4Q415–18, 4Q423), all in a Herodian hand, indicates the ongoing popularity of this work at Qumran perhaps it should be read more in the same way that we read Proverbs or Ben Sira than as a direct source of information about the sect and its views of women.[53]

---

[51] Strugnell and Harrington have one fragment that might run counter to this observation, 4Q418 243 2. They note, however, that the piece "is much shrunken and well on its way to becoming glue." They read line two as "*and a woman abounding* in folly" [italics theirs] (ibid., 451).

[52] E. Schuller, "Evidence for Women in the Community of the Dead Sea Scrolls," *Voluntary Associations in the Graeco-Roman World* (J.S. Kloppenborg and S.G. Wilson, eds.; London and New York: Routledge, 1996) 252.

[53] E. Schuller, "Women in the Dead Sea Scrolls," *The Dead Sea Scrolls After Fifty Years. A Comprehensive Assessment* (P.W. Flint and J.C. VanderKam, eds.; Leiden: Brill, 1999) 2.138.

I absolutely agree with Schuller concerning the difficulty of handling these texts. In fact, one could go a step further than she has and note that there does not seem to be a single wisdom text found at Qumran that deals with women that was composed by the Qumran community itself. That would seem to be a damning realization for anyone trying to find ways into the problem of women and the Qumran community. But I do not think that all is completely lost. In what follows I will make some summary observations and raise a few questions.

Essentially two issues should concern us at this juncture. Can we make anything out of the personifications of Wisdom and Folly as women? Does the practical advice given about women in the sapiential literature found at Qumran tell us anything about women's participation in the sect or about the sect's attitudes toward women generally?

Unfortunately, those texts that personify Wisdom and Folly as women do not take us very far down the road to answers to our questions. C. Camp has made an intriguing argument that the personification of Wisdom in Proverbs actually provides clues about wise women, or even women sages, in Israel during the Persian period.[54] As a development subsequent to Proverbs, Camp argues that Ben Sira's utilization of the idealized image of wisdom most likely functions to repress women, even though it depends to an extent on the description of wisdom in Proverbs. Finally, she concludes that wisdom as woman becomes completely divorced from real women in the later Wisdom of Solomon "in favor of mystical speculation."[55]

In order to make her argument, Camp cannot relegate her study to the personification of wisdom only; she must in addition incorporate the other available information about the cultural and social worlds of the book of Proverbs. What Camp has to work with, however, are complete texts that have cultural and social contexts that can be, at least to some degree, described, and she recognizes that some reconstruction of social context is essential. For example, she notes concerning Proverbs, "The question of whether or not we can discover a real-life female sage behind this poetic form depends in part on our ability to connect the literature with one or more socio-historic contexts."[56] For fragmen-

---

[54] C.V. Camp, "The Female Sage in Ancient Israel and in the Biblical Wisdom Literature," *The Sage in Israel and the Ancient Near East* (J.G. Gammie, L.G. Perdue, eds.; Winona Lake, IN: Eisenbrauns, 1990) 185–203.

[55] Camp, "The Female Sage," 202.

[56] Ibid., 191.

tary texts like 4Q184, 185 and 525 that do not look as if the Qumran sectarians composed them, the original "socio-historic contexts" of these works are obscure at best, and even informed reconstruction of those contexts might be almost impossible. If the texts are non- or pre-Qumranic, they might date from sometime in the second century BCE, perhaps even close to or slightly after the time of Ben Sira (usually thought to be in the 190's–180's BCE). Whatever their exact dates, almost certainly by the time these works were composed the images of Woman Wisdom and Woman Folly had become conventional wisdom motifs. Conventionality allows the image to be used for purposes quite different from its earlier one in Proverbs. So, for example, in the case of Ben Sira an image that in Proverbs reflected "a relatively high status for women in society during the Persian period (especially early on), and the possibility of real social influence for women of experience and wisdom"[57] later gets turned on its head, since the author employs it, not as a symbol of women's influence and status, but as an instrument of control over women.

It might indeed be possible to discover the social functions of these images in the Qumran texts were they more complete and if they had a clearer social context. In 4Q184, Lady Folly is described in very much the same language as that concerning the "strange" woman in Proverbs 1–9. The Qumran fragment starts in the middle of a discussion of this dangerous woman who sets alluring traps, and it ends with a comment about her seductive words. The explicit sexuality of the text reflects the sexual language of Proverbs as well. The length of 4Q184, as long as or longer than any of the individual poems in Proverbs 1–9, represents the gathering together and exegetical expansion of those poems into a single text, but with a very specific agenda, specifically the use of unfettered female sexuality as a powerful metaphor of the poet's "other," as Aubin argues, or as a representation of the demonic as Crawford suggests. In the light of both 4Q184's reading of Proverbs and modern scholarly readings that argue for a metaphorical understanding of the text, I doubt that 4Q184 reveals to us much of anything about the realia of the Qumran covenanters and the presence of women among them. Their use of the text may, however, reflect something of their assumptions about and constructions of women and female sexuality.

---

[57] Ibid., 194.

The early portion of 4Q185 does not contain any indication of a personification of wisdom, but in 1–2 ii 8–14 the text seems to personify wisdom as a woman, although the word חכמה does not appear in the extant portions of this fragment.[58] Wisdom will make happy the one to whom she is given (the macarism in line 8). The one who has her will "take her as a possession," "find her," "get her for an inheritance." Whoever possesses her will have a long life and "fatty bones," among other desirables. All of these sentiments, and some of the actual phrases, are familiar from other wisdom texts. In one interesting phrase, God's mercies are said to be for "her people" (לעמיה). The man who "does her" will be happy. The notion of wisdom as an inheritance reappears in line 15 where it is said that the person who practices wisdom will pass her along to his descendents.

In all of these cases, 4Q185 contains an element of active performance. One *does* wisdom. This performative aspect of the text may indicate that wisdom comports with Torah. Although the text does not explicitly equate Torah and Wisdom, a connection between the two is assumed in the background.[59] In column iii, the text turns to God's judgment, where God knows the innermost workings of human thoughts and deeds. Whereas earlier in column ii wisdom is the subject of the sage's teaching, iii 9 speaks of fulfilling the "words of the covena[nt]," a probable reference to the Torah. This conjunction of wisdom and law may provide confirmation that the author of 4Q185 worked with an understanding that Wisdom and Torah were related.

In 4Q185 the image of Woman Wisdom has become a conventional sapiential trope, and the link between Wisdom and Torah looks similar to that made by Ben Sira. Whether this connection in 4Q185 represents a correspondence that has gained prominence in Jewish wisdom literature of the second to first centuries BCE or whether it reflects some specific social context, like the movement of wisdom out of the domestic sphere and into the male-controlled public sphere as Camp argues for Ben Sira, cannot be determined.[60] My own sense is that it is the former rather than the latter. Part of the difficulty in deciding is that in Proverbs and Ben Sira we also find practical advice about how the budding sage

---

[58] It is, however, reconstructed by García Martínez and Tigchelaar in line 11. See *The Dead Sea Scrolls Study Edition*, 1.378.

[59] Harrington, *Wisdom Texts*, 38.

[60] Camp, "The Female Sage," 199.

should deal with real women, and this advice can inform what may have constituted the content of the image of Woman Wisdom for those authors. 4Q184 and 185 contain no such practical advice.

Much the same could be said about 4Q525. The text's close association between Wisdom and Torah presents nothing especially new. In fact, Wisdom loses some of her personality in being connected with Torah. One must almost speak of Wisdom/Torah together in this text.[61] In short one finds no indication in this text of any specific attitudes toward women, real or imagined.

Perhaps the most that one could make out of those Qumran sapiential texts that personify Wisdom or Folly is that they reinforce and reinscribe, by the continued use of the images, male cultural constructs of women to be desired and women to be avoided. But, of course, ideal construct does not constitute social description. By the time of the second to first centuries BCE the images of Woman Wisdom and Woman Folly appear to have been separated from associations with real women. The nuanced interplay between how the sage treats real women and the personification of wisdom and folly as women described by Camp for Proverbs and Ben Sira is completely obscured in the Qumran texts. The demonization of Folly in 4Q184 even further mythologizes her and probably removes her even farther from any connection to real women.[62] Yes, the Qumran community had copies of Proverbs and Ben Sira where such interplay is important, but their preservation probably does not provide information about the social world of that community. And unlike Proverbs and Ben Sira, the texts I have described above contain in their extant fragments none of the potentially helpful advice (both to an ancient student or us) about how the young sage should treat real women. The reverse is also true; the one major Qumran text that preserves fairly extensive practical instruction, 4QInstruction, shows no evidence of utilizing the image of personified wisdom or folly. Separation has apparently become divorce.

4QInstruction, as part of the practical nature of its advice to the maven, has a lot to say about women. The specifics of what it says about mothers, wives and daughters, however, are less crucial than the

---

[61] Crawford ("Lady Wisdom," 365) speaks of Wisdom being "subsumed" under Torah in 4Q525.

[62] This conclusion would be warranted, I think, whether one reads 4Q184 with Crawford or Aubin.

fact that this wisdom text was preserved in eight copies at Qumran. If the text was indeed considered authoritative by the Qumran community, as Strugnell and Harrington argue, did the practical instruction about women apply to the community members and does it provide any evidence for the possibility that women made up a part of that community?

Strugnell's and Harrington's conclusion, that its basic characteristics make it unlikely to be sectarian, probably, but not certainly, indicates that its advice about women provides evidence for its own original context and not for that of Qumran. Harrington suggests three possible reasons for the presence of the non-sectarian 4QInstruction at Qumran. "[T]he work could be pre-Qumranic—before the movement became sectarian and monastic; or it could be intended for Essenes who lived a life more directly integrated into Second Temple Jewish society; or it could be designed as a step in the education and formation of those who would eventually present themselves for full membership in the movement."[63]

But even if we could determine possible reasons why the text was part of the collection at Qumran, why would the community hold 4QInstruction in such apparent high regard? The most plausible explanation for the authoritative status held by the eight copies of 4QInstruction is that the community at Qumran, whether celibate or not, regarded it as one of its foundational works containing ideas crucial to its self-understanding or its worldview.[64]

4QInstruction's place in the community's literary holdings, however, most likely did not depend on its practical advice about money, women and other mundane matters, but on the importance and centrality of the רז נהיה, "the mystery that is to come." As we saw above, the sage repeatedly encourages the maven to study and to comprehend the mystery. The eschatological warnings in 4Q416 1 are central to the entire work, and the mystery seems to be part of that eschatology. This notion of the "mystery that is to come" is also found in other Qumran texts. The sectarian Rule of the Community calls the mystery (רז נהיה) "the light of my heart" and speaks about the mystery in the same context as God's knowledge, his wonders, his truth, wisdom and judgment (1QS

---

[63] Harrington, *Wisdom Texts*, 41.
[64] Tigchelaar (*To Increase Learning*, 206), for example, argues that 4QInstruction probably influenced the composition of 1QH 5–6.

11:3–6). The Book of the Mysteries refers to the רז נהיה in eschato-logical language (cf. 1Q27). It is almost certain, in my estimation, that "the mystery that is to come" explains the importance of 4QInstruc-tion for the Qumran community. But a group can certainly consider a text foundational and authoritative even when that work assumes a set of social and cultural realities and norms completely different from those of the people using it, as the continued use and reverence for the Jewish scriptures in modernity attests. If this explanation is correct, then the detailed advice the sage of 4QInstruction offers about women tells us little to nothing on its own about the situation in the Qumran community.

We cannot, ultimately, keep the wisdom literature completely iso-lated from the remainder of the Qumran scrolls. 4QInstruction is not the only text at Qumran that has a practical concern for real women. Several non-wisdom Qumran texts have women as an important topic (the Damascus Document and the Temple Scroll are prime examples), and two other texts might even have a woman as the speaker (cf. 4Q414, 4Q502).[65] The relationship between all these documents and what group or groups they might represent is still not clear, however. This lack of clarity has prompted Schuller to remark, "Thus at present, we can say something about women in the *Rule of the Congregation* or the *Damascus Document*, or the *Temple Scroll*—but much caution and further study are required before we can combine the evidence of one or more of these documents, plus the fragmentary bits and pieces, into some comprehensive picture."[66]

While Schuller's observation is certainly true, these texts were, after all, found together and presumably were read and studied by the com-munity who inhabited the settlement at Khirbet Qumran. One reason that we find at Qumran 4QInstruction and other texts that talk about women might simply be that the texts reflect the realities and ideals of the larger social and cultural world of the community. If we momen-tarily hold in abeyance the usual assessment that the people who lived at Qumran were celibate and isolationist, all of these texts that treat women (even if they were not composed at Qumran), both as objects

---

[65] See Schuller, "Women," 120. See more recently, S.W. Crawford, "Not According to Rule: Women, the Dead Sea Scrolls and Qumran," *Emanuel: Studies in Hebrew Bible, Septuagint and Dead Sea Scrolls in Honor of Emanuel Tov* (S.M. Paul et al., eds.; VTSup 94; Leiden, Brill, 2003) 127–50.

[66] Schuller, "Women," 121–22.

of practical advice and of symbolic significance, might have been kept
and read because there actually were women members of the community. Because a work appears to have origins outside of Qumran does
not automatically mean that it could not reflect in some measure the
social situation of Qumran. That might be just the reason it was copied
and used. Of course, other pertinent evidence, such as that from the
nearby cemetery, will necessarily have an important bearing on a case
like this, but as a matter of methodology, we cannot *a priori* rule out
this possibility.[67]

Of course, the most desirable situation would be to have wisdom
texts among the scrolls that treat women and that are clearly sectarian
compositions. Unfortunately, such is not the case. Since the wisdom
texts that we do have are probably imports, they do not offer much
assistance in answering the questions about the presence of women at
Qumran, although they might coincide with the community's attitudes
toward women. And even if the best candidates for inclusion as sectarian
texts, 4Q184, 185 and 525, were admitted, they would tell us very little
on their own. If 4QInstruction originated in a larger movement out
of which the Qumran community developed, or from which it splin-
tered, we might gain some insight into the parent movement's social
world, and perhaps by extension into the social context of Qumran.
But scholars have not as yet satisfactorily sorted out the origins of the
group that lived on the shores of the Dead Sea. 4QInstruction offers
perhaps the most intriguing possibility among the wisdom texts for
trying to address the problem of women at Qumran.

We are left in the end with many more questions than answers.
How significant is it that apparently none of the wisdom texts found
at Qumran were sectarian (at least none is clearly sectarian)? Were all
these texts even read alongside each other throughout the long life of
the Qumran community or did some works fall out of favor and sit on
the shelf collecting dust while other favored texts were avidly read and
studied? How should we read these seemingly disparate texts together
in order to say something sociologically about the people who lived at
Qumran? Ultimately, however, I do not think that the wisdom texts
alone can provide answers to the questions about women's presence
and participation in the Qumran community as much as they put into
relief the difficulty of finding those answers.

---

[67] On women and the Qumran cemetery, see J. Magness, *The Archaeology of Qumran
and the Dead Sea Scrolls* (Grand Rapids, MI: Wm. B. Eerdmans, 2002) 163–87.

CHAPTER TWO

FROM GENERATION TO GENERATION:
THE SAGE AS FATHER IN EARLY JEWISH LITERATURE*

Listen, my child, and accept my judgment;
do not reject my counsel. (Sir 6:23)

Listen to me, my child, and acquire knowledge,
and pay close attention to my words.
I will impart discipline precisely
and declare knowledge accurately. (Sir 16:24–25)

Scattered throughout the Wisdom of Ben Sira we encounter numerous
passages like the two I have cited here in which the sage/teacher takes
upon himself the role of the students' father in order to command attention to his instruction. In the case of this Jewish wisdom book, the sage
is certainly not the addressee's actual parent, but a teacher engaged in
training Israelite young men for successful careers as public servants,
probably as scribes/sages like himself.[1] By assuming the language of a
parent speaking to a child, the sage does more than simply invoke that
relationship, however. He constructs his students as his children and
thereby claims the authoritative leverage with them that a father has
with his sons. The student, who is on the receiving end of the construct,
is subtly coerced into the role of the submissive child. "I am not merely
a teacher to whom you should listen," says the sage, "I am your father
to whom you must listen."

Elsewhere in Second Temple Jewish literature, we find frequent
examples of sages speaking with a father's voice. In some cases, especially

---

* I am delighted to offer this article in celebration of Michael Knibb's scholarly career.
As I have come to know him, Michael has been a colleague in the very best sense of
the word. He has been supportive of my work at the same time as he has engaged it
critically. For that I am grateful and certainly a better scholar. I also extend my appreciation to Sidnie Crawford, Lynn LiDonnici, Robert Rozehnal and Monica Najar, who
read drafts of this paper and offered very valuable comments.
[1] On the term scribe/sage, see R.A. Horsley and P. Tiller, "Ben Sira and the Sociology of the Second Temple," *Second Temple Studies III: Studies in Politics, Class and
Material Culture* (P.R. Davies and J.M. Halligan, eds.; JSOTSup 340; Sheffield: Sheffield
Academic Press, 2002) 99–103 and Chapter 4, "'Who Has Been Tested By Gold and
Found Perfect?' Ben Sira's Discourse of Riches and Poverty."

in texts that have been labeled as wisdom, the "father" (the presumptive author of the text) is a wise sage giving instruction to his "son(s)" (the students/readers are addressed by the singular or plural "you"), as in the examples from Ben Sira above. In other instances, like *Aramaic Levi* and the *Testament of Job*, a father speaking to his children occupies a central place in the narrative. This same device serves as the overarching framework for the *Testaments of the XII Patriarchs*. These scenarios particularly characterize the genre testament, but even apocalyptic texts, such as *1 Enoch*, can employ this device.

Those Second Temple texts in which the author assumes the role of father might be construed at minimum as being dependent on a literary tradition found in earlier Israelite wisdom texts. The biblical book of Proverbs, perhaps the quintessential Israelite wisdom text, presents itself as homegrown wisdom given by a father (and sometimes a mother) to a son. The topics are varied—speech, wealth, relations with women, among others—but all get conveyed as parental instruction to a beloved child. Indeed, some scholars maintain that this literary device may actually reflect the original domestic context of ancient Israelite wisdom instruction.[2] Proverbs, for example, highlights on several occasions the instructional role of parents as teachers and counselors.[3] An Israelite son would have received much of his instruction from his parents in the home, and the sage's adoption of that role indicates the critical importance of that institution as a locus of instruction.[4] The sage, who wants to establish credibility and authority in the eyes of his students, essentially adopts the father's authority. Thus, one could see the central literary frame of a book like Proverbs influencing a sage like Jesus ben Sira, who addresses his own students as sons, even though there is almost no chance that Ben Sira's wisdom originated as family instruction. Ben Sira engages students in a formal context of pedagogy, and his didactic goal is to prepare them to enter into and to cultivate successful

---

[2] For wisdom and the family in Proverbs, see the summary comments and bibliography in R. Murphy, "Israelite Wisdom and the Home," *Où demeures-tu? la maison depuis le monde biblique: en hommage au professor Guy Coutrier* (J.-C. Petit, ed.; Saint-Laurent, Quebec: Fides, 1994) 199–212.

[3] C.R. Fontaine, "The Sage in Family and Tribe," *The Sage in Israel and the Ancient Near East* (J.G. Gammie and L.G. Perdue, eds.; Winona Lake, IN: Eisenbrauns, 1990) 155–64.

[4] On the Israelite family and its functions, see most recently, P.J. King and L.E. Stager, *Life in Biblical Israel* (Louisville: Westminster/John Knox, 2001).

careers. So, in 51:23, he advertises his services, "Draw near to me, you who are uneducated, and lodge in the house of instruction."[5]

To observe that these texts are borrowing a literary device from earlier tradition does not do them justice, however.[6] The direct address to students, for instance, may represent the actual setting and manner of instruction and thus give some clues as to the social location of these texts. While one can imagine a sage instructing his students or parents teaching their children in this manner in a real context of pedagogy, the intentional use of such discourse may work in another altogether different way as well. The author's use of the first-person "I" and the second person "you" (sometimes singular and sometimes plural) in addition to imperative verb forms also draws, even coerces, *whoever reads the te*xt into this same relationship, one in which the author's words possess the force of paternal authority. I would suggest that even if the text might indeed reflect actual pedagogical technique, this particular discourse has as a central aim the extension of this same authority to the reader, whoever he or she might be.

In a short and illuminating article, C. Newsom argues that this is precisely the case in Proverbs 1–9. She explains that the "I" and "you" of the text's direct address are

> linguistic blanks or empty signs filled in only when individual speakers and addressees appropriate them in specific instances of discourse... The striking prominence of the pronouns 'I' and 'you' and the repeated use of vocative and imperative address in Proverbs 1–9 are clear indicators of what is at stake in these chapters: the formation of the subjectivity of the reader.[7]

The author, through the use of ideologically charged discourse, "recruits" the reader, who by responding must take some position vis-à-vis that ideology, a process L. Althusser called "interpellation."[8] All readers

---

[5] The Hebrew of Ms B reads בבית מדרשי. The Greek has ἐν οἴκῳ παιδείας. P.W. Skehan and A.A. Di Lella argue that the original Hebrew probably read בית מוסר (*The Wisdom of Ben Sira* [AB 39; Garden City, NY: Doubleday, 1987] 575). Whatever the case, the phrase certainly indicates some context of formal pedagogy or schooling.

[6] See, for instance, Skehan's and Di Lella's comment on 6:23. "In v 23, Ben Sira appeals to his own authority in addressing his readers in the tone of a father... In so doing, he was modeling himself on Prov 4:10" (*Wisdom of Ben Sira*, 193).

[7] C. Newsom, "Women and the Discourse of Patriarchal Wisdom: A Study of Proverbs 1–9," *Gender and Difference in Ancient Israel* (P.L. Day, ed.; Minneapolis: Fortress, 1989) 143.

[8] Newsom takes the concept of interpellation from Althusser (*Lenin and Philosophy* [London: Monthly Review, 1971] 174–75), who argues that no discourse is ideologically

of Proverbs, according to Newsom, "are called upon to take up the subject position of son in relation to an authoritative father. Through its imitation of a familiar scene of interpellation the text continually reinterpellates its readers."[9] The sage's choice of the setting of the patriarchal family is not a neutral one, argues Newsom; it has ideological force: "Since it is in the family that one's subjectivity is first formed, the malleability called for in the text is made to seem innocent, natural, inevitable. In addition the symbol of the family causes the discourse to appear outside of specific class interests."[10] The discourse further reinforces the hierarchical and authoritative nature of the relationship between father and son and hence of the author and reader since the text denies the literary son an opportunity to talk back, either to question or to challenge that authority. Just as the son does not speak, the reader, who is separated from the author by the text, has no opportunity to speak either. As a result, the teacher/father/author presents his instruction to the student/son/reader not with the expectation of dialogue, but with the anticipation of acquiescence, acceptance and internalization of the instruction.

These same arguments apply to those Second Temple texts that feature a father/son mode of address through the use of first- and second-person pronouns. They employ many of the same discursive and rhetorical devices, not simply because they occur in such an influential text as Proverbs, but because this discourse is pedagogically productive and powerful. Additionally, these sages also exploit avenues of their own that contribute to the effectiveness of this discourse. Second Temple Jewish society remained dominated by the patriarchal family, even if that construction changed somewhat over the years that intervened between the composition of texts like Proverbs 1–9 and Ben Sira.[11] Jewish society at large, like the family, was hierarchical and rigidly patriarchal, structured in such a way that the maintenance of honor

---

neutral. Ideology "recruits" or "hails" a subject, who, responding to the hailing, "takes up a particular position in a particular ideology." This action he calls "interpellation."

[9] Newsom, "Women and the Discourse of Patriarchal Wisdom," 143–44.

[10] Ibid., 144.

[11] Proverbs 1–9 may not be all that remote from Ben Sira, however. Many scholars date these chapters to the post-exilic period, perhaps close to the book of Malachi with which they show some similarity. See C.V. Camp, *Wisdom and the Feminine in the Book of Proverbs* (Decatur, GA: Almond, 1985) 235–54.

and the avoidance of shame determined men's social standing.[12] In this world, the father almost certainly retained his traditional position as his sons' primary teacher and disciplinarian, providing the sage the important social springboard for his claims on his students.

Thus, we can imagine motivations for a sage like Ben Sira to resort to rhetorical strategies that are similar to those that Newsom identified in Proverbs. The author/father controls what gets taught and how it is presented. As part of that agenda, the father of the text determines how undesirable people and actions get characterized.[13] So, in Ben Sira, the loose woman, the fool, the wealthy or the faux-friend all become included in the father's discourse and his portrayal of them. In those verses that begin "Do not say," the same fate befalls even the speech of the son (cf. for example, 5:1, 3, 4, 6). The paternal monologue reinforces the extreme submissiveness/subjectivity of the son/reader and the corresponding and contrasting power of the father/teacher.

Yet as Newsom observes about Proverbs, the attempt to construct a submissive reader is not simply about internalizing teaching; it is also about stifling "recalcitrance before legitimate authority." She writes, "But one may sense behind this supine persona, a shadow figure of significant power. A world made of discourse, a symbolic order, an ideology exists only by consensus. If it cannot recruit new adherents and if those whom it reinterpellates do not recognize themselves in its hailing, it ceases to have reality."[14] In a world of competing discourses, the father's complete control over the discourse is intended to recruit the son into adopting the father's ideology and values, to ensure internalization of those values and to reduce the possibility of their rejection. At the same time it serves to protect the son from those competing discourses that might capture his attention and divert it from the "right" path. In short, the discourse of father/son in wisdom texts like Proverbs and Ben Sira works to reinforce in the reader what Newsom terms the "dominant symbolic order."

---

[12] On honor and shame, see C.V. Camp, "Understanding a Patriarchy: Women in Second Century Jerusalem Through the Eyes of Ben Sira," *"Women Like This:" New Perspectives on Jewish Women in the Greco-Roman World* (A.-J. Levine, ed.; SBLEJL 1; Atlanta: Scholars Press, 1991) 1–39.

[13] Newsom, "Women and the Discourse of Patriarchal Wisdom," 144.

[14] Ibid., 146. In this section, Newsom argues that Wisdom is the public voice "who occupies the places that are physically symbolic of collective authority and power." I think that Wisdom functions a bit differently in Ben Sira, but the point that she makes applies to Ben Sira as well.

With such a potent weapon in their rhetorical arsenal, it should not surprise us that Second Temple authors would rely upon father/son discourse so frequently, especially in instruction or moral exhortation. My purpose is to show that the use of father/son discourse is not an innocent literary borrowing, but that these authors employ it to accomplish similar goals to those of the author of Proverbs 1–9.[15] I will look at three different kinds of texts to explore how they employ the discursive features of Proverbs and how they formulate their own versions of this father-son discourse. The first type is perhaps the clearest—those wisdom texts, like Ben Sira, that adopt father/son discourse as a primary strategy for addressing their readers. While these are the texts in which the discourse identified by Newsom shows up most clearly, we can extend Newsom's analysis to two other kinds of texts. A second group of texts, mostly fragmentary works from Qumran, preserve direct address with the singular or plural second person pronoun without any clear identification of the "I" with a father or the "you" with sons. Do these texts reflect the familial discursive features of Proverbs 1–9? Might any of these fragmentary texts have been framed originally as father/son discourse? Finally, the narrative texts that feature a father and his sons in which the father is a revered figure from the past might also, but in a somewhat different fashion, attempt to achieve the same goals as those texts that use the direct I-you address of father to son.

THE SAGE AS FATHER

Whereas Ben Sira is the most obvious Second Temple period work in which to find the kind of discourse that Newsom identified in Proverbs, the sage in several other wisdom texts also constructs the reader as the child through the explicit use of the vocative "son(s)" and the consistent use of the pronouns "you." Most prominent in this group are 4Q185, 4Q412, 4Q525 and 4QInstruction. One additional work, the *Damascus*

---

[15] Newsom's interest in her article is also how that dominant symbolic order is patriarchal, and she spends a great deal of time explaining the crucial role that the strange woman of Proverbs plays in that discourse. While Ben Sira employs the metaphor of Woman Wisdom, he does not exploit the strange woman or Folly. What turns out to be interesting and could be the subject of separate investigation is that in the Second Temple period some texts use the strange woman of Proverbs (see 4Q184) or the metaphor of Woman Wisdom (see 4Q185) while others do not. On this image at Qumran, see Chapter 1, "Wisdom and Women at Qumran," 6–11.

Document, although it is not a wisdom text, also addresses its readers as sons. Each of these works shares a number of features with Proverbs 1–9. In addition, several other features appear in these texts that reinforce the power of the father's position and hence his authority.

Ben Sira

Although Ben Sira did not compose the kind of extended meditation on wisdom as Proverbs 1–9, he employs almost all of the rhetorical features found there.[16] In addition, other rhetorical schemes work to inscribe the reader's filial subjectivity and hence the authority of the author's teaching. For instance, like Proverbs, Ben Sira relies on the abstract language of righteousness and justice (e.g., 7:5–6, 35:5–9).[17] He presents the image of walking a path or way, playing on the double entendre of a traveler on a real path and of a student on a metaphorical path in life (see especially 32:20–22). This latter image appears frequently in Second Temple literature. Newsom comments on its appearance in Proverbs, "A path is a social product, made by many feet over a period of time…A path does not, in fact, exclude movement in any direction. It only makes its own direction the easiest, most natural, most logical way of proceeding…Customary social behavior, represented by the image of the path, is a type of nonverbal discourse."[18]

One of Ben Sira's primary adaptive strategies for constructing the sinners and their destructive actions, a feature of the discourse in Proverbs, is to begin a teaching with the phrase "Do not say." This device allows him to accomplish two complementary ends. He can portray the sinners and their disregard for proper values and behaviors as he wants the son to hear them. He thus presents the competing discourses of the world that rival those of the patriarchal order as he chooses, and he then takes the opportunity to turn the case around to reinforce his own patriarchal ideology and values, which contrast with those of his rivals. A typical example is 5:4–5: "Do not say, 'I have sinned, yet what has happened to me?' for the Lord is slow to anger. Do not be so confident of forgiveness that you add sin to sin."

---

[16] The Praise of the Ancestors (chaps. 44–50) does have an overall coherence, but it is not a meditation on wisdom in the manner of Proverbs 1–9.

[17] On the place of these abstract nouns in the discourse of Proverbs, see Newsom, "Women and the Discourse of Patriarchal Wisdom," 144.

[18] For a fuller explanation of the metaphor, see ibid., 147–48.

Perhaps most famously, Ben Sira constructs appropriate and inappropriate sexual relationships as either reinforcing or threatening the patriarchal order, a prominent device in Proverbs 1–9.[19] In a society where honor and shame determine a man's status, women possess the frightening ability to destroy a man's honor or the contrasting potential to build it up.[20] It is somewhat curious, then, that, unlike Proverbs where the portrait of the foreign/strange woman who lures the son away occupies a central position in the discourse, Ben Sira does not really exploit this dangerous woman as a symbol of marginality or otherness.

Woman Wisdom, however, acts in Ben Sira in a very similar way to Proverbs to buttress the speech of the father. What Newsom says for Proverbs applies also to Ben Sira. "Where the father is the authoritative voice in the family, *Hokmot* is the corresponding public voice…who occupies the places that are physically symbolic of collective authority and power…She also has the power to save from disaster."[21] In Proverbs, people hear wisdom's public voice "in the streets" (1:20) or "at the entrance to the gates" (1:21). In Sirach 24, wisdom gets one major speech, but she speaks both "in the midst of the people" (v. 1) and "in the assembly of the Most High" (v. 2). Now she resides in the most central of all places, the Temple in Jerusalem (vv. 10–12), and she is embodied in the "book of the covenant of the Most High God" (v. 23). Meanwhile, she calls directly to the student/reader in words of desire and possession (v. 19–20). Even more, though, Ben Sira connects his own teaching directly with wisdom. Sirach 24:23–29 makes a transition between the speech of wisdom and the first-person speech of the author. These verses are replete with mentions of rivers (the Pishon, Tigris, Euphrates, Jordan, Nile and Gihon) as metaphors of sources of wisdom. Verse 30 begins, "As for me I was a canal from a river." Ben Sira, the father who speaks to his sons, has a direct channel to this fluvial source of wisdom, and thus he draws his teaching directly from that wisdom. By making this series of moves from Wisdom to Torah to his own teaching, Ben Sira argues that his values are built into the very fabric of the world. Wisdom's divine nature and Ben Sira's connection with her anchors his own discourse in the "transcendent realm."[22]

---

[19] On this feature of the discourse in Proverbs, see ibid., 153–55.
[20] See Camp, "Understanding a Patriarchy."
[21] Newsom, "Women and the Discourse of Patriarchal Wisdom," 146.
[22] Ibid., 150–51, 157.

One of Ben Sira's most effective strategies for constructing the subjectivity of the reader occurs in the book's opening chapters. Chapters 1 and 2 have as their major themes the grounding of wisdom in creation and the fear of the Lord. Ben Sira uses the phrase "fear of the Lord" seventeen times in these chapters. Chapter 3 then begins, "Listen to me your father, O children," and continues through verse 16 with a poem about proper relationships with parents. As we might expect, Ben Sira affirms unconditionally the authority and position of parents above their children. The conclusion of the poem (vv. 14–16) makes the ultimate connection of the divine and the parental. "For kindness to a father will not be forgotten, and will be credited to you against your sins; in the day of your distress it will be remembered in your favor; like frost in fair weather your sins will melt away. Whoever forsakes a father is like a blasphemer, and whoever angers a mother is cursed by God." By identifying himself explicitly as a father and speaking to the student/reader as a child, Ben Sira effectively assumes the parent's authority, which is linked directly to proper reverence for God. Ben Sira reinforces his position and authority as the reader's father by the repeated use of the vocative, "my child," which occurs eight times in book's first six chapters.

In chapters 44–50, Ben Sira praises a series of famous people from Israel's past.[23] His introduction to this section tacitly enlists the reader as one of the descendents of these righteous ancestors, thus placing the reader in a chain of inter-generational transmission of the patriarchal order. This rhetorical strategy, which Proverbs also employs, helps assure the son that he will not always be at the bottom of the hierarchy. He *will* assume his own place as a bearer of the tradition. Ben Sira begins his praise, "Let *us* now sing the praises of famous men, *our* ancestors (lit. fathers) in their generations" (44:1). Later in verses 10–15, he notes several times that the "wealth" and "inheritance" left by these fathers will remain with their descendents, who will "stand by the covenants." Their progeny "will continue forever." Who else could be the legitimate heirs of this inheritance but those to whom Ben Sira speaks? By framing this entire section with the first-person plural "we" and "us," Ben Sira has placed his sons, both students and readers, in a larger chain

---

[23] On the Praise of the Ancestors and its larger function in the book, see B.M. Mack, *Wisdom and the Hebrew Epic: Ben Sira's Hymn in Praise of the Fathers* (Chicago: University of Chicago Press, 1985).

of father-son relationships in which they are expected to become the fathers who pass on the inheritance to their descendents.

4QSapiential Work (4Q185)[24]

The author of this fragmentary wisdom text specifically invokes patriarchal authority by addressing his readers as sons in 1–2 ii 3, "Listen to me, my sons, and do not defy the words of YHWH." But this is not the only form of direct address in the work. 1–2 i 9 directs a prophetic woe to "you, O sons of men," and i 13–14 appeals to "my people" and "you simple ones." Each vocative assumes a somewhat different, though still hierarchical, relationship between the author and the reader: ruler-subject, teacher-student, father-son.

In the lines following the paternal address, the author employs several features we have seen in Proverbs and Ben Sira. First, he draws on the metaphor of walking a path (ii 1, 4). Second, the father's presentation of the wicked takes the form of a direct quotation of their words, "The wicked persons should not brag saying, 'She [presumably wisdom] has not been given to me and not[…]'" (ii 9). He then leaves the son no room for latitude in response: "Whoever glories in her will say…" (ii 11). These contrasting statements assume that wisdom is a woman that the son can "take as a possession" (יֹ[רו]שה). Here the father of 4Q185 resorts to an old strategy, but with a new twist. Newsom noted about the discourse of Proverbs, "For the young deferral is not endless. So, in Proverbs 1–9, where the reader is continually reinterpellated in the subject position of the son, chapter 4 speaks of the transformation of sons into fathers in the chain of tradition."[25] One way Ben Sira accomplishes that goal is to insert the reader into the chain of the famous ancestors. The author of 4Q185 utilizes a different strategy. He claims that wisdom gets passed down through the generations as an inheritance, and "as she was given to his fathers, so will he inherit her [and hold fast] to her…And he will give her in inheritance to his descendents"

---

[24] For the text of 4Q185, see conveniently F. García Martínez and E.J.C. Tigchelaar, *The Dead Sea Scrolls Study Edition* (2 vols.; Leiden: Brill, 1997) 1.379–80. For the most recent edition of the text, see H. Lichtenberger, "Der Weisheitstext 4Q185—Eine neue Edition," *The Wisdom Texts from Qumran and the Development of Sapiential Thought* (C. Hempel, A. Lange, H. Lichtenberger, eds.; BETL 159; Leuven: Peeters, 2002) 127–50.

[25] Newsom, "Women and the Discourse of Patriarchal Wisdom," 151.

(1–2 ii 14–15). The "he" of these lines is the "whoever glories in her" of line 11, that is, the dutiful son/reader. Wisdom in this text, then, is both the woman with whom the son will have "long days, and greasy bones, and a happy heart, rich[es and honor]" (ii 12), but she is also a possession that can pass from generation to generation as a valuable family heirloom. In the former case, the allusion to wisdom as a good wife reinforces the patriarchal order through the son's proper sexual choices. In the latter case, the father creates the expectation that the son will now become part of the patriarchal order, and he will continue that tradition.

4QBeatitudes (4Q525)[26]

This work is best known for the series of five beatitudes or macarisms contained in 2 ii + 3:1–7. Due to the fragmentary state of the manuscript, the precise context of these beatitudes is uncertain, but they seem to be part of a meditation on the acquisition and benefits of Woman Wisdom in which wisdom is identified with the Torah.[27] The text contains several appeals for the reader to pay attention or listen, and in 2 ii + 3:12 the addressees are called "sons." In fragment 14, however, the discourse becomes second person singular. Exactly when the transition from plural to singular happens and what its significance is remains unclear.[28]

The most prominent feature of the father-son discourse in 4Q525 is the metaphor of walking on paths. References both to good and bad paths occur throughout the various fragments of the work. Three of the five beatitudes speak of paths or walking. Twice the paths lead away from the law and wisdom and so are "perverted" and "insane" (2 ii + 3:2), and once the blessed person "walks in the law of the Most High" (2 ii + 3:3–4). Later in that same fragment keeping wisdom in front of one's eyes keeps one off the wrong path (2 ii + 3:7). Wisdom herself sets out ways for the righteous to follow (5:7, 9) and they "dig her paths"

---

[26] É. Peuch, *Qumrân Grotte 4 • XVIII* (DJD 25; Oxford: Clarendon, 1998) 115–78.

[27] D.J. Harrington, *Wisdom Texts from Qumran* (London/New York: Routledge, 1996) 66–70.

[28] 14 ii 18 is particularly notable because the addressee is called "understanding one" (מבין), a term found with great frequency in 4QInstruction (see below).

(5:12). Altogether the word path or way (דרך) occurs 13 times in the extant fragments of 4Q525.[29]

The text represents wisdom as a woman throughout, and it is clear that the reader is to pursue her. Although the language does not generally have the same double entendre sexual overtones as other texts we have seen, there are occasions where they peek through. Fragment 2 iii, although poorly preserved, seems to be describing the beauty of wisdom. 2 ii + 3 8 may suggest a longing for her on the part of the son. Unfortunately the thing that causes the longing is not extant in the fragment, but "on her account (it) eats away his heart" (ויתם לבו אליה). Fragment 13:5, part of another incomplete fragment, may refer to wisdom as an inheritance.

While the extant text contains no reports of the direct speech of sinners themselves, the author represents their actions, which the son needs to avoid, through a series of "Do not" statements (frag. 5).[30] In fragment 14, the author, as in our previous texts, attempts to situate the reader in a chain of generational transmission of patriarchal values. In this case, however, the author appeals directly to the post-mortem legacy of the reader. The son truly becomes the father here. "[…] he will give you as an inheritance; he will fill your days with goodness, and with abundant peace you will […] you shall inherit honor; and when you are snatched away to eternal rest they will inhe[rit…] and in your teaching, all those who know you will walk together" (14 ii 13–15).

These imperfect tenses (translated as futures in English) form the conclusion of a long passage in which the sage/father reassures the student/son that he will not fail in the difficult times. Those who hate the son will not triumph (14 ii 8–11), and indeed, God will drive away evil and fear (14 ii 12). The voice of the reassuring parent enables the author to warn the child about the possible trials ahead, but at the same time to accept the values he offers since those who hold different views cannot succeed. The ultimate result is the incorporation of the child into the patriarchal order as a transmitter of that order.

---

[29] This number comes from the concordance to DJD 25 (p. 218). See also M.G. Abegg Jr. et al., *The Dead Sea Scrolls Concordance: Volume 1, The Non-Biblical Texts from Qumran* (Leiden: Brill, 2003).
[30] These kinds of statements are especially frequent in wisdom literature. Ben Sira contains a large number of them.

4QInstruction (4Q415–418, 423, 1Q26)[31]

This wisdom book is perhaps the most important one discovered at Qumran, and it survives in at least seven copies. It takes the form of instruction by an older sage to a younger one, who is typically called "understanding one" or "maven" (מבין, hereafter *mevin*), although in one fragment the sage addresses a woman (4Q415 2 ii) and in several passages the "you" is plural rather than singular (e.g., 4Q417 1 i 20, 27). In two places (4Q417 1 i 18; 4Q418 69 ii 15), however, the sage addresses the student directly as "you, O understanding son" (ואתה בן מבין), and in another (4Q417 2 i 25) he calls the *mevin* "sage son" (בן משכיל).[32] While the single term מבין is the sage's preferred mode of address, scholars are almost unanimously agreed that the fragmentary nature of the manuscripts obscures any understanding of its overall scope and structure, if it had one.[33] Yet, the extant passages demonstrate that the sage did resort to the strategy of assuming the role of a father, and indeed several other features of father-son discourse also appear in the work.

Two major themes dominate much of the book: the poverty of the *mevin* and the "mystery that is to come" (רז נהיה). The sage frequently comments on the *mevin*'s poverty, which is clearly material.[34] Yet despite his low estate, the *mevin* has access to the רז נהיה, and the sage exhorts him to study this mystery in order to understand "all the ways of truth" (4Q416 2 iii 14). The רז נהיה perhaps offers an element unique to 4QInstruction among the rhetorical strategies connected with the sage's role as father. Although the text does not spell out its content, it clearly has an eschatological component.[35] Does the eschatological

---

[31] J. Strugnell and D.J. Harrington, *Qumran Cave 4 • XXIV Sapiential Texts, Part 2* (DJD 34; Oxford: Clarendon, 1999).

[32] While these phrases could be taken as referring to a member of a certain class of people or to people who have certain qualities, it seems significant to me that the author departs from his usual designation of the simple מבין for some combination with בן. Thus, the idea of sonship seems implicit in the sage's address.

[33] M. Goff, *The Worldly and Heavenly Wisdom of 4QInstruction* (STDJ 50; Leiden: Brill, 2003) 2–5.

[34] See Chapter 3, "The Categories of Rich and Poor in the Qumran Sapiential Literature" and C.M. Murphy, *Wealth in the Dead Sea Scrolls and the Qumran Community* (STDJ 40; Leiden: Brill, 2002).

[35] On the "mystery that is to come" and its content, see T. Elgvin, "Wisdom, Revelation, and Eschatology in an Early Essene Writing," *SBL Seminar Papers 1995* (E.H. Lovering, ed.; Atlanta: Scholars Press, 1995) 440–63; idem, "Early Essene Eschatology:

promise of the רז נהיה provide an additional incentive for the reader/ son to listen to the teaching of the sage/father? Does the father's anticipation of reward and punishment compel the son to the right course of action? This problem is further complicated precisely because the רז נהיה is never explained. Is the expectation that the reader, like the *mevin*, will know what it is?[36] In any case, the רז נהיה occupies a central place in the teaching that the sage gives.

For my purposes, however, what matters is how the *mevin* learns the mystery. 4Q416 2 iii contains an extended section on honoring one's parents. Two elements of the discourse serve to connect the sage as father to the student/reader as child. First, God is explicitly compared to parents: "For as God is to a man, so is his own father; and as the Lord is to a person, so is his mother" (l. 16). In this same section the sage compares the procreative act of the parents with that of God: "For they are the womb that was pregnant with you, and just as he (i.e., God) has set them in authority over you and fashioned (you) according to the spirit." Second, those same parents taught their child about the רז נהיה: "And as they have uncovered your ear to the mystery that is to come, honor them for the sake for your own honor" (l. 17–18).[37] In another fragment, 4Q418 184, however, it appears that God teaches the mystery to the *mevin*, and the same phrase, גלה אזנכה ברז נהיה, appears in both 4Q418 and 416 2 iii 18.[38] Since parental actions in these

---

Judgment and Salvation according to *Sapiential Work A*," *Current Research and Technological Developments* (D.W. Parry and S.D. Ricks, eds.; STDJ 20; Leiden: Brill, 1996) 126–65; idem, "The Mystery to Come: Early Essene Theology of Revelation," *Qumran Between the Old and New Testaments* (F.H. Cryer and T.L. Thompson, eds.; JSOTSup 290; Sheffield: Sheffield Academic Press, 1998) 113–50; D.J. Harrington, "The *Raz Nihyeh* in a Qumran Wisdom Text (1Q26, 4Q415–418, 4Q423)," *Hommage à Józef T. Milik*, RevQ 17 (1996) 549–53; idem, *Wisdom Texts from Qumran*, chap. 6; and most recently Goff, *Worldly and Heavenly Wisdom*, 30–79.

[36] This question raises the issue of the anticipated audience for these texts. If, for instance, the text were directed to an insider audience who would know the content of the mystery (as it appears here), then eschatology would most likely contribute to the overall agenda of the father working to get the child to adopt his values. Such issues could easily be the topic of a separate study.

[37] The entire passage is very difficult and subject to different translations. For the reasons behind this translation, see DJD 34, 120–22. For a different translation, see Martínez and Tigchelaar, *Study Edition*, 2.853.

[38] The editors have taken God as the subject here, because God apparently is the subject in the previous line. The subject could have changed, however. Without any broader context, we cannot know with certainty. The most likely alternative here is the *mevin's* parents, as in 4Q416. In any case, this ambiguity does not affect my overall argument.

texts are compared and even conflated with God's, by directly addressing the *mevin* as "son," the sage inserts himself into that relationship,
effectively claiming the same authority that he has urged between the
mevin and his "real" parents. At the same time, the linkage of the sage
to the *mevin*'s parents to God essentially grounds the sage's teaching
in the divine order. "Your father is like God to you, and I am a father
to you," says the sage. How could one fail to listen?

The concept of inheritance, denoting an important family possession
that is passed from the father to his legitimate heirs, plays an important
role in 4QInstruction. In some cases, like 4Q416 2 ii 18 or 4Q416 2 iv
11–12, the term probably refers to material inheritance, but far more
frequently it is connected with words like "glory" or "truth." Several
examples illustrate the point. In 4Q417 2 i 10–11, an eschatological
inheritance contrasts with the things of this life: "Lest you have trouble
in your life [gaze upon the mystery] that is to come and comprehend the
birth-times of salvation, and know who is to inherit glory and toil." In
4Q416 4:3 the sage encourages the *mevin* to "rejoice in the inheritance
of truth" (שמחה בנחלת אמת). One passage suggests that the "mystery
that is to come" contains an inheritance for the wicked (and, I imagine, for the righteous as well, although such a statement is not extant).
4Q417 1 i 18–24, which begins with the sage calling the *mevin* "son,"
is a long passage on the "mystery that is to come" and knowledge of it.
Lines 23–24 speak of evildoers: "Do not be contaminated by evildoing
[...for everyone who is contaminated] with it shall not be treated as
guiltless. According to his inheritance in it [i.e., the mystery] he shall be
tr[eated as wicked...]." For the sage of 4QInstruction, God distributes
an inheritance to all humankind, but he is the "portion" (חלק) and
"inheritance" (נחלה) of the *mevin*. 4Q418 88 ii 7–8 may even suggest
that in death there is an inheritance: "Then you shall be gathered in
(your) sorrow [into death...] and in truth your in[her]itance shall be
fulfilled." A single passage employs the idea of inheritance to place the
mevin in the chain of patriarchal tradition. 4Q416 2 iii 7–8 claims that
if the *mevin* is faithful and uncorrupted by money "then (at death) you
will sleep in faithfulness, and at your death your memory will flow[er
forev]er, and your posterity will inherit joy."

Inheritance serves an import rhetorical function in the sage's strategy
of constructing the *mevin* (and the reader) as his child. By appealing to
this idea, the sage accomplishes more than one end. First, the language
of inheritance makes concrete the hierarchical nature of the relationship, particularly in this text, since the author compares God to one's

father, and so the metaphor serves to reinforce the readers' subjectivity. Second, by highlighting that one can inherit good and bad from God in the eschaton, the reader essentially must choose to hear and to obey his legitimate father, one who will give a desirable inheritance, or essentially be disinherited and abandoned to destruction. The stark reality of the choice is clear. Finally, as we have seen, the father's appeal to the receipt of an inheritance assures the son that he will take his place in the patriarchal order, if he adopts the values of the father. Each of these uses of inheritance furthers the aim of having the student/reader adopt the dominant symbolic order.

4QInstruction also utilizes a number of other features of father-son discourse that Newsom identified. The metaphor of walking correctly and on the right paths appears at several points in the extant fragments, although sometimes simply the verb "walk" alone serves to elicit the metaphor (see 4Q416 2 iv 7; 4Q417 1 i 10–12, 18–19; 4Q417 1 ii 11; 4Q418 87:10–11). Although they do not feature prominently in the work, the sage does frame rival discourses through the use of "do not say" (4Q416 2 iii 12) or direct report (4Q418 69 ii 10–11). While a number of passages in the extant fragments advise the *mevin* how to have a good relationship with the "wife of your bosom" (4Q416 2 iv 5), one fragmentary passage may suggest that the sage also referred to the dangers of illicit sexuality (4Q418 243). The notable feature lacking in 4QInstruction is any idealization of wisdom or her counterpart, folly, as a woman.[39]

The Damascus Document (CD; 4Q266–273)[40]

The *Damascus Document* begins with a call for "all who know justice" to "listen and understand the actions of God" (1:1). The text continues with the claim that God has a dispute (ריב) with all flesh, after which the author narrates the early history of the group for whom the text is written. In 2:2, the author again appeals for his readers to listen. This time the addressees are called "all who enter the covenant." In this sec-

---

[39] On women in 4QInstruction and other Qumran wisdom texts, see Chapter 1, "Wisdom and Women at Qumran."

[40] I am grateful to Charlotte Hempel for this reference. For the text of CD, see M. Broshi, *The Damascus Document Reconsidered* (Jerusalem: The Israel Exploration Society/The Shrine of the Book, Israel Museum, 1992). For the cave 4 manuscripts, see J.M. Baumgarten, *Qumran Cave 4 • XIII The Damascus Document (4Q266–273)* (DJD 18; Oxford: Clarendon, 1996).

tion the author will "open your ears to the paths of the wicked." In a third call to listen (2:14), the author moves to addressing the readers as "sons." Now, after having described the group's beginnings, those who opposed it, and the paths of the wicked, the author plans to "open your eyes so that you can see and understand the deeds of God so that you can choose what he is pleased with and repudiate what he hates." He then frames the choice before the readers in the language of walking paths. His "sons" are expected to follow perfect paths, while at the same time avoiding "the thoughts of a guilty inclination and lascivious eyes" (2:16), presumably the wrong path. Many have strayed because of these things, says our author, who then embarks on a long review of history beginning with the fall of the Watchers and extending to his present and then to the eschatological future. In the first two instances of the call to listen the author describes the situation before the readers as he assesses it. When he wants to present his readership with a choice to make, he calls them "sons." Here he adopts the language of the parent who understands that his children have a choice to make, but he has a clear preference for which option they select, or using the metaphor of the text, which path they decide to tread. He uses his presumed authority as the readers' "parent" to bias their decision in his favor. The decision is not really a free one since the author/parent expects that the readers/sons will see that what lies before them is really not a choice at all, but an expectation that they will walk the path to which the author/father directs them.

Texts Addressed to "You"

A number of works from Qumran address the reader as "you," but their extant fragments do not contain any explicit mention of the addressee(s) as "son(s)." In a couple of these, the addressee's identification is explicit, however. 4Q298 preserves in its first line what was presumably the title of the work, "Words of a sage, which he spoke to all the Sons of Dawn," and it begins with a familiar call, "Listen to me, all men of heart and pursuers of justice, understand my words, and seekers of truth hear my words." Unfortunately, not much of the work survives, but it contains a reference to the "path of life" (i 3). The work also preserves a call to the addressee to "understand the end of the ages" (iii 9–10). 4Q302, another short and fragmentary work, uses the second person plural, and its author calls out, "Understand

this, O wise ones" (2 ii 2). The rest of these works are extremely fragmentary and little can be made of them. Yet, every so often in them as
well some features of father-son discourse survive. One text, however,
deserves a more detailed examination.

4Q424 is a wisdom work whose three largest fragments contain warnings about various kinds of people to avoid. Fragment 3 ends with the
beginning of a list of people who are approved by the sage. The constant
refrain of "Do not do *x* with *x sort of person* because…" presents in
an explicit and unmistakable fashion those whom the sage regards as
sinners. The metaphorical use of "path" occurs one time, when the sage
warns against using a lazy person to help with one's business "for he
will not take care of your paths" (1:7). The list of approved people is
dominated by such abstract terms as justice (3:10, "sons of justice") and
righteousness (3:9 "righteousness for the poor ones") together with the
adjectives "wise," "prudent" and "upright." The sage presents a clear
contrast for the student to see.

The most prominent feature of this text, however, is its division of
the self into a series of body parts and adjectives describing them, all
of which are used metaphorically to identify moral categories. Newsom
highlights the strategy of rewriting the self as its parts in Proverbs 4,
and she comments, "The self is not presented as a simple entity. Or
perhaps it is better to say that the various parts of the body can represent the whole by synecdoche. The individual's subjectivity can be
seen as invested in each of these parts, any of which has the power to
work his ruin."[41] In 4Q424 individuals become symbolized by a single
body part, thus, reinforcing the ways that any individual body part can
control a person. So, the text warns against the "person with twisted
lips" who distorts the truth (1:8–9), the "person with an evil eye" who
will squander or steal one's wealth (1:10–12). One should not "send
a dim-sighted person to observe the upright" (3:3) nor the "hard of
hearing…to investigate a case" (4–5). The "fat of heart" should not be
asked to "unearth thoughts, because the wisdom of his heart is hidden…" (3:6–7).

In such a small amount of extant text, just three fragments, we find
a number of aspects of the father-son discourse that we have seen
elsewhere. Finding such a dense use of these devices in such limited
remains suggests that the sage of this work may have explicitly presented
himself as a father to a son.

---

[41] Newsom, "Women and the Discourse of Patriarchal Wisdom," 152.

Narrative Fathers Speaking to Sons

The narrative device of a father giving his sons advice, especially as he is about to die, appears with relative frequency in Second Temple Jewish literature. In some cases, like the *Testaments of the XII Patriarchs* or *Testament of Qahat (4Q542)*, the father's deathbed testament to his sons frames the entire work.[42] In other instances, like Tobit 4 and 14 or *1 Enoch* 82:1–4, the scene is incorporated into a larger and more diverse work. In each case, however, the speech of the father is characterized by the "I-you" of the wisdom texts I examined above. What makes a considerable difference is that the narrative frame of the speech distances and separates the reader from the father of the text, because the "I" and the "you" are no longer "linguistic blanks or empty signs," to use Newsom's phrase. These pronouns now have specific *dramatis personae* as their referents.

When we look at the speeches themselves, we can see many of the same features of the father-son discourse that we have already noted. It would certainly be possible to create a laundry list of where these features occur in these texts, but my purpose here is not to detail their presence in each work. Several examples will suffice to demonstrate the point. (1) The metaphor of walking paths occurs often. In *1 Enoch* 82:4 Enoch blesses the righteous "who walk in the path of righteousness." *Aramaic Levi* (4Q213 3 + 4:8) presents the patriarch as warning his sons that they will "forsake the paths of justice and all the ways of [. . . ." The *Testaments* are replete with references to walking either on paths or in God's commandments, in simplicity, etc. (i.e., *T.Sim.* 5:2; *T.Jud.* 13:2, 26:1; *T.Iss.* 4:1, 6, 5:1; *T.Naph.* 4:1; *T.Ash.* 1:3; *T.Jos.* 18:1). (2) All these texts rely on abstract notions of righteousness, justice, etc. The clearest example of how these terms can function is in the *Testament of Qahat* (4Q542 1 i 11–13), ". . . because you have carried on [the] inheritan[ce] which your fathers gave you, truth, justice, and uprightness, and

---

[42] While I recognize that not all scholars agree that the *Testaments* were originally Second Temple Jewish works, all concur that the work is heavily dependent, at the least, on Jewish sources. The best example is, of course, *T.Levi* and *Aramaic Levi*. On that relationship, see M.E. Stone, "Aramaic Levi Document and Greek Testament of Levi," *Emanuel: Studies in the Hebrew Bible, Septuagint, and Dead Sea Scrolls in Honor of Emanuel Tov*, (S.M. Paul et al., eds.; VTSup 94; Leiden/Boston: Brill, 2003) 429–37. Since these works contain many of the features of the discourse I have outlined above, they contribute to the overall argument of this paper. See H.W. Hollander and M. de Jonge, *The Testaments of the Twelve Patriarchs: A Commentary* (SVTP 8; Leiden: Brill, 1985).

perfection, and puri[ty and ho]liness, and the priest[ho]od...." (3)
Many texts emphasize the difference between approved and disap-
proved sexual relationships, which work to replicate or threaten the
patriarchal order. Thus, women often function as symbols of otherness
and marginality. This theme stands out especially in the *Testaments* and
Tobit. (4) Generally in these testamentary scenes the sons do not have
an opportunity to reply to the father's words, and thus the patriarch
gets to present the sinners and their behaviors and values in his terms
(cf., e.g., *1 Enoch* 82:4b–6; *Aramaic Levi*).

The topics purveyed in these works, such as moral exhortation, proper
cultic practice or warnings about eschatological rewards and punishments, suggest that these narrative father-son discourses are aimed at
influencing the readers' behavior and values. Thus, a crucial question
is whether these texts contain any features that bridge the gap between
the narrative "I" and "you" and the reader so that the reader can "take
up the subject position of son" in relation to the father of the narrative.[43] If readers found themselves in the same subject relationship to
the text that we saw above, then the elements of father-son discourse
contained in them potentially could affect the readers and encourage
their adoption of the values of the text's patriarch.

One feature of these texts that might accomplish such an aim is the
command on the part of the textual father for his sons to transmit his
teachings to their children. This obligation on the part of the textual
sons has the potential to place the reader at the end of a chain of transmission of the father's teaching through the generations. In a sense,
the reader would become one of the descendents of the narrative patriarch. To this end, the device that probably creates the highest degree
of obligation in the reader to adopt the father's teaching is when he
gives *writings* to his sons and obligates them to transmit them to their
sons throughout subsequent generations. In this case, the recipient,
who reads or listens to the book being read, has physical possession
of the legacy of the father's instruction, which creates a link between
the patriarch and the reader. The readers then may perceive that the
"I-you" discourse of the father is directed at them. Other features of
this discourse will most likely function as they do in those works in
which the sage addresses the reader directly through the text. We find

---

[43] The quote comes from Newsom, "Women and the Discourse of Patriarchal Wisdom," 143.

this strategy in *1 Enoch, Aramaic Levi Document* and the *Testament of Qahat* (4Q542). In *1 Enoch* 82:1–2 Enoch, who has seen heavenly visions, transmits records of them to Methuselah:

> And now my son Methuselah, all these things I recount and write for you, and all of them I have revealed to you, and I have given you books about all these things. Keep, my son Methuselah, the books of the hand of your father, that you may give them to the generations of eternity. Wisdom I have given you and to your sons and to those who would be your sons that they may give to all the generations until eternity this wisdom that surpasses their thought.[44]

Enoch's command for Methuselah to pass on these books "to those who would be your sons" contains the implication that *anyone* who receives this wisdom is a son of Methuselah, and hence of Enoch. Thus, Enoch speaks to the reader directly through the "I-you" discourse contained in his written legacy.[45]

Both *Aramaic Levi* and *Testament of Qahat* give strong indication that their teaching is to be handed down in written form. In *Aramaic Levi* (4Q213 1 i 9–10 and Cambridge col. e 18–19) the patriarch requires his sons to "teach reading and writing and the teaching of wisdom to your children and may wisdom be eternal glory for you."[46] Here reading and writing are connected with wisdom that is to be handed to a next generation. While this passage is not as clear as *1 Enoch*, the implication is that written material is to be transmitted by the patriarch's sons. Although fragmentary, one passage in the *Testament of Qahat* (4Q542 1 ii 9–13) has the patriarch say, "And now to you, Amram my son, I comma[nd...] and [to] your [son]s and to their sons I command [...] and they have given to Levi, my father, and which Levi, my father, has gi[ven] to me [...] all my writings as witness that you should take care of them [...] for you; in them is great worth in their being carried on with you." Elsewhere in the work (4Q542 1 i 3–4) Qahat refers to "your sons in the generations of truth forever." Although the details are

---

[44] The original place of this passage is a matter of dispute. In the version of the work that we have it forms part of the conclusion of the Astronomical Book. See G.W.E. Nickelsburg, *1 Enoch 1* (Hermeneia: Minneapolis: Fortress, 2001) 333–44.

[45] While the claims of the text gain authority from the fact that they are written and passed down from the patriarch, the texts themselves probably derive authority by taking on the voices of known and revered patriarchs.

[46] 4Q213 2 ii + 2:12–13 contains the phrase "in the books read," but there is no context. It is not clear if these are written books from Levi or something else entirely. This passage does not appear to have a parallel in the Geniza manuscripts.

somewhat obscure, it appears as if Qahat is passing down his literary legacy to Amram so that he can pass it on to future generations.

A variant of this notion may be found in the *Testaments of the XII Patriarchs*. Each of the twelve separate deathbed speeches from the patriarchs to their sons begins with the claim that it is a copy of the patriarch's words that he spoke to his sons before his death. Five of these also contain in them some additional command that the sons transmit the patriarch's teaching and wisdom to their sons (*T.Iss.* 6:3; *T.Dan* 6:9; *T.Naph.* 8:2; *T.Gad* 8:1; *T.Ash.* 7:4). This combination of a claim to the exact words of the patriarch and the command to transmit them may position readers at the end of the chain of transmission and thus obligate them to hear and adopt the father's teaching. Three of the testaments, *Simeon*, *Levi* and *Benjamin*, make more explicit reference to time after the patriarch's grandsons. *T.Sim.* 7:3 reads, "Therefore, I give you these commands, that you may command your children that they may observe them through their generations." *T.Jud.* contains the notice at the very beginning, "A copy of the words of Levi, which he enjoined on his sons before his death according to all that they would do and that would befall them until the day of judgment." *T.Levi* contains other references to transmission beyond the patriarch's sons (4:5; 13:2) as in other testaments. Finally, *T.Benj.* 10:4 has, "For I teach you these things instead of any inheritance. And do you also, therefore, give them to your children for an everlasting possession." These three combine the command to transmit or possess the patriarch's teachings over periods of time that extend well beyond a generation or two. In these, readers are certainly included as the descendents of the patriarch who should observe his teaching.[47]

Conclusion

What Newsom brought to light in Proverbs was that the sage was not content simply to offer instruction and see what happened. He resorted to a discourse that limited the ability of his students or his readers to decide on their own whether or not to adopt his values and symbolic

---

[47] In the case of Tob 14:8–9, Tobit commands his children to command their children "to do what is right, to give alms, and to be mindful of God, and to bless his name at all times." He does not bequeath a written legacy to his children, and this case is not as compelling as those in which written texts get handed down.

order. By constructing students and readers as children of an authoritative father, he placed obligations on them to accept those values just as they would those of their "real" fathers. In order to accomplish this end, the sage of Proverbs employed a variety of strategies to recreate and reinforce the subjectivity of those who engaged the text. Each of these strategies served to bolster the authority of the sage and the power of the values and symbolic order he presented to his students/readers.

The sages represented in these Second Temple wisdom texts moved beyond trading on a literary device they found in the tradition; they clearly found it effective for accomplishing their own similar goals. Thus, they did more than borrow. They adopted and adapted this father-son discourse and created additional strategies, like 4QInstruction's emphasis on the centrality of inheritance or Ben Sira's use of historical review to enlist the son as a potential father, that enabled them to claim the paternal authority that they employed as instructional tools. All these sage fathers had themselves once been sons, figuratively as well as literally, who had been integrated into the values of their own fathers. They had been successfully transformed from sons into fathers, and they in turn bequeathed their legacy to their children and to their children's children. Because of the open and inclusive nature of readership, the preservation of these texts has enabled these textual parents to speak to innumerable readers as their children in times and places they could never have imagined.

CHAPTER THREE

THE CATEGORIES OF RICH AND POOR IN THE QUMRAN SAPIENTIAL LITERATURE

In his article, "Ten Reasons Why the Qumran Wisdom Texts are Important," D.J. Harrington has argued a case for the value of the corpus of wisdom books found near the Dead Sea.[1] Undoubtedly many more than ten reasons could be mustered in support of their importance to scholars of Judaism in the Second Temple Period, and several studies have set out the general scope and problems of these texts.[2] The recent publication of 4QInstruction, the most extensive wisdom book found at Qumran, by J. Strugnell and D.J. Harrington in DJD 34, puts scholars in the advantageous position of having practically all of the Qumran wisdom texts available.[3] The foundation is now laid for further and more detailed studies of this literature.

One observation that scholars have made about the Qumran texts is that they cover a number of subjects familiar from other Jewish wisdom literature. Indeed, the third of Harrington's ten reasons is that "[t]hey provide further treatments of standard wisdom topics."[4] Along with women and speech, the subject of riches and poverty, and attitudes toward those who are rich or poor, constitutes one of the most pervasive topics in Jewish wisdom. The frequency with which the ancient sages addressed issues connected with wealth, poverty and

---

[1] *DSD* 4 (1997) 245–54. This entire fascicle is devoted to "Wisdom at Qumran."

[2] The most important to this point is D.J. Harrington, *Wisdom Texts from Qumran* (London and New York: Routledge, 1996). See also Harrington's earlier article, "Wisdom at Qumran," *The Community of the Renewed Covenant* (E. Ulrich and J.C. VanderKam, eds.; Christianity and Judaism in Antiquity 10; Notre Dame, IN: University of Notre Dame Press, 1994) 137–52. See also the long chapter "Wisdom in the Dead Sea Scrolls," in J.J. Collins, *Jewish Wisdom in the Hellenistic Age* (OTL; Louisville: Westminster John Knox, 1997) 112–31.

[3] See J. Strugnell and D.J. Harrington, "4QInstruction," *Qumran Cave 4.XXIV: Sapiential Texts, Part 2* (J. Strugnell, D.J. Harrington, T. Elgvin, eds.; DJD 34; Oxford: Clarendon, 1999) 1–503. T. Elgvin contributed the publication of 4Q423 ("423. 4QInstruction^g," DJD 34.505–33). Strugnell and Harrington also include a re-edition of 1Q26 published originally by J.T. Milik in DJD 1 (Oxford: Clarendon, 1955); see "Appendix: 26. 1QInstruction (Re-Edition)," DJD 34, 535–40.

[4] Harrington, "Ten Reasons," 248.

financial dealings demonstrates just how important they thought it was for someone receiving instruction to have a proper understanding of matters concerning money.

The ways that the producers of Jewish wisdom talk about wealth and poverty inform modern scholars as well, since oftentimes these ancient discussions seem to reflect the complex social and cultural realities of those who promulgated wisdom instruction. Even though investigation into the social origins of wisdom literature is notoriously difficult, scholarly analysis of this pervasive topic could provide some entrée into these ancient social and cultural worlds. Examination of the language of rich and poor and the sages' advice about riches and poverty has already helped elucidate a variety of issues in the study of two Jewish wisdom texts, including their social locations. In separate studies, J.D. Pleins and H.C. Washington have looked at the use of the language of riches and poverty in Proverbs.[5] In a separate study, C.V. Camp and I have argued that Ben Sira's instruction about wealth and poverty reveals that he occupied a precarious social position. On the one hand, he reinforces for his students the Jewish covenantal obligation to assist the poor, even to the extent of rendering judgments in their favor. On the other hand, he must continually exercise caution when dealing with the rich, who are clearly his social superiors. Finding himself in this intermediary position, he is faced with conflicting social loyalties and obligations.[6]

In this paper I want to ask questions about the Qumran sapiential texts similar to those Camp and I asked about Ben Sira, in order to see if any answers might be ventured.[7] Does the language of riches, poverty and financial dealings provide access to the social contexts of the Qumran wisdom texts? Do the sages who produced these texts intend the terms to denote actual circumstances of rich and poor? Is the language ever used metaphorically? Do the sages represented in the Qumran texts think that God favors one group or the other?

---

[5] J.D. Pleins, "Poverty in the Social World of the Wise," JSOT 37 (1987) 61–78; see also his recent book, *The Social Visions of the Hebrew Bible* (Nashville: Abingdon, 2001). Likewise see H.C. Washington, *Wealth and Poverty in the Instructions of Amenemope and the Hebrew Proverbs* (SBLDS 142; Atlanta: Scholars Press, 1994).

[6] Chapter 4, "'Who Has Been Tested by Gold and Found Perfect?' Ben Sira's Discourse of Riches and Poverty."

[7] See now C.M. Murphy, *Wealth in the Dead Sea Scrolls and in the Qumran Community* (STDJ 40; Leiden: Brill, 2002). Murphy examines the issue of wealth across the entire Qumran corpus.

Rich and Poor in the Qumran Wisdom Texts

Although the Qumran scrolls contain a number of wisdom texts, many are fragmentary and difficult to understand. Those manuscripts usually included in the category are:[8] 4Q184 (the so-called "Wiles of the Wicked Woman"); 4Q185; 4Q298; 4Q413; 4Q415–418, 423 (formerly Sapiential A, but now known as 4QInstruction of which 1Q26 is also a copy); 4Q420–421 (4QWays of Righteousness); 4Q424; 4Q525 (4QBeatitudes); 11Q5 26:9–15 (*Hymn to the Creator*). Harrington notes that scholars have identified a number of other manuscripts as sapiential, on the basis of their style and vocabulary (4Q307–308; 4Q408; 4Q410–412; 4Q425–426; 4Q472–476; 4Q486–487; 4Q498); but, "in all cases there is not enough running text preserved to make a substantial contribution to our understanding of Qumran wisdom."[9]

As in other Jewish wisdom texts, Qumran wisdom employs a number of different terms for rich and poor. The major words that indicate poverty are the usual ones found elsewhere—אבון, דל, מסור and רש (with its variant ריש). עני/ענוה, meaning "humble," often refers to those of poor economic circumstance in Jewish wisdom, but except for a very few instances, it does not generally have the meaning "poor" in our group of texts. In non-Qumran wisdom literature the terms טובה, חרוץ, חיל, הון, עשר and מחיר can indicate wealth, money or riches. In the Qumran scrolls הון is far and away the most frequent.

In what follows, I provide notes on all the places I could identify where the language of wealth, poverty and financial matters appear in the scrolls listed above. I will give the shorter, more fragmentary texts first and then treat the more substantial ones, about which I will make more extensive comments.

4Q184:[10] This text, which warns against the scandalous behavior of Lady Folly, who pursues the righteous to lead them astray, contains no unambiguous references to wealth or poverty. Fragment 1 line 16

---

[8] These correlate closely with the texts cited by Harrington in *Wisdom Texts from Qumran*. I have not listed here wisdom texts that were already known before the finds at Qumran.

[9] Harrington, *Wisdom Texts from Qumran*, 73–4. Some of these text designations have changed upon publication in the DJD series and others may change in the future.

[10] See J.M. Allegro, "184," *Qûmran Cave 4.1 (4Q158–4Q186)* (DJD 5; Oxford: Clarendon, 1968) 82–5; J. Strugnell, "Notes en marge du volume V des 'Discoveries in the Judaean Desert of Jordon,'" *RevQ* 7 (1969–70) 163–276, pp. 263–68.

speaks about Folly's attempt to make the "humble (עָנוים) rebel against God." In this instance, the meaning of "poor" found elsewhere in Jewish wisdom literature for עָנוה (cf. many instances in Ben Sira and also 4Q424 below) does not seem to apply.

4Q185: This fragmentary work primarily concerns the search for Lady Wisdom. Two mentions of riches appear here. Fragment 1–2 ii 4–5 poses the question, "Is not one day in his house better than riches? ([...]מעשר)" In this question, one of the most desirable things in life, riches, fails in comparison with being "in his house" [= the Temple?]. Later in line 12 the sage says that the one who eventually finds wisdom and holds fast to her will have "long days and greasy bones and a happy heart and rich[es and honor] ([עשׁ]ר וכבוד])."[11] Contrary to 4QInstruction, where עשׁר does not appear at all in the extant fragments, in 4Q185 it is the only word used for wealth. The more general sentiment of this passage, that contentment and prosperity are the result of the successful pursuit of wisdom, is shared with other Jewish wisdom literature (cf., for instance, Prov 8:18, 22:4 where riches are the reward of humility and fear of the Lord; cf. also Sir 51:28).

4Q412: Published by A. Steudel in DJD 20, 4Q412 is a fragmentary, wisdom-type text.[12] Fragment 4 contains the phrase [...]עשׁרי ינחיל[...], which could be translated "my wealth he will give as an inheritance."[13] The phrase has no context that would assist in understanding it further. It is, like 4Q185, another one of the few places in the wisdom texts at Qumran where עשׁר is the Hebrew term designating wealth.

4Q525:[14] Most notable for its series of macarisms or beatitudes (Fragment 2 ii) that can be compared to those in Matthew's Sermon on the Mount, 4Q525 refers to gold and poverty separately in two fragmentary

---

[11] The texts and translations are taken from F. García Martínez and E.J.C. Tigchelaar, *The Dead Sea Scrolls Study Edition* (2 vols.; Leiden: Brill, 1998) 1.378. The references are partially restored. Harrington's translation in *Wisdom Texts from Qumran* makes no mention of riches in either place.

[12] "412. 4QSapiential-Didactic Work A," *Qumran Cave 4.XV: Sapiential Texts, Part I* (T. Elgvin et al., eds. in consultation with J.A. Fitzmyer, S.J.; DJD 20; Oxford: Clarendon, 1997) 163–67.

[13] García Martínez and Tigchelaar, *Study Edition*, 2.843.

[14] For the text see É. Puech, "525. 4QBeatitudes," *Qumrân Grotte 4.XVIII: Textes Hébreux (4Q521–528, 4Q576–579)* (DJD 25; Oxford: Clarendon, 1998) 115–78. Translation as in García Martínez and Tigchelaar, *Study Edition*, 2.1053–59.

passages. Although wisdom is not specifically mentioned, Fragment 2 iii 2, "she cannot be obtained with gold" (לוא תלקח בזהב), claims that Wisdom cannot be bought. This sentiment contrasts with the remarks made earlier in the work (Fragment 2 ii) that one acquires wisdom by doing things like adhering to the Law, always thinking about her (i.e., wisdom), searching for her with "pure hands."

The one mention of poverty in 4Q525 comes in Fragment 15, which mentions a burning serpent and vipers and eternal curses. Perhaps it concerns eschatological judgment. The first line of the fragment says, "You will gather poverty (אגר ריש[ת...])." Exactly what this statement means or to what it refers remains unclear.

4Q424: Although four fragments of this work survive, only three provide text that is usable, since Fragment 4 contains a scant seven letters. The extant portion of the work preserves two types of practical wisdom— sayings about people with whom one should not associate or to whom one should not give responsibility and sayings describing people who have valuable qualities that should be imitated.[15]

References to riches and poverty appear several times in these fragments, and if their frequency provides any indication, these topics were an important concern of the whole work. Fragment 1:7–8 proffers the trenchant advice, "A man who is always complaining about his luck, do not expect money (הון) from him when you are in need (למחסורך)." הון, "money," and מחסור, "need/want," constitute two of the most frequent words used in the Qumran wisdom texts to connote riches and poverty. They are particularly frequent in 4QInstruction (see below).

Line 10 admonishes the recipient of this wisdom not to put a greedy person "in a position of authority over your mo[ney]/we[alth] (בהו]נך)." Line 11 is more fragmentary, but it seems to continue the thought. S. Tanzer suggests that a possible reconstruction of these lines might be, "A man who is greedy do not put in a position of authority over your we[alth, for never] will he mete out your surplus to your satisfaction, but [he will keep (it all)] for those who have more than enough[...]."As

---

[15] On this text, see S. Tanzer's edition, "424. 4QInstruction-like Composition B," *Qumran Cave 4.XXVI: Cryptic Texts* (S.J. Pfann, ed.); and *Miscellanea, Part 1* (P. Alexander et al., eds. in consultation with J.C. VanderKam and M. Brady; DJD 36; Clarendon: Oxford, 2000) 333–48; and three articles by G. Brin: "Studies in 4Q424, Fragment 3," *VT* 46 (1996) 271–95; "Studies in 4Q424 1–2," *RevQ* 69 (1997) 21–43; "Wisdom Issues in Qumran: The Types and Status of the Figures in 4Q424 and the Phrases of Rationale in the Document," *DSD* 4 (1997) 297–311.

she observes, if this reconstruction approximates what was in the full text, the passage would present a contrast between how the greedy money manager would treat the poor and how he would regard the rich.[16] That is, he would not give the surplus wealth to the poor, as the owner desires, but redirect it to the rich, perhaps in order to ingratiate himself with them.

Fragment 2:3 contains a familiar sapiential admonition: "One who is a hypo]crite, do not give surety for him among the poo[r] (עָנ[י])." In this saying the meaning of the more allusive עָנָוה as "poor" corresponds to its use in other wisdom books like Ben Sira, where the term often connotes people of low economic status. The topic of giving surety is a standard wisdom subject that recurs many times in Jewish wisdom texts (cf., for example, Prov. 6:1; Sir 8:13; and a number of times in 4QInstruction, see below). Whereas the primary concern of 4Q424 1 was protecting the addressee's wealth from potentially unscrupulous people, the saying in this fragment focuses on guarding the poor against abuse.

Further down this fragment at the beginning of line 5, Tanzer reconstructs the word אב[יונים, but the broken context does not allow one to say much about it. She does, however, suggest the possibility, "A man who despises the poor, do not set him in authority."[17] If this saying, or something close to it, were the actual text, then both sayings in this fragment would focus on protecting the poor.

Assistance for the poor is also the subject of Fragment 3:9–10 and perhaps line 11, which concludes the fragment's extant text. These three lines come in the second section of the work, which characterizes people of integrity and values. Lines 9–10 read, "A man of generosit[y perfo]rms charity for the poor (לאביונ°[]) [...]/[...]he takes care of all who lack property/money (הון)." Thus, the generous person is the opposite of those described earlier who are greedy or hypocrites; he will take care of the poor when they will not. This same topic perhaps continues in the fragmentary line 11, which contains the phrase "in all wealth (בכול הון)," but it is difficult to know since the line contains this phrase alone.

---

[16] Tanzer, DJD 36, 340.
[17] Ibid., 342.

The passages concerning riches and poverty that I have discussed so far
do not allow us to make much headway regarding (1) the ever-vexing
question of whether any of these texts is "sectarian," that is, a product
of the Qumran community and (2) the social location of the texts.
Although some scholars have tried to advance arguments that would
place the origins of particular wisdom texts within the sphere of Qumran
or the sectarian community out of which the *yaḥad* emerged, none has
as yet won the day. J.C.R. de Roo, for instance, has argued that 4Q525
is a sectarian document, while É. Puech thinks it more likely that it
predated and influenced some of the authors at Qumran.[18]

Two major difficulties attend any attempt to rely on the remarks about
wealth and poverty as a basis for making judgments about the social
context of these works. First, in many cases there simply is very little
or even no context to provide any clear indication of how these terms
and ideas are functioning. A passage like that in 4Q412, "my riches he
will give as an inheritance," tells us very little beyond which term for
wealth appears in the text. Second, many passages that do have some
context turn out to contain conventional sentiments about wealth and
poverty. To say that wisdom cannot be purchased with money as in
4Q525, or that one should not put a greedy person in charge of one's
money as in 4Q424, is neither revelatory nor even surprising in this
literature. In fact a good number of the statements about wealth and
poverty find ready parallels in other Jewish wisdom texts. Thus their very
conventionality becomes an obstacle to determining if they represent
the particular social context of these documents.

Yet, even though much of the advice about wealth and poverty does
not come unexpectedly, one might still be able to venture some remarks
about the texts. The different ways in which the sages represented in
them invoke wealth and poverty might say *something* about their social
locations. For instance, the instruction given in 4Q424 comes from
a sage to a singular "you" as is the often the case with Ben Sira and

---

[18] J.C.R. de Roo, "Is 4Q525 a Qumran Sectarian Document?" *The Scrolls and the
Scriptures: Qumran Fifty Years After* (S.E. Porter and C.A. Evans, eds.; Roehampton
Institute London Papers 3; JSPSup 26; Sheffield: Sheffield Academic Press, 1997)
338–67. É. Puech, DJD 25, 119. On the beatitudes in 4Q525, see Puech, "4Q525 et les
péricopes des béatitudes en Ben Sira et Matthieu," *RB* 98 (1991) 80–106; and idem,
"The Collection of Beatitudes in Hebrew and in Greek (4Q525 and Mt 5,3–12)," *Early
Christianity in Context. Monuments and Documents* (F. Manns and E. Alliata, eds.;
Studium Biblicum Franciscanum, Collectio Maior 38; Jerusalem: Franciscan Printing
Press, 1993) 353–68.

Proverbs. The sage advises his charge about use of his money and care for the poor. Even though the advice he gives conforms to what we see elsewhere, the practical nature of that advice suggests that the recipient of the instruction needs to be taught about money matters. One could conclude, then, that the character of the wealth and poverty discussion at the least indicates that the recipient likely lives in a world where he has to make monetary decisions. This life situation, of course, contrasts with the usual picture of communal life at Qumran. 4Q424, however, also contains language, like the phrase רודפי דעת, that has sectarian connotations, a fact that potentially complicates matters.[19] This same problem accompanies analysis of 4QInstruction.

Texts like 4Q185 work differently. They do not address a wisdom recipient, nor do they contain instruction about the practical use of wealth or care for the poor. They employ the language of wealth and poverty in the service of some other end. To claim that wisdom cannot be bought, but that she must be sought, or that holding fast to wisdom brings riches, differs in kind from the practical advice given in texts like 4Q424. In cases like 4Q185, the author employs the language using different rhetorical strategies, and though not strictly metaphorical, such language does not signal advice about how to use one's money properly, or how to avoid becoming impoverished, or how to provide for the poor. In such instances, the use of the categories of rich and poor does not as readily provide insight into the possible life situation as it does in a work like 4Q424. In general, texts of this sort lack extended reflections on material circumstances, and as a result much less can be said about them on the basis of their use of the categories of rich and poor.

4QInstruction (4Q415–418, 418a, 423, 1Q26)

The seven (or possibly eight) extant, although fragmentary, copies of this work demonstrate that it was held in high regard among the members of the Qumran community. It is the most extensive wisdom text that survives among the Qumran scrolls, and one could claim that it is the most interesting as well.

What distinguishes 4QInstruction from many other wisdom texts is that it frames wisdom advice, much of it standard, with cosmological

---

[19] Tanzer, DJD 36, 336.

and eschatological matters.[20] Such interests form a stark contrast with a work like Ben Sira, whose disinterest in eschatology is often noted. In fact, 4QInstruction apparently began with a third person section featuring the judgment pronounced by God on all the wicked (4Q416 1).[21] This fragment contains no wisdom teaching, and it may well be intended to provide the motivation for following the instruction given to the recipient later in the work. The interest in and concern for eschatology continues throughout the book, especially in the references to the elusive רז נהיה, or "mystery that is to come," whose content, although never made explicit in the fragments that survive, almost certainly is at least partially eschatological.[22]

The text switches from the third person of the beginning to second person singular address when the sage gives wisdom instruction to the *mevin*.[23] In several places the addressee shifts from the *mevin* to someone else. This occurs most notably in 4Q415 2 ii where second person singular feminine pronouns show the addressee to be a woman.[24] 4QInstruction does not contain in isolation many short pithy proverbs about behavior à la the biblical Proverbs; rather, the short proverbs are mixed with longer, topically oriented wisdom instructions. Among the usual wisdom topics covered in the work, wealth, poverty and financial matters stand out as exceptionally prominent. Several of the larger fragments have money as a central concern, and they contain sometimes

---

[20] The inclusion of eschatology in wisdom writing can also be seen in 4Q525 and other texts from Qumran.

[21] Strugnell and Harrington, DJD 34, 80.

[22] On the "mystery that is to come" and its content, see T. Elgvin, "Wisdom, Revelation, and Eschatology in an Early Essene Writing," *SBL Seminar Papers, 1995* (SBLSP 34; Atlanta: Scholars Press, 1995) 440–63; idem, "Early Essene Eschatology: Judgment and Salvation according to Sapiential Work A," *Current Research and Technological Developments on the Dead Sea Scrolls: Conference on the Texts from the Judean Desert, Jerusalem, 30 April 1995* (D.W. Parry and S.D. Ricks, eds.; STDJ 20; Leiden: Brill, 1996) 126–65; idem, "The Mystery to Come: Early Essene Theology of Revelation," *Qumran Between the Old and New Testaments* (F.H. Cryer and T.L. Thompson, eds.; JSOTSup 290; Sheffield: Sheffield Academic Press, 1998) 113–50; D.J. Harrington, "The *Raz Nihyeh* in a Qumran Wisdom Text (1Q26, 4Q415–418, 4Q423)," *Hommage à Józef T. Milik*, *RevQ* 17 (1996) 549–53; idem, *Wisdom Texts from Qumran*, chap. 6.

[23] מבין, the recipient of the wisdom teaching of 4QInstruction, translated "maven" by Strugnell and Harrington.

[24] Strugnell and Harrington, DJD 34, 48, suggest a "female associate" of the *mevin* or perhaps his wife or daughter. Some other sections give teaching using second person plural forms. On this issue, see E.J.C. Tigchelaar, "The Addressees of 4QInstruction," *Sapiential, Liturgical and Poetic Texts from Qumran: Proceedings of the Third Meeting of the International Organization for Qumran Studies* (D.K. Falk, F. García Martínez, E.M. Schuller, eds.; STDJ 35; Leiden: Brill, 2000) 62–75.

lengthy instructions about it. Words having to do with riches and
poverty are scattered throughout even the very small fragments.

Several general features of 4QInstruction's teaching about riches and
poverty stand out. First, the work concentrates much more on poverty
and the conditions that result in impoverishment than on wealth or
the wealthy. Even the vocabulary used reflects this emphasis. The only
word used by 4QInstruction for wealth or money is הון. עשר, which
occurs frequently in other wisdom texts like Ben Sira and which might
be expected in a text that focuses on money matters, does not appear
at all in the extant fragments of our text. One possible explanation for
this absence might be that 4QInstruction betrays no concern at all for
the rich as a social class. Whereas Ben Sira advises his protégés about
how to deal with the rich, 4QInstruction contains no such advice. This
observation has ramifications for understanding the possible social
location of the text, which I will treat below.

The terms meaning "poor" or "poverty," however, are quite diverse.
4QInstruction uses מחסור ,ריש ,אביון and דל. The only occurrence
of עני in the extant fragments comes in 4Q417 2 i 14 (overlapped by
4Q418a 22). Strugnell and Harrington translate the line, "Be like a
humble [emphasis mine] man when you contend for a judgment in
favor of him."[25] There is no indication that the term as it is used here
connotes poor economic status as it can in other wisdom texts. 4QIn-
struction's favorite words for poverty are אביון and ריש (and its variant spellings רש, ראש, רוש), which are practically synonyms. מחסור,
"deficiency," "lack," or "want," is frequent and most often indicates
conditions of poverty. In at least one instance, however, the phrase לפי
מחסור צבאם "according to the deficiency of their host" (4Q416 1:6),
denotes something lacking in the host, but its/their economic status
does not seem to be the issue. דל occurs one time (4Q418 126 ii 7) in
what looks to be an eschatological context, where God will "raise up
the head of the poor."

One of the consistent emphases of 4QInstruction is the connection
between the *mevin* and poverty. The sage in the text reminds the *mevin*
repeatedly, "You are poor" (cf. אביון אתה 4Q415 6:2; 4Q416 2 iii 12;
ראש אתה 4Q416 2 iii 2; רש אתה 4Q418 177:5). Such designations

---

[25] Strugnell and Harrington use a King James-like English for their translation.
Although I have used their translations throughout, I have also substituted "you" and
"your," etc. for words like "thee" and "thou."

might be thought to denote the humility of the *mevin* rather than his low economic status. Perhaps the author wanted to play on the possible multivalence of the terms, but all the evidence points to some relationship between the language of 4QInstruction and the *mevin*'s actual or at least potential impoverishment.

In a number of places, 4QInstruction refers to the *mevin*'s poverty, sometimes in contexts immediately surrounding the "you are poor" phrases. In the fragmentary 4Q415 6, for example, line 2 begins with the familiar אביון אתה and then line 3 starts with רישכה, "your poverty." 4Q416 2 iii 15–16 gives the admonition, "Honor your father in your poverty (ברישכה) and your mother in your low estate." And later in line 20, "you have taken a wife in your poverty (ברישכה)." Sometimes, however, the advice is given in a conditional form, "if you are poor," and seems to refer to the *mevin*'s potential impoverishment (cf. 4Q416 2 iii 19; 4Q417 2 i 19). Using 4Q416 2 iii 19 as a central text, E.J.C. Tigchelaar argues that all the "you are poor" clauses in this section of 4QInstruction should be read as conditionals. He concludes, "Thus one should not translate: 'You are poor. Do not…,' but 'If you are poor do not….' The section as a whole should be read as an instruction on how to behave *if*, or *when*, one is poor, but the resumption of the theme of poverty in the next section is somewhat strange."[26]

Other scholars, such as Collins and Harrington, accept the "you are poor" statements as evidence of the *mevin*'s actual poverty.[27] Indeed, in the quote given above, Tigchelaar notices the strangeness of the reference to "your poverty" in 4Q416 2 iii 15–16, the admonition to honor one's parents. His solution to the problem, that "the reference to poverty in these commandments serves to smooth the transition from the theme of financial matters to that of family affairs," is less than satisfactory, however.[28] Yet, his argument does at least attempt to resolve the real incongruity between statements that seem to indicate the *mevin*'s poor circumstances and those that anticipate potential impoverishment.

Several observations, however, indicate that the references in 4QInstruction to the *mevin*'s poverty reflect the real nature of his economic situation and its ongoing precarious nature. First, most of the references

---

[26] Tigchelaar, "Addressees," 71.
[27] Collins, *Jewish Wisdom*, 118; Harrington, *Wisdom Texts from Qumran*, 45.
[28] Tigchelaar, "Addressees," 71.

to poverty or potential poverty are directed at the *mevin*. By contrast, the text contains no evidence that he should be counted among the wealthy. The references to poverty in 4QInstruction only apply infrequently to poor people generally, and it contains practically no discussion of the wealthy as a social class. In fact, a social class of the wealthy is conspicuous by its absence from the extant portions of this wisdom text. I would maintain that the *mevin*, however we describe him, cannot be situated among the well-to-do. In fact, he is taught repeatedly about how to avoid being their economic victim.

Second, several passages outside of the "you are poor" clauses seem to refer to the *mevin*'s actual poverty. The fact that they do not appear in conditional contexts is what prompted Tigchelaar's remark that they appeared strange. Several instances occur in larger fragments that have some reasonable context and do not appear to be intended to be conditional (cf. 4Q416 2 ii 20 [במחסורכה]; 4Q416 2 iii 6, 15, 20 ברישכה, רישכה, ברישכה; 4Q417 2 i 17, 21 [למחסורכה, מחסורכה]; 4Q418 126 ii 13 [למחסורכה]). In a case like 4Q416 2 iii 5–6, for example, the *mevin* is warned not to take money from someone he does not know, "lest he increase (*or*: make worse) your poverty (פן יסיף על רישכה)." The poor economic position of the *mevin* seems taken for granted here, and the warning aims to keep that situation from becoming even worse. Other occurrences of "your poverty" or "your need" come in more fragmentary passages where it is not possible to tell whether or not the context was conditional (cf. 4Q418 88 ii 5 [ממחסורכה]; 4Q418 107:3 [למחסורכה]; 4Q418 148 ii 4 [איש אתה רו° "you are a poor(?) man"]).

Third, 4QInstruction also provides evidence congruent with statements in Ben Sira that being poor is not the same as being destitute. Both wisdom texts indicate that to be poor is not necessarily identical with being penniless. Sirach 29:21–22, for example, says, "The necessities of life are bread, water, clothing, and also a house to assure privacy. Better is the life of the poor under one's own roof than sumptuous food in the house of others." Ben Sira distinguishes the poor person who has *something* from the destitute person who must resort to begging. "It is better to die than to beg," he says in 40:28.[29] Like Ben Sira's poor, the *mevin* of 4QInstruction is assumed to have some possessions, and he should safeguard them in order to keep from falling into more abject

---

[29] On this issue in Ben Sira, see "Who Has Been Tested by Gold?" 79–80.

circumstances (cf., for example, 4Q416 2 ii 5). The encouragement given in 4Q417 2 i 20 to eat what God gives him assumes that the *mevin* has food, but ought not to desire more than he has. It thus may not be contradictory to picture the addressee of 4QInstruction as having some possessions and at the same time being described as poor.

It does not appear to me, then, that the "you are poor" or "if/when you are poor" clauses are necessarily exclusive of each other. In any case one certainly gets the general impression that the *mevin*, who is not well off and may already be in poverty, continually teeters on the edge of falling into increasingly difficult economic circumstances, even destitution. The sage of 4QInstruction thus intends his advice to rescue the *mevin* from the oppressive results of poverty, such as falling into the hands of creditors, lenders and others who would take advantage of him.

Indeed, the theme of how to deal with creditors and debt seems something of a preoccupation of 4QInstruction, a preoccupation that might reflect the social world of the work. Three significant sections, 4Q416 2 ii and iii and 4Q417 2 i (and their overlaps in other fragments), have this theme as their primary focus.[30] 4Q416 2 ii 4–6 reads:

> (4) As much as a man's creditor has lent him money (הון), hastily pay it back, and you will be on equal footing with him (sc. the creditor). If the purse (5) containing your treasures (כיס צפונכה) you have entrusted to your creditor, on account of your friends you have given away all your life with it. Hasten and give what (6) is his, and take back your purse, and in your speech do not act feeble-spirited.

Two different matters are at stake here. First, the sage enjoins the *mevin* to pay back quickly any loans he has taken. The reason is simple—that way the creditor will have no power over the *mevin*, and he and the creditor will be on equal footing. The second issue apparently concerns some kind of loan or deposit made on behalf of friends that the *mevin* is now responsible to repay. The *mevin* should, as in the first case, make repayment quickly, because in the eyes of the sage, by giving up his purse he has given away his life. In this latter case the *mevin*

---

[30] In these cases I am relying on the composite text of the fragments given in Strugnell and Harrington, DJD 34. In each of these places they give the fragment numbers and the exact places where textual overlaps have been used to fill in a lacuna in the larger fragment. For the information on the overlaps, see Strugnell and Harrington on these two sections.

should also not shrink from defending himself or his friends.[31] The second part of the passage also bears on the problem of putting up collateral, a practice against which the sage warns the *mevin* in other places (cf. 4Q415 8; 4Q416 2 ii 18[?]=4Q417 2 ii 23). Another passage in this fragment apparently warns the *mevin* against selling himself into indentured servitude (line 17).

One finds similar emphases in a lengthy passage featuring poverty in 4Q416 2 iii. In lines 3–8 the sage admonishes the *mevin* about several matters relating to borrowing and creditors. If he has had a loan deposited with him, he is to be sure to be honest and return it as he has received it. The sage says, "Do not lay your hand upon it, lest you/your hand(?) be scorched, and your body burnt in its fire" (line 4). Subsequently the *mevin* is told not to take money from any person because the lender will "increase your poverty" (line 6). Line 8 provides perhaps the ultimate advice to keep the *mevin* out of the hands of creditors. "You are needy; do not desire something beyond your share/inheritance..." (cf. 4Q417 2 i 20).

What follows in 4Q416 2 iii 9–15 is connected to line 8 through the "share" and brings in the "mystery that is to come." The sage says,

> (9) But if men (or perhaps God) restore(s) you to splendor (?), walk in it (the share/inheritance of line 8) and by the mystery that is to come study the origins thereof (i.e., of the mystery). And then you shall know (10) what is allotted to it, and in righteousness you shall walk, for God will cause his c[ountenanc]e to shine upon all your ways. To him who glorifies you give honour, (11) and praise his name continually, for out of poverty (מראש) he has lifted your head, and with the nobles has he made you to be seated, and over a glorious heritage (12) has he given you authority; seek out his good will continually. You are needy (אביון אתה); do not say, "I am needy (רש אני), and I will n[ot] (13) study(?) knowledge." Bring your shoulder under all instruction and with all[ ]...refine(?) your heart, and with abundance of understanding (14) (sc. refine) your thoughts. Study the mystery that is to come, and understand all the ways of Truth, and all the roots of iniquity (15) you shall contemplate.

The initial section of this passage actually begins in line 8 with the words, "You are needy." The meaning of the conditional sentence in line 9, however, depends on resolving a textual problem. 4Q416 2 iii 9 has the verb in the singular ישיבכה (or perhaps read יושיבכה). This line has an

---

[31] This is how Strugnell and Harrington understand the clause about speech. See DJD 34, 97.

overlap in 4Q418 9:7 where the verb is in the plural, יושיבוכה. Strugnell and Harrington read with 4Q418 and translate "If (men) restore you to splendor." If one accepts the singular verb of 4Q416, however, the subject of the clause would not be the indefinite plural "men," but some singular entity, either "one" or "God." If men do the restoring, then the remainder of lines 9–11 could be describing, as Strugnell and Harrington suggest, "the proper reactions of the poor man when he has been promoted in rank" most likely by a human benefactor.[32] That is, he should study the origins of the mystery, he should walk in righteousness, and he should praise God's name continually because as line 11 says, "he (i.e., God) has lifted your head out of poverty, And with nobles he has made you to be seated." The entire section, then, might represent a possibility for real social advancement for which the *mevin* should be prepared and for which he should thank God.[33]

One problem with this interpretation is that nowhere else in the work do we have any indication that the *mevin* might be in a position to receive such social elevation. Line 11, in fact, runs directly counter to what 4QInstruction reveals of the *mevin*'s social status elsewhere and its apparent possibilities. Might we read the passage, especially if God is the subject of the verb in line 9, as the sage's version of the familiar wisdom assertion that ultimately God is in control of all things? God has the ability, if he chooses, to bring down the rich and to elevate the poor, and he can place the poor and humble who have wisdom on a par with princes and nobles. Strugnell and Harrington note the difficulty of interpreting this entire section. Although they translate line 9 using the plural "men," they appeal to 1 Sam 2:8, "He raises up the poor from the dust; he lifts the needy from the ash heap, to make them sit with princes and inherit a seat of honor," as a close parallel, which, they note, argues in favor of God rather than "men" as the benefactor of the *mevin*.[34] Sirach 11:1 expresses a similar thought in very much the same words as 4QInstruction, "The wisdom of the poor raises up his head and seats him among nobles." If we also keep in mind that lines 9–11 depend on the conditional "if," these lines might be read not as a claim about any real expectation that the *mevin* might advance socially, but as an expression of confidence about what is possible with God.

---

[32] Strugnell and Harrington, DJD 34, 118.
[33] Ibid.
[34] Ibid.

The second section of the passage begins with "You are needy" in line 12. Here the sage reminds the *mevin* that poverty is no excuse for neglecting the study of knowledge and instruction. Of course, as elsewhere in 4QInstruction, the object of that study is the "mystery that is to come." Strugnell and Harrington comment about this passage, "It is even more unclear in general how the fact of being רש would excuse one from a quest for knowledge—unless that activity is reserved for those whose wealth allows them such a luxury."[35] Perhaps we see in this section the sage's reaction to what might be perceived as a more elitist vision of the pursuit of knowledge and wisdom. Sirach 38:24–34 maintains that only the person with little business and lots of leisure can get wisdom. Although tradespersons "maintain the fabric of the world" (38:34), they cannot sit in judgment; they cannot be counselors to the powerful, etc. Given the constant reminders of the *mevin*'s poverty, I imagine that any notion like Ben Sira's of the acquisition of wisdom would leave a bad taste in the mouth of the sage of 4QInstruction. A lack of material wealth and leisure time does not provide exemption from understanding the "mystery that is to come." This passage probably indicates as well, as Tigchelaar has concluded and as I will argue further below, that the addressee of 4QInstruction "was not a professional sage, but could be anyone in society."[36]

The text of 4Q417 2 i (and the overlapping fragments that fill it out) has poverty as its main idea. The sage makes a number of important observations and claims about poverty in this section. In keeping with the theme of borrowing and lending, the sage, perhaps surprisingly, tells the *mevin* to borrow: "And if you are in poverty (ואם תחסר), for what you lack (מחסורכה), borrow without having any money (הון), for your/his treasure house [God] will not make (to be empty lacking anything)" (l. 19). The meaning of this admonition is not completely clear to me, but it seems that the *mevin*, if he does borrow money, is advised to borrow it without giving up as collateral what meager resources he has.[37] Perhaps this passage relates to the advice in 4Q416 2 ii about the danger of entrusting one's purse to creditors. The sage further advises the *mevin* to eat only what God gives him for food and

---

[35] Ibid., 119.
[36] Tigchelaar, "Addressees," 75.
[37] Perhaps the advice is based on Isa 55:1–2, especially "You that have no money, come, buy and eat! Come buy wine and milk without money and without price." I am grateful to S.W. Crawford, who pointed out the possibility.

not any more, "lest by gluttony you shorten your life." Finally he returns in lines 21–24 to familiar ideas about borrowing:

> (21) If you borrow men's money (הון) for your poverty (למחסורכה), let there be no sleep for you (22) day or night, and no rest for your soul, until you have restored to your creditor his loan. Do not lie (23) to him, lest you should bear guilt (for it). Moreover, because of reproach to/from your creditor[…]And you will not any more entrust it to his neighbor. (24) Then against/to your poverty (ובמחסורכה) he (the lender or neighbor) will close his hand.

As I noted above, most of the remarks about poverty in 4QInstruction are directed toward the *mevin* and *his* circumstances. There are almost no passages that focus on poor people generally or care for the poor, especially the *mevin*'s individual responsibility in that regard. This situation contrasts with Ben Sira's continued insistence to his students on the importance of care for the poor.[38] Strugnell and Harrington fill out a lacuna in 4Q416 2 ii 3 to read "[And in his poverty you shall not make the poor stumble because of it]. Nor because of his shame shall you hide your face."[39] This statement, if it were part of 4QInstruction, would at least suggest concern for the position of the poor, and Strugnell and Harrington may have reconstructed it this way since poverty is a theme of this section of the work. If that were the case, however, the next clause, "And because of his shame you shall hide your face," would seem to imply that poverty is somehow shameful, a position taken nowhere else in the work that I can find.

Elsewhere, two difficult passages in 4Q417 2 i also seem to have the poor as their subject. In line 9 through the beginning of line 11, written in the second person singular, the sage tells the *mevin*, "And not for yourself alone shall you increase [your appetite when you are in poverty,] for what is more insignificant than a poor man (כיא מה צעיר מרש)? And do not rejoice in mourning, lest you have trouble in your life. (11) [Gaze on the mystery] that is to come." Further down in lines 15–17, in a section where the *mevin* is advised to be cognizant of his own sins, the sage says (with a lacuna filled in by Strugnell and Harrington), "[Fo]r before [His anger] none will stand, and who will be

---

[38] Although begging appears to be a different story for him. See "Who Has Been Tested by Gold?" 79–80.

[39] The phrase "stumble because of it" comes from 4Q417 2 ii 5. Strugnell and Harrington conjecture the prior phrase, "And in his poverty thou shalt not make the poor." See Strugnell and Harrington, DJD 34, 90, 93, 95.

declared righteous when He gives judgment? And without forgiveness [h]ow [can any] poor man [stand before Him?] (ובלי סליחה[] א[יכה יקום לפניו כול [] אביון]).”

In the first instance, the insignificance of the poor is most likely in the eyes of human beings rather than those of God. The poor person who desires more than it is possible to have will have trouble in life. The second passage could be read as a declaration that the poor have no special considerations from God when judgment comes. No one will be able to stand before God's anger without forgiveness, not even the poor. In order to avoid judgment, the *mevin* is encouraged not to overlook his own sins (l. 14) but to "gaze on the mystery that is to come" and to "comprehend the birth-times of salvation" (l. 11). In 4Q418 126 ii 7, a passage about judgment, the sage asserts that God will act "to shut (the door) upon the wicked, but to raise up the head of the poor (דלים)."[40] The contrast between shutting out the wicked and raising up the poor intimates that God will vindicate those poor who have been wronged by the wicked, not that their poverty excuses them. Poverty, then, for the sage of 4QInstruction, does not seem to be valued intrinsically for its own sake or as a way of avoiding sin and judgment.

What can we make of these various references to poverty and wealth in 4QInstruction? When we consider questions of the social location of the text, these passages provide some clues, but they also raise a number of other questions. I essentially agree with Torleif Elgvin, who notes that in addition to the "you are poor" mode of address, the frequency of terms for poverty give some indication of the social status of the *mevin* and his community.[41] I think, however, that the material on poverty and wealth in 4QInstruction allows us to go a bit further than Elgvin does.

Certainly the way that the *mevin* is understood as able to be involved in the world of financial affairs, with all its attendant dangers, fits with other instruction in the work to evoke a picture of the addressee as one who walks in the larger society, not in some isolated sectarian commu-

---

[40] Other fragments of 4QInstruction have words for poverty and what look to be matters of eschatology or judgment together in the same context. Cf. 4Q415 6; 4Q418 123(?); 4Q418 177(?). It is interesting to note that 4Q416 2 iii 9–11 has very similar sentiments to this fragment, but without the judgment theme and in the second person singular, not in the third person.

[41] Notwithstanding Tigchelaar's caveats about the function of this phrase. See Elgvin, "Wisdom, Revelation, and Eschatology," 444.

nity.[42] Several factors indicate that 4QInstruction may have originated in some sort of school context, although one that differs radically from the kind that we see in Ben Sira. First, as Elgvin shows, the work utilizes a number of literary traditions, particularly material from the Jewish scriptures, such as Genesis, Deuteronomy and Isaiah, among others.[43] Second, its emphasis on studying the "mystery that is to come" probably originates in some kind of formal teaching environment, like a school, although the sage of the text admonishes his charge to honor his father and mother because they "have uncovered your ears to the mystery that is to come" (4Q416 iii 18). Third, Strugnell and Harrington argue that the "rhetorical situation of instruction" points to a school setting "though what sort of 'school' is to be imagined is not at all clear (since generally only one person is being instructed)."[44]

In this regard, 4QInstruction is often compared to Ben Sira, which explicitly originates in a school context (Sir 51:23). Ben Sira's teaching about wealth and poverty, however, reveals that he was probably instructing young men who would make their way into public service and who would occupy a social position below that of the rich and above that of the poor, whom they were obligated to help. In our study of this language in Ben Sira, C. Camp and I concluded,

> The scribe/sage, as a member of a retainer class, occupies a sometimes insecure social position and is faced with conflicting loyalties and obligations. Thus the watchword for Ben Sira and his students in relating to the rich and powerful is caution. If the scribe/sage remains wary and observes proper etiquette and appropriate behavior he will succeed with the powerful. When it comes to the poor, Ben Sira's attitude seems primarily conditioned by his understanding of the covenantal responsibilities to care for the poor, widows, and orphans. Ben Sira exhorts the rich, as well as his students, to fulfill their obligation to the poor through almsgiving. For his budding scribes, he makes clear that if they find themselves in positions of rendering judgments, they must be fair and not prefer the case of the rich because of their influence and power.[45]

---

[42] Several scholars have reached this conclusion. See Elgvin, "Wisdom, Revelation, and Eschatology," 443; Harrington, *Wisdom Texts from Qumran*, 41; Strugnell and Harrington, DJD 34, 36; Tigchelaar, "Addressees," 74–5.

[43] See Elgvin, "Wisdom, Revelation, and Eschatology," 446–48.

[44] Strugnell and Harrington, DJD 34, 20. It should also be noted here that other wisdom texts generally, although not exclusively, address mainly one person. Cf., for example, Ben Sira, *passim*.

[45] "Who Has Been Tested By Gold?" 95.

The same cannot be said for 4QInstruction. The sage of this work apparently counts the *mevin* as among the poor—but yet not among the destitute. Although he is not one of the wealthy, the *mevin* still can participate in financial dealings, sometimes even having a loan or collateral deposited with him (4Q416 2 iii 3). In addition, being counted among the poor may be the reason that 4QInstruction contains no instruction to the *mevin* about caring for the economically disadvantaged. The *mevin*, who must be concerned for his own survival, simply may not be in a position to do this.

In their public service careers, Ben Sira's students would of necessity have to deal with the rich on an almost daily basis, and his book offers them much advice about how to behave around them. Such teaching is completely absent from the extant portions of 4QInstruction. The *mevin* will have to deal with creditors if he borrows money for his needs, but, in contrast to Ben Sira's teaching to his charges, there is no evidence in 4QInstruction that he should prepare to be invited to be master of a banquet (cf. Sir 31:12–18) or to be placed in a position of counsel to the powerful. It does not appear that the instructional or school context of the *mevin* is intended to produce the same professional class of scribes as Ben Sira envisions coming out of his school.[46]

One very suggestive, although incomplete and fairly poorly preserved, passage, however, hints that some kind of community or public activity might be possible for the *mevin*. 4Q417 2 i might indicate the potential availability of some judicial or administrative role for him.

> (12) Be an advocate for your own interests, And let not [your soul be contaminated] (13) by every perversity of yours. Pronoun[ce] your judgments (משפטיכה) like a righteous ruler. Do not ta[ke…] (14) And do not overlook your own sins. Be like a humble man when you contend for a judgment in favor of him.

Unfortunately, the text is not clear about how, where, and for or against whom the *mevin* would render or contend for judgments. Might the *mevin*, who has received instruction and has studied the mystery that is to come (which is mentioned in lines 10–11), act as a judge in his own community? If the passage does mean this, would it reflect some

---

[46] On the school context generally, Tigchelaar concludes his article by saying that "[t]he composition apparently intends to admonish people from all layers of society to behave according to their God-given ordained position, and promises them everlasting glory" ("Addressees," 75). He does not, however, indicate whether or not he thinks this teaching was part of some wisdom curriculum.

kind of sectarian interest? Does the passage simply refer to the *mevin*'s behavior in his personal relationships? It is impossible to tell from this passage. Ben Sira, for his part, recognizes that his students can reasonably expect to become judges and administrators who would adjudicate all manner of cases, and he warns them against preferential treatment of the rich (Sir 4:28). He even cautions them about becoming judges at all—"do not seek to become a judge, or you may be unable to root out injustice; you may be partial to the powerful, and so mar your integrity" (Sir 7:6).

Of course, 4Q416 2 iii 9–15, which I discussed above, is another text one might want to adduce as evidence supporting the idea that the *mevin* of 4QInstruction may not be in quite the disadvantaged position that the work makes out for him. But as we saw, rather than a statement about real upward mobility, the passage might just as easily be a claim about what God could do if he wished, a remote possibility, not a social probability.

All the factors outlined above lead me to the conclusion that the *mevin* of 4QInstruction cannot be found in the same kinds of social groups as Ben Sira's clientele. In fact, the information given in the two works about the social contexts of Ben Sira's students and the *mevin* of 4QInstruction appear to situate them very differently. Ben Sira's students cannot be reckoned among the poor; the *mevin* seems to belong to a social stratum that could be categorized as such, and he certainly seems to have much in common with the poor. Ben Sira's students are being trained to serve in public and official administrative capacities as judges, counselors and scholars; the teaching of 4QInstruction does not appear to envision the *mevin* as destined for such official administrative roles. Ben Sira constantly advises his students about their behavior in relation to the rich; the sage of 4QInstruction does not even mention a class of rich people as such. Ben Sira explicitly links the wisdom that he teaches to the Torah; the sage of 4QInstruction focuses attention on the "mystery that is to come" and its content.

Can we move from these observations to a description of the *mevin*'s social world? I do think we need to take the claims to the *mevin*'s poverty seriously, even while recognizing the difficulty introduced by those statements about poverty that can be read as conditionals. The text pictures the *mevin* constantly poised to fall into more abject poverty or even indentured servitude. I see no other way to read these assertions than as reflections of social realities. Can we understand the lack of references to rich people as an indication that the *mevin*'s social world is isolated from these classes of society? Are the creditors or the "oppressors" mentioned in 4Q416 2 ii 17 equivalent to the "rich" of other wisdom texts? These are more difficult questions to answer with much certainty. Elgvin and Strugnell and Harrington make the suggestion that 4QInstruction perhaps stems from an Essene community like those well known from Josephus's descriptions, living in towns and cities, marrying and engaging in everyday social life. Such may indeed be the case, but the instruction about wealth and poverty taken on its own does not seem to give much additional insight into that problem.

One final question to be asked is: Does poverty constitutes an ideal value for 4QInstruction? 4QInstruction teaches that the poor are indeed considered insignificant in the eyes of others, and they are not justified before God by the fact of their poverty. As we saw above, the poor who sin require God's forgiveness (4Q417 2 i). God will, however, raise up the poor who have been wronged (4Q418 126—interestingly enough, not explicitly by the rich). One fragmentary line might indicate that the sage of 4QInstruction prefers a way of life characterized by poverty. 4Q416 2 ii 20–21 reads, "Do not esteem yourself highly for your poverty (במחסורכה) when you are (anyway?) a pauper (רוש), lest *vacat* you bring into contempt your (own way) of life." Is the sage concerned that if the *mevin* were to boast about his poverty, he would bring such a life, one that he values highly, into disrepute? Unfortunately one can do no more here than suggest this reading as a possibility.

The frequency with which financial matters and especially poverty appear in 4QInstruction, however, demonstrates in a *prima facie* way their importance for the work, and the document includes a wide range of teaching on these issues. On its own, the use of this language in 4QInstruction enables us to draw some tentative conclusions about its social context and also to raise some important questions, but as one component of a relatively long and complex literary work, many more questions remain to be asked. We are really only at the beginning of the task of understanding the social and cultural contexts of this unique wisdom text.

CHAPTER FOUR

"WHO HAS BEEN TESTED BY GOLD AND FOUND PERFECT?" BEN SIRA'S DISCOURSE OF RICHES AND POVERTY

(with Claudia V. Camp, Texas Christian University)

The rich and the poor have always been part of the fabric of human society. Yet how societies have constructed the relative values of wealth and poverty and how they have treated rich and poor people have varied over time and geography. The sages of ancient Israel were well aware of the socio-economic disparities between rich and poor, and Israelite and Jewish sapiential literature has as one of its major concerns these disparities and how people ought to respond to them.

In the Wisdom of Ben Sira, the sage's discourses on riches and poverty occur almost exclusively in material that A.A. Di Lella has called "recipe wisdom," that is, wisdom that "deals with everyday attitudes, beliefs, customs, manners and forms of behavior one should have toward God, one's fellows, and the world at large if one is to live fully and well as a faithful Israelite."[1] For Ben Sira riches and poverty are not metaphorical concepts that apply, for instance, to those who are spiritually wealthy or impoverished in the way that the author of the gospel of Matthew redacts the Beatitudes in his Sermon on the Mount. When Ben Sira speaks of wealth and poverty, he talks almost exclusively in terms of people who do or do not have material wealth. The ways in which he constructs his discourse allow insight into his own attitudes toward these conditions as well as how he wants his students to respond to them. They also provide a glimpse into the social world of the sage, the rich and the poor in second-century BCE Judea, and the ideology that supports these complex relationships.

---

[1] P.W. Skehan and A.A. Di Lella, *The Wisdom of Ben Sira* (AB 39; New York: Doubleday, 1987) 32.

THE VOCABULARY OF RICHES AND POVERTY IN BEN SIRA

Since the Wisdom of Ben Sira is not fully extant in Hebrew, one must look both at the surviving Hebrew texts and at the Greek translation of Ben Sira's grandson in order to get as complete an understanding as possible of the vocabulary of riches and poverty in the entire book.[2]

In general the terminology in the surviving Hebrew texts is what one would expect to find when one compares it to other wisdom texts like Proverbs, for example.[3] The major terms for poverty all appear in Sirach, רש, ענוה/עני, מחסור, דל, אביון. Ben Sira prefers the terms דל and עני/ענוה, however, to indicate poverty. מחסור only occurs once in the extant portions of the Hebrew (40:26), and it means "lack" or "want."[4]

The Greek translation employs two major word groups to translate the Hebrew words for poverty; these are derived from the stems πτωχ- and ταπειν-. The Greek translator, however, often seems to regard the two roots as synonymous. One example will suffice at this juncture. In Sir 13:20–23 Ben Sira writes of the rich and the poor. He notes that "humility (ענוה/ταπεινότης) is an abomination to the proud; likewise the poor (אביון/πτωχός) are an abomination to the rich (עשיר)."[5] The surrounding context of the verse shows that the translator was not consistent in his renderings. At the end of verse 19 he rendered דל with πτωχός. The same Hebrew word, דל, appears in verse 21 as ταπεινός, in verse 22 as ταπεινός again, and in verse 23 as πτωχός as in verse 19. What complicates matters even more is that the Greek translator, while

---

[2] After the completion of this paper, we became aware of V.M. Asensio, "Poverty and Wealth: Ben Sira's View of Possessions," *Der Einzelne und Seine Gemeinschaft bei Ben Sira* (R. Egger-Wenzel and I. Krammer, eds.; BZAW 270; Berlin: Walter de Gruyter, 1998) 151–77. In this article Asensio's description of Ben Sira's general attitude toward riches and poverty is in essential agreement with the one we set out here. His analysis, however, views the material as essentially reflecting a dichotomy between rich and poor throughout Ben Sira's teaching and does not take into consideration Ben Sira's own ambiguous status vis-à-vis his rich superiors. See below for our remarks on this problem, which we view as central to understanding Ben Sira. For the Hebrew manuscripts and the places where they are extant, see P.C. Beentjes, *The Book of Ben Sira in Hebrew: A Text Edition of All Extant Hebrew Manuscripts and a Synopsis of All Parallel Hebrew Ben Sira Texts* (VTSup 68; Leiden: Brill, 1997). For the Greek, see J. Ziegler, *Septuaginta: Vetus Testamentum Graecum Auctoritate Academiae Litterarum Gottingensis editum; vol. XII, 2: Sapientia Iesu Filii Sirach* (Göttingen: Vandenhoeck & Ruprecht, 1965).

[3] On the language of poverty in Proverbs, see J.D. Pleins, "Poverty in the Social World of the Wise," *JSOT* 37 (1987) 61–78.

[4] In this single instance, the Greek has ἐλάττωσις.

[5] In Hebrew the passage is only extant in Ms A.

using these two word groups for *most* of the Hebrew references, also used a variety of other terms to render single instances of the Hebrew words. For instance, in 4:4 θλιβόμενον, "one who is afflicted," translates דל. Thus, in those sections of Ben Sira where no Hebrew survives, one must use caution when trying to reconstruct what Ben Sira may have written in Hebrew.[6]

When Ben Sira wants to refer to rich people, he uses the term עשיר, for which the Greek always uses πλούσιος or πλοῦτος.[7] When, however, Ben Sira writes about the material goods possessed by the rich, the situation becomes much more complicated. He uses several Hebrew terms indicating material wealth that are rendered by a variety of words in Greek. Other than words from the root עש"ר, Ben Sira uses טובה הון, חיל, חרוץ and מחיר. Unfortunately, the Greek translator did not render any of these terms stereotypically with any single Greek word. The most frequently occurring Greek equivalent is χρῆμα, which renders seven different Hebrew words, including חיל, הון, חרוץ and טובה. At the same time, חיל, for example, is translated by at least six different Greek words. The lack of consistency on the part of the translator for words indicating goods or possessions means that for those parts of the book lacking Hebrew one can get a good idea that such goods are the topic of interest, but what specific Hebrew terms lie behind the Greek may not be altogether certain.

BEN SIRA'S ATTITUDE TOWARD WEALTH AND POVERTY

In his analysis of poverty in the biblical book of Proverbs, J.D. Pleins argues that the understanding of poverty in this book is quite different from that of the biblical prophets. He remarks that in contrast to the prophetic critique of wealth, "[t]he teachings of the wise support their concerns for social status, class distinction, and the proper use of wealth—concerns which are rooted in the values cultivated by the ruling elite from which the literature comes."[8] Di Lella notes that although Pleins was talking about Proverbs "much of what he writes applies also

---

[6] For a detailed look at translation technique and the problems of reconstructing the Hebrew of Sirach, see B.G. Wright, *No Small Difference: Sirach's Relationship to Its Hebrew Parent Text* (SBLSCS 26; Atlanta: Scholars Press, 1989).

[7] In 13:2 there is a doublet in Greek for the Hebrew עשיר. ἰσχυρός appears in the doublet with πλούσιος.

[8] Pleins, "Poverty," 72.

to such vocabulary in Ben Sira."[9] We will return to the issue of social location below, but in this section we want to look at Ben Sira's general attitude toward wealth and poverty in order to see if it is similar to that which Pleins finds in Proverbs. This overview will also provide background for the discussion of the social location of Ben Sira and his students in relationship to the rich and the poor. We will find that the sage walks a fine line in his interpretation and theological evaluation of wealth and poverty, one that disappears on occasion into outright contradiction.

Wealth

Ben Sira recognizes that much of everyday living revolves around economic activity. People buy and sell, borrow and lend, acquire wealth and lose it. Yet in this daily activity of acquisition and loss, Ben Sira attributes one's fortunes to God. "Good things and bad, life and death, poverty and wealth (ריש ועושר), come from the Lord," he says (11:14).[10] In the next breath, however, Ben Sira can also claim that "The Lord's gift remains with the devout, and his favor brings lasting success" (ורצנו יצלח לעד 11:17 Ms A). Whatever success God's favor brings, this verse does not seem to be a blanket endorsement of wealth *per se*. At the least, one's economic condition in this life is fleeting. In this same poem, Ben Sira encourages trust in God "for it is easy in the sight of the Lord to make the poor rich, suddenly in an instant" (11:21).

When he speaks about riches, Ben Sira is both cautionary and critical. Most of his cautions have to do with the use of wealth and the potentially corrupting nature of money and its acquisition. His criticism of wealth, however, is not directed at simply having money. In fact having wealth can be a good thing; what is important is the behavior of the wealthy person and what is done with wealth. In chapter 40, Ben Sira writes about the good things in life. Speaking of wealth he says, "Riches (חיל) and strength build up confidence" (40:26 Ms B). But even though no criticism of wealth is implied in this colon, the next continues "but the fear of the Lord is better than either." These two cola in short epitomize

---

[9] A.A. Di Lella, "The Wisdom of Ben Sira: Resources and Recent Research," *Currents in Research* 4 (1996) 172.

[10] Most translations are taken from the New Revised Standard Version. In each case, we have consulted both the Hebrew and Greek texts for text-critical difficulties that affect the overall meaning of the passage. In some cases we have also used or adapted the translation given in Skehan and Di Lella's Anchor Bible Commentary.

Ben Sira's understanding of wealth and riches. "Riches (העושר) are good if they are free from sin" (13:24 Ms A).

Unfortunately, Ben Sira realizes, such is all too often not the case, not only individually, but corporately. International and political strife can be caused by wealth (10:8). Riches and money by their very nature can be corrupting and lead one to transgress, especially where the poor are concerned. Thus, it is the rich person who sins that God despises; he does not hate the rich person because he/she is rich. But, Ben Sira knows that "gold has ruined many and has perverted the minds of kings" (8:2).

The business arena presents constant temptations for the ancient entrepreneur. A number of passages in Sirach emphasize caution and proper conduct in commercial activity. One should not be ashamed "of accuracy of scales and weights and acquiring much or little; of profit from dealing with merchants" (42:4–5). Thus, acquiring wealth in business is perfectly acceptable. In fact, Ben Sira indicates that becoming wealthy is even desirable. Sir 19:1 comes in the middle of a passage on self control. If one lacks self control, Ben Sira says, he will not become rich. Business relationships breed sin, however, and gold can be a stumbling block even for the upright. In perhaps his most direct passage on the problems of business, Ben Sira says in 26:29–27:3,

> 26:29 A merchant can hardly keep from wrongdoing,
> nor is the tradesman innocent of sin.
> 27:1 Many have committed sin for gain,
> and those who seek to get rich will avert their eyes.
> 27:2 As a stake is driven firmly into a fissure between stones,
> so sin is wedged between selling and buying.
> 27:3 If a person is not steadfast in the fear of the Lord,
> his house will be quickly overthrown.[11]

---

[11] M. Hengel, *Judaism and Hellenism* (Philadelphia: Fortress, 1974) 137, remarks about this passage that Ben Sira "is particularly critical of the merchant, who is presumably often still non-Jewish and whose profession, unlike that of divinely sanctioned agriculture (7.15; 20.28), brings with it extreme danger." We are not sure what the evidence is that would establish that these merchants are "presumably often still non-Jewish." Ben Sira is generally critical of thoughtless rushing after wealth. The two passages that Hengel cites here, 7:15 and 20:28, although they speak positively of farm labor and hard work, are not enough, in our estimation, to sustain a social reconstruction of the Jewish farmer versus the largely non-Jewish merchant, which seems to be where Hengel is going in his analysis.

The potential pitfalls of wealth are not only inherent in the process of its acquisition. Once one has wealth numerous difficulties remain. Many who acquire wealth become miserly, and Ben Sira condemns the wealthy miser in chapter 14. "Riches (עושר Ms A/ὁ πλοῦτος) are inappropriate for a small-minded person, and of what use is wealth to a miser…The miser is an evil person; he turns away and disregards people. The eye of the greedy person is not satisfied with his share; greedy injustice withers the soul. A miser begrudges bread, and it is lacking at his table" (14:3, 8–10 Ms A). Chapter 31 contains a long poem on the difficulties of being rich. It begins by noting that wealth creates anxiety and loss of sleep (31:1–2) and goes on to indict the greedy. "The lover of gold will not be free from sin; whoever pursues profit will be led astray by it. Many have they been who were entrapped by gold, who put their confidence in corals" (31:5–6).[12] Yet for Ben Sira, some are rich who are also blameless, and they will be blessed (31:8). But through a series of rhetorical questions at the end of the poem, Ben Sira seems to indicate the rarity of someone who is both rich and blameless.

31:9   Who is he [who is rich and blameless] that we may praise him?
          For he has done wonders among his people.
31:10   Who has been tested by it [gold] and found perfect?
          Let it be for him a ground for boasting.
          Who has had the power to transgress and did not transgress,
          and to do evil and did not do it?
31:11   His property will be established,
          and the assembly will proclaim his acts of charity.

How then should one respond to having wealth? Ben Sira seems to enjoin two attitudes. The first is implicit in the passages we discussed above. Wealth should be kept in perspective. Human fortune is determined by God, and it can change rapidly (11:14–21). Not all wealth is good, only that acquired justly. The wealthy who unjustly accumulate their riches will both lose what they have gotten and experience God's judgment. "Do not depend on dishonest wealth; it will not benefit you in the day of wrath" (5:8).[13] Wealth gotten dishonestly will "dry up

---

[12] We have followed Skehan and Di Lella's translation here because of the textual difficulties attached to this section. For an explanation of the problems, see Skehan and Di Lella, *Wisdom of Ben Sira*, 380.

[13] We have followed Hebrew Ms A here for "day of wrath." The Greek has "day of calamity." Sirach 5:7 concerns the sudden nature of God's judgment in the "time of punishment" (ביום נקם Ms A, בעת נקם Ms C). The context, then, argues for a picture of God's judgment, not simply an unfortunate circumstance.

like a river" (40:13). What is more important is the keeping of God's commandments—in Ben Sira's language, "the fear of the Lord" (40:26). We shall return to the larger ideological force of this phrase in the sage's system. But even mundane matters, like one's health, may occasionally take precedence over having riches. In 30:14–17, the sage teaches that when it comes to one's health, poverty and health are to be preferred to wealth and sickness.

The second response desired by Ben Sira is the proper use of what one has. The primary responsibility of those who have is almsgiving. Ben Sira explicitly connects the obligation to give alms to the poor with the biblical commandments. In 29:8–13, a short poem on giving to the poor, Ben Sira says that one should help the poor "for the command-ment's sake" (v. 9).[14] One should "store up almsgiving in your treasury and it will rescue you from every disaster" (v. 12). The background of this poem is most likely Deut 15:7–11, which promises in verse 10, "Give liberally and be ungrudging when you do, for on this account the Lord your God will bless you in all your work and in all that you undertake." In 17:22 Ben Sira compares almsgiving to a "signet ring" with God. In contrast to liberal giving, one is not to take away the little that the poor have. Sirach 4 begins with a short litany of "do not's." Among other things, one should not "cheat the poor of their living," "grieve the hungry," or "turn your face away from the poor," because if one of these should curse you "their creator will hear their prayer."[15] In a more severe indictment of taking from the poor, Sir 34:24–27 calls the one who would impoverish the poor a murderer.

> 34:24 Like one who kills a son before his father's eyes
>   is the person who offers a sacrifice from the property of the poor
>   (χρημάτων πενήτων).
> 34:25 The bread of the needy is the life of the poor (πτωχῶν);
>   whoever deprives them of it is a murderer.
> 34:26 To take away a neighbor's living is to commit murder.
> 34:27 To deprive an employee of wages is to shed blood.

---

[14] In this short poem, Sirach has the second person pronoun, indicating that Ben Sira is speaking to his students. In other passages one finds third person pronouns. Ben Sira's students are probably not to be counted among the wealthy, but they apparently have enough means to warrant Ben Sira's encouragement to take care of the poor. More on the social issue will be said below.

[15] This passage most likely has Exod 22:21–23 in the background.

Poverty

In much the same way that he does not condemn nor exalt the rich for being wealthy, Ben Sira does not despise the poor for being poor, nor does he elevate their status by virtue of their poverty. Ben Sira is very realistic about the place of the poor in his world, and although he nowhere indicates that the poor are pious because they lack an abundance of possessions, in the face of their low status he recognizes that they have some special place in God's eyes. The life of the poor is difficult. Whereas the rich person, when he rests, can enjoy the finer things of life, the poor person "works hard to make a meager living, and if he ever rests he becomes needy" (31:4). Unlike the mourner who recovers from sorrow, "the life of the poor weighs down the heart" (38:19).

In addition to the difficulties inherent in a life of poverty, Ben Sira observes that those who are rich often make the lot of the poor worse, and thus, the poor often have hardship piled upon hardship. Sirach 13–14 constitutes a major block of material concerned with rich and poor. One needs to read these two chapters and other passages like them with caution, however, since in the beginning of chapter 13, in which he uses the second person singular "you," Ben Sira is addressing his students, who are almost certainly not poor themselves, about the dangers of interacting with rich people.[16] Later in the chapter, beginning in verse 15, he switches to third person singular, which probably indicates more general observations about the nature of the relationship between rich and poor. We shall return below to the significance of this distinction for understanding Ben Sira's social location. Here we focus on the general reflections in verses 15–24, where he concentrates on the favorable predisposition of society toward the rich. He begins by observing that all creatures prefer their own kind; this includes rich and poor. "What peace is there between rich and poor?" he asks (v. 18). Generally the poor are "an abomination to the rich" (v. 20). The rich, however, receive preferential treatment by those around them.

> 13:21   When the rich person (עשיר) totters, he is supported by a friend,
>   but when the poor (דל) falls he is pushed away even by friends.

---

[16] The mistake of reading passages of this sort as concerning simply the relationship between rich and poor is made, for example, by Asensio, "Poverty and Wealth" and by V. Tcherikover in *Hellenistic Civilization and the Jews* (New York: Atheneum, 1982, reprint of 1959 Jewish Publication Society edition). On p. 147, Tcherikover takes Sir 8:1–2, a passage clearly addressed to Ben Sira's students, to indicate the tenuous position of the poor vis-à-vis the rich.

13:22   If the rich person slips, many come to the rescue,
        he speaks unseemly words, but they justify him.
        If the poor person (דל) slips, they even criticize him,
        he talks sense, but he is not even given a hearing.
13:23   The rich person speaks, and all are silent; they extol to the clouds
        what he says.
        The poor person (דל) speaks and they say, "Who is this fellow?"
        And should he stumble, they even push him down.
13:24   Riches are good if they are free from sin;
        poverty (העוני) is evil only in the opinion of the ungodly.

Because of their lowly place in life, Ben Sira argues that God, though
not counting their poverty as piety, does give the poor a special hearing
when they pray. The "do not's" of chapter 4 conclude with "for if in
bitterness of soul some should curse you, their creator will hear their
prayer." In a long section of chapter 35, Ben Sira is concerned with
God's justice, especially toward the poor and oppressed. He insists
that God shows no partiality, not even to the poor. It is the prayer of
the wronged that he hears. The prayer of the widow and the orphan
he will not ignore (vv. 16–17). In verse 21 he returns to the poor. "The
prayer of the poor (דל) pierces the clouds, and it will not rest until it
reaches its goal. It will not desist until the Most High responds and
does justice for the righteous, and executes judgment." It seems as if
Ben Sira is trying to accomplish two goals in this section while walking a rather thin line. The first is to insist that God does not prefer
one person over any other. The second, however, stands somewhat in
contrast to the first. He wants to say at the same time that God does,
in fact, listen particularly to the prayers of the oppressed and downcast.
This latter position affirms the claims made in places like Exodus 22
that God listens and responds to the prayers of the marginalized, and
he judges those who oppress them.

Being in poverty, however, is not the worst thing that could happen
according to Ben Sira. As we saw above, to be poor and healthy is to be
preferred to being rich and diseased. In Sir 29:28 Ben Sira decries the
necessity of living off of borrowed means. In fact, he says in 29:21–22,
"The necessities of life are water, bread and clothing, and also a house
to assure privacy. Better is the life of the poor (πτωχοῦ) under one's
own roof than sumptuous food in the house of others."[17] Poverty is
certainly not a desirable condition, but there are apparently worse fates.
The one whom Ben Sira calls "poor" has *something* at least—a roof,

[17] The passage is not extant in any of the Hebrew manuscripts.

some bread or clothing. The kind of destitution that leads to begging is a worse situation than being in poverty. "My child," Ben Sira writes, "do not live the life of a beggar; it is better to die than to beg. When one looks to the table of another, one's way of life cannot be considered a life" (40:28–29).[18] The idea that it is better to die than to beg gives considerable force to his claim that depriving the poor of their bread is akin to murder. Begging seems to constitute a kind of social death in Ben Sira's eyes that is as horrifying to him as actual starvation. The intensity of his reaction to begging deserves attention.

The poor who avoid this fate, however, can sometimes do more than just survive; they can find honor as well. Whereas the rich person is accorded honor for wealth, the poor person's knowledge brings acclaim. "One who is honored in poverty, how much more in wealth! And one dishonored in wealth, how much more in poverty" (10:31).[19]

OBSERVATIONS ON BEN SIRA'S ATTITUDES TOWARD WEALTH AND POVERTY

When one looks at Ben Sira's attitudes toward rich and poor, his outlook is similar in certain respects to that which Pleins describes for Proverbs. There are occasions where Ben Sira recognizes the class conflict that is inherent in his world. There is no peace between rich and poor, he observes. But despite his understanding that the rich and poor are at odds, Ben Sira is no social critic. He does not blame the rich for creating the circumstances that oppress the poor, nor does he advocate any measures, other than almsgiving, that would redress the economic disparities that he sees around him. God decrees one's place in life, and what sets one person apart from another before God is not

---

[18] The Hebrew is very difficult. On the textual problems in Ms B and Masada, see Skehan and Di Lella, *Wisdom of Ben Sira*, 467. They adopt the reading of Masada as corrected by J. Strugnell, "Notes and Queries on the 'Ben Sira Scroll from Masada,'" *W.F. Albright Volume, Eretz Israel* 9 (1969; A. Malamat, ed.) 112. The Greek text uses ἐπαίτησις "begging" and ἐπαιτέω "to beg."

[19] On the larger poem in which this verse is embedded, see A.A. Di Lella, "Sirach 10:19–11:6: Textual Criticism, Poetic Analysis, and Exegesis," *The Word of the Lord Shall Go Forth: Essays in Honor of David Noel Freedman in Celebration of His Sixtieth Birthday* (C.L. Meyers and M. O'Connor, eds.; Winona Lake, IN: ASOR-Eisenbrauns, 1982) 157–64 and M. Gilbert, S. J., "Wisdom of the Poor: Ben Sira 10,19–11,6," *The Book of Ben Sira in Modern Research* (P.C. Beentjes, ed.; BZAW 255; Berlin: Walter de Gruyter, 1997) 153–69.

station in life, wealth or poverty, but keeping the commandments, fearing the Lord. Ben Sira is not engaging in the kind of social critique that the biblical prophets are.

This situation becomes a little curious when one looks at Ben Sira's view of himself, because he clearly sees himself somewhat in the model of the biblical prophet. He understands his own teaching as being "poured out like prophecy" (24:33). The prayer of chapter 36 has a number of prophetic features. The famous section on the sage in chapter 39 also has prophetic elements woven into the sage's role.[20] But when Ben Sira looks at rich and poor as categories of existence, his analysis is pretty standard wisdom fare. He does not seek to change the status quo, but rather he is more pragmatic. He does, however, have the biblical commandments in front of him, and they exhort care for the poor and oppressed. He specifically enjoins his students, who are apparently in a position to do so, to fulfill the commandments, to look out for those who are marginalized. Ben Sira's and his students' own social positions seem to enable them to do little more than that. They are not agents of social change.

To some extent, then, Ben Sira's advice offers the practical morality glossed with traditional piety that one associates with the conventional wisdom of Proverbs. Yet he lacks the comfort level of the Proverbs sages, their confidence in the observable moral order of the world and their place in it. Tension is evident here between, for example, the generalized negativity of 31:5 ("whoever pursues profit will be led astray by it") and the sage's more typical expression of the moral neutrality of wealth. He perceives, furthermore, the difficulty the rich clearly have in abiding by his admonitions to fear the Lord and care for the poor. This awareness might have suggested a more systemic critique of the structures of wealth and power and, perhaps, a more critical stance toward the one in ultimate charge of it all. The slippage toward a blanket condemnation of pursuing profit in 31:5 suggests that Ben Sira has withheld the full force of his wisdom in this matter, perhaps even from his own consciousness. Likewise, although Proverbs admits that the divine will may supersede human plans, the earlier book is much more wedded to a theologized logic of material retribution than is Ben

---

[20] The terminology in 39:6–8 recalls the prophetic image of chapter 24. See R.A. Argall, *1 Enoch and Sirach: A Comparative Literary and Conceptual Analysis of the Themes of Revelation, Creation and Judgment* (SBLEJL 8; Atlanta: Scholars, 1995) 87–8.

Sira. Our sage manifests a distinct tension between the ideal and the real: the Lord's favor is said to bring lasting success while ill-gotten gain is but temporary; yet meanwhile, God seems to give wealth and take it away in morally random ways. Ben Sira, one might say, *notes* this incongruity but does not *notice* it.

Ben Sira's distinction between the merely "poor" and the utterly destitute is also quite revealing. Apparently his compassion, and his application of the law's demands, only reaches so far down. His failure to include those at the very bottom of the economic ladder in his moral calculus of wealth and poverty suggests a blindness, not to say hardness of heart, that is surely related to difficulties in the practical and ideological negotiation of his own class-status. The same is true for his assumption that honor is available even to the poor, or at least to those who avoid the shame of begging. Like "fear of the Lord," the language of honor and shame plays a larger role in Ben Sira's discourse than merely conveying piety. The interconnection and ideological function of these concepts will require further exploration.

RICHES, POVERTY AND SOCIAL LOCATION:
EDUCATING A RETAINER CLASS

Ben Sira's comments on riches and poverty and on relationships with rich and poor people provide important material for trying to sketch his and his students' social location as well as that of the people whom he calls rich and poor, people who occupy social positions different from those of the scribes. Of course, Ben Sira as a scribe/sage, and one who apparently trains budding scribes/sages, has a very elevated view of the role of the sage in Jerusalemite society.[21] It is possible, however,

---

[21] P. Tiller in an unpublished paper, "Politics and the High Priesthood in Pre-Maccabean Judea" (Dec. 1997 draft; our thanks to the author for making available a copy of the paper), notes that the term "class" is not the most appropriate term to use. Ben Sira is really concerned with power relationships rather than social class in any modern sense. We use the term "class" here for convenience. R.A. Horsley and P. Tiller use the term "scribe/sage" as a description of Ben Sira's office. For an explanation, see their jointly authored article, "Ben Sira and the Sociology of the Second Temple," *Second Temple Studies III: Studies in Politics, Class and Material Culture* (P.R. Davies and J.M. Halligan, eds.; JSOTSup 340; Sheffield: Sheffield Academic Press, 2002) 74–107. (Originally presented in The Sociology of the Second Temple Group, Society of Biblical Literature Annual Meetings, San Francisco, 1992). Other scholars prefer either scribe or sage. We use the designation scribe/sage here in order to try to avoid any terminological confusion.

to penetrate some of Ben Sira's language to see where he and his train-ees fit in the social landscape. Several studies have suggested that the scribe/sage is essentially part of a "retainer" class that is in the employ of the rich and powerful and dependent on them for livelihood.[22] It is precisely the betwixt-and-betweenness of this social position, we would suggest, that accounts for the ambivalent social and theological assess-ment of wealth and poverty evident in our discussion above. There are, moreover, two foci to this ambivalence. The first is more social and external, having to do with the precariousness of the sage's own social status and material prosperity. The second focus is more psychologi-cal and identity-related; it concerns the dissonance between this status insecurity and his theologically elevated view of his profession.

On the political level, the scribe/sage functions as "a kind of counselor or technical expert for the powerful; he seems to be ready and willing to adjudicate disputes even in foreign lands."[23] He may well achieve a certain social status and recognition, and perhaps become famous as a judge or ambassador (39:4). Like those worthies whom Ben Sira describes in chapters 44–50, he may even gain eternal renown (39:9–11). Yet neither fame nor fortune is assured.

Ben Sira often addresses his students about their attitude toward and behavior in the presence of their social superiors. In these passages he is not talking directly about the conflict between poor and rich; his comments derive from a school context where he is training future scribes and sages in the way that *they* must navigate these treacherous relationships. Ben Sira's students interact with these people as mem-bers of a retainer class, not as poor people. The teacher must struggle, however, to define and valorize the identity of this group over against both rich and poor.

It is clear that, in Ben Sira's thought, the scribe/sage is socially supe-rior to ordinary workers, farmers, smiths, potters and the like (cf. Sir 38:24–34), and it is most likely from among these that Ben Sira's poor come. The poor who concern him are not those who are destitute and reduced to begging. As we saw above, they may well have some material

---

[22] Although he does not use the sociological category "retainer class," this is, in effect, what D.J. Harrington seems to suggest in his article "The Wisdom of the Scribe Accord-ing to Ben Sira," *Ideal Figures in Ancient Judaism* (G.W.E. Nickelsburg and J.J. Collins, eds.; SBLSCS 12; Chico, CA: Scholars Press, 1980) 184–85. Horsley and Tiller explicitly use this language of Ben Sira in "Ben Sira and the Sociology of the Second Temple," as does Tiller in "Politics and the High Priesthood in Pre-Maccabean Judea."

[23] Harrington, "Wisdom of the Scribe," 185.

means. Ben Sira condemns those who sacrifice "from the property of the poor (ἐκ χρημάτων πενήτων)" (34:24). It is better to be poor under one's own roof than to depend on the luxuries of others (29:22). Ben Sira and his students clearly stand above these classes of Jews. Sirach 4:7 and 7:6 demonstrate the possibility that Ben Sira's students could achieve the position of a judge. The scribe/sage could sit on the councils, achieve public prominence, expound God's law and sit among rulers (cf. 15:5; 21:17; 39:4); tradespersons and craftspersons could not, even though they "maintain the fabric of the world" (38:31–34).

In the same way, Ben Sira and his students do not belong to the class of the rich and powerful. These are clearly a rung above the scribes/ sages, who may be closer to the rich than to the poor, but do not themselves make up the aristocracy.[24] The ability of Ben Sira's students to aspire to positions of leadership shows that they were or at least thought themselves to be more akin to the powerful and rich. For Ben Sira power and wealth are practically synonymous, and in at least one place he puts the two notions in parallel cola. "Do not contend with a powerful person (איש גדול/ἀνθρώπου δυνάτσου), lest you fall into his hands. Do not quarrel with a rich person (ἀνθρώπου πλουσίου), lest he pay out the price of your downfall" (8:1).[25] For the most part, those in the ruling classes and the rich, "would have been members of the priestly aristocracy of Jerusalem or their retainers."[26]

As persons in a social middle position between the rich and powerful and the tradespersons, craftspersons and poor, but mostly beholden to the powerful, Ben Sira's advice to his students about dealing with both rich and poor provides a good window into the social world of the sage in third- and second-century BCE Jerusalem. A large portion of Ben Sira's advice to his young trainees is about how to deal with those higher up on the social ladder. The practical necessities involved in keeping in the good graces of the rich and powerful and the self-perception that the scribe/sage is more like them than the "lower classes" may also explain the larger proportion of the book that Ben

---

[24] Horsley and Tiller ("Ben Sira and Sociology," 85–6; also Tiller, "Politics," 15) show that Ben Sira uses a variety of terms for the ruling elite, but that they all "refer to local rulers of the Judean temple-state." They have excellent discussions of Ben Sira's terms for these powerful rulers and the social reconstructions one can make from them. Our brief remarks here depend largely on their analysis.

[25] The translation here depends on Skehan and Di Lella, *Wisdom of Ben Sira*, 209. See their note on p. 210 on the textual difficulties of this verse.

[26] Tiller, "Politics," 16.

Sira devotes to relationships with the powerful than to dealings with social inferiors. Although the relationship of the scribe/sage with the rich and powerful is important, it is not without its inherent dangers, and Ben Sira is careful to warn his charges about them. Some of these warnings reflect general circumstances and others involve advice for specific social situations.

In general Ben Sira counsels that his students be wary of rich people and their motives. The rich and powerful most often act out of self interest and the scribe/sage should not be misled into thinking otherwise. Sirach 13:4–7 epitomizes this kind of warning.

13:4　A rich person (עשיר) will exploit you if you can be of use to him, but if you are in need he will abandon you.

13:5　If you own something, he will live with you, he will drain your resources without a qualm.

13:6　When he needs you he will deceive you and smile at you and encourage you; he will speak kindly to you and say, "What do you need?"

13:7　He will embarrass you with his delicacies until he has drained you two or three times, and finally he will laugh at you. Should he see you afterwards, he will pass you by and shake his head at you.[27]

One of the apparently more important social situations in which the sage was likely to find himself together with the rich was the banquet, and Ben Sira provides extensive advice on one's comportment at such a meal. Two major blocks of material deal with banquets, 31:12–18 and 32:1–13. Sirach 13:8–13 may also be concerned with banquets, and 41:19 has at the least to do with meal etiquette in general. Sirach 31:12–18 advises that the scribe/sage invited to a banquet "at the table of the great" (על שלחן איש גדול)[28] be careful not to be greedy, to eat what is put before him, to be the first to stop and the last to take. To overstep these bounds is to risk causing offense (31:16, 17). Sirach 32:1–9 tells the scribe/sage-in-training what to do if the host of the banquet makes him "master of the feast."[29] In this case the advice is not about

---

[27] We give here the NRSV translation, but the text has a number of problems. See Skehan and Di Lella, *Wisdom of Ben Sira*, 248, 251–53 for their translation and textual notes.

[28] We use Ms Bmg which corrects Ms B's שלחן גדול to שלחן איש גדול.

[29] This clause is not extant in the Hebrew manuscripts. The Greek has ἡγούμενόν σε κατέστησαν.

eating at the banquet, but it concerns the proper times for speaking. The banquet is at the same time an opportunity for enjoyment and praise and a minefield of potential hazards. If the scribe/sage takes care of the banqueters first and fulfills his duties, he can then be seated "so that you may be merry along with them and receive a wreath for your excellent leadership." But he must be careful not to interrupt the music or "display cleverness at the wrong time" (vv. 3–4). He should speak briefly and only if asked (v. 7). When "among the great" (בין שרים)[30] he should not be "too forward" (v. 9). Sirach 13:8–13 contains a message similar to that of chapter 32, but it does not specifically set the scene as a banquet. The invitation of an important person (נדיב) is an opportunity and a danger. Ben Sira concludes this section, "Be on your guard and be very careful, for you are walking about with your own downfall" (v. 13).[31]

Ben Sira's language of caution in dealing with the rich and powerful appears to be in some tension with his construction of the place of the scribe/sage in Jewish society, who devoted himself to the study of the Jewish law and ancient wisdom and was in that sense the guardian of the tradition. Such a position was not achieved by a disinterested study of the text. According to Ben Sira, such study served to set the scribe/ sage apart from others. "How different the one who devotes himself to the study of the law of the Most High" (39:1). The sage approaches God in prayer and repentance and "[i]f the Lord is willing, he will be filled with the spirit of understanding. He will pour forth wisdom of his own and give thanks to the Lord in prayer" (39:5–6).[32] His is a divinely inspired wisdom.

The scribe/sage acted as a kind of mediator between his rich and powerful patrons (primarily priests, according to Horsley and Tiller) and ordinary Jews. The potential for social status and rewards are clearly evident, but religious issues also came into play, and with it the potential for conflict between the scribe/sage's values and his self-interest. In his role as guardian and interpreter of the law, the scribe/

---

[30] The Greek translation ἐν μέσῳ μεγιστάνων in verse 9a indicates that the subject nouns in Ms B probably have been transposed.

[31] The Hebrew and Greek of this verse are very different. We prefer the Greek here. Ms A reads "Be on guard and be careful, and do not walk with men of violence."

[32] On 38:24–39:11 concerning the trades and the sage, see J. Marböck, "Sir. 38,24–39,11: Der schriftgelehrte Weise. Ein Beitrag zu Gestalt und Werk Ben Siras," *La Sagesse de l'Ancien Testament* (M. Gilbert, ed.; BETL 51; Gembloux/Louvain: Duculot/ University, 1979) 293–316.

sage sometimes had obligations to go beyond mediation to advocacy.[33] These two competing functions, service to his aristocratic patrons and guardianship of the Israelite religious tradition, most likely created some rather ticklish situations. It was the scribe/sage's responsibility to blunt the desires of the rich and powerful against the poor. In his own life not only must he give to the poor from what he has, but if called upon he must also ensure that the poor are treated justly in the face of pressure to favor the powerful. Ben Sira is very conscious of the inherent dangers. In 4:7 he teaches his students to be deferential to the powerful, "Endear yourself to the congregation; bow your head low to the great (שלטון; μεγιστᾶνες)," but at the same time they should "[r]escue the oppressed from the oppressor and do not be hesitant in giving a verdict." Later in verses 27–28 he concludes, "Do not subject yourself to a fool or show partiality to a ruler (מושלים; δυνάστης). Fight to the death for truth, and the Lord God will fight for you." But despite such assurances of God's approval, in 7:6, Ben Sira can say, "Do not seek to become a judge, or you may be unable to root out injustice; you may be partial to the powerful, and so mar your integrity."

Perhaps, then, we might summarize Ben Sira's highly ambivalent advice to his students on their future prospects as follows: "Become a judge! Here lies your highest God-given authority and your greatest potential to serve God's law in society." "Do not become a judge! Here lies your greatest potential for your own social and theological undoing."[34] The conventional maxims to which the sage appeals to teach about being a good rich person or a worthy poor person fail him utterly when he confronts the conflict between his religious values and his need for status preservation.

On the one hand, then, Ben Sira's ideology of the sage should conceivably place him at the top of the social heap. The scribe/sage is endowed with divine inspiration and pours out his teaching like prophecy. He is an indispensable advisor and counselor to the powerful. But on the other hand, the reality appears to be that the social position of the scribe/sage is conditioned by the precarious balancing act of proper behavior and support of those who employ him and advocacy on behalf of those who are the socially and economically disadvantaged. The

---

[33] Horsley and Tiller, "Ben Sira and Sociology," 29–30; Harrington, "Wisdom of the Scribe," 185.

[34] Compare the contrasting admonitions regarding responding to a fool in Prov 26:4–5.

combination of Ben Sira's perception of the scribe/sage as fundamental
to the functioning of society and the tenuous social position that he in
fact occupies might well produce some insecurity, which would neces-
sitate a way of constructing an alternative understanding of the power
relationships that create the insecurity. In more specific terms, the sage
is the expert in God's law and the guardian of the ancient tradition of
wisdom who has a certain power dependent on his knowledge. Yet he
still has to be very careful what he says and does when at a banquet,
and, by rendering fair judgments, he risks alienating people who have
power over him. This ambiguous social position could produce a kind
of dissonance that had to be resolved.

To describe Ben Sira's social situation this way is not, as already
noted, to say that there are no social rewards for the scribe/sage.[35] Yet
the temporal social rewards that are accorded to him do not seem to
compensate for his lack of power and position when compared to those
above him, among them the priests. Tiller notes,

> From Ben Sira's extensive reflection on the activities of his own "profes-
> sion" it is clear that the sages were retainers with scribal, legal, cultural
> and religious functions, some of which may have overlapped with those of
> the priests. According to Ben Sira's ideology of the priesthood, the func-
> tion of teaching the law originated with Moses (45:5) and belonged to the
> Aaronide priesthood (45:17). In second temple Judea the priesthood must
> have, in effect, over a period of generations, delegated that authority and
> function to the sages, both with regard to the people generally (37:23),
> and with regard to the exercise of their own governmental authority
> (8:8; 9:17–10:5; 38:32–33; 38:34–39:4). In 9:17–10:5 it seems particularly
> clear that it is the scribe who stands behind "the wise judge" and "the
> government of the intelligent one." It appears, in fact, that one of Ben
> Sira's goals was to enhance the authority and honor of the scribal class.
> His book is full of claims that the greatest honor is for the wise, those
> who fear the Lord and obey his commands.[36]

Thus, Ben Sira is faced with a real dilemma. He is a strong supporter of
the priesthood, at least that in Jerusalem.[37] The priests have been chosen
by God to minister before him at the altar. Yet, certain priestly func-

---

[35] See M.E. Stone, "Ideal Figures and Social Context: Priest and Sage in the Early
Second Temple Age," *Ancient Israelite Religions: F. M. Cross Festschrift* (P.D. Miller, Jr.,
P.D. Hanson, S.D. McBride, eds.; Philadelphia: Fortress, 1988) 575–86.

[36] Tiller, "Politics," 21–22.

[37] See Chapter 5, "'Fear the Lord and Honor the Priest': Ben Sira as Defender of
the Jerusalem Priesthood."

tions, like teaching and interpreting the law have become much more the responsibility of the scribe/sage. In 15:1, Ben Sira uses the phrase תופש תורה ("practiced in Torah"), which Jer 2:8 applies to the priests, to refer to the scribe who may not be a priest.[38] As Tiller puts it, "The role of the priests as authoritative interpreters and teachers of the law is being supplanted by the sage."[39] The scribe/sage thus increasingly has a priestly role without the benefits of being a member of the priestly class, adding one further turn of the screw to Ben Sira's already conflicted position with respect to wealth, power and religious authority.

Honor, Shame and Fear of the Lord: Ben Sira's Class Ideology

One possible way to enhance the honor, if not the authority, of the scribe/sage would be to maintain that those things which seem to determine the prevalent social order are not in actuality the most meaningful or important, to propose a different hierarchy of values. One of the ways Ben Sira accomplishes this goal is through the idea of the "fear of the Lord." This important theme is a complex one in Sirach, but it seems that achieving a proper fear of the Lord functions here, at least in part, as a mechanism for leveling some of the power and social inequities that he perceives in the social position of the scribe/sage. As Ben Sira articulates it, fear of the Lord supersedes all social status and class, and a number of passages suggest that anyone can achieve it. He makes it quite clear in his book, for example, that the fear of the Lord is what truly makes one worthy of honor (10:19). For both rich and poor, "their glory is the fear of the Lord" (10:22). "No one is superior to the one who fears the Lord. Fear of the Lord surpasses everything; to whom can we compare who has it?" (25:10–11).

---

[38] Skehan and Di Lella, *Wisdom of Ben Sira*, 264; cited also in Tiller, "Politics," 22.

[39] Tiller, "Politics," 22. According to the book of Ezra, the interpreting and teaching of the Law had already been taken over by the Levites. Ezra's ostensible fifth-century date is currently much disputed by scholars, and it is noteworthy that Ben Sira's list of famous men does not include this apparently important figure, though it does mention Ezra's literary counterpart, Nehemiah. These facts raise the interesting question of the relationship of the scribes/sages of Ben Sira's day to the Levites and invite speculation that the struggle for authority may have been multi-faceted, involving not just "priests vs. scribes," but different groups of priestly claimants, temple functionaries and retainers jockeying for power through alliances and efforts at self-legitimation.

Yet when we look more carefully at Ben Sira's discourse about rich and poor, the powerful and the humble, it appears that the scribe/sage is in the best position to achieve such a fear of the Lord. Fear of the Lord for Ben Sira is primarily identified with wisdom and fulfilling of the commandments. "The whole of wisdom," he says, "is fear of the Lord, and in all wisdom there is the fulfillment of the Law" (19:20). Who is better able to fulfill the law and learn wisdom than the scribe/sage who is the recognized expert in the law and the guardian of wisdom? The acquisition of wisdom depends on much leisure time and having little business. Those who are laborers and artisans do not have such time (38:24–34). The poor cannot rest because when they do, they find themselves in need (31:4). By contrast, those who have power and wealth and are righteous are a rare breed, according to Ben Sira. The rich and powerful may have the time, but they find the demands of their wealth and power more pressing. Thus, we find the introduction to the poem on the scribe/sage to be very significant. "How different the one who devotes himself to the study of the Law of the Most High!" (38:34). How different indeed! It may be theoretically possible for all to fear the Lord, but practically the one best able to achieve proper fear of the Lord is the scribe/sage. Ben Sira thus grounds his understanding of himself in a different system of values, his ability to pursue wisdom and fear of the Lord, that which surpasses all else, including riches, poverty and social status. This set of values he holds out to his students as a way for them to understand themselves and to find true honor in their place in life.

Appeal to fear of the Lord, then, provides an ideological alternative to conventional material values, but also an ideological cover-up, a masking of the systemic incongruities that underlie these teachings. As such, its effectiveness is but partial. Harsher realities—both social and theological— bubble under the surface and require yet more complex ideological manipulation. As we have seen, Ben Sira's different system of values produces conflict on several levels, not simply that *observed* by the sage between rich and poor, but that *experienced* by the sage between his value of care for the poor, based on his guardianship of the Israelite religious tradition, and his obligations of service and sub-servience to his aristocratic patrons. And conflict on top of conflict: although Ben Sira identifies more closely with his patrons than with the poor, his ideology of the divinely inspired, Torah-pious sage tells him he is their superior—their superior, unfortunately, in spiritual, but hardly in material and political reality. His fear of the Lord masks but does not erase the sage's anxiety regarding his dependent social position. Poverty does not, as in the gospel of Matthew, get metaphorically spiritualized, but middle-class anxiety certainly gets dosed with its own prescription of theo-ideological Valium.

As a final move in our analysis, then, we shift our focus from the sage's teachings about wealth and poverty, and their negotiations by his retainer class, to the discourse beneath the discourse, the problematic rhetorical effort to suppress the contradictions experienced by this class. The cover-up involves appeal to transcendent values, specifically fear of the Lord; yet, as other details suggest, the Lord is also part of Ben Sira's problem. The conflict that underlies and exacerbates all the others in this book's ideology is that between the man and his God. How does this play out?

A key might be found in a pair of verses cited earlier in our analysis:

> Good things and bad, life and death,
> poverty and wealth, come from the Lord. (11:14)
> The Lord's gift remains with the devout,
> and his favor brings lasting success. (11:17)

But which is it, really? The second verse does not imply a spiritualization of poverty, *à la* Matthew, but its opposite, a theologization of wealth *à la* Proverbs and the Torah—just what one would expect from a Torah-pious sage like Ben Sira. The first verse, on the other hand, is a sample of skeptical wisdom *à la* Qohelet, resigned about the moral inexplicability of God's work in the world. In contrast, then, both to Proverbs' theological optimism and Qohelet's worldly skepticism, Ben Sira seems to want to have his cake and eat it too. He knows the world does not work according to the divine justice his tradition leads him to expect, but he tries desperately to make himself and his readers believe it is so. This is the paradox playing out in his fitful effort to explain how wealth, which ought to be not simply good, but in fact a sign of God's favor, ends up being such a problem, leading to anxiety at best, corruption at worst (and often). We see it too in his shilly-shallying about how God doesn't really play favorites with respect to the poor, but nonetheless accords their prayers a special hearing. Is the latter teaching a warning to the greedy rich or a proleptic word of comfort to that proportion of his students who might be expected to fall from the tightwire of their class? Or perhaps both. Ben Sira's God, at any rate, can both give and remove wealth with the same arbitrary and breath-taking speed (11:21–25).

Better than consolation, though, is if one can construct a special place for oneself in God's economy over against the economy of the world. The fear of the Lord that transcends worldly treasure—available to all, but the special prerogative of the sage—seems like the perfect alternative. Even here, however, Ben Sira ends up tying himself in ideological knots because fearing the Lord, that is, keeping the commandments, is supposed to buy one something: according to the tradition, wealth and success. But now we're back where we started. What about the pious poor and the corrupt rich? To deal with this, Ben Sira introduces another ideological component: honor and shame. We have noted this topic in passing, but it needs to be foregrounded in order to understand fully the way in which the sage's discourse constructs and legitimates the leaning tower of his class in relationship to the rich, the poor and to God. Honor and shame constitute a crucial linchpin between the tension Ben Sira experiences as the result of his social location and the theological tension we have just highlighted. Here the conflicts and their masking are in clear, if convoluted, view.

Ben Sira states that knowledge and wisdom bring honor to the poor (10:30). Indeed, "the wisdom of the poor/humble (דל) lifts their heads high, and seats them among the great" (11:1). Yet honor and shame are social values, matters not simply of objective truth, but also of appearances and calculations, negotiated in that world of politics and power in which Ben Sira seeks to make his way. When he urges his student not to seek "from the Lord the highest office nor the seat of honor from the king" (7:4), this is not advice based on some ideal of modesty, but on self-preservation; honor brings responsibility and with responsibility comes the possibility of offending the powerful, hence of disgrace (7:6–7). "It is not right," says the sage, "to despise an intelligent poor man, nor is it proper to honor a violent man" (10:23), but Ben Sira knows it happens, and acknowledges, a few verses later, that while knowledge may bring honor to the poor man, "a rich man is honored for his wealth" (10:30). At his least idealistic he observes that rich people receive recognition from others even if they "speak unseemly words," while at the same time, "when the poor man speaks, they say, 'Who is this fellow?' " (13:21–23). Further, while the rich and powerful may experience disgrace at the hand of the Lord (11:4–6), the poor live in danger of falling into the shameful abyss of beggary (40:28–29). The poor may strive for honor, but the playing field is hardly level.

Honor and shame, then, partake in Ben Sira's discourse of the same moral tension as his evaluation of wealth and poverty. Yet the ante has been upped here in a couple of different ways. First, honor and shame form an ideological matrix that connects one's material well-being with other crucial elements of social standing. Social honor is based on

> the ability of a man to control the defining attributes of his life over against the challenge of others to subvert that control. The defining attributes may be seen as socially determined signs of value and power: one's women, one's property (i.e. one's household in both personal and impersonal dimensions), one's political influence, one's body, one's reputation or name.[40]

These factors contribute further to the anxiety expressed in this book, for the sage has no more guarantee of success in preventing the members of his household from bringing shame down upon his head than he has security in his position and prosperity.[41] In Ben Sira's discourse, that is to say, wealth and poverty are just one component of a larger ideological system of honor and shame, a system pervaded with the anxiety of losing control and thus losing status.

The sage appeals to honor, moreover, not only as a social value that should compensate for lack of deserved prosperity, but also as the כבוד/δόξα of God (or personified wisdom), the ultimate value of values that will protect one from shame (15:4–6) and provide the ultimate justification, namely, a good name at the time of death. It is, finally, God's honor on the line. Honor demands control, which Ben Sira not surprisingly insists belongs to God in fullest measure (see, e.g., the hymn in 42:15–43:33). Honor also demands the *appearance* of control, however, and this requires a great deal of faith, given the erratic moral evidence of the world. The possibility of a dishonorable God is one that threatens to undo what ideological coherence the sage has managed to manufacture.

Analysis of the rhetoric of honor and shame in Sirach shows that this discourse, which seeks to cover over the disjunctions in the sage's evaluations of wealth and poverty, in fact opens up fissures that run to the depths and breadths of his theo-ideological system. This analysis

---

[40] C.V. Camp, "Honor and Shame in Ben Sira: Anthropological and Theological Reflections," in Beentjes, *The Book of Ben Sira in Modern Research*, 173.

[41] On honor and shame in Sirach, see in addition to the study cited in the preceding note, C.V. Camp, "Understanding a Patriarchy: Women in Second Century Jerusalem Through the Eyes of Ben Sira," *Women Like This: New Perspectives on Jewish Women in the Greco-Roman World* (A.-J. Levine, ed.; SBLEJL 1; Atlanta: Scholars Press, 1991) 1–39 and D.A. daSilva, "The Wisdom of Ben Sira: Honor, Shame and the Maintenance of Minority Cultural Values," *CBQ* 58 (1996) 433–55.

illuminates the discussion of Ben Sira's social location from another angle as well, in terms of the position of the scribes relative to the priests. We argued above that fear of the Lord, a trait most readily available to the Torah-pious scribe, provides a mechanism for leveling some of the power and social inequalities that exist between the two. While this may be the case for fear of the Lord, כבוד/δόξα has rather the opposite effect. Honor can easily be tainted by the ambiguities and arbitrariness of the social situation. Yet it retains its powerful position in Ben Sira's teaching because of its theological content, its ultimate expression of the Lord's power and glory. In the human world, the one place this divine glory is fully manifest is in the person of the priest before the altar (chap. 50). In the rapturous rhetoric that concludes the book, the ambiguities of life are swept away, along with any consciousness of the tensions that pervade the book's ideological underpinnings.[42] The remarkable thing is that this happens by means of the very language—of honor/glory—that constitutes these tensions in their most profound form. If, then, the idea of fear of the Lord serves to equalize the status of priest and scribe, that of honor accords to the priest not only the status of highest mediator between humans and God, but also an iconic quality, the image under which human reality is redefined as the reflection of God's glory. Whether this re-definition served the poor or harmed them is another matter altogether.

CONCLUSIONS

The discourse of rich and poor in Sirach is derived from the real-life circumstances of third- and second-century BCE Jerusalem. V. Tcherikover expresses it eloquently. "For Ben Sira describes rich and poor, not in the conventional formula known to him in literature, but as an artist who draws the material he needs direct from life."[43] One does not find metaphorical uses of the categories in Ben Sira's book. Ultimately Ben Sira does not view riches and/or poverty in and of themselves as

---

[42] For further development of this argument, see Camp, "Honor and Shame."

[43] Tcherikover, *Hellenistic Civilization*, 146. Indeed, he suggests on p. 148 that Ben Sira "may well have been born and educated in poverty and have gradually climbed to prominence by force of his natural intelligence and of his devotion to the study of Torah and practical wisdom." We do not doubt that Ben Sira was gifted intellectually. Given what he says about artisans and tradespersons in chapter 38, we find it less likely that Ben Sira's own origins were that humble.

signs of piety or impiety, of God's favor or disfavor. God may hear the prayer of the poor, but Ben Sira maintains that it is not *because* they are poor that God listens. Although they might be rare, Ben Sira does not rule out the possibility that rich people could be righteous. What transcends both of these categories is fear of the Lord and the keeping of the commandments.

The scribe/sage, as a member of a retainer class, occupies a sometimes insecure social position and is faced with conflicting loyalties and obligations. Thus the watchword for Ben Sira and his students in relating to the rich and powerful is caution. If the scribe/sage remains wary and observes proper etiquette and appropriate behavior he will succeed with the powerful. When it comes to the poor, Ben Sira's attitude seems primarily conditioned by his understanding of the covenantal responsibilities to care for the poor, widows and orphans. Ben Sira exhorts the rich, as well as his students, to fulfill their obligation to the poor through almsgiving. For his budding scribes, he makes clear that if they find themselves in positions of rendering judgments, they must be fair and not prefer the case of the rich because of their influence and power.

These competing demands of social status maintenance and religious obligation create incoherencies at the ideological level. In certain respects Ben Sira continues in the economic vein of his predecessors in the wisdom tradition, advocating care for the poor without engaging in the class criticism of the prophets. Yet his situation seems more precarious. He is unable to maintain the consequential relationship of righteousness and wealth found in Proverbs; neither can he treat their disconnection with Qohelet's detached irony. When he asserts that fear of the Lord is better than wealth, this appears to be no mere platitude, but rather a bulwark against real possibilities. Such teaching is also, however, an ideological weapon in his battle for status maintenance, offense as well as defense for the scribe/sage who can direct his professional life to that end as few others can. It may have had a particular value in establishing the status claims of the scribe/sage over against the priest.

Fear of the Lord intersects with another element of Ben Sira's economic ideology, however, in a problematic way. Wealth and poverty are also tied to the system of honor and shame that pervades his society and conditions his theological anthropology. One should be able to gain social honor and avoid shame through proper acquisition and dispersal of wealth. If all else fails, one's wisdom, closely associated with fear of the Lord, should earn one honor enough. But it is not so. A man in Ben Sira's position can lose everything in the blink of an eye. Here the priest has an advantage over the scribe/sage, in the form of ritual access to the honor of the Lord that overshadows the values conflicts of the social world and suppresses the nagging question of theodicy these conflicts produce.

The Israelite wisdom tradition was practical as well as philosophical, and young scribes/sages needed to learn how to make their way through life. As a result we hear Ben Sira reflecting on the everyday realities facing these young men. Through his advice concerning riches and poverty Ben Sira has transmitted to us an important snapshot of the social world of Jews in third- and second-century BCE Judea. An analysis of this discourse helps us to see a bit more clearly not only the specific social location of the scribe/sage, but more generally the complex social and ideological matrix of real people doing their best to negotiate real lives.

CHAPTER FIVE

"FEAR THE LORD AND HONOR THE PRIEST": BEN SIRA AS DEFENDER OF THE JERUSALEM PRIESTHOOD*

From the early years after the people of Israel returned from exile in Babylon to the land of their forefathers, the conduct of the priesthood that served in the Temple constituted the principal reason for the dissatisfaction of some Jews with the worship of God in Jerusalem, and it became a lightning rod for criticism. Upon his return to Palestine, for example, the scribe Ezra in the fifth century BCE found that the priests and the Levites, as well as ordinary Israelites, had married foreign women, and stopping this practice became one of the cornerstones of his religious reforms (Ezra 9–10). The post-exilic prophet known as Malachi excoriated the priests for offering defective animals as sacrifices in the Temple cult (Mal 1:6–14). He further indicted them for divorcing their wives and producing polluted offspring with other women (2:13–16).[1]

In the turbulent political world of the late third to early second century BCE, it should not be a surprise to see that the priesthood and thus the Temple are still seen by some as corrupt institutions that God would punish or replace. The discovery and publication of the literature of the Qumran *yaḥad* brought into bold relief a group that rejected the Jerusalem priesthood.[2] But already for several decades before the

---

* I presented some preliminary thoughts on these issues in a paper entitled "Seeking the Sublime: Aspects of Inner Jewish Polemic in the Wisdom of Ben Sira" to the Hellenistic Judaism Section of the 1993 Annual Meetings of the Society of Biblical Literature in Washington, D. C. The general argument given here can also be found in my paper "Putting the Puzzle Together: Some Suggestions Concerning the Social Location of the Wisdom of Ben Sira," *SBL Seminar Papers 1996* (Atlanta: Scholars Press, 1996), which was later republished in B.G. Wright and L.H. Wills, *Conflicted Boundaries in Wisdom and Apocalypticism* (SBLSymS; Atlanta: SBL, 2005) 89–112. I have adapted portions of the original argument in this paper.

[1] On priests in general, see L.L. Grabbe, *Priests, Prophets, Diviners, Sages: A Socio-historical Study of Religious Specialists in Ancient Israel* (Valley Forge, PA: Trinity Press International 1995) 41–65 and M. Stern, "Aspects of Jewish Society: The Priesthood and Other Classes," *The Jewish People in the First Century* (S. Safrai and M. Stern, eds.; CRINT I.2; Philadelphia: Fortress, 1976) 561–630.

[2] On the origins of the Qumran community and its relationship with the priests in Jerusalem, see J.C. VanderKam, *The Dead Sea Scrolls Today* (Grand Rapids, MI: Eerdmans,

Maccabean Revolt, prior to the composition of the sectarian literature
from Qumran, there was a lively, oftentimes acrimonious, war of words
being waged in Palestine over the legitimacy of the Jerusalem priesthood. Some of the critical voices from this period, like the anonymous
authors/compilers of *The Book of the Watchers* (*1 Enoch* 6–36), the
Astronomical Book (*1 Enoch* 72–82) and the *Aramaic Levi Document*,
have been identified and their criticisms outlined by scholars.[3] Other
Jews, however, did not see the priesthood in such a negative light, but,
in fact, believed that God's approbation rested on those who served in
the Jerusalem Temple.

In the early second century BCE, perhaps the most prominent of those
who supported the Jerusalem priests was a Jerusalemite named Jesus
ben Eleazar ben Sira. Indeed, many scholars of the Wisdom of Jesus
ben Sira have commented on his positive valuation of the Jerusalem
priests and cult.[4] One scholar, H. Stadelmann, has tried to make the
case that Ben Sira was himself a priest.[5] In this paper, however, I want
to go another step. I believe that a case can be made on the basis of
certain pieces of circumstantial evidence, that Ben Sira's positive view of
the Jerusalem priesthood did not take shape in an ideological vacuum,
but that he was deeply engaged in that ongoing war of words as one
who actively took the side of the Temple priests in polemical opposition
against those who criticized them.

The argument of this paper is that Ben Sira was aware of and intended
some passages to respond polemically to complaints that had been
lodged against the Jerusalem priestly establishment and those who sup-

---

1994) 101–2 and L.H. Schiffman, *Reclaiming the Dead Sea Scrolls* (Philadelphia: Jewish
Publication Society, 1994) 87–9.

[3] See, for example, D. Suter, "Fallen Angel, Fallen Priest: The Problem of Family
Purity in 1 Enoch 6–16," *HUCA* 50 (1979) 115–35; G.W.E. Nickelsburg, "Enoch, Levi
and Peter: Recipients of Revelation in Upper Galilee," *JBL* 100 (1981) 575–600; idem,
Jewish Literature Between the Bible and the Mishnah (Philadelphia: Fortress, 1981)
52–4; M.E. Stone, "Enoch, Aramaic Levi and Sectarian Origins," *JSJ* 19 (1988) 159–70;
R.A. Kugler, *From Patriarch to Priest: The Levi-Priestly Tradition from Aramaic Levi to
Testament of Levi* (SBLEJL 9; Atlanta: Scholars Press, 1996).

[4] See, for example, T. Maertens, *L'éloge des pères (Ecclésiastique XLIV–L)* (Bruges:
Abbaye de Saint-André, 1956) 121, 156; G. Maier, *Mensch und freier Wille: Nach der
jüdischen Religionsparteien zwischen Ben Sira und Paulus* (WUNT 12; Tübingen: Mohr
Siebeck, 1971) 52–4.

[5] H. Stadelmann, *Ben Sira als Schriftgelehrter: Eine Untersuchung zum Berufsbild des
vor-Makkabäischen Sofer unter Berücksichtigung seines Verhältnisses zu Priester- Propheten-
und Weisheitslehretum* (WUNT 2/6; Tübingen: Mohr Siebeck, 1981).

ported it. These complaints can be found in the works mentioned above, which are roughly contemporary to Ben Sira.[6] He had a strategy for addressing these concerns that consisted of (1) writing positively about the priesthood and encouraging Jews to pay the priests in the Temple the honor due them and (2) confronting some of the means by which the communities who produced and used these works that opposed the Temple priests legitimated or gave authority to their criticisms. I believe that Ben Sira knew the specific criticisms of those whom he supported and came to their defense.

This last claim highlights the inevitable circumstantial character of this argument. Ben Sira does not mention the targets of his polemic but embeds his remarks against them in the middle of other discussions. Likewise, some of the critics of the Jerusalem establishment couched their criticisms in the heavily symbolic language of apocalyptic without any specific references to their contemporary agenda. Consequently, the social situations reflected in these documents must be reconstructed from precious few clues, which present a difficult obstacle. Do the literary devices, themes and issues provide a firm enough basis to reconstruct a social world where real people and communities are struggling to realize their own visions for the Israel of God? Can we see here communities of Jews in conflict with each other? In other words, even though Ben Sira and the communities represented in the Enochic works and *Aramaic Levi* may be contemporary and even treat the same themes and issues, can we move from those "facts" to envisioning a social world in which these people know about one another and attack or respond to one another? Given the indirect and ambiguous nature of the evidence, can one move from literary theme to social reality? I think that the cumulative effect of all the pieces of evidence when

---

[6] The *Book of the Watchers* and the *Astronomical Book* probably date to at least the third century BCE. J.T. Milik dates the Qumran manuscripts of these sections to the second century BCE [*The Books of Enoch* (Oxford: Clarendon, 1976)]. Since they are surely not the autographs, the composition of the books must be earlier. On the dating of the Enochic corpus, see Nickelsburg, *Jewish Literature*, 46–55, 150–51. On a third century BCE date for *Aramaic Levi*, see Stone, "Enoch, Aramaic Levi," 159 note 2 and Kugler, *From Patriarch to Priest*, 222–24. Sirach is usually dated to somewhere around 180 BCE. See P.W. Skehan and A.A. Di Lella, *The Wisdom of Ben Sira*, (AB 39; Garden City, NY: Doubleday, 1987) 8–10. On the relationship between the *Aramaic Levi Document* and the Greek *Testament of Levi*, which used *Aramaic Levi*, see H.W. Hollander and M. de Jonge, *The Testaments of the Twelve Patriarchs: A Commentary* (SVTP 8; Leiden: Brill, 1985) and also Kugler's discussion and the literature cited therein.

they are drawn together will enable a plausible scenario to emerge of a continuing confrontation among different Jewish groups over what they consider to be foundational issues for Jews in the period before the Maccabean Revolt.

BEN SIRA'S SUPPORT OF THE JERUSALEM
PRIESTHOOD AND TEMPLE

Sirach contains several passages that demonstrate the author's outspoken enthusiasm regarding the Jerusalem priesthood and the Temple cult. Since these have been treated elsewhere, I will outline only the most important passages in this section.[7] I cannot review in detail in this paper the problem of whether Ben Sira is simply giving lipservice to the importance of the cult while really being concerned about ethical living or whether he does think that the cult is important in and of itself. S. Olyan has provided a good summary discussion of these issues and concludes that for Ben Sira the cult really matters. I am convinced by his overall argument and his conclusion that "Ben Sira's positive view of the cult is as obvious as are his ethical concerns. There is no conflict between the two."[8]

Ben Sira expresses his views on the priesthood most succinctly in the critical passage 7:29–31.[9] Here he adapts the language of Deut 6:5, part of the Shema, in order to encourage giving the priests their due. "With all your heart (בכל לבך) fear the Lord and regard the priests as holy (הקדיש). With all your might (מאודך) love your maker and do not forsake his servants. Give glory to God and honor the priest, and give their portion as you are commanded." As Olyan remarks, "the parallelistic structure of this passage is striking."[10] Each action intended for God is paralleled by one intended for the priests. Ben Sira's use of Deuteronomy lends tremendous symbolic and rhetorical weight to how important honoring the priests is. Giving the priests honor is the

---

[7] See especially Stadelmann, *Ben Sira als Schriftgelehrter*; S. Olyan, "Ben Sira's Relationship to the Priesthood," *HTR* 80 (1987) 261–86 and the literature cited in these studies.

[8] Olyan, "Ben Sira's Relationship to the Priesthood," 263. The full discussion can be found on pp. 261–63, 265 note 13, 266–67.

[9] For a full discussion of this passage, see Stadelmann, *Ben Sira als Schriftgelehrter*, 56–68.

[10] Olyan, "Ben Sira's Relationship to the Priesthood," 264.

symbolic equivalent of fearing and loving God. Thus, the command to give the priests their portion of the sacrifices (which are listed in verse 31) also takes on greater rhetorical importance in the context. Performance of the cult and giving the priests their due is elevated to the level of extending to God his proper honor.

Sirach 34:21–35:12 deals more specifically with the performance of the cultic sacrifices.[11] In this passage, Ben Sira contrasts the abuse of the cult with its proper performance. What distinguishes the one from the other is proper ethical conduct. Ben Sira states forthrightly that God does not accept the sacrifices of the ungodly (34:23) and that "the sacrifice of the righteous is acceptable" (35:9). But his other comments about the cult in this passage do not seem to spiritualize it in favor of ethics.[12] In 35:1–12 Ben Sira repeatedly notes the importance of performing the sacrifice. The sacrificial offerings "fulfill the commandment." Sirach 35:1–2 connects intimately the cult with righteousness. "The one who keeps the law makes many offerings; one who heeds the commandments makes a peace offering."

Although Ben Sira in this passage stresses the importance of the relationship between ethics and sacrifice, he does not do so to the diminution of the sacrificial system practiced in the Temple. Proper sacrifice "enriches the altar" (35:8). The Jew who fulfills the law, a matter of crucial importance to Ben Sira, acts properly *and* performs the necessary sacrifices in the Temple.[13]

Returning to the priesthood, many have remarked on the greater amount of attention that Ben Sira devotes to Aaron as compared to his more famous brother Moses. The long section on Aaron (45:6–22) is followed by one on Phinehas (45:23–25), and later in chapter 50 Ben Sira closes the Praise of the Ancestors section by glorifying the high priest Simon II. God makes an eternal covenant both with Aaron and with Phinehas, the everlasting covenant being mentioned twice in Aaron's case. Olyan notes that in these passages Ben Sira "alludes to P passage after P passage…ignoring for all intents and purposes other Pentateuchal narrative."[14] He goes on to argue that Sirach reflects a

---

[11] On this section, see Stadelman, *Ben Sira als Schriftgelehrter*, 68–138.

[12] Ibid., 119. Stadelman compares his understanding of Ben Sira's position to the one later found at Qumran.

[13] Sirach 38:9–11 also enjoins the offering of sacrifices, in this case in time of illness. One should offer sacrifice and then call a doctor.

[14] Olyan, "Ben Sira's Relationship to the Priesthood," 270.

position in which, like the Priestly narrative in the Pentateuch, Aaron and his descendents are the true priests. According to Olyan, Ben Sira maintains a "pan-Aaronid" view of the priesthood, while at the same time neglecting the Levites entirely and never mentioning the sons of Zadok.[15] Since Ben Sira's praise of Simon II harks back to that of Aaron, Simon becomes the epitome of the high priest who fulfills the covenant made with Aaron and Phinehas.[16] Ben Sira's pan-Aaronid views find further confirmation in the description of Simon exiting the Temple and blessing the people in which those priests who accompany him are called "sons of Aaron" (50:13, 16).[17] By deliberately choosing one particular priestly ideology over other possible ones, like those in Deuteronomy and Jeremiah or in the work of the Chronicler, Olyan concludes that Ben Sira rejects the exclusivistic claims to the high priesthood made by Zadokites.[18]

The Temple itself also finds approbation in Sirach. In the famous Praise of Wisdom found in chapter 24, God sends wisdom to dwell in Israel where she ministers in "the holy tent" (24:10). He then establishes her in Jerusalem, but specifically in Zion, that is, in the Temple.[19] In 49:12 Joshua and Zerubbabel are remembered as having "raised the holy temple destined for everlasting glory."[20]

Apart from the textual affirmations of the priests, cult and Temple given by Ben Sira, R.A. Horsley and P. Tiller suggest that Ben Sira's position in Jerusalem society provides strong motivation for him to support the Jerusalem Temple establishment. In their jointly authored article, "Ben Sira and the Sociology of the Second Temple," they utilize the insights of the sociologist Gerhard Lenski in an attempt to sketch the contours of Judean society in the time of Ben Sira and to understand

---

[15] Ibid., 275. Olyan implies that Ben Sira's "pan-Aaronid" views may also account for the absence of Ezra from the Praise of the Ancestors since he was a Zadokite and that balancing the absence of Zadokites in Sirach might explain the addition of the hymn after 50:12 where a specific praise of the sons of Zadok appears. See also P. Höffken's conclusion in "Warum schwieg Jesus Sirach über Ezra?" *ZAW* 87 (197) 184–202 cited by Olyan, "Ben Sira's Relationship to the Priesthood," 275 note 40.

[16] Olyan (ibid., 270) remarks that even Simon's Zadokite lineage is ignored by Ben Sira.

[17] Ben Sira probably had personal experience of Simon officiating in the Temple, even though the book was probably written after the high priest's death. See Skehan and Di Lella, *Wisdom of Ben Sira*, 9.

[18] Olyan, "Ben Sira's Relationship to the Priesthood," 272, 275–76.

[19] Skehan and Di Lella, *Wisdom of Ben Sira*, 333.

[20] This translation reflects Ms B from the Geniza, which is missing "to the Lord" found in the Greek.

where he fits in the network of social relations revealed in his book.[21] They conclude that the first-person descriptions given by Ben Sira reveal him to belong to what they call the "scribe-sage" class, a class categorized by Lenski as a retainer class.[22] They argue that Ben Sira would have belonged to a retainer class that acted as mediators between the rulers, primarily priests in ancient Judea, and ordinary Jews. Some of the functions of this class would necessarily overlap with those of the priests, especially teaching the law (a responsibility given to Aaron in 45:17), which would have been delegated by priests to the scribe-sage class. Horsley and Tiller remark, "In Ben Sira's Judea, the sages performed the functions that Lenski ascribes to 'the clergy' in societies of limited literacy: officials and diplomats as well as educators."[23]

Consequently, this scribe-sage class would be heavily dependent on the priests for its livelihood and social status; it would be both politically and economically vulnerable to the priests. Horsley and Tiller argue that such a social position would account well for Ben Sira's admonitions about how to deal with the ruling class. But, in addition, scribes would have some independence from the priests and retain some authority as those who guard, teach and interpret the divine commandments. Their presumed authority might even bring them into conflict with their priestly superiors. "The sages had a clear sense of their own, independent of their patrons, of how the temple-state should operate in accordance with (their interpretation of) the covenantal laws. Their high priestly superiors, however, had regular dealings with the Hellenistic imperial officials and were susceptible to greater influence from the wider Hellenistic culture."[24]

Thus, whatever Ben Sira's precise social position was, priest, scribe-sage or priest *and* scribe, he shows himself to be thoroughly on the side of the Jerusalem priestly establishment. He enjoins his charges to honor the priests, to give them their proper portions of the sacrifices, to offer

---

[21] This work was originally presented to the Sociology of the Second Temple Group, San Francisco, 1992. The paper was later published as "Ben Sira and the Sociology of the Second Temple," *Second Temple Studies III: Studies in Politics, Class and Material Culture* (P.R. Davies and J.M. Halligan, eds.; JSOTSup 340; Sheffield: Sheffield Academic Press, 2002) 74–107. Subsequent references will be to the published version. For Lenski's thought they rely on *Power and Privilege* (New York: McGraw-Hill, 1966).

[22] Horsley and Tiller, "Ben Sira and Sociology," 99–103.

[23] Ibid., 100.

[24] Ibid., 102. This might also explain to a degree Ben Sira's support of the priests, on the one hand, and some of his apparently negative attitudes towards Hellenistic culture, on the other.

the proper sacrifices at the right time. If he were actually a priest as Stadelmann argues, he would have a deep investment in viewing the Temple priesthood in this manner. Yet even if he were not a priest, but a member of a social group retained by the priests, as Horsley and Tiller claim, he would have cause as well to stand behind the legitimacy of the Jerusalem priests. These views on the priesthood did not take shape in some esoteric realm of theological detachment, but they were formed as a response to those whose views on the Jerusalem establishment were quite opposite Ben Sira's.

CRITICISMS OF THE PRIESTS IN *1 ENOCH* AND *ARAMAIC LEVI*

Two sections of *1 Enoch*, the *Book of the Watchers* and the *Astronomical Book*, together with the *Aramaic Levi Document* are roughly contemporary with our Jerusalemite sage. Even if these third century BCE works slightly predate Ben Sira, they were clearly prized and in use in communities at his time.[25] Thus, the way that they view the priests in Jerusalem provides an excellent window through which to see Ben Sira's antagonists. Two questions surface regarding these works: what is the nature of the criticism and out of what kinds of groups do they arise?

Both D. Suter and G.W.E. Nickelsburg have argued that the *Book of the Watchers* contains veiled criticism of the Jerusalem priesthood, and by extension the legitimacy of the Temple cult, over the issue of improper marriages.[26] Suter examines *1 Enoch* 6–16. Chapters 6–11 have as a central part of the myth of the fallen Watchers a concern that they have been defiled by contact with women and blood and that the offspring of the unions between the women and the Watchers are *mamzerim*. Chapters 12–16, a commentary on the preceding chapters, demonstrate interest in the same problem, but also here there is the implication that the sexual contact "is defiling *per se* since it represents an illegitimate degree of family relationship... The incongruity of marriages of angels and women is underlined by 1 En. 15:4–12." The giants are "hybrids"

---

[25] The author of *Jubilees* knew the *Book of the Watchers*, and of course, portions of all three works were found among the Qumran manuscripts.

[26] Suter, "Fallen Angel" and Nickelsburg, "Enoch, Levi and Peter." See also M. Himmelfarb, *Ascent to Heaven in Jewish and Christian Apocalypses* (New York: Oxford University Press, 1993) 9–29.

just as the offspring of the illicit priestly marriages are. For the *Book of the Watchers* "the concern for the purity of the angels in both sections [6–11 and 12–16], taken with the treatment of the giants as *mamzerim*, suggests that the myth needs to be examined in light of rules concerning family purity in Second Temple Judaism."[27] This preoccupation with family purity in *1 Enoch*, according to Suter's analysis, is about priestly purity, which was a primary concern for Jews in the Second Temple period. He concludes, "There is a parallel between the separation that the myth seeks to draw between the angelic and human realms and the tendency toward endogamy in priestly marriages."[28]

In addition other clues point to the priesthood as the critical problem in *1 Enoch* 6–16. In these chapters the Watchers pervert priestly responsibilities. Because they teach forbidden knowledge, the Watchers subvert the priest's role as teacher. The illegitimate marriages of the Watchers further result in their expulsion from heaven, which is depicted as a temple. For the author of these chapters, like the Watchers expelled from the heavenly Temple, the priests in Jerusalem who contract illegitimate marriages should be prevented from serving in the earthly Temple.[29]

This interest in and concern for priestly purity may well indicate that the *Book of the Watchers* originated in circles of priests who were convinced that the Jerusalem priests had violated purity rules, were defiled as a result, and should be expelled from the Temple service. Several pieces of evidence indicate a priestly origin for this work. M.E. Stone argues that the "scientific" speculations contained in the early parts of *1 Enoch* must have originated in groups of "educated men and may possibly have been associated with the traditional intellectuals, the wise and the priests." He notes in addition that the calendrical interests so notable in both the *Book of the Watchers* and the *Astronomical Book* are traditionally matters dealt with by priests.[30]

In his SBL paper, "The Priesthood and Apocalyptic," Suter looks to the sociological analysis of Edward Shils, who studied the roles of intellectuals in society, for indications as to who might have produced the *Book of the Watchers*. Shils's analysis shows that the center of society is made

---

[27] Suter, "Fallen Angel," 118–19.

[28] Ibid., 122.

[29] Ibid., 123–24. On heaven as a Temple in *1 Enoch*, see Nickelsburg, *Jewish Literature*, 53 and Himmelfarb, *Ascent to Heaven*, 14–6.

[30] M.E. Stone, "The Book of Enoch and Judaism in the Third Century B.C.E.," *CBQ* 40 (1978) 489. See below for a more detailed treatment of the calendar.

up of two systems, "a *central institutional system*, which wields power, and a *central cultural system*, which develops the myths legitimating the exercise of power." Suter combines this insight with the connection made by Stone between apocalyptic and Jewish intellectual traditions. He concludes, "Since the interests of the central institutional system are not completely identical with those of the central cultural system, it is possible to account for friction within the priesthood itself within Judean society, since priests are undoubtedly in the forefront of both systems."[31] That is, the criticisms in evidence in *1 Enoch* are not simply *about* the priesthood, they originate *within* priestly groups.

The roles ascribed to Enoch, the protagonist of this mythic drama and likely representative of the community, also provide evidence of the group that produced the work. Enoch is called "scribe of righteousness" (15:1), and in drawing up the petition of the Watchers he acts as a scribe. But, Enoch also plays the role of priest when he intercedes for the Watchers before God, intercession being a priestly function. Enoch has extraordinary access to the heavenly Temple, the Temple being a place that is the absolute domain of the priests.[32] As Suter notes regarding the role of scribe and priest, "a scribal role need not preclude a priestly one, and may even point in that direction."[33]

Nickelsburg concentrates specifically on the cultic language contained in *1 Enoch* 15:2–4, where Enoch is to tell the Watchers that their plea to God has been rejected. Rather than someone petitioning God for them, they should be interceding for humankind. The indictment of the Watchers follows in verses 3–4, "Why have you [the Watchers] left the high heaven and the eternal holy one and lain with women and defiled yourselves with the daughters of men and taken to yourselves wives and acted like the children of earth…yet you defiled yourselves with the blood of women." The description of heaven in this work as a Temple and the angels as priests has prompted Nickelsburg, like Suter, to identify the Watchers as priests who have fallen and united themselves with women by marrying illegitimately. As a result, God has banned the Watchers from the heavenly Temple, and those priests who have married women forbidden to them should be barred from the earthly

---

[31] D. Suter, "The Priesthood and Apocalyptic," 11. The paper was presented in the Worship/Cult in Ancient Israel Section of the 1981 Annual Meetings of the SBL in San Francisco. My thanks to the author for making his paper available to me.
[32] Himmelfarb, *Ascent to Heaven*, 23–5.
[33] Suter, "The Priesthood," 9. Ezra is himself called scribe and priest.

Temple. This kind of anti-priestly polemic is consistent with several other Second Temple Jewish texts that report similar difficulties, and it demonstrates that the character of the priesthood is a fundamental concern for many Jews in this period.[34] Nickelsburg concludes that "the easiest explanation [of the myth in *1 Enoch* 12–16] appears to be that the mythmaker has a grievance against the priesthood in his own time... [W]e have here in *1 Enoch* 12–16 an apocalyptic tradition emanating from circles in upper Galilee who view the Jerusalem priesthood as defiled and therefore under the irrevocable judgment of God."[35]

The situation in *Aramaic Levi* is very similar to that of *1 Enoch*. This work also contains elements of polemic against exogamous marriages. The specific comments of the fragmentary passage in 4Q213 2 about virgins ruining their names and bringing shame on their brothers, which Levi apparently sees in a vision, would seem to indicate that priestly exogamy in particular is the problem.[36] Later in *Aramaic Levi* 82–106, Levi's testamentary speech to his children predicts that in later generations they will cease to follow his instructions. The section begins with an admonishment by Levi that his children learn and teach wisdom. In 102–106 Levi makes clear that his descendents will abandon this wisdom and will "walk in the darkness of satan... will become fools." They will turn to wickedness and evil (106).[37]

A number of other characteristics of the work also point to a priestly milieu for its origins. Levi's position as the ancestor of priests sets up a glorification of the priesthood as an institution while at the same time there is a condemnation of particular groups of priests; the polemic concerning illegitimate marriages and the wickedness of some priests recalls *1 Enoch*. The centrality of the figure of Levi also points in this direction. Several of the emphases of *Aramaic Levi* reflect priestly interests. *Aramaic Levi* is interested in the calendar and seems to use a solar year. The work includes detailed sacrificial instructions (13–60), and it emphasizes the levitical line.[38] Indeed the levitical line is so important that *Aramaic Levi* transferred to Levi the biblical verses referring to

---

[34] Nickelsburg, "Enoch, Levi and Peter," 584–85.
[35] Ibid., 586. Nickelsburg identifies the upper Galilee as the place where these groups live, primarily on the basis of descriptions of the places of revelation in *1 Enoch, Aramaic Levi* and the New Testament gospels.
[36] Kugler, *From Patriarch to Priest*, 36, 77.
[37] For the text and translation see ibid., 120, 122.
[38] In contrast to Ben Sira who emphasized a pan-Aaronid priesthood. See above.

Judah that later took on messianic interpretations.[39] The *Testament of Levi*, which used *Aramaic Levi* as a source, attributes scribal characteristics to Levi (8:17; chap. 13; 14:4).[40] Stone assesses *Aramaic Levi* this way: "[T]he circles responsible for *Aramaic Levi* laid a very strong emphasis on the instructional function of the priesthood and this aspect of the priesthood attracted sapiential motifs."[41] As in the case of Enoch in the *Book of the Watchers*, the two roles, scribe and priest, are subsumed under one figure, here Levi.

Thus, we find in roughly contemporaneous Jewish works quite opposite views of the priesthood. Ben Sira takes a positive stance toward the priests and encourages their support through the cultic performance in the Temple. He may even, in his pan-Aaronid views, be implicitly opposing levitical or Zadokite claims. *1 Enoch* and *Aramaic Levi* are quite harsh in their critical stance vis-à-vis the priests who are in control in Jerusalem, precisely the people whom Ben Sira honors.[42] These views are certainly enough to establish that the priesthood in the late third to early second century is a contentious issue in Second Temple Judaism. Is there evidence that Ben Sira and the groups who produced and used *1 Enoch* and *Aramaic Levi* may have been aware of each other? To this problem I now turn.

The Relationship Between Sirach, *1 Enoch* and *Aramaic Levi*

Several recent studies have shown that Sirach and *1 Enoch* have important literary similarities, and these similarities have suggested to some a possible social relationship. Nickelsburg, on the basis of Sirach's and

---

[39] M.E. Stone, "Ideal Figures and Social Context: Priest and Sage in the Early Second Temple Age," *Ancient Israelite Religions: F. M. Cross Festschrift* (P.D. Miller, Jr., P.D. Hanson, S.D. McBride, eds.; Philadelphia: Fortress, 1988) 580.

[40] Himmelfarb, *Ascent to Heaven*, 30.

[41] Stone, "Ideal Figures," 580.

[42] Ithamar Gruenwald expresses a similar view about works like *1 Enoch* and *Aramaic Levi*, "Moreover, if we take into consideration that Apocalypticism was to a large extent the product of levitic, or priestly circles, then the polemical tones struck therein do not merely have an anti-priestly orientation, but they do in fact echo an inner-priestly struggle for hegemony and authority" (*From Apocalypticism to Gnosticism: Studies in Apocalypticism, Merkavah Mysticism and Gnosticism* [BEATAJ 14; Frankfurt am Main 1988] 139).

the *Epistle of Enoch*'s treatments of the rich and poor, has speculated that perhaps "the *poor* of Ben Sira's time" produced the Epistle.[43] The two most detailed treatments of the issue come from R.A. Argall in his study *1 Enoch and Sirach* and from G. Boccaccini in his *Middle Judaism*.[44] Argall's book is concerned with the literary themes and forms in common between Sirach and *1 Enoch*. He demonstrates that these two Second Temple Jewish works treat identical themes—revelation, creation, judgment—and articulate them similarly. At the end of his book he ventures several possibilities about a social connection between the works. He remarks about their differing views, "Such differences are the stuff of conflict...[I]t is enough to make the case that each tradition views the other among its rivals."[45]

Boccaccini also examines the theological similarities and differences between Sirach, the *Book of the Watchers* and the *Astronomical Book*.[46] He claims that this literary relationship reveals that Ben Sira is aware of apocalyptic theologies and that he is writing against them. His literary analysis of the theologies of these works makes him think that there might be some direct literary confrontation between Ben Sira and these apocalyptic groups. Commenting on the theme of covenant in Sirach, Boccaccini writes,

> Ben Sira is intent on reaffirming the centrality of the covenant and the retributive principle, overcoming the aporias and doubts of Job and Qohelet. At the same time he *directly* [emphasis mine] confronts the

---

[43] G.W.E. Nickelsburg, "Social Aspects of Palestinian Jewish Apocalypticism," *Apocalypticism in the Mediterranean World and the Near East* (D. Hellholm, ed.; Tübingen: Mohr Siebeck, ²1989) 651.

[44] R.A. Argall, *1 Enoch and Sirach: A Comparative Literary and Conceptual Analysis of the Themes of Revelation, Creation and Judgment* (SBLEJL 8; Atlanta: Scholars Press, 1995); G. Boccaccini, *Middle Judaism: Jewish Thought 300 B.C.E. to 200 C.E.* (Minneapolis: Fortress, 1991). Argall's assessment of the dates of the different portions of *1 Enoch* relies on that of Nickelsburg. He uses those portions of *1 Enoch* that are contemporary with Sirach, as I do here. Primarily for reasons of space, I have limited this paper to the *Book of the Watchers* and the *Astronomical Book* while Argall has included in his study the *Epistle of Enoch* (*1 Enoch* 92–105). On the *Epistle of Enoch*, see also G.W.E. Nickelsburg, "Revealed Wisdom as a Criterion for Inclusion and Exclusion: From Jewish Sectarianism to Early Christianity," *"To See Ourselves as Other See Us:" Christians, Jews, "Others" in Late Antiquity* (J. Neusner and E.S. Frerichs, eds.; Chico, CA: Scholars Press, 1985) 74–7. A connection between Sirach and the *Epistle of Enoch* was originally suggested by Victor Tcherikover, *Hellenistic Civilization and the Jews* (New York: Atheneum, 1982 [reprint of 1959 edition]) 151. See also, Nickelsburg, "Social Aspects," 651.

[45] Argall, *1 Enoch and Sirach*, 250.

[46] Boccaccini, *Middle Judaism*, chapter 2, "Ben Sira, Qohelet and Apocalyptic."

suggestions of the apocalyptic movement. The calm and systematic style of this wisdom book should not lead us to lose sight of the terms of a bitter debate, addressing such precise referents and urgent questioning.[47]

Finally, in two brief but suggestive remarks, S. Olyan links the polemics of the *Testament of Levi* and *1 Enoch* with Sirach. Olyan believes that both the *Testament of Levi* and *1 Enoch* witness to claims of the Levites to the priesthood against what they consider to be the pretensions of the Aaronids/Zadokites.[48] This position contrasts with Ben Sira's "refusal to recognize the Levites as a group," and Olyan further notes that "we may have evidence here [in *1 Enoch* 89:73] of a contemporary Levitic theology opposed to Ben Sira's pan-Aaronid exclusivism."[49]

Several passages in Sirach seem to me to treat very specifically issues found in *1 Enoch* and *Aramaic Levi*, and the way that Ben Sira addresses these problems shows his awareness of apocalyptic groups and their ideas. Four, in particular, the calendar, the inner workings of the universe, dreams and visions and the person of Enoch, suggest to me that Ben Sira in his instruction to his students is voicing his concern about the claims of these people.

Problems of the Calendar

43:6 It is the moon that marks the changing seasons,
      governing the times, their lasting sign.
43:7 By it we know the sacred seasons and pilgrimage feasts,
      a light which wanes in its course.
43:8 The new moon like its name renews itself;
      how wondrous it is when it changes!
      An army signal for the cloud vessels on high,
      it paves the firmament with its brilliance.

"It is difficult to overstress the importance of the calendar." So M.E. Stone concludes about the character of third century BCE Judaism.[50] Calendrical concerns are certainly in evidence in the documents under consideration here, and the problem of the calendar is addressed polemically in some of them. The fundamental issue at stake is whether one reckons the year on the basis of the sun alone or by the moon (or, sun and moon together). Control of the calendar means control of the set-

---

[47] Ibid., 80.
[48] Olyan, "Ben Sira's Relationship to the Priesthood," 279–80.
[49] Ibid., 280.
[50] Stone, "Enoch, Aramaic Levi," 166.

ting of the Jewish festivals and observances, and Jewish groups who reckoned the calendar differently would fix different days for the same celebrations. The Qumran community, in a period slightly later from the one I am considering here, used a solar calendar, but the origins of that calendar are clearly much earlier than the Qumran *yaḥad* itself.[51]

The *Astronomical Book*, the *Book of the Watchers* and *Aramaic Levi* all evidence use of a solar calendar. The *Astronomical Book* preserves the most extensive and detailed treatment of a 364-day solar year.[52] In this section of *1 Enoch*, the angel Uriel shows Enoch a vision in which he sees the intricacies of the movements of the sun, moon and stars through the heavens. The revelation given to Enoch provides the basis for the solar year, and thus the reckoning of seasons and festivals. Although the *Astronomical Book* was apparently not originally intended to be a polemic, two passages in the present form of the book, 75:2 and 82:4–7, and one eschatological addition to the book, 80:2–8, seem to polemicize against those who do not use the Enochic solar calendar.[53] *1 Enoch* 75:2 and 82:4–7 decry those who do not reckon the four epagomenal days that bring the calendar to 364 days. O. Neugebauer remarks that 75:2 "could refer to the lunar calendar of the Jews (which has no intercalary days)."[54] *1 Enoch* 82:4–7 blesses the righteous who "do not err in counting all their days in which the sun travels in the sky…together with the four (days) that are added." *1 Enoch* 80:2 begins by saying that "in the days of the sinners years shall become shorter.

---

[51] On the Qumran calendar, see S. Talmon, "The Calendar Reckoning of the Sect from the Judean Desert," ScrHier 4 (1958) 162–99. See also R. Beckwith, "The Earliest Enoch Literature and Its Calendar: Marks of Their Origin, Date and Motivation," *RevQ* 10 (1981) 365–403.

[52] The Aramaic fragments of the *Astronomical Book* found at Qumran show that the version used by the Qumranites was more extensive than that preserved in the Ethiopic *1 Enoch*. See Milik, *The Books of Enoch* and M. Black, *The Book of Enoch or 1 Enoch: A New English Edition* (SVTP 7; Leiden: Brill, 1985). The solar year constitutes an integral part of both forms of the book.

[53] On these passages, see Black, *Book of Enoch*, 252, 411 and Nickelsburg, *Jewish Literature*, 48. On *1 Enoch* 80–81, see J.C. VanderKam, *Enoch and the Growth of an Apocalyptic Tradition* (CBQMS 16; Washington, D. C.: Catholic University of America, 1984) 106–9. On the date of chapter 80, VanderKam (107) remarks, "When and why they [the passages in chap 80] were spliced in the AB remains an enigma."

[54] Black, *Book of Enoch*, 402. J. VanderKam notes, however, that the polemic about the four epagomenal days does not necessarily oppose a lunar calendar. He argues that the original *Astronomical Book* presented a 364-day calendar apparently without any active opposition to the calendar governing the cult in Jerusalem. See "The 364-Day Calendar in the Enochic Literature," *Society of Biblical Literature 1983 Seminar Papers* (K.H. Richards, ed.; Chico, CA: Scholars Press, 1983) 164.

And their seeds shall be late in their lands and fields." This is a prelude to various eschatological tribulations. The "sinners" may be those who do not abide by the solar calendar revealed to Enoch, but who use a lunar or soli-lunar calendar that rapidly falls out of sync with the solar year. The same 364-day calendar is utilized later in clearly polemical contexts by the book of *Jubilees* (which knows *1 Enoch*) and by the people of Qumran. Nickelsburg's comment on these texts is apt here. "Behind all this [the problems concerning calendar evidenced in these works] appears to have been a bitter calendrical dispute with the Jewish religious establishment."[55]

The *Book of the Watchers*, although lacking the detail about the calendar of the *Astronomical Book*, also preserves clues that this calendar was an important facet of the Enochic visionary tradition generally. The solar calendar is not even explicitly mentioned in the *Book of the Watchers*, but the work clearly assumes such a calendar. Chapters 33–36 appear to be a summary account intended to end the work, and 33:2–4 specifically look like a condensed version of the material in the *Astronomical Book*. As was the case there, herc Uriel shows Enoch the "gates of the heavens" and the determination of the calendar.[56] Chapters 34–36 also refer to these gates, even though the astronomical scheme is slightly different from the *Astronomical Book*.[57]

The fragmentary condition of *Aramaic Levi* makes it difficult to determine exactly how the calendar functioned in that work, but a calendar like that used at Qumran is recognizable. This conclusion depends primarily on the reports about Levi's children in *Aramaic Levi* 65–72.[58] M.E. Stone and J.C. Greenfield conclude that the data given about the births of Levi's children are consistent with the Qumran solar calendar. These include: (1) the numbering of months as opposed to naming them, (2) the births of the children exactly three months apart putting them on the same date and day of the week, (3) two cases, where dates are provided, in which the births fall on a Wednesday, an important day in the Qumran calendar, (4) Kohath's birth on the morning of the

---

[55] Nickelsburg, *Jewish Literature*, 48.
[56] Argall, *1 Enoch and Sirach*, 52. See the notes to these chapters in Black, *Book of Enoch*, 180–81.
[57] Ibid.
[58] On the various Greek and Aramaic portions of *Aramaic Levi*, see M.E. Stone and J.C. Greenfield, "Remarks on the Aramaic Testament of Levi from the Geniza," *RB* 86 (1979) 214–15 and Kugler, *From Patriarch to Priest*, chapter 2.

first day of the month, morning being the time that the day begins at Qumran.[59]

Ben Sira's comments about the heavenly bodies reveal a position directly in contrast to that found in the works just examined. In the large section about the works of God's creation that acts as a preface to the Praise of the Ancestors (42:15–43:33), several important verses treat the celestial bodies. What Ben Sira has to say about the sun and moon especially should be read, in my estimation, as a polemic against the solar year found in *1 Enoch* and *Aramaic Levi*. His interest in the sun is actually quite mundane—it is hot. Four of the five verses devoted to this heavenly orb describe its fiery nature. It "parches the earth and no one can endure its blazing heat" (43:3). It is hotter than a furnace, and it "breathes out fiery vapors" (43:4). Nowhere does Ben Sira attribute to the sun any calendrical function. In fact, he notes quite specifically how it speeds on its course "at his (the Lord's) command."[60]

In diametrical opposition is Ben Sira's discussion of the moon, which centers almost exclusively on its role as the body that establishes the seasons and festivals. The moon governs the changing seasons (עתות), the festivals (מועד) and the pilgrimages (חג). As its name indicates, the moon gives the month its name, and it serves as an "army beacon" (כלי צבא).

A second text, 50:6, also displays the same contrast between sun and moon. In the description of Simon II, Ben Sira compares him to both sun and moon. Simon is "like the full moon in the festival season" (וכירח מלא בימי מועד).[61] The description of the sun is consistent with that of 43:2–5. Here Simon is "like the sun shining on the Temple of the king" (וכשמש משרקת אל היכל המלך). Although the shining of the sun connotes Simon's glory for Ben Sira, the disparity between the brightness of the sun and the calendrical function of the moon is striking.

What is particularly notable about these statements is that Ben Sira not only denies the sun its primary function in the Enochic scheme, he does so in contrast to the role it plays in the Priestly creation account, which he certainly knows. This is all the more remarkable when one

---

[59] Stone and Greenfield, "Remarks," 224.

[60] This is the NRSV translation. Skehan and Di Lella, *Wisdom of Ben Sira*, 485, 488, translate, "at whose orders it urges on its steeds." For the translation of אבירֿיו as "his steeds" they refer to Jer 8:16; 47:3; 50:11.

[61] This is a reconstructed Hebrew. Ms B has an additional מבין from verse 6a that overloads the present colon. See Skehan and Di Lella, *Wisdom of Ben Sira*, 549. My thanks to Alon Goshen-Gottstein for alerting me to this passage.

remembers Ben Sira's reliance on the Priestly narrative for his theology of the priesthood. In Gen 1:14–15 the sun and the moon *cooperate* in governing the calendar. "God said, 'Let there be lights in the vault of the heavens to separate the day from the night, and let *them* serve as signs both for festivals and for seasons and for years.'"[62] I take Ben Sira's ignoring of Genesis in this way to indicate a deliberate attempt on his part not to make even an apparent concession to the calendrical schemes used by those Jews who produced and used the *Astronomical Book*, the *Book of the Watchers* and *Aramaic Levi*, Jews who claimed the priority and foundational character of the solar calendar.

The Secrets of God and Creation

For Ben Sira, the Law contains God's revelation and wisdom. Its fulfillment is paramount (cf. 15:1; 32:15, 24; 33:2–3). The polemic against the use of a solar calendar in chapter 43 reflects his more overarching suspicions about inquiring into matters that go beyond what is in the Law. One passage in particular, 3:21–24, reveals Ben Sira's unwillingness to delve into things inscrutable, notably the secrets of the created order and what will be in the future.

> 3:21   What is too marvelous for you, do not investigate,
>   and what is too difficult/evil for you, do not research.
> 3:22   On what is authorized, give attention,
>   but you have no business with secret things
> 3:23   And into what is beyond you, do not meddle,
>   For that which is too great has been shown to you.
> 3:24   For many are the thoughts of the sons of men,
>   evil and erring imaginations.[63]

---

[62] A. Rofé, "The Onset of Sects in Postexilic Judaism: Neglected Evidence from the Septuagint, Trito-Isaiah, Ben Sira and Malachi," *The Social World of Formative Christianity and Judaism* (J. Neusner, et al., eds.; Philadelphia: Fortress, 1988) 43–4.

[63] Except for 3:21, I have used the translation of Argall, *1 Enoch and Sirach*, 75. Argall argues for adopting the reading of Ms C from the Geniza for 3:21b against Skehan and Di Lella, *Wisdom of Ben Sira*, who use Ms A. To judge from the Greek translation, however, the situation is more complicated than simply following one manuscript or the other. I follow Ms A for the verbs since elsewhere in Sirach ἐκετάζω (Gk. colon b) only translates Hebrew חקר (11:7; 13:11), but I prefer the adjectives used in Ms C where Greek χαλεπώτερα seems to reflect a *Vorlage* more like Ms C's רעים. The Hebrew of Ben Sira (except for Ms F) can be most conveniently found in The Historical Dictionary of the Hebrew Language, *The Book of Ben Sira: Text, Concordance and an Analysis of the Vocabulary* (Jerusalem: Bialik, 1973 [Hebrew]). For Ms F from the Geniza, see A.A. Di Lella, "The Newly Discovered Sixth Manuscript of Ben Sira from the Cairo Geniza," *Bib* 69 (1988) 226–38.

This passage has often been understood as a polemic against Jewish participation in Greek philosophical inquiry and discussion. P.W. Skehan and A.A. Di Lella summarize the issue this way:

> Ben Sira cautions his readers about the futility of Greek learning, its goals and techniques, and also reminds them of what the Lord has bestowed on them…Hence it is better for the enlightened Jew to follow the certainties and true wisdom of the Law revealed to Moses than to strive after the often contradictory musings and uncertain opinions of the Greek thinkers.[64]

Of course, Ben Sira's ultimate desire is that his students adhere to the Law of Moses, but I think that the passage ought to be understood as well against the backdrop of the mysteries of the cosmos and the eschaton revealed to Enoch and Levi.[65]

Sirach 3:21–24 is both clear and ambiguous at the same time. Ben Sira clearly wants his students to refrain from certain kinds of inquiry. The subjects at issue are "too marvelous," "too difficult/evil" or "hidden," and Ben Sira forbids investigation into them.[66] But the passage is also characterized by a pervasive vagueness. What exactly are those things that are "too marvelous" or "hidden"? Two Hebrew terms used in this passage may indicate what these forbidden subjects are.

The first, the adjective פלאות (3:21; Gk. is probably ἰσχυρότερα), seems to describe the "works of God" generally and the secrets of the universe in particular.[67] The term appears two other places in Sirach. In 11:4 it modifies "the works of God" (מעשי יהוה) and refers to the way that human fortunes can unexpectedly change. פלאות in 43:25, which is part of the poem on the wonders of creation, also describes the "works of God," but in this case these works are the marvelous/incredible sea monsters. Elsewhere in the poem on creation, the related term נפלאות appears, which indicates the unfathomable wonders of God's creation.

---

[64] Skehan and Di Lella, *The Wisdom of Ben Sira*, 160–61. See also Martin Hengel, *Judaism and Hellenism* (Philadelphia: Fortress, 1974) 139–40.

[65] Several scholars have noted that this passage might be directed against apocalyptic thought. Most notably see Gruenwald, *From Apocalypticism to Gnosticism*, 17–8.

[66] On this passage, see Argall, *1 Enoch and Sirach*, 74–6, 250.

[67] Elsewhere in Sirach the phrase "works of God" refers to God's creation. In a reference to Genesis, 16:26 speaks of God who created his works from the beginning, using ברא as does Genesis 1:1. Sirach 33:15 speaks of God's works coming in pairs, which probably includes the created order. Sirach 39:33 follows a long section treating the reasons that God made various things, such as wind and fire. Ben Sira says, "All the works of the Lord are good." Finally, in 43:28 in the poem on creation, it is said that God is greater than "his works," clearly meaning creation.

At the outset of the poem (42:15), Ben Sira exclaims, "I shall recall the works of God (מעשי יהוה)...through the word of the Lord are his works (מעשיו)." These works are filled with God's glory (v. 16), and are impenetrable; even the "holy ones of God" cannot adequately describe "the wonders of God (נפלאות יהוה)." The poem concludes with Ben Sira extolling God for his power and inscrutable nature. In 43:32–33 he reprises his praise of God's works, "Many more things than these are marvelous (נפלא?) and powerful. Only a few of his works have I seen. It is the Lord who has made all things and to those who fear him he gives wisdom."[68]

In one passage where no Hebrew text has survived, Ben Sira appeals to God's role as creator of wondrous things to establish his position as judge. In 18:4–7, he again claims that God's creation cannot be fathomed. No one is able to describe "God's works" or to measure his power. One cannot penetrate the "wonders of the Lord" (καὶ οὐκ ἔστιν ἐξιχνιάσαι τὰ θαυμάσια τοῦ κυρίου). This is a sentiment identical to that found in the poem on creation.

The second term, נסתרות (3:22; Gk. κρύπτα), probably refers to what the future holds. This word also occurs in the poem on creation that begins in chapter 42. God plumbs the depths of the human heart, and "he discloses the past and the future, and he reveals the deep secret things (נסתרות)" (42:19). The two verbs in this verse, מחוה and מגלה, connote revelatory activity, and נסתרות occurs in parallel with matters of the past and the future. This term, used as it is in the context of a poem on creation, connects both with revelation and with creation. The universe comprises not only the created order of visible and invisible things, but also the things that God has ordained to happen. These are all things that God has made, his works.

The poem culminates, as I noted above, in the claim that the creator gives wisdom to those who fear him. Is part of this wisdom the revelation of matters yet to happen, eschatology? Indeed, the same term, נסתרות, is used in 48:25 of those things revealed to the prophet Isaiah, "who foretold what should be till the end of time, hidden things (נסתרות) that were yet to be fulfilled." Here, Ben Sira believes that Isaiah has

---

[68] Skehan and Di Lella, *The Wisdom of Ben Sira*, 487, 490, follow the Greek here because of the fragmentary nature of Ms B, which only has the first word and part of the last word fully legible. On the basis of the traces on the manuscript, the Hebrew Language Academy edition of the Hebrew reconstructs the verse, רוב נ[פ]ל[ל]א וחז[ק] [מ]אלה. I have translated on the basis of this reconstruction.

been shown eschatological realities. Thus, the most likely content of the נסתרות into which 3:22 prohibits inquiry is the eschatological future. Does Ben Sira's apparent distrust of looking for revelation of the future reflect an awareness on his part of the eschatological focus found in works like the *Book of the Watchers* or *Aramaic Levi*?

For his part, even though he understands himself to have a prophet-like inspiration, Ben Sira admits that he has seen only a small portion of God's works (43:32), and he does not make any pretensions about knowing the future. It is not that God completely withholds such revelation; he has, for example, revealed such things to Isaiah. What God has already given, however, is for Ben Sira's students plenty to contemplate, and these are the only things "authorized."

I do not think it entirely coincidental that the secrets of creation and revelation of the future are precisely two of the more conspicuous elements found in the *Astronomical Book*, the *Book of the Watchers* and *Aramaic Levi*. Certainly the foundation of the solar calendar in *1 Enoch* depends on the revelation to Enoch about the workings of the celestial bodies. In *1 Enoch* 14, Enoch's encounter with God in the heavenly Temple, God reveals to Enoch the impending judgment of the Watchers, that is, the Jerusalem priesthood.[69]

The eponymous hero of *Aramaic Levi* also knows the future. If R. Kugler's arrangement of the Qumran fragments is correct, 4Q213 2 constitutes Levi's heavenly vision, which was initially reported in 4Q213 1 ii in which Levi sees the gates of heaven.[70] The extant text breaks off with mention of an angel. 4Q213 2, which may follow, concerns matters of priestly exogamy. Levi is thus shown in a vision that priests will enter into illegitimate marriages.[71] Later in the work Levi predicts the disobedience of his descendents in the text cited above.

Thus, the admonitions given by Ben Sira in 3:21–24 to his students forbid them to investigate the inner workings of the universe, which cannot be fathomed, or to try to divine future events, probably eschatological happenings. By contrast, he directs their attention to what is authorized, almost certainly a reference to the Law. He intends to keep

---

[69] On this interpretation of the *Book of the Watchers*, see Nickelsburg, "Enoch, Levi and Peter"; Suter, "The Priesthood" and "Fallen Angel." The eschatology found in the *Astronomical Book* is in chapters 80–1, which are probably not original to the book. See VanderKam, *Enoch and the Growth*, 106.

[70] Kugler, *From Patriarch to Priest*, 77.

[71] A major aspect of Kugler's analysis of the fragment has to do with its similarity to *Jub* 30:5–17. For the complete argument, see ibid., 83–4.

his charges grounded, to confine their study to the Law, in which is contained the only acceptable revelation of God. Rather than a polemic against Greek philosophy, this passage confronts unauthorized interest in things that God has decided to withhold from human understanding. Ben Sira is worried about what he considers to be an unhealthy concern for matters too difficult, too great and perhaps even too dangerous to investigate, the secrets of God's created order and the revelation of the future.[72]

Dream Visions and Ascents

At the same time that Ben Sira forbids delving into certain subjects he attacks the mechanisms by which this knowledge is acquired. In 34:1–8, Ben Sira takes on dreams and visions.

> 34:1 Empty and false are the hopes of the senseless,
> and fools are sent winging by dreams.
> 34:2 Like one grasping at shadows or chasing the wind
> is whoever puts his trust in dreams.
> 34:3 What is seen in dreams is a reflection
> that mirrors the vision of the onlooker.
> 34:4 Can the clean produce the unclean?
> Can the liar ever speak the truth?
> 34:5 Divination, omens, and dreams are unreal;
> what you already expect, the mind depicts.
> 34:6 Unless it be a vision specially sent from the Most High,
> fix not your heart on it.
> 34:7 For dreams have led many astray,
> and those who base their hopes on them have perished.
> 34:8 Without deceit the Law is fulfilled,
> and well-rounded wisdom is the discourse of the faithful.[73]

Although the target in this passage is reliance on dreams and visions, Ben Sira says little about what is revealed in them. M. Hengel thinks that the passage is concerned with mantic traditions or magical practices, and Skehan and Di Lella refer to the prohibition of divination

---

[72] If Argall's translation of 3:23 is accepted, Ben Sira is even aware that these matters have "been shown" to some of his students or are being promulgated in rival wisdom schools. See Argall, *1 Enoch and Sirach*, 76. It should be noted here that b. Hag 13a understands Sir 3:21–4 as referring to the secrets of creation.

[73] The only Hebrew extant for this section is Ms E, which preserves portions of verse 1. The Greek constitutes the major witness for the remainder of the passage.

and paying heed to omens as "pagan and untrustworthy."[74] The passage could very well be read as a general admonition about the uncertainty of understanding dreams and their meanings, a widespread concern throughout antiquity.[75] Since Ben Sira appears to have in his sights various matters connected with Jewish apocalyptic traditions, like differing calendars and unlawful revelation, the question arises as to whether this passage has a more focused concern on the specific vehicles by which that forbidden revelation is obtained.

The mention of "divination" and "omens" most likely indicates Ben Sira's use of the Mosaic proscriptions against such practices, but they are not the central theme of the passage. Since they are mentioned in verses 1, 2, 3, 5 and 7, dreams would appear to be the intended target.[76] Those who depend on these vehicles are "senseless" and "fools." Ben Sira recognizes the self-fulfilling nature of dreams; they simply mirror the one dreaming (vv. 3, 5).

When we move from Ben Sira's anti-visionary remarks to the Enoch and Levi materials, we notice that dreams play a central role in how these patriarchal figures get their revelations. Three times in *1 Enoch* 13 and 14 Enoch says that his visions come in his sleep, and Ben Sira's caustic remark that "fools are sent winging by dreams" might even directly attack heavenly ascents in dreams, like Enoch's ascent and heavenly tour.[77] Although *Aramaic Levi* is fragmentary, in 4Q213 1 Levi lies down and, after a lacuna in the text, he has a vision. It seems likely that some mention of sleep and/or a dream belongs in this unpreserved section. If so, Levi's vision, like Enoch's, also comes in a dream.[78]

Whatever the object of Ben Sira's scorn, whether it is specifically apocalyptic dream visions or a more general distrust of nocturnal sights, he paints himself into something of a corner. Dreams and dream visions are frequent occurrences in the Hebrew scriptures, and most of the major biblical characters have them. The exception that he

---

[74] Hengel, *Judaism and Hellenism*, 240; Skehan and Di Lella, *Wisdom of Ben Sira*, 409.

[75] On dreams and dream interpretation generally, see N. Lewis, *The Interpretation of Dreams and Portents* (Toronto: Stevens, 1976) and P.C. Miller, *Dreams in Late Antiquity: Studies in the Imagination of a Culture* (Princeton: Princeton University Press, 1994).

[76] Argall notes that by linking dreams with divination and omen reading, Ben Sira connects these practices with those of the nations found in Deut 18:10–1. He also wonders whether the rhetorical question of 34:4 about purity indicates that the dreamers have separated themselves from the Temple (*1 Enoch and Sirach*, 82).

[77] Ibid., 81.

[78] On 4QTLevi[a] see, M.E. Stone and J.C. Greenfield, "The Prayer of Levi," *JBL* 112 (1993) 247–66.

carves out for dreams, those sent from the Most High, seems to me to
refer to these biblical events, but he nowhere says how one can tell a
divinely inspired dream from one that simply "mirrors the vision of the
onlooker." The passage does, however, end in verse 8 with the antithesis
of "grasping at shadows," the fulfillment of the Law. The Law is placed
together with "well-rounded wisdom," probably the kind that Ben Sira
dispenses. Thus his rhetorical strategy here is like we have seen in other
cases, the Law and its wisdom are the concern of his students, not the
flights of fancy and fleeting visions found in the dreams of people like
Enoch and Levi.

The Person of Enoch

Sirach contains within the Praise of the Ancestors, two mentions of the
patriarch Enoch (44:16; 49:14). What Ben Sira has to say about Enoch
is clearly important in the context of other passages that may indicate
his awareness of groups who appeal to traditions that have Enoch as
their legitimator.

Sirach 44:16 is a very well-known problem since the Masada scroll and
the Syriac are missing this reference to Enoch, and its presence in Ms
B from the Cairo Geniza is certainly corrupt as it stands. Despite arguments contesting its authenticity, I think that some mention of Enoch
at the head of the Praise of the Ancestors is called for.[79] It is present in
the Greek translation and although the Greek translator at times used
a Hebrew that was apparently corrupt, an appeal to a corrupt text here
does not seem a sufficient explanation.

The fact that the text is missing in the Masada scroll is often seen as
conclusive evidence of the inauthenticity of the verse. One could easily
posit, however, that its absence from the scroll found by Y. Yadin can
be accounted for by parablepsis on the part of the scroll's copyist. The
scribe's eye would only have to skip from חנוך in 44:16 to נוח (as it is
spelled in the Masada scroll) in 44:17 for the verse to drop out of the
text.[80] Without the negative evidence of the Masada scroll, the presence
of the verse in Greek and Ms B from the Geniza and the literary use

---

[79] For arguments against the authenticity of 44:16 see T. Middendorp, *Die Stellung
Jesu Ben Siras zwischen Judentum und Hellenismus* (Leiden: Brill, 1973) 53–4, 109, 112,
134 and Skehan and Di Lella, *Wisdom of Ben Sira*, 499. Several scholars, most notably B.
Mack, *Wisdom and the Hebrew Epic: Ben Sira's Hymn in Praise of the Fathers* (Chicago:
University of Chicago Press, 1985), follow Middendorp.
[80] I am grateful to Michael Stone for this suggestion.

of Enoch as an inclusio for the entire section up until Simon II would seem to be strong reason to consider 44:16 original.[81] The Greek translation used in conjunction with Ms B would seem, then, to constitute the best basis from which to work. As almost all commentators recognize, the phrase נמצא תמים, which appears in Ms B, is an intrusion from the reference to Noah in verse 17. Based on the Greek and Ms B, the resulting passage should probably be reconstructed something like:

אות דעת לדור ודור[82]   חנוך התהלך עם ייי ונלקח

If the passage is original to Sirach, what does it tell us about Ben Sira's view of Enoch? Both verbs in the first colon clearly derive from Gen 5:24 and represent no more than the reporting of that tradition.[83] The second colon, however, is a different story. Several scholars argue that the phrase אות דעת betrays an awareness of extrabiblical tradition about Enoch. The strongest argument is made by Argall, who argues that the use of "the complete sign of wisdom" in *1 Enoch* 92:1, the beginning of the *Epistle of Enoch*, is essentially the same phrase. Argall also contends that this phrase "implies that Enoch has returned from heaven with revelation."[84] This phrase might simply be an elaboration on the

---

[81] J. Marböck argues that 44:16 is authentic because it forms an inclusio to the Praise of the Ancestors and because, since David is mentioned twice, two mentions of Enoch do not disqualify it ("Henoch—Adam—der Thronwagen: Zu frühjüdischen pseudepigraphischen Traditionen bei Ben Sira," *BZ* N. F. 25 [1981] 104).

[82] Argall, *1 Enoch and Sirach*, 9. My reconstruction is similar to Argall's. He has וילקח at the end of the first colon and omits the *waw* before דור in the second colon. I now agree with those commentators who see Y. Yadin's reconstruction of 44:16 originally belonging with 49:14 (*The Ben Sira Scroll from Masada* [Jerusalem: Israel Exploration Society, 1965] 38) as incorrect, despite my acceptance of this scheme previously (*No Small Difference: Sirach's Relationship to its Hebrew Parent Text* [SBLSCS 26; Atlanta: Scholars Press, 1989] 289–90).

[83] The first verb in the Greek of Sirach, εὐηρέστησεν, also reflects the LXX translation. The second, μετετέθη, does not, probably because, although the Hebrew of Sirach is the same root as the Hebrew of Genesis, Genesis is *qal* and Sirach is *niphal*. On the Greek translator's use of the Jewish-Greek Scriptures for his translation of Sirach, see Wright, *No Small Difference*, chapter 3.

[84] Argall, *1 Enoch and Sirach*, 11. This latter claim seems to me to be based on *1 Enoch* 92:1, and I am not sure that a return from heaven is implied in Sirach. Marböck ("Henoch—Adam," 105–8) and P. Grelot ("La légende d'Henoch dans les apocryphes et dans la Bible: origine et signification," *RSR* 46 [1958] 181–83) also argue that this phrase reveals knowledge of Enochic tradition. Based on the dates of the Qumran Enoch fragments, Marböck (106) notes: "Ben Sira konnte also bereits Henoch*literatur* vor sich haben." He concludes, "So kann Sir 44,16 ebenfalls als zusammenfassende Aussage über Henochs umfassendes Wissen verstanden werden; noch dazu begegnet an beiden Stellen das Wort vom 'Zeichen,' für die künftigen Generationen."

first colon, however, and indicate that Enoch was the prime example of
what it means to know God and to walk with him.[85] Nevertheless, even
if the phrase reveals that Ben Sira was aware of Enochic lore—part of
the central argument of this paper—it represents little more than a tip-
ping of the hat to Enoch, a somewhat veiled acknowledgment of these
traditions. It certainly does not constitute approbation of the extensive
tradition that has built up around this biblical figure.[86]

The second passage, 49:14, also depends on Gen 5:24. Ben Sira notes
that "few have been created like Enoch," since Enoch is not the only
person to have been taken by God. Elijah was as well, and this recognition is made clear by Ben Sira's use of the verb הנלקח of Elijah in 48:9.
So the fact that Enoch was not alone in being taken by God is consistent
with the biblical testimony. The end of verse 19, however, does present
a bit of a dilemma. The Hebrew of this colon, וגם הוא נלקח פנים is not
altogether clear about where Enoch was taken. Argall maintains that
פנים is a reference to the heavenly Temple that *1 Enoch* says that the
patriarch visited and thus shows "some appreciation" for Enochic lore.[87]
I think that this is overstating the case. The natural curiosity would,
of course, be about where it was that Enoch was taken, but פנים here
more likely means "into the presence [of God]," a less specific reference
to Enoch's final destination.[88] The colon again says little more than the
biblical notice in Genesis 5.

Thus, I think that what Ben Sira is doing in these verses is domes-
ticating the image of Enoch. Almost the entirety of Ben Sira's remarks
about Enoch reflects the biblical notice of this enigmatic figure. If 44:16
betrays any knowledge by Ben Sira of extra biblical tradition, he almost
downplays it by its brevity. Enoch was for Ben Sira an extraordinary

---

[85] This seems to be part of the point of M.H. Segal, *The Complete Book of Ben Sira*
(Jerusalem: Bialik, 1958) 307 [Hebrew].

[86] The interpretive translation of the grandson, ὑπόδειγμα μετανοίας, is another
problem altogether. D. Dimant thinks that the Hebrew phrase refers to Enoch's role as
a witness against humankind (cf. *Jub* 4:24), but the Greek translator understood אות
to mean "example" ("'The Angels That Sinned' in the Scrolls from the Judean Desert
and in the Apocryphal Books Related to Them," Ph.D. Dissertation, Hebrew University,
1974, 120 note 332 [Hebrew]). On the Greek phrase, see also F.V. Reiterer, *"Urtext" und
Übersetzungen: Sprachstudie über Sir 44,16–45,26 als Beitrag zur Siraforschung* (Arbeiten
zu Text und Sprache im Alten Testament 12; St. Ottilien: EOS Verlag, 1980) 84–5.

[87] Argall, *1 Enoch and Sirach*, 12–3.

[88] S.D. Fraade, *Enosh and His Generation: Pre-Israelite Hero and History in Postbiblical
Interpretation* (SBLMS 30; Chico, CA: Scholars Press, 1984) 12 note 21.

figure, who, because of his "walking" with God, was considered worthy to be taken into his presence.[89]

BEN SIRA AND HIS OPPONENTS:
THE SOCIAL SITUATION

The pieces of evidence adduced above show that where criticisms of the Jerusalem priests are concerned, Ben Sira takes both a positive and a negative tack. On the positive side, he directly and unequivocally maintains his support of the Temple priesthood and provides a strong theological case for that position. On the negative, he attempts to discredit several ways in which the groups who mount these attacks legitimize them. If one reads these two different tacks as two sides of the same coin, then several aspects of Jewish society in the late third to early second century BCE begin to take shape. In general, Sirach, *1 Enoch* and *Aramaic Levi* reflect people and communities that care about the priesthood primarily because all apparently were priests or were closely connected with them. The most contentious issues seem to be the legitimacy of marriages contracted by the priestly class in Jerusalem and the use of varying calendars. We are presented then in these works with competing groups/communities who most likely know about each other, who don't really like one another and who actively polemicize against one another.

More specifically, as I reconstruct the social situation reflected in these works, it seems probable that the people who stand behind the *Astronomical Book*, the *Book of the Watchers* and *Aramaic Levi* represent groups of priests and scribes who feel marginalized and even disenfranchised vis-à-vis the ruling priests in Jerusalem. They contend that the repercussions of transgressions of family purity, specifically the contracting of illegitimate marriages by the Jerusalem priests and the use of an incorrect calendar, have rendered the ritual conducted in the Temple corrupt and defiled. In *1 Enoch* part of the attack on those in

---

[89] T.R. Lee argues that Enoch and Joseph are being compared here, but he uses Yadin's reconstruction of the Enoch reference in 49:14, which brings 44:16 back to chapter 49. Lee concludes that "it is stated that he [Enoch] was such a remarkable figure that even if he had died like other men, his corpse would have received the exceptional treatment given to Joseph's bones" (*Studies in the Form of Sirach 44–50* [SBLDS 75; Atlanta: Scholars Press, 1986] 231–32).

power is veiled in the myth of the fallen Watchers in *1 Enoch* 6–16. This group, like Ben Sira himself, legitimates its understanding by a particular concept of wisdom. The wisdom of those competing with Ben Sira, however, depends on a different authority from his, namely the ascent vision where the seer obtains his wisdom directly from God, unmediated. These visions provide the foundation for the critical stance taken by these groups, just as Ben Sira's concept of wisdom embodied in Torah grounds his position.[90]

The wisdom granted to Enoch is handed down as a sort of counter-wisdom to that offered by teachers like Ben Sira. For the authors of *1 Enoch* this wisdom has chronological precedence to that given to Moses in the Sinaitic Law. It is apparently even transmitted in written form that is legitimated by a prophetic inspiration. The "account" of Enoch's transmission of this knowledge to his son Methuselah in *1 Enoch* 82:1–3 makes this clear.

> And now, my son Methuselah, all these things I am recounting to you and writing down for you; and I have revealed to you everything, and given you writings of all these things. Keep, my son, Methuselah, the writings of your father's hand, that you may deliver them to the generations of eternity. Wisdom I have given to you and to your children, and to those who will be your children, that they may transmit it to their children, and to generations of generations forever, to whoever is endowed with wisdom; and they shall celebrate all the wise. Wisdom shall slumber, (but) in their mind those who have understanding shall not slumber, but they shall hearken with their ears that they may learn this wisdom, and it shall be better for those that partake of it than rich food.[91]

Ben Sira is aware of the attacks and the methods for legitimating them, and he returns the polemic. His wholehearted support of the priests and his treatment of the calendar, dreams and visions and inquiring into the workings of the universe are all intended to counteract these critical attacks. Ben Sira is a scribe, perhaps even a priest, who imparts *his* wisdom in *his* school (51:23). But his wisdom is different, being based on fulfillment of God's Torah through disciplined study.[92] Ben

---

[90] The connection of Law and Wisdom is thoroughgoing in Sirach, and the amount of scholarly literature on this subject is immense. For bibliography on these subjects see Skehan and Di Lella, *Wisdom of Ben Sira*. See also J. Marböck, *Weisheit im Wandel: Untersuchungen zur Weisheitstheologie bei Ben Sira* (BBB 37; Bonn: Hanstein, 1971). For a view different from the usual identification of Law and Wisdom in Sirach, see Boccaccini, *Middle Judaism*, 88–98.

[91] Translation taken from Black, *Book of Enoch*, 70–1.

[92] On the importance of discipline in Ben Sira, see Wright, "Putting the Puzzle Together."

Sira expects his students to be thoroughly established in the study of the Law, where the only legitimate wisdom is found. If Argall's translation of 3:23b is correct ("for that which is too great for you was shown you"), then Ben Sira's students may even have come from some of these other groups and told him their teachings.[93]

A major difficulty, however, is the nature of the polemic involved in these works; it is mostly indirect. That is, it is contained in literature that is not supposed to be read by the targets of the criticism but by those inside the group that produced and used the literature. Rather than changing the minds of outsiders, this literature more probably promotes the stability and cohesion of the group's insiders and confirms their belief systems. The wisdom that Enoch transmits to Methuselah is for those who have not "slumbered," presumably the members of the Enochic community. The fragmentary condition of *Aramaic Levi* makes conclusions more difficult, but the emphasis on Levi as the primary actor may indicate its intended audience as dissaffected priests. Ben Sira intended his teachings for his students, the scions of Jerusalem society.

This, then, raises the question that if these books were so intended, how would the antagonists become aware of each other's criticisms and responses? I can only offer some informed speculations. It is certainly possible that, since the traditions seem to have been transmitted in writing, these people somehow acquired and read each other's literature. Priests, perhaps more so than other Jews, were required to be in Jerusalem, and criticism of other priestly groups did not necessarily preclude going to the city. No doubt these people came into direct contact and debate with each other within the city itself.[94] Finally, there was almost certainly some mobility of students among wisdom groups, and new students might communicate the teachings of previous teachers.[95] Without any substantial clues, however, the ways in which these groups knew about each other remains obscure.

But the polemic probably worked well internally. Ben Sira was certainly trying to inculcate certain views in his disciples. In order to accomplish that, he did not have to resort to direct social or even

---

[93] Argall, *1 Enoch and Sirach*, 75. Argall's book is an extended and detailed argument that Sirach and *1 Enoch* engage each other over the problem of competing wisdoms.

[94] This, of course, assumes that some of these groups came from outside of Jerusalem as seems likely. For example, Nickelsburg argues for a Galilean provenance for *1 Enoch* 12–16 ("Enoch, Levi and Peter," 586).

[95] Josephus, for instance, in *Life* 2 narrates his peripatetic youth, moving between different Jewish philosophies.

direct literary confrontation. He may not have wanted to draw what he considered unnecessary and unwarranted attention to the teachings of others. He had his own divinely inspired wisdom to pass on. Those students who received warnings to pay no heed to fleeting dreams or admonitions against seeking the secrets of the universe were less likely to do such things later. Ben Sira was a student of the Jewish scriptures, and Solomon's wisdom does counsel after all to "train up a child in the way he should go, and when he is old he will not depart from it" (Prov 22:6).

Ben Sira's social world was one in which differing and competing notions of scribal wisdom and priestly legitimacy were hotly contested. Jews lived in a complicated world where foreign cultural influences clamored for attention, where international politics intimately affected Jews in Palestine and where groups of priests battled each other for control of the political and religious establishment. Ben Sira was not isolated from that world, and in this complex book he addressed the pressing issues of the world around him. He could apparently view Hellenistic ideas with favor, at times enlisting Hellenistic philosophy in his service.[96] He also saw the dangers of those who criticized the Jerusalem religious establishment, and he confronted them.

Although some of the details will differ, this basic assessment of the situation generally complements and confirms the impressions of scholars like Boccaccini and Argall who have suggested some mutual awareness between *1 Enoch* and Sirach. Continued intertextual study of works that are contemporary with each other such as those considered here will continue to enrich our reconstructions of Judaism in the Second Temple period. Reading Sirach, *1 Enoch* and *Aramaic Levi* together sheds valuable additional light on a critical period in the history of ancient Judaism.

---

[96] See for instance J.T. Sanders, *Ben Sira and Demotic Wisdom* (SBLMS 28; Chico, CA: Scholars Press, 1983) who describes Ben Sira's use of the Hellenistic philosopher Theognis, or R. Bohlen, *Die Ehrung der Eltern bei Ben Sira: Studien zur Motivation und Interpretation eines familienethischen Grundwertes in frühhellenistischer Zeit* (TThSt 51; Trier: Paulinus-Verlag, 1991) who argues that Ben Sira used Hellenistic views about the family in conjunction with traditional Israelite morality. Middendorp has made the most vigorous claims about Ben Sira's positive views toward Hellenism (*Die Stellung Jesu Ben Siras*). In contrast several studies have argued that Ben Sira had a more negative approach to Hellenism, even if he enlisted some Hellenistic ideas in this argument. See, for example, A.A. Di Lella, "Conservative and Progressive Theology: Sirach and Wisdom," *CBQ* 28 (1966) 139–54 and Hengel, *Judaism and Hellenism*, 138–53.

CHAPTER SIX

"PUT THE NATIONS IN FEAR OF YOU":
BEN SIRA AND THE PROBLEM OF FOREIGN RULE*

Ben Sira must have lived in exciting times—exciting being a relative term. He was active as a scribe/sage in Jerusalem during a *very* turbulent time in the political history of the ancient Near East. He probably grew up during the period of Ptolemaic rule in Palestine and watched as his native land was taken from the Ptolemies by the Seleucid king Antiochus III. Although he most likely did not live to see the reign of Antiochus IV and its attendant turmoil, his own times must have been difficult enough.

As one who lived in Jerusalem, he was, like other residents of the city, able to feel the effects of the constant tension between the Ptolemies and Seleucids on his everyday world. But as a scribe/sage, Ben Sira also worked for the political elite of Jerusalem while at the same time he trained young sages. He was part of a retainer class who served the rich and powerful, and he had entrée into circles of influence in Jerusalem, doubtlessly witnessing first hand a great many of the political maneuverings happening in the Jewish capital.[1]

This kind of access to the political world of Jerusalem undoubtedly made an impression on Ben Sira, and one would expect to find some traces in his book of his assessment of the position that Judah and Jerusalem occupied vis-à-vis the two great foreign powers of his time. Indeed his book contains a number of passages that mention the Gentiles/

---

* The paper is a revised version of a paper originally given to the Wisdom and Apocalypticism in Early Judaism and Christianity Group at the SBL Annual Meetings in Boston. The original was published in the *Seminar Papers* volume of that year (Atlanta: SBL, 1999, 77–93).

[1] On the scribe/sage as part of a retainer class that was employed by the wealthy and aristocratic classes, see P. Tiller, "Politics and the High Priesthood in Pre-Maccabean Judea" (unpublished paper; Dec. 1997 draft; my thanks to the author for making available a copy of the paper). R.A. Horsley and P. Tiller use the term "scribe/sage" as a description of Ben Sira's office. For an explanation, see their jointly authored paper, "Ben Sira and the Sociology of the Second Temple," *Second Temple Studies III: Studies in Politics, Class and Material Culture* (P.R. Davies and J.M. Halligan, eds.; JSOTSup 340; Sheffield: Sheffield Academic Press, 2002) 74–107.

nations; these may reveal both his attitude toward the rule of foreigners over Israel and his explanation of why God allows them this sovereignty. Several of these texts mention "the nations" in general admonitions. It is difficult to determine the extent to which in these places Ben Sira is presenting his students with generic life lessons, or he is commenting on some specific contemporary problem without coming right out and saying so, or both. Ben Sira does, in fact, appear in some cases to cloak warnings about specific contemporary people or situations in the more universal language of admonitions and proverbs.[2] But concerning the nations, there is at least one passage, the prayer in 36:1–22, where Ben Sira seems to allow his genuine feelings about the matter of foreign rule to surface. When one examines the regional politics of Ben Sira's time and then reads his comments about foreign nations, kings and Israel's enemies in the light of those events, Ben Sira's attitude about foreign rule over Israel begins to emerge.

PTOLEMAIC AND SELEUCID COMPETITION
FOR PALESTINE

For most of the third century BCE, Palestine fell under the control of the Ptolemaic dynasty, which reigned in Egypt. A number of sources, such as the Zenon papyri and Josephus's report of the Tobiad family (*Ant.* 12.154–236), give a reasonably good picture of the conditions in Palestine under Egyptian domination.[3] Most of this century was essentially peaceful, and the Ptolemies administered Palestine as an imperial province, farming the tax burden to local strong men like the Tobiads and keeping troops there to guard against Seleucid incursions. A protracted period of political and military turmoil ensued during the reign of Ptolemy IV Philopater (221–203 BCE), when the Seleucid king, Antiochus III, resolved to take Palestine and the surrounding areas, known together as Coele-Syria, from the Lagid king. Antiochus

---

[2] For another possible example, see Chapter 5, "'Fear the Lord and Honor the Priest': Ben Sira as Defender of the Jerusalem Priesthood."

[3] For more detailed description of the relations between the Ptolemies and the Seleucids than is possible here, see D. Gera, *Judaea and Mediterranean Politics, 219 to 161 B.C.E.* (Brill's Series in Jewish Studies, Vol. 8; Leiden: E.J. Brill, 1998); V. Tcherikover, *Hellenistic Civilization and the Jews* (New York: Atheneum, 1982 [reprint of the 1959 Jewish Publication Society edition]; M. Hengel, *Judaism and Hellenism* (Philadelphia: Fortress, 1974); S.K. Eddy, *The King is Dead: Studies in the Near Eastern Resistance to Hellenism 334–31 B.C.* (Lincoln: University of Nebraska Press, 1961).

launched a military campaign that encountered encouraging initial success, and he successfully wrested control of the area from Ptolemy IV for a brief time. But in 217 BCE, Antiochus was defeated in battle at Raphia in the south of Palestine and had to abandon all that he had won from Ptolemy.

The Seleucid king bided his time, however, and after the death of Ptolemy IV, his son, Ptolemy V Epiphanes, who was still a young boy, succeeded him. Egypt was clearly in a weakened state, and Antiochus saw his chance once again to take control of Coele-Syria. In 201 BCE Antiochus III reinvaded Ptolemaic Palestine; again he succeeded in gaining control of it. But again, just as in his earlier campaign, he suffered a military setback, this time at the hand of Ptolemy V's general, Scopas. Antiochus had no choice but to retreat. Only a year later, however, in 200 BCE Antiochus's forces soundly defeated Scopas at Paneas, and by 198 Palestine had passed into Antiochus's hands yet another time—on this occasion for good.

During this period of reversals of fortune for the Seleucid ruler, there was a significant pro-Seleucid faction among the upper classes of the Judean state, most likely led by the high priest Simon II.[4] When Antiochus ultimately gained final control of Judah and Jerusalem, he rewarded the Jews who had supported him, according to Josephus (*Ant.* 12.142), with, among other things, permission for the Jews to live "according to their ancestral laws."[5] It appears that Antiochus was prepared to allow the Jews to live relatively unhindered by Seleucid rule as long as the taxes were paid and there was no trouble. But in 190 BCE Antiochus fought the Romans at Magnesia, where he suffered a decisive defeat. In the treaty of Apamea, concluded in 188 BCE, the Romans left Coele-Syria in Antiochus's hands, but they placed a heavy financial indemnity upon him, one that would play an important role in the subsequent relationship between the Seleucids and the Jews.

A year later in 187 BCE Antiochus died and was succeeded by his son Seleucus IV Philopater. Even though Seleucus seems to have continued the general policies of his father toward the Jews, the Roman financial burden fell squarely on his shoulders. The Seleucid-leaning

---

[4] On the pro-Seleucid faction led by Simon II, see Tcherikover, *Hellenistic Civilization*, 79–82. See also J.C. VanderKam, *From Joshua to Caiaphas: High Priests after the Exile* (Minneapolis: Fortress, 2004, 182), who argues on the basis of Josephus's positioning of Simon II in the events of the Tobiad family that he was pro-Seleucid.

[5] On the meaning of this phrase, see Tcherikover, *Hellenistic Civilization*, 82–4.

high priest Simon II had died in about 196 BCE, and his son Onias III became high priest in Jerusalem. Onias seems to have shared his father's political sympathies initially, but some evidence suggests that his support might have turned toward Egypt, perhaps because of the higher tax debt imposed on the Jews by Antiochus III and continued by Seleucus IV as a means of acquiring the necessary funds to pay an indemnity to the Romans.[6] These political leanings eventually would contribute to Onias's undoing, but that almost certainly occurred after Ben Sira's death. The years leading up to Onias's eventual assassination during the reign of Antiochus IV, however, must have been filled with political intrigue in Jerusalem, and they probably created anxiety in Jerusalem during the last years of Ben Sira's life. It is this unsettled military and political atmosphere that Ben Sira breathed for most of his professional life and that any reader of his book must keep in mind when looking at what Ben Sira has to say about foreign nations and their relationship to Israel.

Ben Sira and the Nations: The Texts

Ben Sira's comments about the Gentiles/nations appear at several points in his book. As I noted above, some of them appear in the middle of larger sections that contain general admonitions, and one wonders whether any mention of the nations in those contexts is any more than a generic example of how the world works. But there are several places where Ben Sira may be talking about specific political events of which he is aware, and there are still others that I find hard to read as anything but Ben Sira's references to contemporary political realities (or at least wisdom lessons drawn from them). The following list contains those passages in which Ben Sira talks about the nations or which need to be considered in any discussion of his attitude toward foreign rule.

Sirach 4:15: This verse falls in the middle of a short section on the rewards of following wisdom and illustrates well Ben Sira's references to nations in contexts of general instructions. Wisdom is the subject of

---

[6] See VanderKam, *Joshua to Caiaphas*, 192, who thinks that the opposition to Onias by the Tobiads and Menelaus together with 2 Macc 3:10–11, which notes that Hyrcanus the Tobiad maintained large deposits in the Temple, indicate that Onias at some point held pro-Ptolemaic sympathies.

verse 11, and verses 11–14 tell of the benefit of holding to her teaching. Verse 15 in Hebrew Ms A from the Cairo Geniza shifts to Wisdom as speaker who says, "Whoever obeys me will judge nations; whoever will listen to me will dwell in my innermost chambers."[7] There is no particular element of this passage, when it is considered in isolation from others that mention the nations, to indicate that Ben Sira was doing anything other than articulating the kinds of things that the scribe will do if he follows the path of Wisdom. Yet, if one were to interpret this verse and those like it in conjunction with the other passages and ideas in the book that concern "the nations," these verses begin to look more like valid indicators of Ben Sira's dissatisfaction with foreign rule.

Sirach 8:2: As part of a series of "do not's," Ben Sira warns his students about the problems of the rich and riches.[8] He remarks that gold "has perverted the minds of kings." Like the previous passage, this verse, by itself, could be understood to be part of Ben Sira's assessment of life generally, rather than any allusion to some specific situation. Dealing with the rich and powerful is important for his students, since it is from them that they will find work. In a number of places Ben Sira notes his own service to kings, and he reminds his students that they will appear before and serve the rich and powerful (e.g., 7:5; 8:8; 34:12–13).

Sirach 10–11: These two chapters reveal quite a bit about Ben Sira's ideology of rule, whether it be Jewish or foreign. Just as we saw with the previous two texts, his comments in these chapters do not bear the undeniable stamp of reaction to contemporary events, although some have read a couple of verses as disguised commentary on commonly known occurrences.

In 10:1–5 Ben Sira contrasts the wise ruler with the poor one, making no distinction between Israel and the nations. He notes that all human

---

[7] The translation is that of P.W. Skehan and A.A. Di Lella, *The Wisdom of Ben Sira* (AB 39; New York: Doubleday, 1987) 169. The Greek has, "Those who obey her will judge nations, and all who listen to her will live secure" (NRSV). The major textual issue with this verse is that the Hebrew ends colon a with the consonants אמת, which some scholars read as *'emet* in agreement with the Syriac translation (see especially, M. Segal, *The Complete Book of Ben Sira* [2nd ed; Jerusalem: Bialik Foundation, 1958], 24 [Hebrew]). Skehan and Di Lella (*Wisdom of Ben Sira*, 170) argue that the consonants should be read as the defectively spelled *'ummōt*, which is apparently how the Greek understood the word.

[8] For Ben Sira's thoughts on poverty and riches, see Chapter 4, "'Who Has Been Tested by God and Found Perfect?' Ben Sira's Discourse of Riches and Poverty."

government is "in the hand of the Lord" (ביד אלהים ממשלת תבל,
Ms A), who will establish the ruler at the proper time (ואיש לעת יעמד עליה,
Ms A; v. 4). In the end, "Human success is in the hands of the Lord,
and it is he who confers honor on the lawgiver" (v. 5).[9] Even though
this passage contains no historical specifics, P.W. Skehan and A.A. Di
Lella suggest that Ben Sira is referring to the Ptolemaic and the Seleucid
kings, especially to their claims to divine honors, but they suggest that
his criticisms "are sufficiently veiled so as not to get him into trouble."[10]
The notion is one to which Ben Sira will return in several places—
governments and rulers exist only by the permission of God.

In the next section of chapter 10 Ben Sira turns his attention to arro-
gance and pride. Here too he finds examples from politics. "Because of
injustice and insolence and wealth" rule has passed from one nation to
another (v. 8). This verse may well be a reference to the loss of Palestine
by the Ptolemies to the Seleucids. With such a momentous event in
the not-too-distant past, I find it hard to think that Ben Sira did not
intend this as a reference to that time; I imagine that anyone reading his
book would have understood it that way also. This verse almost seems
to introduce a second short section on pride that has rulers, perhaps
specifically Gentile kings, as its focus. In verses 9–11 Ben Sira reminds
his audience that death comes even to kings. Skehan and Di Lella take
the specific note in verse 10 about illness and the king as a reference
to the sudden death of Ptolemy IV in 203 BCE.[11]

The verses that follow (14–18) lay the groundwork for what will
come in chapters 35 and 36. In these later chapters, Ben Sira anticipates
that God will destroy the nations, that is, the foreign powers who were
bedeviling the Jews during Ben Sira's lifetime. In 10:14–18 he seems to
be saying that this is the way God has always worked. God, because of
the pride of the nations, overthrows their thrones (v. 14), uproots them
(v. 15), lays them waste (v. 16a), destroys them (v. 16b) and erases their
memory from the earth (v. 17). Whereas one could interpret these verses
in the same way as I interpret chapters 35 and 36 below, as Ben Sira's

---

[9] Following the text of Ms A here. Sirach 10:1–5 treats government and rule. The
Hebrew מחוקק in verse 5 was read as "scribe" by the Greek translator, but because of the
context should probably be understood with the NRSV to be the ruler or lawgiver.

[10] Skehan and Di Lella, *Wisdom of Ben Sira*, 224. I will speak below about the problem
of this interpretation in light of chapter 36. Suffice it to say at this juncture that if there
were trouble awaiting those who criticize the rulers, chapter 36 would have potentially
gotten Ben Sira into a lot of hot water.

[11] Ibid.

indictment of the Ptolemies and the Seleucids, I think they probably function here as a sort of veiled historical review. When oppressive rulers have arisen in Israel's past, God has destroyed them. One thinks immediately of the Babylonians and the stories of God's humbling of king Nebuchadnezzar.[12] Ben Sira's non-specific language here allows the reader to call to mind his/her own examples.

The theme of humbling the powerful returns in 11:5–6, this time in a section on boasting. Ben Sira remarks that the one who boasts never knows when he will come to naught. "Many kings have had to sit on the ground, but one who was never thought of has worn a crown. Many rulers have been utterly disgraced, and the honored have been handed over to others" (v. 6).

Sirach 17:17: This verse is part of a long section on the creation of humans and their relationship with God. Fundamentally God is in control of human life. God created humans out of earth and makes them return to it (17:1). God made humans aware of him and put fear of him into their hearts. God revealed his laws to them. The Lord knows their ways and will repay their deeds (17:19–24; cf. also 16:5–14). Sirach 17:17 comes in the middle of this discussion and says simply, "He appointed a ruler for every nation, but Israel is the Lord's own portion." Although not a direct statement about foreign rule, the ideology found in this one verse reveals the basis for Ben Sira's thoughts on the matter. The nations have their individual rulers, but Israel belongs to God alone. He rules over his people. In making such a claim, Ben Sira reflects an old Israelite tradition that Israel is set apart for God (cf. Deut 32:9) and that he himself is Israel's king (cf. for example, 1 Sam 8:4–9). Anyone who would rule over God's people is usurping God's rightful place. The difficulty raised by this theology, of course, is that the historical reality was that foreigners *did* rule over Israel, and Ben Sira has to account for it. I will consider below how he does that.

Sirach 35:22–26: These four verses really form the transition from the long poem that begins in 34:21 to the prayer in 36:1–22. Sirach 34:21–35:21 focuses on proper worship of God and treatment of the oppressed. Ben Sira connects responsibility to care for the poor, widows and orphans with proper fulfillment of God's covenant with Israel as in

---

[12] Indeed the verbs in this passage are reminiscent of Jer 1:10.

the Hebrew scriptures (cf. Exod 22:21–24).[13] The claim in 35:21 that the prayer of the humble reaches God and that he responds with justice and judgment might well have prompted Ben Sira's shift in verse 22 from the oppressed of Israel to Israel the oppressed. Sirach 35:22–26 expresses Ben Sira's confidence that God will not delay, that he will "repay vengeance on the nations" (ולגוים ישיב נקם; v. 23b). The "scepter of the unrighteous" (מטה רשע [Gk. σκῆπτρα, pl.]) he will break (v. 23c). God will "judge the case of his people" (ב ריב עמו[...], Ms B; ἕως κρίνῃ τὴν κρίσιν τοῦ λαοῦ αὐτοῦ) and "make them rejoice in his mercy" (ושמחם בישועת; καὶ εὐφρανεῖ αὐτοὺς ἐν τῷ ἐλέει αὐτοῦ; v. 25b). Here it seems that Ben Sira's expectation that God will stand on the side of the oppressed has brought to his mind his own nation that is under the "scepter of the unrighteous." In this case God not only shows mercy to the poor, widows and orphans but to "his people." How else would God show his mercy but by crushing the nations who oppress Israel?

Sirach 36:1–22: Ben Sira's claim in 35:22–26 that God will show mercy to his people is followed by his passionate prayer for the Deliverer of Israel to do just that. The emotional and nationalistic tone of the prayer has caused some like T. Middendorp to argue that 36:1–22 was not part of the original book of Ben Sira. J. Marböck, however, has argued persuasively that the prayer does, in fact, fit in the book. While it is true that Ben Sira's emotion in these verses might seem somewhat out of character with the rest of the book, most elements of the passage are consistent with Ben Sira's thought elsewhere, and there is really no good reason to excise it.[14] The challenge is to find the motivation for Ben Sira's passion in this instance.

The prayer consists of a series of petitions addressed to God that have a decidedly prophetic ring to them. Indeed, other places in Ben Sira's book suggest that he sees himself in a prophetic role (cf. 24:33; 39:1).[15] Many of the themes and much of the language of this prayer

---

[13] See "Who Has Been Tested by Gold?" 80–2.

[14] T. Middendorp, *Die Stellung Jesu ben Siras zwischen Judentum und Hellenismus* (Leiden: E.J. Brill, 1973) 125–32. For the arguments that the prayer belongs in the book, see J. Marböck, "Das Gebet um die Rettung Zions Sir 36,1–22 (G: 33,1–13a; 36,16b–22) im Zusammenhang der Geschichtsschau ben Siras," *Memoria Jerusalem. Freundesgabe Franz Sauer* (J.B. Bauer and J. Marböck, eds.; Graz, Austria: Akademisches Druck-u. Verlaganstalt, 1977) 93–115, esp. 103–4 and the literature cited there.

[15] On the prophetic role of Ben Sira, see Hengel, *Judaism and Hellenism*, 134–35

are paralleled in the Hebrew scriptures.[16] The main theme of the prayer, however, is clear and is expressed already in verse 1—"Have mercy on us, O God of all, and put all the nations in fear of you." The plea for God to "give new signs and work wonders" (חדש אות ושנה מופת; ἐγκαίνισον σημεῖα καὶ ἀλλοίωσον θαυμάσια; v. 6a) is an allusion to the wonders performed against Egypt in the Exodus story (see, for example, Exod 7:3). Ben Sira thus explicitly makes his own situation equivalent to the Hebrews' enslavement in Egypt that became so fundamental to Israel's understanding of itself.

Several places in the prayer have an eschatological ring about them and probably represent Ben Sira's hope, not that God will bring time as he knows it to an end, but that he will reestablish a revitalized nation of Israel, free from foreign oppression, with Israel's God as its sovereign.[17] Verse 10 requests that God "hasten the end (קץ) and remember the appointed time (מועד)." This language of time combined with the petitions to "gather the tribes of Jacob and give them their inheritance" (v. 13), to "fill Zion with your majesty" (v. 19), to "fulfill the prophecies spoken in your name" (v. 20) and to "let your prophets be found trustworthy" (v. 21) all reinforce the impression that the prayer contains a nationalistic eschatology.

In the revelation of God's wrath against the nations, they will all see the glory of God. But two verses suggest that perhaps part of what Ben Sira hopes for God to do is intended for Israel's benefit as well. Verses 3–4 read, "As you have used us to show your holiness to them so use them to show your glory to us. Then they will know as we knew that there is no God but you." God's glory will become as apparent to Israel as it will be to the nations.

---

and M.E. Stone, "Ideal Figures and Social Context: Priest and Sage in the Early Second Temple Age," *Ancient Israelite Religions: F.M. Cross Festschrift* (P.D. Miller, Jr., P.D. Hanson and S.D. McBride, eds.; Philadelphia: Fortress, 1988) 577–78.

[16] On the several phrases that appear in this prayer that are parallel to biblical phrases, see Marböck, "Das Gebet" and J.G. Snaith, "Biblical Quotations in the Hebrew of Ecclesiasticus," *JTS* 18 (1967) 8–9. I am not as convinced as Snaith is that these phrases are necessarily "quotations." On Ben Sira's use of the Hebrew Bible, see B.G. Wright, *No Small Difference: Sirach's Relationship to Its Hebrew Parent Text* (SBLSCS 26; Atlanta: Scholars, 1989) chap. 3.

[17] For more on the eschatology of this passage, see J. Corley, "Seeds of Messianism in Hebrew Ben Sira and Greek Sirach," *The Septuagint and Messianism* (M.A. Knibb, ed.; BETL 195; Leuven: Peeters, 2006) 301–12 and B.G. Wright, "Eschatology without a Messiah in the Wisdom of Ben Sira," in the same volume, 313–23.

The form of a prayer of lament[18] and the intensity of the language both leave the distinct impression that here we have Ben Sira's true feelings about the domination of Israel by foreign powers. Petitions such as "Crush the heads of hostile rulers who say, 'There is no one but ourselves'" (v. 12) or "Let survivors be consumed in fiery wrath, and may those who harm your people meet destruction" (v. 11) reveal an intensity of feeling that goes beyond the general admonitions about kings and rulers that we saw elsewhere in the book. The major question about this chapter, however, is not necessarily its message; that is pretty clear.[19] What is the reason for the emotional and passionate outburst of prayer here? In other places Ben Sira may be alluding to contemporary events (see above on 10:8, 10), but he apparently disguises the allusions for reasons that, in the light of this passage, are now not so evident. Although below I will try to make some suggestions about the possible solutions to this problem, I do not yet have a definitive one.

Sirach 39:23: This passage is in a sense a reprise of several others that we have seen. In a poem that treats matters of the blessings of God, Ben Sira remarks, "His blessing overflows like the Nile; like the Euphrates it enriches the surface of the earth. Again, his wrath expels the nations and turns fertile land into a salt marsh."[20] The reference to land turning to salt marsh is most likely an allusion to the destruction of Sodom and Gomorrah, but the nations that are the intended target of the expulsion are not immediately identifiable. Skehan and Di Lella think this verse refers to the expulsion of the Canaanites from the land, since the combination of Sodom and Gomorrah and the Canaanites probably occurs earlier in the book at 16:8–9, which says that God "did not spare the neighbors of Lot" and "showed no pity on the doomed nation."[21] All I can say is that in this passage the combination is not so transparent and that if one reads this passage with others like it in the light of 36:1–22 it takes on a different hue.

Sirach 44–50: In the so-called "Praise of the Ancestors" section, Ben Sira does not come right out and criticize foreign rule, but the way in which he talks about the different figures in this section helps to illuminate the

---

[18] See Marböck, "Das Gebet," 102 and Skehan and Di Lella, *Wisdom of Ben Sira*, 420.
[19] Marböck gives a detailed discussion of the various themes in the prayer (ibid.).
[20] The translation is that of Skehan and Di Lella, *Wisdom of Ben Sira*, 454.
[21] Ibid., 459.

reason that he thinks Israel has fallen under foreign domination. One subtheme that runs through Ben Sira's discussion of a number of the figures in this section is what happens when enemies oppress or when foreign ways intrude on Israel, usually in the form of idolatry.[22] The following Israelites are said by Ben Sira either to triumph over enemies or to remain faithful in the face of idolatry.

Moses (45:1–5): Sirach 45:2 is a difficult verse primarily because of its textual problems. Skehan and Di Lella adopt the reading of Ms B(mg) and translate, "God made him like the angels in honor and strengthened him with fearful powers."[23] The Greek has for colon b, "And he (God) magnified him (Moses) in the fear of his enemies." Sirach 45:3, though, makes a clear reference to the "signs" that Moses did in Egypt and the fact that God "glorified" Moses before Pharaoh. However one chooses to read 45:2, the clear context of the two verses together is the contest between God (through Moses) and the Egyptian pharaoh, a contest that God wins. It is Moses' faithfulness that prompts God "to choose him out of all flesh," and it is presumably that faithfulness that enables Moses to triumph over the Egyptians. Thus, Ben Sira establishes an early connection in this section of the book between faithfulness to God and defeat of enemies.

Aaron (45:6–22): It is something of a commonplace to observe that Ben Sira spends more time on Aaron than on any other ancient Israelite. Ben Sira is a staunch supporter of the priesthood in Jerusalem, and it was the brother of Moses who was given the eternal covenant of the priesthood.[24] God chose him "out of all the living" to be his minister, and this responsibility has continued through all his descendents. When Dathan, Abiram and the Korahites, called "outsiders" (זרים) by Ben Sira (v. 18), conspired against Aaron, God became angry and destroyed them

---

[22] The form of this section is still something of a question mark. For detailed discussions of the form of chaps. 44–50, see T.R. Lee, *Studies in the Form of Sirach 44–50* (SBLDS 75; Atlanta: Scholars, 1986) and B.L. Mack, *Wisdom and the Hebrew Epic: Ben Sira's Hymn in Praise of the Fathers* (Chicago Studies in the History of Judaism; Chicago: University of Chicago Press, 1985).

[23] Skehan and Di Lella, *Wisdom of Ben Sira*, 506, 509.

[24] On Ben Sira's support of priests, see Chapter 5 "'Fear the Lord and Honor the Priest'" and the literature cited there.

with "wonders" (אות).[25] Although Ben Sira does not single out Aaron for his "faithfulness," he does call Moses' brother "exalted" and "holy," making clear in several places his special status with God.

Phinehas (45:23–25): Although no specific enemies are mentioned in the section on Phinehas, the covenant that God made with him is attributed to his "zeal for the Lord" (v. 23). This verse is a clear reference to the story found in Numbers 25 where God makes a covenant specifically with Phinehas because he killed an Israelite man and a Midianite woman during a purge of all Israelites who had begun to worship Ba'al Peor. Because he helped to turn the people from idolatry, Phinehas was rewarded.

Joshua (46:1–10): It is not surprising, when one considers the biblical stories about Joshua, that over half of the space devoted to him by Ben Sira concerns his success in war. Verse 1 says that he took vengeance on Israel's enemies. "He called upon the Most High, the Mighty One, when enemies pressed him on every side, and the great Lord answered him with hailstones of mighty power" (v. 5). The result was that Joshua defeated his enemy, "and on the slope he destroyed his opponents" (v. 6). In 46:6e Ben Sira explicitly calls Joshua God's "devoted follower" (כי מלא אחרי אל).

The Judges (46:11–12): Like Phinehas, the judges did not turn to idolatry nor did they turn away from God. "May their memory be blessed!"

Samuel (46:13–20): Samuel, like those Israelite heroes before him, was faithful to God, his faithfulness proving his prophethood (v. 15). When describing their predicaments, Ben Sira uses identical wording for both Joshua and Samuel.[26] When he was "pressed about by enemies on every side" (v. 16), Samuel called out to God who answered him and

---

[25] An interesting side note is that in verse 13 Ben Sira notes that no "outsider" ever put on the priestly vestments, only the sons of Aaron. Ben Sira is presumably dead by the time the priestly clothes are more or less put up for sale under Antiochus IV. In this verse, Ben Sira is most likely asserting the theological legitimacy of the high priestly line and not necessarily responding to any contemporary problem with the priestly vestments.

[26] Ms B is damaged in both 46:5 and 46:16. The Greek, however, has the same wording in these verses as the Hebrew most likely did.

destroyed "the leaders of the enemy and all the rulers of the Philistines" (cf. 1 Sam 7:7–11).[27]

David (47:1–11): When David was faced with the giant, Goliath, he called on God who gave him strength to defeat his enemy (v. 5). Ben Sira notes that as king, David defeated his enemies "on every side," and he wiped out "his adversaries, the Philistines" (v. 7). It is interesting to note that Ben Sira does not emphasize David's faithfulness. To a degree he cannot in light of the king's infamous liaison with Bathsheba and his plot to kill her husband (cf. 2 Samuel 11). He does, however, make special note of God's forgiveness of David's sin, which permits him to list David in 49:4 as one of three kings who were not sinners. Forgiveness thus serves as the functional equivalent of the faithfulness that Ben Sira has noted for other ancestors.

Elijah (48:1–11): Although enemies are not specifically mentioned in the section on this prophet, Ben Sira does remark that he "sent kings down to destruction" (v. 6) and that he "anointed kings to inflict retribution" (v. 8). The latter statement is a reference to the anointing of Jehu, who would ultimately end the Omrid dynasty in the Northern Kingdom (cf. 1 Kgs 19:15–18; 2 Kgs 9:4–26). It was this family that produced the hated king Ahab, who brought the worship of foreign gods into Israel by his marriage to the infamous Jezebel.

Elisha (48:12–14): The brief notice of Elisha does not contain any reference to enemies, although Ben Sira does say that Elisha never "trembled before any ruler" (v. 12).

Hezekiah and Isaiah (48:17–23): Ben Sira treats these two figures together, because in the most important event he recounts about them, the two of them were the primary actors. He notes that in addition to fortifying Jerusalem and bringing water into the city (v. 17), Hezekiah pleased God and was faithful to him. He held to the ways of his father David, and he did as the prophet Isaiah advised him (v. 22). Isaiah, for his part, is called "great" and "trustworthy" (v. 22). The result was that, when the Assyrians besieged Jerusalem, the people "called upon the

---

[27] Reading "enemy" with Skehan and Di Lella, *Wisdom of Ben Sira*, 516. Greek has "the leaders of the Tyrians."

Lord…The Holy One quickly heard them from heaven and delivered them through the prophet Isaiah" (v. 20). God struck down the Assyrians by sending an angel to wipe them out (cf. 1 Kgs 19:14–37).

Josiah (49:1–3): Ben Sira shares the deuteronomic historian's unreserved praise for both Hezekiah and Josiah. Whereas Hezekiah fortified Jerusalem, Josiah restored proper worship of God and eliminated idolatry by removing "the wicked abominations" (v. 2; cf. 2 Kgs 23:4–25). According to Ben Sira, "He kept his heart fixed on the Lord; in lawless times he made godliness prevail" (v. 3).

Simon II (50:1–21): After reviewing the history of Israel, Ben Sira focuses on one contemporary figure, the High Priest Simon II.[28] Simon is clearly a hero for Ben Sira. He praises him not only for his service in the Temple, but for his repair of God's house and its enclosure and the fortification of the walls of the city, all of which must have been damaged in the struggles between the Ptolemies and the Seleucids for control of Palestine. Of the twenty-one verses that Ben Sira devotes to Simon II, he lavishes sixteen of them on a description of Simon's temple service.

Others of the ancestors do not fare as well at the hands of Ben Sira as those listed above. The consequences that Ben Sira gives for the faithlessness of some of the ancestors provides insight into how Ben Sira can reconcile his belief that Israel is God's portion and that the nations have no right to rule over Israel with the fact that the Jewish people as he knows it is firmly under the control of foreigners. The consequences of faithlessness come into even bolder relief when they are compared with the results of the faithfulness of Moses, Aaron, David and the rest. In this context Ben Sira mentions three kings specifically. Solomon (47:12–22) was wise in his youth, and he built the Temple in Jerusalem. Ben Sira recounts Solomon's fame due to his songs, proverbs and parables (v. 17). It was "in the name of the Lord God" that Solomon amassed great fortune (v. 18). But Solomon became foolish because he married foreign

---

[28] J.C. VanderKam has argued that the Simon the Just referred to in Jewish sources is not Simon II as is often claimed, but rather Simon I. In the course of his argument he maintains that Simon I is also the subject of Sirach 50. Whether or not VanderKam's arguments about Simon the Just have any merit, I do think, in contrast to VanderKam, that the activities attributed to the high priest in Sirach 50 reflect Simon II's actions taken to restore Jerusalem after Antiochus III successfully wrested control of Judea in 200–198 (*From Joshua to Caiaphas*, 147–155).

women who "stained" his honor. He subjected his body to his wives, and this act probably represents for Ben Sira the subjection of Israel to foreign powers. Solomon's legacy was "a rebel kingdom in Ephraim" (v. 21) and a son "broad in folly and lacking in sense"—the opposite of the young Solomon. This son, Rehoboam, "drove the people to revolt" (47:23), a reference to the division of Solomon's kingdom into two. In the north, Jeroboam (47:24–25), who established the cult shrines in the north at Dan and Bethel, "caused Israel to sin." Because of Jeroboam's actions, according to Ben Sira, the people's sins increased and culminated in exile from the land and vengeance coming upon them (v. 25). Here Ben Sira recalls the Assyrian destruction of the Northern Kingdom in the eighth century BCE.

Several additional comments emphasize the point that faithlessness to God results in sin and foreign domination. In a transitional passage between the section on Elisha and that on Hezekiah (48:15–16), Ben Sira observes that the people did not repent or cease from sinning. The result was that "they were carried off as plunder from their land and were scattered over all the earth" (v. 15). This passage, placed where it is between Elijah and Hezekiah is most likely a second reference to the Assyrian destruction of the north. Verse 16 claims that a remnant remained faithful, but Ben Sira is quick to note that the majority continued to sin.

The end of the Praise of the Ancestors in chapter 49 is an interesting hodge-podge of a sort. Verses 4–7 strengthen the interpretation that Ben Sira connects faithlessness to God, primarily through transgression of the Law, and foreign rule. All of the kings except for David, Hezekiah and Josiah were great sinners because they "abandoned the Law of the Most High" (v. 4). Consequently, "they gave their power to others and their glory to a foreign nation who set fire to the chosen city of the sanctuary and made its streets desolate" (vv. 5–6). This notice refers to the Babylonian destruction of Jerusalem and the Southern Kingdom. Ben Sira, then, accounts for both Israel's and Judah's loss of land and sovereignty by connecting the Assyrian destruction of the north and the Babylonian exile of the south to the people's sin. These twin destructions thus function as the primary paradigms for how Ben Sira understands the reality of foreign rule—Israel sins and the result is that God gives the nation over to foreigners (cf. above on 10:14–18).[29]

---

[29] After this Ben Sira mentions in rapid succession Ezekiel, Job, the Twelve, Zerubbabel, the high priest Joshua, Nehemiah, Enoch, Joseph, Shem, Seth, Enosh and Adam.

The theology that faithfulness is the condition necessary for God's deliverance is for Ben Sira both national and individual. A very personal expression of this theology, with similar vocabulary to the national example in 36:1–22, is found in the prayer of thanksgiving in 51:1–12.[30] In this chapter Ben Sira thanks and praises God for delivering him from his adversaries. His enemies surrounded him on every side, and he was near death (v. 6–7). "Then I remembered your mercy," he says, "…and I sent up my prayer from the earth…My prayer was heard for you saved me from destruction and rescued me in time of trouble" (vv. 6–12).

Ben Sira and Foreign Rule:
Ptolemies and Seleucids

Ben Sira's basic understanding of foreign rule is essentially consisent with the theological outlook found in the deuteronomic history. That is, faithfulness results in success; faithlessness brings punishment. For Ben Sira that translates into faithfulness resulting in defeat of enemies; faithlessness brings foreign domination. When foreigners succeed against Israel, it is because the rulers and the people have abandoned the Law. But how does Ben Sira apply this thinking to his own contemporary situation, and how can this theology help to make sense of it? The answer to this question presents something of a problem.

It seems clear that Ben Sira has a fundamental difficulty with foreigners ruling over God's people at any time; such a situation is simply not the natural order of things. Israel is God's own possession that he created at the beginning (17:17; 36:20). God sent Wisdom to dwell in Jerusalem in the Temple (24:10). Yet, Ben Sira himself has known no other reality than foreigners having political and military domination over Israel, and the various comments about the nations in his book, I think, reveal his dissatisfaction with that contemporary situation.

Several facets of that historical situation and Ben Sira's response to it require some further examination, however. The first is Ben Sira's unmitigated praise of Simon II. It is likely that Ben Sira is writing after the time of Simon's priesthood, since his descriptions of Simon seem

---

None of Ben Sira's remarks about these biblical personages bears on the theme of this paper.

[30] Without the long addition found in Ms B from the Cairo Geniza.

to presume that his activity is in the past.[31] Simon, however, would appear to present something of an enigma to Ben Sira. He was intimately involved in the events that led to the changeover of Palestine from Ptolemaic to Seleucid control, perhaps even the leader of the party supporting the Seleucids.[32] From a political perspective, he undoubtedly saw the increasing strength of the Seleucids and the corresponding weakness of the Ptolemies. In addition, I imagine that Simon might also have seen the Seleucids as a way out from under the tax burden of the Ptolemaic bureaucracy. Indeed, that seems to have been precisely the result of his support of Antiochus III, at least initially. After Antiochus's victory at Paneas, not only did he allow the Jews to live "according to their ancestral laws," a policy the Ptolemies probably followed as well, he gave his supporters among the Jews tax relief as a reward for their support. He also, according to Josephus (*Ant.* 12.139–141), intended to help rebuild Jerusalem and the Temple, both of which had apparently been severely damaged in the wars between Egypt and Syria. Ben Sira most likely refers to this rebuilding in his praise of Simon in 50:1–4.[33]

As far as we know, however, Simon never attempted to shake off foreign rule as much as he probably tried to get the best deal he could. Yet although there is plenty of evidence that he is unhappy with Israel's subjection to foreigners, Ben Sira never even implies any criticism of Simon for acceding to Seleucid domination. Why? Perhaps Ben Sira thought that Simon's success with Antiochus III would enable Israel eventually to reestablish its independence or, at least, would allow for a kind of *de facto* independence under a passive Seleucid rule.

This brings me to the second issue that requires some discussion, the tone of the prayer in 36:1–22. The emotion of Ben Sira's prayer for God to crush the nations seems very out of character with the rest of his book. Ben Sira's method of operation in other matters is often to mask his criticisms as parts of general admonitions. I have argued elsewhere that he does exactly this against groups of marginalized priests who are criticizing the Jerusalem priesthood and against the rich and powerful.[34] As I noted above, Skehan and Di Lella suggest that this is the intent of chap. 10 in order to stay out of trouble. Yet, the trouble is that anyone

---

[31] Skehan and Di Lella, *Ben Sira*, 9, 550; Segal, *Complete Book of Ben Sira*, 348.
[32] Tcherikover, for instance, says that Simon "stood at the head" of the pro-Seleucid faction in Jerusalem (*Hellenistic Civilization*, 80).
[33] See Tcherikover, *Hellenistic Civilization*, 80–1.
[34] Chapter 5 "Fear the Lord and Honor the Priest."

reading 36:1–22 can hardly fail to sense the emotion and passion of that passage. If Ben Sira had been trying to stay out of trouble, this would not seem the best way to do it.

The one context I can imagine for this uncharacteristic outburst, and I admit to the speculative nature of this reconstruction, is the series of events following Simon II's death in 196 BCE. Onias III, Simon's son, followed his father, but he seems eventually not to have shared his father's political allegiances. It is easy to picture the internal political maneuverings that must have gone on between those who supported Seleucid rule and those who favored Ptolemaic influence, some of which Ben Sira most likely observed himself. The situation could only have gotten worse during and after 190–188 BCE when the Romans defeated Antiochus at Magnesia and forced him into the treaty of Apamea that placed a very heavy burden of financial reparations on him, one that was undoubtedly passed along to his subjects.[35] The honeymoon was certainly over. If it is in this period or slightly later that Ben Sira is writing, as many think, then the years of Simon II *must* have seemed like a golden age to him—the city and Temple repaired, taxes lightened, Jews able to live according to their law. The political crises of the years after Simon's death might all have been too much for Ben Sira, who must have seen a lot in his life already. The tone of the prayer may be the outcome of his disappointment at the way things had developed.[36]

The prayer in 36:1–22, as I understand it then, is Ben Sira's own cry to God. He is doing exactly what those ancient heroes of Israel did; he is calling to God in a time of national trouble and beseeching him to rescue his people. God answered those ancestors who were faithful by delivering them from their enemies. Ben Sira hoped he would do the same now.

There is one element missing in the prayer, however, that I find hard to understand. Ben Sira's theology constructs foreigners ruling over Israel to be the result of faithlessness and sin. The prayer, though, does not contain any mention of either. Ben Sira petitions for God's mercy and pity, but not his forgiveness. Despite the machinations of the politically powerful, Ben Sira nowhere in the book intimates that the high priest

---

[35] After writing an initial draft of this paper, I discovered that Marböck, "Das Gebet," 105, also connects 36:1–22 with these same events. He also brings in the events described in 2 Maccabees 3 when Heliodorus attempts to rob the Temple treasury.

[36] Marböck remarks that Ben Sira's prayer could be understood as a reaction to "newly growing pressure from the foreign masters" (Ibid., 106).

specifically or priests in general, those who were in control of state and cult, had been faithless and thus had brought Israel to its present condition. In fact, the opposite is the case. Ben Sira expresses nothing but admiration and support for the priests. Does he blame the current conditions on the rich (many of whom must have been priests)? He certainly criticizes wealth and finds it difficult to think that there are very many righteous wealthy people, but there is no clear connection in the book that I can see between wealth and the contemporary political fortunes of Israel. Does he understand the sins of the ancestors to be the cause of this foreign rule? It was certainly true that Judah had been under foreign domination since the time of the Babylonian destruction of Jerusalem, despite the brief respite under Zerubbabel, Joshua and Nehemiah to which Ben Sira alludes (49:11–13). What bearing does the claim he makes in 48:16 that the majority continued to sin have on this issue? At this juncture I am not confident about any particular resolution to this quandary.

Yet, when one examines the Praise of the Ancestors section, the opposite side of that coin might provide a clue to Ben Sira's thinking here. Faithless rulers and people may forfeit Israel's political sovereignty, but righteous rulers who call to God bring rescue for the people. Is Ben Sira's paean of Simon II an attempt on his part to equate him with the righteous rulers of the past? Not only did Simon rebuild the Temple and city and bring water in (in these tasks he is like Nehemiah and Hezekiah), but the greater part of Ben Sira's description concerns the magnificence of his worship in the Temple (in which he resembles his ancestor Aaron). Indeed, the Hebrew of Ms B closes the section on Simon with a benediction connecting Simon's actions with Phinehas's on behalf of Israel: "May he grant you wisdom of heart and may he abide with you in peace; may his kindness to Simon be lasting; may he establish for him Phinehas's covenant so that it may not be abrogated for him or for his descendents for the days of heaven" (50:23–24).[37]

---

[37] Verses 23–24 differ between the Hebrew and the Greek. The Greek has, "May he grant us joy of heart, and may there be peace in our days in Israel, as in the days of old. May his kindness remain constantly with us and may he save us in our days" (translation is from Skehan and Di Lella, *Wisdom of Ben Sira*, 548). Skehan and Di Lella see the Greek as reflecting the later situation of Ben Sira's grandson who translated the book. He was undoubtedly aware that Onias III had been assassinated, and thus Simon's high priestly line had come to an end. The original benediction was no longer appropriate (Skehan and Di Lella, *Wisdom of Ben Sira*, 554).

Although Simon is probably dead by the time Ben Sira writes, he does not make any apparent reference in the book to Onias III who would have been the current high priest. Did Simon's accomplishments put him on a par with the righteous ancestors of Israel's past? Should God rescue Israel because of Simon's faithfulness? Admittedly, the prayer of chapter 36 and the praise of Simon are not connected in the book. Yet Marböck has shown some similar themes in the prayer and the Praise of the Ancestors, and given Ben Sira's theological understanding of why foreigners rule over Israel and how God ends that domination, connecting the two passages is an attractive option.[38] Such a connection helps to make sense of the prayer, the emphasis on the faithfulness of those righteous ancestors whom God delivered from their enemies and the attention Ben Sira pays to the glories of Simon II.

What is not at issue, however, is that Ben Sira hoped for a time when foreign rule would end, when God would restore sovereignty to his people under his own kingship. Unfortunately, Ben Sira's plea would not be answered in the way that he hoped, and his people would remain subject to foreigners long after the Ptolemies and Seleucids had disappeared from the scene.

[38] Marböck, "Das Gebet," 104–8.

CHAPTER SEVEN

WISDOM, INSTRUCTION AND SOCIAL LOCATION
IN BEN SIRA AND *1 ENOCH**

In his seminal article, "Lists of Revealed Things in the Apocalyptic Literature," Michael Stone addressed, among other matters, the relationship between apocalyptic and wisdom literature as evidenced in the lists of secrets revealed to apocalyptic seers.[1] In that article and several others, Stone also commented more specifically on the relationship between the Wisdom of Ben Sira, *1 Enoch* and *Aramaic Levi*.[2] His provocative comments led me some years ago to give close readings to a number of passages in Sirach that struck me as attempts to refute ideas like those made in certain sections of *1 Enoch*, especially the *Book of the Watchers* (*1 Enoch* 1–36) and the *Astronomical Book* (*1 Enoch* 72–82), as well as the *Aramaic Levi Document*.[3] I was spurred on further when I encountered R.A. Argall's work on the relationship between *1 Enoch* and Sirach.[4] While Argall argued very persuasively that there was a literary

---

* I have learned more than I probably realize from Michael Stone—from his published works, in seminars with him and in collegial conversation. I am pleased to offer this contribution in honor of an esteemed teacher and friend. It is an extensive revision of my paper, "Wisdom and Instruction in Ben Sira and *1 Enoch*" presented in the "Wisdom and Apocalypticism in Early Judaism and Christianity Group" at the SBL Annual Meeting in Toronto, 2002. In that seminar G.W.E. Nickelsburg and J. Kampen offered very cogent responses to my paper. The authors have generously allowed me to include material from their responses in this article. I refer to them below as Nickelsburg, "Response" and Kampen, "Response."

[1] *Magnalia Dei: The Mighty Acts of God. Essays on the Bible and Archaeology in Memory of G. Ernest Wright* (F.M. Cross Jr., W.E. Lemke, P.D. Miller, eds.; Garden City, NY: Doubleday, 1976) 414–52; reprinted in M.E. Stone, *Selected Studies in Pseudepigrapha and Apocrypha: With Special Reference to the Armenian Tradition* (SVTP 9; Brill: Leiden, 1991) 379–418.

[2] "Lists," *passim*; "Enoch, Aramaic Levi and Sectarian Origins," *JSJ* 19 (1988) 167 (reprinted in *Selected Studies*, 247–58); "Ideal Figures and Social Context: Priest and Sage in the Early Second Temple Age," *Ancient Israelite Religion: Essays in Honor of Frank Moore Cross* (P.D. Miller, P.D. Hanson, S.D. McBride, eds.; Philadelphia: Fortress, 1988) 578–82 (reprinted in *Selected Studies*, 259–72).

[3] Some of these ideas also appear in the *Epistle of Enoch* (*1 Enoch* 92–105), which I did not treat in my earlier work, but which I will examine below.

[4] *1 Enoch and Sirach: A Comparative Literary and Conceptual Analysis of the Themes of Revelation, Creation and Judgment* (SBLEJL 8; Atlanta: Scholars Press, 1995).

and conceptual relationship between the two, my research focused on trying to detect any specific social connections between people like Ben Sira, who supported the priestly establishment in Jerusalem, and others like those represented especially in the *Watchers* and *Aramaic Levi* who apparently criticized those in power in the Temple.[5]

The extent to which one can identify a specific group standing behind any ancient Jewish text presents a major methodological obstacle to this kind of inquiry, however. Warnings abound against assuming that a text represents a social group, and on more than one occasion Stone himself has noted the perilous nature of moving too blithely from understanding a text to imagining a social group responsible for it. As he wrote in *CBQ* in 1978, "Caution in such matters is wise, for the movement from tendencies of thought discerned in the analysis of texts to the positing of the existence of otherwise unattested social groups is fraught with peril. Yet that danger is one that the scholar must brave if his analysis is conducted in terms that imply a sociological matrix of the development of ideas."[6]

In this paper, I want to think about "a sociological matrix of the development of ideas" in the Wisdom of Ben Sira and in three sections of *1 Enoch* (the *Astronomical Book*, the *Book of the Watchers*, the *Epistle of Enoch*) without trying to posit identifiable social groups behind them and thus falling into the group-identification morass. Here I want to ask some questions not about what social groups might have produced the texts, but in what social locations these works may have originated or at least been used. The argument essentially breaks down into three parts. First, Stone, G.W.E. Nickelsburg and Argall have all offered strong cases that parts of *1 Enoch* employ sapiential forms, language and ideas, although they are frequently invested with different content and meaning.[7] In my own work I have argued that the authors/redac-

---

[5] "Putting the Puzzle Together: Some Suggestions Concerning the Social Location of the Wisdom of Ben Sira," *Society of Biblical Literature 1996 Seminar Papers* (Atlanta: Scholars Press, 1996) 133–49 (Reprinted in B.G. Wright and L.M. Wills, *Conflicted Boundaries in Wisdom and Apocalypticism* [SBLSymS; Atlanta: SBL, 2006] 89–112); Chapter 5, "'Fear the Lord and Honor the Priest': Ben Sira as Defender of the Jerusalem Priesthood."

[6] "The Book of Enoch and Judaism in the Third Century B.C.E.," *Emerging Judaism* (M.E. Stone and D. Satran, eds.; Minneapolis: Fortress, 1989) 65–6 [originally in *CBQ* 40 (1978) 479–92]. More recently, see L.L. Grabbe, "The Social Setting of Early Jewish Apocalypticism," *JSP* 4 (1989) 27–47.

[7] For discussion of various wisdom elements in *1 Enoch*, see Stone, "Lists"; "Enoch, Aramaic Levi"; 162–63; G.W.E. Nickelsburg, "Enochic Wisdom: An Alternative to the

tors of the *Watchers* and the *Astronomical Book* presented their work as wisdom to be handed down from generation to generation.[8] To what extent can we characterize the Enochic books as wisdom?

Second, those Israelite and Jewish works traditionally included in the category "wisdom" have a clear pedagogical/instructional function. The use of the short maxim or proverb meant to condition behavior, what we might call ethical training and character formation, and the transparent mentoring relationship of father to son (even, as in Proverbs 31, mother to son) or teacher to student (often articulated in a fictive father/son relationship) point to some pedagogical context. When compared with a book like Sirach, does the use and reformulation of wisdom elements in the Enochic works indicate that their authors/redactors intended them as instruction?

Third, scholars have variously situated ancient instruction as taking place in the family, the "school," the temple or the royal court.[9] If we are warranted in characterizing the Enochic books as containing wisdom that is offered as instruction, might we then situate the genesis and subsequent life of these texts in any of those traditional ancient contexts where pedagogy routinely took place?

THE ENOCHIC BOOKS OF WISDOM

In my article "Fear the Lord and Honor the Priest" I tried to make the case that we can read parts of Sirach as polemical comments about matters of calendar, revelatory visions and priestly legitimacy such as we find in the *Watchers*, the *Astronomical Book* and *Aramaic Levi*. The authority for Ben Sira's teaching rests on the foundation of the Israelite sapiential tradition—the Torah and the accumulated wisdom of the sages. Disciplined study of the Torah and attentiveness to the sages' words constituted for him the vehicles for acquiring wisdom and knowledge

---

Mosaic Torah?" *HESED VE-EMET: Studies in Honor of Ernest S. Frerichs* (J. Magness and S. Gitin, eds.; BJS 320; Atlanta: Scholars Press, 1988) 123–32; Argall, *1 Enoch and Sirach*, 17–52. In this paper I only discuss the three sections of *1 Enoch* that look to be contemporary with Sirach or that predate it. One could also examine the *Book of Dreams* and the *Parables*, but these postdate Sirach.

[8] See Wright, "Putting the Puzzle Together," 146–49 and "Fear the Lord," 123–26.

[9] On the problem of the school as the setting of biblical wisdom, see A. Lemaire, "The Sage in School and Temple," *The Sage in Israel and the Ancient Near East* (J.G. Gammie and L.G. Perdue, eds.; Winona Lake: Eisenbrauns, 1990) 165–81 and the literature cited therein.

and for leading a life pleasing to God and other people. Indeed, in Sir 38:34b–39:11 Ben Sira compares his wisdom to prophecy, which he receives through prayer. The sage's wisdom thus constitutes inspired wisdom and, as Stone notes, in that respect brings "Ben Sira's conception of the sage close to the apocalyptic seer, particularly in actions and attitudes relating to inspiration."[10]

The Enochic authors/redactors bolster their claims by articulating a notion of wisdom that relies on a different authority from that claimed by sages like Ben Sira. They anchor their claims to authority in an "esoteric revealed wisdom" received directly from heaven through Enoch's dreams and visions and handed down from predeluvian times.[11] Those who would read and understand Enoch's wisdom/knowledge would learn proper calendar reckoning and priestly conduct, and they could know that the events foreseen by the ancient patriarch—that some would act impiously—referred to those in power in Jerusalem.[12] Thus, the wisdom granted to Enoch could function for those who used his books as a counter-wisdom to that proffered by sages like Ben Sira. The "account" of Enoch's transmission of this knowledge to his son Methuselah in *1 Enoch* 82:1–3 establishes the antiquity and written continuity of his wisdom.

> And now, my son Methuselah, all these things I am recounting to you and writing down for you; and I have revealed to you everything, and given you writings of all these things. Keep, my son, Methuselah, the writings of your father's hand, that you may deliver them to the generations of eternity. Wisdom I have given to you and to your children, and to those who will be your children, that they may transmit it to their children, and to generations of generations forever, to whoever is endowed with wisdom; and they shall celebrate all the wise. Wisdom shall slumber, (but) in their mind those who have understanding shall not slumber, but they shall hearken with their ears that they may learn this wisdom, and it shall be better for those that partake of it than rich food.

In this passage, the handing down of Enoch's wisdom from father to son recalls the home and family setting of much ancient wisdom instruction (see Proverbs, for example) or even the artificial family relationships invoked by the sage in the school, who can address his charge as "my son." This passage thus evokes two of the principal ancient contexts where wisdom would be transmitted.

---

[10] Stone, "Ideal Figures," 581.
[11] The phrase comes from Argall, *1 Enoch and Sirach*, 251.
[12] "Fear the Lord," 104–8.

1 Enoch does more than employ the image of the transmission of wisdom from father to son or sage to student. It routinely incorporates forms, language and ideas of the Israelite sapiential tradition, and in these respects it demonstrates an affinity with wisdom texts. In "Lists of Revealed Things," to cite one example, Stone demonstrated the connections between lists of natural and cosmological secrets revealed to apocalyptic seers and the cosmological elements of the wisdom tradition, even though the apocalyptic lists reformulate the older wisdom material. *1 Enoch* 93:11–14 does just that when it adopts the sapiential rhetorical device of using an interrogative to emphasize the inscrutability of God's wonders. In taking over the sapiential form, Stone argues, the apocalypticist adapts it to its new context.

> [T]he significance of 1 Enoch 93 is that an interrogative formulation can be moved from a pure Wisdom context to one in which, in both content and form, it refers to and is relevant to the secret tradition of apocalyptic speculation. This particular transformation of a Wisdom form and of Wisdom language is part of a general movement in the apocalyptic writings toward interpretation and reuse of wisdom language. "Wisdom" is invested, therefore, with a new meaning.[13]

Even though he concludes that the origins of some apocalyptic speculations about natural phenomena "are to be sought in wisdom passages, or in hymns of praise to God as Creator," Stone explicitly distinguishes his position from that of G. von Rad, who maintained that apocalyptic had its origins in the wisdom tradition.[14] He notes that the wisdom material does not help

> directly to explain the more curious and less obvious objects of apocalyptic speculation. It seems most probable that part of this speculative concern of the apocalyptic lists derived from Wisdom sources, although the lines of connection may prove difficult to trace. It is impossible, however, to see wisdom tradition as the only source from which the interest in these subjects sprang.[15]

Yet the wisdom given to the predeluvian wisdom figure, Enoch, differs dramatically from traditional Israelite wisdom. The Enochic authors presented their texts as *revealed* wisdom, not acquired through study

---

[13] Stone, "Lists," 426.

[14] Ibid., 431. G. von Rad, *Wisdom in Israel*, (Nashville/London: Abingdon/SCM, 1972).

[15] Ibid., 438. The same can probably be said of the relationship between wisdom and apocalyptic more broadly. Although I argue here for influence and use of wisdom in apocalyptic texts, Stone's conclusion is certainly correct.

or human reflection, even if in doing so they appealed to the familiar language of Jewish sapiential tradition.[16]

Argall offers a variety of elements throughout the Enochic corpus as evidence that these works employ wisdom forms and ideas and that the corpus, as a collection, is portrayed as a book of wisdom. Right at the beginning, the framework of the *Book of the Watchers* is reminiscent of a testament, a form of instruction in which wisdom gets transmitted from parent to child.[17] In what may have originally been the conclusion to the *Book of the Watchers*, 81:5–82:3 provides a testamentary closing, which explicitly interprets the book's revelation as wisdom that Enoch writes down for transmission to future generations.[18] As an additional framing device, *1 Enoch* 1:2, 3 also describe the content of the patriarch's visions as a משל or παραβολή, a common wisdom term.[19] Argall argues that several other features of the *Watchers*—the teaching of forbidden knowledge by the angel Asael (chaps. 6–11), Enoch's role as "scribe of righteousness" (12:1), the Tree of Wisdom (chap. 32)—all reflect sapiential language and motifs.[20]

Argall demonstrates that both the narrative bridge to the *Epistle* (91:1–10, 18–19) and the *Epistle* itself (92–105) reveal strong wisdom connections as well. The superscription describes it as "this complete sign of wisdom" addressed to "all my sons upon the earth, and to the last generation who will observe truth and peace" (92:1). Its author explicitly utilizes the wisdom categories of the wise and the foolish in 98:9–99:10 and 104:9–105:2 to describe his own community and those whom he opposes. Argall identifies the most important indicators of the *Epistle*'s central concern with wisdom as: (1) the wise are teachers who are in some conflict with those who teach others to disregard their words. (2) This conflict involves written texts—"Woe to those who write lying words and words of error; they write and lead many astray with their lies when they hear them" (98:15); disputes over differing

---

[16] On Enoch as a wisdom figure, see Stone, "Enoch, Aramaic Levi," 162–63 and literature cited therein. On revealed wisdom, see Argall, *1 Enoch and Sirach*, 35.

[17] The opening chapters of *1 Enoch* allude to Moses' testament in Deuteronomy 33. Argall, *1 Enoch and Sirach*, 18; G.W.E. Nickelsburg, *1 Enoch 1* (Hermeneia; Minneapolis: Fortress, 2001) 135.

[18] On these verses as a conclusion to *Watchers*, see Nickelsburg, *1 Enoch 1*, 334–37.

[19] This initial section of *1 Enoch* is based on Balaam's oracle. On the term משל/παραβολή in this context, see Nickelsburg, *1 Enoch 1*, 138–39 and Argall, *1 Enoch and Sirach*, 19–20.

[20] For detailed argument, see Argall, *1 Enoch and Sirach*, 24–35.

interpretations of the Torah most likely lie at the heart of the problem. (3) At the end, the superiority of the wisdom of the wise will become plain for all to see.[21] Argall concludes about the *Epistle*:

> This approach by the author(s) of the Epistle serves to reinforce the notion that the words of Enoch are grounded in what he learned from his tour of the upper, unseen world and in the authority he received to reveal it to his children and the last generation. In the Epistle, this perspective is used to shed light on a controversy between teachers who possessed Enoch's books of revealed wisdom and teachers who possessed books that advocated a different way. Enoch foresaw the controversy and addressed it in the strongest possible terms. Those who follow another way are fools and idolaters. They must abandon their lies or they will perish in the judgment of God. Only the wisdom books of Enoch, the Epistle now included, reveal the paths of righteousness and truth, paths that lead to eternal salvation.[22]

The *Astronomical Book* turns out to be somewhat different from the *Watchers* and the *Epistle* in that it does not employ sapiential language and forms in any consistent and obvious manner. Yet, the book in its current form is presented in its entirety as revealed cosmological knowledge that Enoch wrote down and passed on to Methuselah (82:1–5).[23] This perception is reinforced in several other passages. *1 Enoch* 74:2 claims that Enoch wrote down his revelations, and in two places, Enoch mentions that he "showed" them to Methuselah (76:14; 79:1).

The transmission of revealed wisdom from heaven to earth with Enoch after his ascent recalls the sapiential myth of the descent of Wisdom found in Ben Sira 24 and Baruch 4. Its use in *1 Enoch* differs dramatically from these other two, however. As in Sirach 24 and Baruch 4, the authors of *1 Enoch* take up an idea found in Proverbs 8, but whereas Ben Sira and Baruch localize wisdom in the Torah, *1 Enoch*'s readers are assured that they have access to this divine wisdom through Enoch's written legacy (82:3; 104:12–13).[24] Other major themes as well point to what Nickelsburg calls *1 Enoch*'s "roots in the sapiential tradition."[25]

---

[21] Ibid., 46–7. For most of this section Argall relies on the analysis of G.W.E. Nickelsburg, "The Epistle of Enoch and the Qumran Literature," *Essays in Honour of Yigael Yadin* (= *JJS* 33 [1982]; G. Vermes and J. Neusner, eds.) 333–48.

[22] Ibid., 49.

[23] Ibid., 52.

[24] On Enoch and the myth of Wisdom's descent, see Nickelsburg, "Enochic Wisdom," 127 and Argall, *1 Enoch and Sirach*, 53–98.

[25] Nickelsburg, "Enochic Wisdom," 126.

1 Enoch takes its own fictive setting seriously. Since Enoch received his revelation generations before God gave the Torah to Moses, *1 Enoch* downplays Moses' importance so that "its putative author received full and definitive divine revelation millennia before the birth of Moses."[26] Indeed *1 Enoch* contains "the written repository of heavenly wisdom, received by the ancient patriarch Enoch and transmitted for the salvation of the last generations who were to live before the final judgment," and it lacks the legal forms characteristic of the Mosaic Law.[27] So, for example, the author of the *Epistle* can describe human behavior using the metaphor of the "two ways," a common sapiential ethical motif, rather than appealing to any legal proscription.[28] He construes obedience as walking the right path and disobedience as straying from it and treading the path of wickedness. Throughout the *Epistle* sapiential motifs and language appear instead of formal legal language and forms. Nickelsburg concludes, "Thus the Enochic texts provide a window into a time and place in Israel's religious history in which the Mosaic Torah is known, but revealed instruction, necessary for salvation, is tied to Enoch rather than Mosaic authority."[29] Indeed the Enochic books stand so much closer to the Israelite wisdom tradition than to the Pentateuch that Nickelsburg can assert that wisdom is an "almost all-encompassing" category in them.[30]

THE INSTRUCTIONAL FUNCTION OF WISDOM

The sapiential character of so many elements of the Enochic works and the framing of them as wisdom books raise the question of whether texts so infused with wisdom language, forms and ideas, no matter how reformulated, have some instructional or pedagogical function

---

[26] Ibid., 129.

[27] Ibid.

[28] For recent discussion of two-ways wisdom, see R.A. Kraft, "Early Developments of the 'Two-Ways Tradition(s),' in Retrospect," *For a Later Generation: The Transformation of Tradition in Israel, Early Judaism and Early Christianity* (R.A. Argall, B.A. Bow, R.A. Werline, eds.; Harrisburg: Trinity Press International, 2000) 136–43 and G.W.E. Nickelsburg, "Seeking the Origins of the Two-Ways Tradition in Jewish and Christian Ethical Texts," *A Multiform Heritage: Studies on Early Judaism and Christianity in Honor of Robert A. Kraft* (B.G. Wright, ed.; Scholars Press Homage Series 24; Atlanta: Scholars Press, 1999) 95–108.

[29] Nickelsburg, "Enochic Wisdom," 130.

[30] Ibid., 125.

similar to that of the traditional didactic wisdom of the Israelite sages. Does the sapiential character of a work like *1 Enoch* indicate that it was intended to provide instruction/teaching for those who read it, and if so, for what purpose?

Before discussing whether *1 Enoch* might be intended as instruction and, if so, where it might be located, I want to think a little about these issues using Sirach, a traditional Jewish wisdom book whose pedagogical intent is not a matter of dispute. In his response to my Toronto SBL paper, Nickelsburg outlined four interrelated characteristics of instruction that I have found helpful in my subsequent thinking about the issue. He says that instruction can be thought of as "(1) the imparting of knowledge, (2) by means of certain literary or oral forms (and perhaps through certain kinds of action or activity), (3) within particular concrete social circumstances, (4) to accomplish specific purposes or objectives."[31] As he observes, the content of that knowledge and the forms that it takes (#1 and #2) are often much easier to identify than the setting and purpose (#3 and #4).

For Ben Sira, identifying these characteristics does not appear to present insoluble difficulties. The book is obviously didactic; its central focus is instructional, with character formation and success in life as its central goals (#4). Ben Sira frequently characterizes his teaching using the terms παιδεία/מוסר (cf. 23:2, 7; 24:27, 32; 33:18; 41:14; 51:28), and he delivers it in a teacher/student relationship in some sort of formal pedagogical setting, what the text calls a "house of instruction" (51:23; #3). Those who receive that instruction and put it to use will achieve a happy and secure life. Character formation, using instruction to shape students' behavior and their way of relating to the world, provides the basis for achieving and maintaining that "good life." In the honor/shame society in which Ben Sira lived, his teaching equipped his students to maintain and even enhance their honor in the face of attempts to undermine it.[32]

---

[31] Nickelsburg, "Response."

[32] On Ben Sira and honor/shame, see C.V. Camp, "Understanding a Patriarchy: Women in Second Century Jerusalem Through the Eyes of Ben Sira," *"Women Like This:" New Perspectives on Jewish Women in the Greco-Roman World* (A.-J. Levine, ed.; SBLEJL 1; Atlanta: Scholars Press, 1991) 1–39; idem, "Honor and Shame in Ben Sira: Anthropological and Theological Reflections" *The Book of Ben Sira in Modern Research* (P.C. Beentjes, ed.; BZAW 255; Berlin: Walter de Gruyter, 1997) 171–87; and Chapter 4, "'Who Has Been Tested by Gold and Found Perfect?' Ben Sira's Discourse of Riches and Poverty."

Instruction and character formation have in Sirach a definite present-world and practical focus (#1), and Ben Sira delivers his teaching through the medium of the wisdom saying or maxim, often connecting several together in short poems about topics like friendship, riches, powerful patrons and women (#2). He does not encourage his students to behave in a particular fashion so that they might avoid some post-mortem punishment or achieve an eschatological reward. Their reward comes in the good things that accrue to them in this life, benefits such as social status, honor and family.[33]

The content of Ben Sira's teaching and the authority for it are founded on a particular notion of wisdom. God has indeed revealed wisdom to humankind, but that revelation is not apprehended in a revelatory encounter with God.[34] Ben Sira claims that God sent Wisdom from heaven to dwell with his people in the Jerusalem Temple (24:8–12). No one went to heaven to get Wisdom; God sent her to Jerusalem where the Temple cult and the priests who officiate there mediate her to the community at large. Ultimately, however, Ben Sira claims that Wisdom became embodied in the "book of the covenant of the Most High God, the law that Moses commanded us as an inheritance for the congregations of Jacob" (24:23). Despite the fact that there are no direct citations from the Law in Sirach, divine wisdom flows like a great river from the Mosaic Torah (24:23–29).

That wisdom, mediated to humans in the Mosaic Law, requires additional mediation, found in the teaching of inspired sages, which is how Ben Sira describes his own teaching (24:30–34). Our Jerusalemite sage sees himself as the custodian and transmitter not only of the wisdom embodied in Torah, but also of an inherited tradition of scribal wisdom. Additionally, Ben Sira has acquired wisdom on his own by observation of human behavior and the workings of the natural world. So, for example, Ben Sira's teaching on riches and poverty can depend on the Torah and life experience at the same time. "The prayer of the humble pierces the clouds, and it will not rest until it reaches its goal" (34:21) affirms claims made in Exod 22:21–27 that God hears the pleas of the

---

[33] The major underlying reason for this emphasis is undoubtedly that Ben Sira's view of the afterlife does not allow for any other possibilities. According to Ben Sira, and here he is in agreement with the Hebrew scriptural tradition, every human being inherits the identical post-mortem shadowy world of Sheol where there are no luxuries and all people suffer the same fate (14:16). This life, then, is what there is to enjoy.

[34] In fact he seems to dismiss the legitimacy of such encounters. See "Fear the Lord," 114–18.

oppressed and vindicates them.[35] Yet, "A merchant can hardly keep from wrongdoing, nor is a tradesman innocent of sin" (26:29) recognizes the real-life risk of doing business in the marketplace. Ben Sira anticipates reward and blessing from God for obedience, which takes the form of success in this world, characterized by material benefit and enhanced honor, not some deferred future salvation in the time of judgment. God's judgment also occurs in the here-and-now, and the wicked will not escape it in their lifetimes (cf. 11:14–28; 14:11–16).

The situation in the *Astronomical Book*, the *Watchers* and the *Epistle* differs from that in Sirach in several crucial respects, and thus the question of whether their authors intended them in whole or in part as instruction is more difficult to sort out. While we can reconstruct a social setting for Sirach, the Enochic works are pseudonymous, and their social settings must be extrapolated from their fictional ones.[36] Whereas the topics and literary form of Sirach make its didactic function clear, *1 Enoch*'s use of revelatory visions and extended narrative in and of itself does not immediately signal an instructional purpose, although Enoch's visions do serve as a vehicle for imparting knowledge.

The *Astronomical Book* may be perhaps the clearest case of instruction in *1 Enoch*. In essence, the *Astronomical Book* almost exclusively contains data—that is, cosmological, astronomical and meteorological information set out in excruciating detail. In a rather straightforward manner, the work provides the details of the movements of the sun and moon throughout the years, months and days, especially information about the way in which the solar and lunar years become increasingly out of sync with one another (#1). This compendium comes to the reader in the form of revelation that the seer Enoch has received from the angel Uriel (#2). While the revelatory instruction about these astronomical phenomena does not give any indication of a specific social setting, one can at minimum say that "[i]ts setting appears to have been some venue where persons concerned with astronomical observation and calendrical observance carried out their activity" (#3).[37]

The work's "specific purposes or objectives" (#4) get spelled out to some extent in the text. Its author attempts to counteract the incorrect calendrical practices used by "the sinners," who do not reckon the four

---

[35] See "Who Has Been Tested," 79.
[36] Nickelsburg, "Response."
[37] Ibid.

epagomenal days that bring the calendar to a total of 364 rather than 360. Observing these days is equivalent to walking "in the way of righteousness" (82:4). Nickelsburg summarizes the material in the *Astronomical Book* this way, "We have [in the *Astronomical Book*] instruction pure and simple, presented as ancient revelation, intended to change religious (rather than social or ethical) practice, undergirded by an explication of the consequences of contrary practice."[38]

The *Watchers* presents a more difficult set of circumstances to disentangle. Unfortunately, the work provides few clues as to its social setting, although it may have some connections with priests (#3).[39] The content of the work chronicles Enoch's heavenly journeys in which an angel conveys to him knowledge of cosmological secrets and eschatological realities, particularly places of punishment of the stars and the angels that transgressed God's command (*1 Enoch* 18–21) as well as the fates of righteous and wicked people (*1 Enoch* 22–27) (#1). From the opening oracle, the *Watchers* employs its sapiential language and motifs, especially observations about nature, in the service of warnings about eschatological salvation and judgment. By means of such teaching, the author of the *Watchers*, through interpreted apocalyptic visions, encourages his readers to remain on the path of righteousness (#4). This road, however, does not lead to the "good life" of traditional Israelite wisdom, but to future, eschatological reward through faithfulness to God.

When we look at the *Epistle*, its condemnation of false teachers who write lying words points to some conflict over right and wrong instruction (98:15; #3?).[40] For the author of the *Epistle*, the foolish possess "neither knowledge nor wisdom" (98:3), and they do not listen to the teaching of the wise (98:9). The righteous, by contrast, will listen to the "words of the wise and understand them" (99:10). Additionally, the *Epistle*'s use of traditional wisdom forms that convey ethical teaching, such as two-ways material, suggests some didactic function, although the *Epistle* also employs prophetic "Woes" extensively in its vituperations against the impious (#2).

But the *Epistle* differs somewhat from Ben Sira and the other two Enochic books in that it does not explicitly enumerate the positive behaviors that put one on the path of peace. Despite the fact that in

---

[38] Ibid.

[39] Wright, "Fear the Lord," 123–24 and the literature cited therein.

[40] On the nature of this conflict, see R.A. Horsley, "Social Relations and Social Conflict in the *Epistle of Enoch*," in Argall, et al., *For a Later Generation*, 100–15.

91:18, the *Epistle* says that Enoch will show to his sons "the paths of righteousness and the paths of wrongdoing," it never really spells out what actions constitute righteousness. Rather than providing teachings that explicate righteous behavior, the *Epistle* enumerates the actions of the wicked, so that the righteous know the paths to avoid, and, in fact, the *Epistle* details quite a number of wicked deeds (e.g., *1 Enoch* 99). The teaching of the false teachers constitutes the counterpart to the teaching of the wise of the *Epistle* (#1). The example of the wicked is clear, "And now I say to you righteous, 'Do not walk in the wicked path, nor in wrongdoing, nor in the paths of death, and do not draw near to them, lest you be destroyed' " (94:3). The *Epistle*'s main emphasis comes through loudly and clearly; the righteous must remain faithful, shunning the wicked thoroughfares and walking on the paths of peace. The *Epistle*'s author admonishes his readers so that they will not end up sharing the harsh eschatological judgment to befall the wicked, but rather that they will receive a reward for their faithfulness (#4).

If we compare instruction in the *Astronomical Book*, the *Watchers* and the *Epistle* to a clearly didactic work like Sirach, we might say that while the purpose and goals of the teaching seem similar, the payoff is very different. I used the phrase "character formation" earlier to describe Ben Sira's goal of shaping his students' behavior and their manner of relating to the world. In this sense, all three of the Enochic works have character formation as a central concern. Each of them seeks to inculcate certain behaviors and values and to make them part of the readers' daily lives. The *Astronomical Book* seeks to establish a particular religious practice in order that its readers keep to the path of righteousness, which, beyond simply possessing the right calendar, presumably leads to salvation. The *Watchers* does not focus its attention on the "good life" in the present, but faithfulness to God that leads to eternal reward. Its use of the myth of the fallen Watchers that leads up to the extensive sections describing Enoch's heavenly journeys may function at the same time as critique of the Jerusalem priesthood and as admonition to proper (priestly?) behavior.[41] The *Epistle*'s instruction reflects something like the Torah-oriented teaching of Ben Sira, although the two works certainly differ in their understanding of what happens as a result of keeping the Law. The wicked deeds condemned in the *Epistle* violate specific elements of the Mosaic Torah, and certainly the *Epistle*'s passionate denunciations

---

[41] Wright, "Fear the Lord," 104–8, 123–25.

of riches (94:8–10), of consuming blood (99:11) and of idolatry (99:7–8) seek to shape the reader's routine behavior.[42] Yet, whereas Ben Sira advocates living according to the Law in order to obtain happiness and security in this life, the *Epistle*'s author, in view of the impending judgment, instructs his readers and exhorts them to faithfulness so that they receive an eschatological reward. Nickelsburg's assessment of *1 Enoch* in its entirety also applies individually to these three Enochic works: "Thus in contrast to the received paradigm of a Judaism centered around the authoritative Mosaic Torah, we find an Enochic corpus, presented as sacred scripture, embodying the divine wisdom necessary for salvation for those who live in the last times."[43]

Not only is the payoff of Enoch's instruction different from traditional wisdom, the manner in which knowledge gets acquired differs as well. While those living in the last times—that is, those who read and used the Enochic books—received the written Enochic wisdom, the source of that wisdom was God via revelation to the patriarch. Enoch did not acquire his wisdom through some earthly sage; it does not reside in a Torah needing to be unpacked by some teacher. In this sense, Enoch the sage is more akin to a wisdom figure like Job, whose questions about theodicy elicited a response from heaven. Whereas Enoch goes up to heaven and descends with wisdom, Job has heaven come to him. The result is essentially the same, however—an encounter with the Almighty.[44] This mechanism of acquiring knowledge does not characterize the Israelite sapiential tradition of which Sirach is more representative. While Ben Sira may regard his teaching as in some sense "inspired," he receives it in a more mundane manner, through study of the Law and the accumulated wisdom of the sages and through observation of the way that the world works.

WISDOM, INSTRUCTION AND SOCIAL LOCATION

With respect to the problem of social location, Sirach almost certainly derives from a formal pedagogical context, however we might imagine

---

[42] Kampen, "Response."

[43] Nickelsburg, "Enochic Wisdom," 127.

[44] On Job as a sage, see S. Terrien, "Job as a Sage," in Gammie and Perdue, *The Sage in Israel*, 231–42 and on revelatory knowledge in Job, see R. Albertz, "The Sage and Pious Wisdom in the Book of Job: The Friends' Perspective," in Gammie and Perdue, *The Sage in Israel*, 251–52.

the particular institution of instruction. Much of the context of Ben Sira's teaching indicates that this wisdom sage trains aspiring young scribe/sages for careers in public service.[45] Topics such as behavior at banquets, in law courts, etc. suggest a location of formal career training rather than a family context. Ben Sira appeals explicitly to the uneducated to come to his "house of instruction" (51:23) so that they might gain wisdom, and thereby "silver and gold," i.e., success. The term "wisdom school" would seem a most appropriate description of Sirach's social location, if by the term "school" we simply mean a formal pedagogical context in which teachers instruct students. Like more traditional Jewish wisdom material, might the constituent parts of *1 Enoch* have been transmitted in similar social contexts, i.e., the family, the royal court, the temple, or the "school"?

Scholars have increasingly come to understand apocalyptic literature as the product of learned circles.[46] If these texts do come from educated elites, there is a limited range of places in the social landscape of ancient Judaism to find such learning. The royal court, the Temple or the school are the most likely places, since these institutions would have had the most invested in writing, interpreting and teaching ancient texts and traditions. We should consider cult and education together in this instance, since in the period of the Second Temple scribes and priests appeared to have had a close association, with the traditional priestly function of teaching the Law perhaps moving more into the purview of the learned scribe, who worked as a priestly retainer.[47] This conclusion echoes Stone's suggestion that the sorts of "scientific" speculations found in parts of *1 Enoch* may well have originated with circles "of educated men and may possibly have been associated with the traditional intellectuals, the wise and the priests."[48]

---

[45] For the designation scribe/sage, see R.A. Horsley and P. Tiller, "Ben Sira and the Sociology of the Second Temple," *Second Temple Studies III: Studies in Politics, Class and Material Culture* (P.R. Davies and J.M. Halligan, eds.; JSOTSup 340; Sheffield: Sheffield Academic Press, 2002) 99–103.

[46] See, for example, Stone, "Book of Enoch and Judaism"; J.Z. Smith, "Wisdom and Apocalyptic," *Map is Not Territory: Studies in the History of Religions* (SJLA 23; Leiden: Brill, 1978) 67–87; J.J. Collins, *The Apocalyptic Imagination* (New York: Crossroad, 1984) 30; Horsley, "Social Relations," 100–15; Grabbe "Social Setting," 32–5.

[47] Horsley and Tiller "Ben Sira," 99–103; Horsley, "Social Relations," 106; "Who Has Been Tested," 82–7. For an argument that scribes did not constitute a class independent of priests, see S. Fraade, "'They Shall Teach Your Statutes to Jacob': Priest, Scribe and Sage in Second Temple Times" (unpublished paper). I am grateful to the author for making the paper available to me.

[48] Stone, "Book of Enoch and Judaism," 73.

Even though *1 Enoch* is pseudonymous and lacks specific information about social location(s), I think the cumulative evidence points to a school context, that is, circles of teachers and students, for this material. The individual Enochic works that I have examined give evidence of the transmission and adaptation of various "scholarly" matters, especially astronomical, cosmological and meteorological lore. The incorporation of sapiential language and forms, the presence of instruction with the purpose of character formation and the emphasis on transmission to future generations in the form of books all constitute signposts going down that road. Enoch's own roles as ancient wisdom figure and as "scribe of righteousness" (12:4) may provide further indication of the importance of the learned scribe/sage in the generation and transmission of Enochic revelatory wisdom. Even though the content of the teaching and the authority that gives it status may differ from traditional Israelite wisdom, the school remains the most prominent social location where all of the factors outlined above coalesce.

Yet to suggest a social location for this material is not the same thing as identifying a social group to which those teachers and students might belong. So, while it might be enticing to go the next step and see *1 Enoch* and Ben Sira as representing antagonistic wisdom schools hotly contesting their different and competing views of wisdom—as tempting as such a recreation might be—the analysis pursued here cannot really lead us there. John Kampen has offered a persuasive argument for why we might hesitate to take this tantalizing step. Kampen sees "no evidence to suggest that Jewish groups used wisdom as a category for differentiating themselves from one another in ways that led to concrete social manifestations."[49] That is, Jews in the Second Temple period disagreed about a number of issues—one could cite Temple, calendar, eschatology or Torah as possibilities. Disagreements over these matters would have been fundamental to the formation of concrete political and social divisions within Jewish society. Whereas wisdom's content may make a decisive difference, wisdom *per se* does not appear to fall into this category of possible areas of divisive disagreement. Kampen argues that "wisdom and instruction are merely readily available and comprehensible servants" to those competitions and disagreements.[50] As such wisdom and instruction do not constitute categories for self-

---

[49] Kampen, "Response."
[50] Ibid.

definition in a text; they are tools to express, articulate or formulate that self-definition.

So, I return briefly to Stone's caution about identifying social groups behind texts with which I began this paper. While I think that the presence of wisdom and instruction in parts of *1 Enoch* provide a plausible location for these works in the social landscape of ancient Judaism, we cannot take that same evidence of wisdom and instruction as offering testimony for knowing who those teachers and students were, with what group or community they might have been associated, or what their relationship was to other teachers, schools, or learned circles. Scholars will have to look elsewhere for the clues to brave answers to those questions.

CHAPTER EIGHT

BEN SIRA ON THE SAGE AS EXEMPLAR

> Autobiography is overrated.
>
> —Susan Werner, October 30, 2007

In the Fall of 2007, Susan Werner, a well-known singer and songwriter, came to Lehigh University, where I teach, to perform music from her newest project, "The Gospel Truth," in which she adopts the voices of different types of people—believers to sort-of believers to agnostics—in order to comment on and challenge aspects of contemporary Christianity in America.[1] When one of my students, blithely assuming that all the lyrics represented Ms. Werner's own beliefs, asked her how she could hold these different positions at the same time, Ms. Werner replied with the quote that serves as the epigram above. At the time of her appearance at Lehigh, I was writing this paper, and Ms. Werner's caution about presuming that what someone says or writes is first and foremost autobiographical prompted me to think more intently about the extent to which scholars have focused on autobiography in the Wisdom of Ben Sira, an attention that potentially obscures any rhetorical functions such passages might have. That is, scholars often take certain features of the book, particularly the use of first-person pronouns, at their face value, but when given a close reading, these passages, whether or not they reflect Ben Sira's personal experience, work to construct an ideal sage who is lifted up before the student/reader of the book as an exemplar to be emulated. Moreover, the way the first-person passages function in Ben Sira might be compared to the way that pseudepigraphical authorship works in a book like *Jubilees*.

In current scholarly literature and conversation, Hindy Najman has written about the pseudepigraphical attribution of Second Temple Jewish works to figures from the ancient past. In *Seconding Sinai*, she questioned the extent to which, in the Second Temple period, we can

---

[1] For Susan Werner, go to www.susanwerner.com. This article is a thoroughly revised version of the paper I gave in the Hellenistic Judaism Section at the 2007 Annual Meetings of the SBL in San Diego.

distinguish sharply "between the *transmission* and the *interpretation* of biblical traditions."[2] There she describes the appearance in texts such as *Jubilees* of what she calls Mosaic discourse, "a discourse tied to a founder," in which "to rework an earlier text is to update, interpret, and develop its content in a way that claims to be an authentic expression of the law already accepted as authoritatively Mosaic."[3] In this manner, attribution to a pseudonymous author legitimizes the attendant interpretations and ideologies that the pseudepigraphical text's "real" author expresses. Pseudepigraphy, then, plays a central role in establishing the authority of the text, its contents and claims.

More recently, Najman has extended this work on pseudepigraphy to ask how these authorizing figures—people like Moses, Enoch or Ezra—serve as exemplars and how they function in text-production and text-interpretation.[4] Exemplary figures work on two levels. On the primary level, the exemplar, someone such as Moses, does more than simply confer authority on the pseudepigraphical text. The author's act of effacing himself via the use of "pseudonymous attribution should be seen as a metaphorical device, operating at the level of the text as a whole, whereby the actual author emulates and self-identifies as an exemplar." His emulation of the exemplar in pseudepigraphy should be considered "a spiritual discipline, an asceticism of self-effacement."[5] The exemplar thus plays a *revelatory role* and thereby produces a *prophetic text*. So, in the case of *Jubilees*, both the Angel of the Presence and Moses are the exemplary figures to whom the discourse of *Jubilees* is attributed. The angel dictates the heavenly tablets to Moses, the exemplary scribe, who accurately writes what he hears—so, as Najman observes, "at the level of authorship the text is both angelic and Mosaic."[6] Whereas we understand *Jubilees* to be *interpreting* previous texts, the self-presentation is as prophetic revelation. Whereas in much biblical scholarship, the categories of revelation and interpretation are often considered distinct

---

[2] H. Najman, *Seconding Sinai: The Development of Mosaic Discourse in Second Temple Judaism* (JSJSup 77; Leiden: Brill, 2003) 8.

[3] Ibid., 13.

[4] See, for example, "How Should We Contextualize Pseudepigrapha? Imitation and Emulation in 4 Ezra," *Flores Florentino: Dead Sea Scrolls and Other Early Jewish Studies in Honour of Florentino García Martínez* (A. Hilhorst, É. Puech, E. Tigchelaar, eds; JSJSup 122; Leiden: Brill, 2007) 529–36 and her paper delivered at the Fourth International Enoch Seminar, "Reconsidering *Jubilees*: Prophecy and Exemplarity."

[5] Najman, "How Should We Contextualize," 535 (both quotes).

[6] Najman, "Reconsidering *Jubilees*," 14.

from one another, Najman challenges us to take the pseudepigraphical self-presentation of works like *Jubilees* and *4 Ezra* seriously and to
see revelation *as* interpretation, however paradoxical that might sound
initially.

Such a reconceptualization of revelation in texts that appeal to exemplary figures is deeply connected with a longing to reestablish intimacy
with the divine that was lost in the destruction of the first temple—a
destruction that was never really overcome. As Najman puts it, "One
goal of revelation in the second temple period is to recover a lost relationship between God and humanity. Thus, the desire for revelation is
the aspiration to approach and perhaps even imitate divine perfection
by recovering an idyllic past and imagining an inspired future."[7]

On the secondary level, exemplars can function *within* texts. So, in
Jubilees even though Enoch, Noah and Abraham do not *author* the
work, they act as "exemplars to the reader of how to be worthy of the
heavenly tablets."[8] In the way that he casts these figures, *Jubilees'* author,
in toto, argues for what it means to be exemplary and to be worthy of
the revelation of prophecy.

In her work on *4 Ezra*, Najman explains most fully what she intends
by invoking the idea of exemplarity. There, "Ezra," the pseudonymous
author of the text, imitates other exemplars, such as Moses, Jeremiah
and Daniel, but in that *4 Ezra's* "real" author identifies himself as Ezra, he
also emulates the founder of the discourse. In that sense, then, Najman
distinguishes between imitation and emulation—being like someone or
identifying with someone. Emulation of an exemplar is akin to metaphor;
it is "pregnant with indeterminate implications."[9]

Although Najman has developed and employed the concepts of a
discourse tied to a founder and exemplarity in order to take seriously
the pseudepigraphical frameworks that are associated with founding
figures, as I have thought about the idea of exemplarity, I have wondered
about the extent to which it might help to clarify or provide insight into
the discursive strategies employed in texts that might not be so obviously linked to a founder. One such text is the Wisdom of Ben Sira,
and in what follows I want to engage in a bit of a thought experiment
to see how exemplarity might illuminate certain rhetorical features of

---

[7] Ibid., 6.
[8] Ibid., 15.
[9] Najman, "How Should We Contextualize," 534.

this important wisdom text. One of Najman's observations about *4 Ezra* provides a good place to begin: "So, we seem to be able to identify a thread here [i.e., in the pursuit of perfection] of using exemplary figures to construct paths of living—in texts and in people. The two, we might say are inextricably linked."[10]

If a wisdom text like Ben Sira is meant to do anything at all, it is to "construct paths for living." Indeed, even in a surface reading of the book we encounter an abundance of "practical" proverbs meant to proscribe certain actions—so, for example, 5:8, "Do not rely on dishonest wealth, for it will not benefit you on the day of calamity"—or to prescribe certain ways of behaving—e.g., 7:32, "Stretch out your hand to the poor, so that your blessing may be complete." But as many scholars have pointed out, the book is much more than a collection of dos and don'ts. Ben Sira also incorporates into his instruction hymns, prayers, a centrally located discourse where wisdom praises herself (chap. 24) and, of course, the Praise of the Ancestors in which he praises selected heroes of Israel's past (chaps. 44–50). Whereas there might not be any obvious overall structure to the book, Ben Sira employs an array of strategies that are designed to coerce his reader, albeit subtly, to adopt and internalize his teaching.[11] As one way of achieving that larger goal, he holds up the ideal sage, with whom he identifies, as someone to be emulated. That is, the ideal sage, and perhaps Ben Sira himself, serves as an exemplar to his students. In some crucial ways in Sirach, the sage plays a very similar role to that of Moses in *Jubilees* or of Ezra in *4 Ezra*. Moreover, in Sirach exemplarity works on the same two levels that Najman describes. On the primary and authorial plane, the ideal sage (Ben Sira) is the producer of the text and the founder of the discourse, who claims to have prophetic inspiration (see below). On the secondary level within the text, the Praise of the Ancestors invokes various figures from Israel's history as exemplars. For reasons of space, I will focus in this paper only on the primary level, that of the ideal sage who is both author and exemplar.

---

[10] H. Najman, "The Quest for Perfection in Ancient Judaism." Forthcoming essay in French and English. ["La Recherche de la Perfection dans le Judaïsme Ancien," where the English is translated, "Ainsi on est capable d'identifier une trame ici de personnages exemplaires pour tracer des chemins de vie à la fois dans les textes et dans la réalité. On peut dire des deux qu'ils sont liés de manière inextricable."]

[11] See Chapter 2, "From Generation to Generation: The Sage as Father in Early Jewish Literature."

Three distinct features of Ben Sira's book illuminate how he employs exemplarity and how he constructs the ideal sage as an exemplar: (1) the discourse of the father-son language of instruction; (2) the first-person speeches; and (3) the famous meditation on the activity of the scribe in 38:34c–39:11. Two of the three are characterized by use of first-person pronouns. While it is tempting to see the "real" or autobiographical Ben Sira as the primary subject of these passages, and most scholars read the book this way, we cannot assume that this is the case. Besides whatever personal experience might be reflected here, these sections offer a deliberate *self-presentation*. That is, through his authorial "voice" we hear how Ben Sira wants his reader to perceive the "I" who speaks here, and, as we shall see, the "I" passages serve a specific function in the book. Consequently, we should exercise caution when claiming that we can gain any significant insight into Ben Sira's personality, since upon reflection we find the "I" of Ben Sira to be just as constructed as the "I" of Moses in *Jubilees* or the "I" of Ezra in *4 Ezra*.

The Sage as Father

Throughout his book, Ben Sira adopts the mantle and voice of his students' father. Although a common feature of wisdom literature, this device is not used innocently, and Ben Sira employs this identification to great effect. The various features that feed into this larger rhetorical strategy limit the ability of his students (or his readers who are also by extension adopted as children) to decide on their own whether or not to adopt the values that he propounds. As a claimant to the role of father, he obligates his students to internalize his values just as they ought to adopt those of their "real-life" fathers.[12] So, for example, in chapters 1 and 2, Ben Sira emphasizes that true wisdom is grounded in creation and in "fear of the Lord," a phrase that appears seventeen times in those chapters. Chapter 3 then begins, "Listen to me, your father, O children," which introduces a long poem on parents' unconditional authority over children. By identifying himself as a father to these students, the sage effectively assumes the parental authority over them, a relationship that he connects directly with proper reverence for God: "Whoever forsakes

---

[12] For more details on how Ben Sira accomplishes this goal, see Chapter 2 "From Generation to Generation."

a father is like a blasphemer, and whoever angers a mother is cursed by the Lord" (3:16).

This fictive parental relationship appears in numerous passages, introducing poems on important practical and theological subjects. Some of these connect with the sage's first-person accounts elsewhere in the book. I will offer just a few examples here. The poem in 6:23–31 begins with "Listen, my child, and accept my judgment; do not reject my counsel," an appeal that stands at the head of a poem on submission to wisdom in language and images that anticipate the sage's own search for Wisdom described in the first-person poem in 51:13–22. Sirach 16:24–25 ("Listen to me, my child, and acquire knowledge, and pay close attention to my words. I will impart discipline precisely and declare knowledge accurately") opens a long poem on the nature of creation. Similarly in 42:15, the beginning of another poem on creation that leads into the Praise of the Ancestors, the sage says, "I will now call to mind the works of the Lord, and will declare what I have seen." The address, "Listen to me, my child," stands in the middle of a short section of practical wisdom teaching on moderation in 31:19–24. Finally, 39:12–13 ("I have more on my mind to express; I am full like the full moon. Listen to me, my children, and blossom like a rose growing by a stream of water") introduces a hymn in praise of God. Furthermore, these two small verses contain language reminiscent of Wisdom's self-praise in chapter 24, a central passage for understanding exemplarity in Sirach, as we shall shortly see.

Ben Sira's assumption of parental authority over his students goes well beyond simply trading on a stock wisdom image. It is part of a larger discourse, the use of which enables him to present his instruction to the student/reader with the unstated expectation that the student will acquiesce to it, accept it and internalize it. How could a son do otherwise and still fulfill the commandment to honor one's parents, one emphasized so early in the book? In short, as Ben Sira merges the pedagogical with the parental and adopts the role of his students' father, the students are rhetorically coerced to make a similar identification—to place themselves in the position of children who are obligated to obey. With respect to the construction of the sage as an exemplar, father-son discourse contributes to that enterprise. The sage sets himself up as one who should be emulated. In other words, his goal is for students not only to do as he says, but to do as he does. Fathers expect their children to internalize their values in order to resist any external attempts to subvert them, and ultimately the children will be able to take their father's place and preserve their father's memory in the community (see

30:4–6). In this manner, the sage's adoption of the role of father is closely linked with the first-person passages in which Ben Sira constructs his ideal sage, an ideal that also serves as an exemplar. These passages, to which I now turn, operate on two levels: (1) they speak directly to the student of the accomplishments of the sage and (2) they are Ben Sira's self-presentation as the ideal sage who has himself reached the goal of acquiring wisdom.

Speeches Using First-person Pronouns

Somewhat surprisingly, we do not encounter first-person speech very frequently in Sirach, but those passages where we find the authorial "I" have an importance that outstrips the amount of space they occupy. As we shall see, each of these passages is reflected in Ben Sira's comments about the sage and his activities in 38:34c–39:11. But before moving to that famous passage, we need to review briefly each of the "autobiographical" passages.

22:25–23:6: The first-person speech of 22:25–26 makes the transition from the preceding poem on friendship to the prayer of petition that follows in 22:27–23:6. The prayer itself asks God to protect the sage from various sins, especially sins of speech and thought, and from enemies. Several aspects of the passage are notable. First, it treats speech, an important topic in Sirach. Second, and more importantly, the prayer twice invokes God as Father. The first time in 23:1 the sage beseeches God to preserve him from sins in speech and thought, "otherwise my mistakes may be multiplied and my sins abound, and I may fall before my adversaries, and my enemy may rejoice over me." The second time is verse 4, where it precedes a petition that God remove evil desire from the sage. We find in 51:1–12, a prayer of thanksgiving in which the author thanks God for rescue from enemies, especially from those who have used slanderous speech, that God has answered the sage's petitions (see below). These two prayers are the only ones in the book that employ first-person speech. The other major prayer, 36:1–22, contains no first-person speech.

24:30–34: This famous chapter is critical to understanding the sage's self-presentation and the idea of exemplarity in Sirach. Wisdom's famous self-praise finds her first ministering in the temple and second becoming embodied in the "book of the covenant of the Most High God, the

law that Moses commanded us." In verses 25–33, Ben Sira plays out
an extended metaphor for the law featuring water.[13] The law *overflows*
with wisdom (v. 25), *runs over* with understanding (v. 26), *pours forth*
instruction (v. 27). Wisdom's thoughts are "more abundant than the
sea, and her counsel deeper than the great abyss" (v. 29). At verse 30,
the discourse shifts to the authorial "I":

> 30   And as for me, I was like a canal from a river
>   like a water channel, into a garden.
> 31   I said, "I will water my garden,
>   and drench my flower beds."
>   And lo, my canal became a river,
>   and my river a sea.
> 32   I will again make instruction shine forth like dawn,
>   and I will make it clear from far away.
> 33   I will again pour out teaching like prophecy,
>   and leave it to all future generations.
> 34   Observe that I have not labored for myself alone
>   but for all who seek wisdom.

By using water as the basic metaphor, Ben Sira argues for continuity
between his teaching and Wisdom. As his small canal *becomes* a river,
then *becomes* a sea, the metaphor finally links "the sea" of heavenly
Wisdom described in verse 29 directly with wisdom/teaching of the
sage, who serves as a channel for Wisdom. Verse 32 changes the metaphor from water to one of light—"I will again make instruction shine
forth like the dawn, and I will make it clear from far away." Ben Sira
reprises his fluvial metaphor in verse 33, only this time prophecy gets
drawn into the picture—"I will again *pour out* teaching (διδασκαλία)
like prophecy (προφητεία) and leave it to all future generations." Verse
34 concludes with the claim that the sage's labors are "for all who seek
wisdom."

Two points are of note in this passage. First, the "I" of the text claims
to have tapped into primordial, heavenly Wisdom, which authorizes the
sage's teaching. Second, although in this verse the sage stops short of
claiming outright that his teaching is the product of revelatory activity,

---

[13] After writing this section of the paper, I read L.G. Perdue's article, "Ben Sira and
the Prophets," in which he makes several similar points to the ones I make in this section [*Intertextual Studies in Ben Sira and Tobit* (J. Corley and V. Skemp, eds.; CBQMS
38; Washington, DC: Catholic Biblical Association of America, 2005) 132–54]. On this
passage see also my paper, "*Jubilees*, Sirach, and Sapiential Tradition," presented at the
Fourth International Enoch Seminar, Camaldoli, Italy, July 9, 2007.

the comparison "like prophecy" comes very close. If we consider the sage's claims in the light of the wisdom poem in 4:11–19, we see that he almost certainly understands the source of his instruction as revelation. In 4:17–18, Ben Sira notes the tortuous discipline that Wisdom exacts. The results of perseverance, however, are that Wisdom will gladden and will reveal (גליתי) her secrets (מסתרי) to her followers.[14] The verb is significant for the construction of the sage, in that elsewhere it denotes divine revelation, particularly in 42:19 where God "reveals (מגלה) the traces of hidden things."[15] As J. Aitken notes about this passage, "As he [i.e., Ben Sira] presumably saw himself as a true disciple of Wisdom, he would expect Wisdom to reveal her 'secrets' to him (cf. 4:18)."[16]

Both of the foregoing claims reinforce even more dramatically the sage's calls throughout the book for his students/children to listen to him—after all, the source and authority of his teaching is Wisdom herself, who has revealed things to him, and it has the status of prophecy! We can see a similar authorizing mechanism in the book of *Jubilees*, a work usually thought to be quite different from Sirach. There the halachic prescriptions that the author advocates exist primordially on the heavenly tablets, and the revelation to Moses links heavenly authority with earthly instruction. In a comparable manner, primordial Wisdom in Sirach connects heaven and earth, authorizes Ben Sira's teaching and serves as the vehicle of revelation to the sage.[17] The effect is that Ben Sira's claim in verse 33 that he "will pour out teaching like prophecy" places him, if not in the line of prophets, at least as the recipient of heavenly revelation not dissimilar from that of the prophets.[18]

---

[14] The Greek translation uses the third person here, but the Hebrew has Wisdom speak in the first person. On the importance of this passage, see J.K. Aitken, "Apocalyptic Revelation and Early Jewish Wisdom Literature," *New Heaven and New Earth, Prophecy and the Millennium: Essays in Honour of Anthony Gelston* (P.J. Harland and R. Hayward, eds.; Leiden: Brill, 1999) 181–93.

[15] For more detail, see ibid., 189–90.

[16] Ibid., 190.

[17] For more detailed argumentation, see Wright, "*Jubilees*, Sirach and Sapiential Tradition."

[18] Perdue draws the conclusion from 24:30–33 that "Ben Sira sought to restore prophecy to a legitimate place in religious history (although not his contemporary present), not only by claiming that its inspiration had passed to the sage, but also by asserting that some of their unfulfilled statements awaited divine enactment, known only to the inspired sages" ("Ben Sira and the Prophets," 137). P.C. Beentjes thinks that verse 33 refers to the sage as "a kind of inspired mediator," whose interpretations of Torah are "like prophecy" ("Prophets and Prophecy in the Book of Ben Sira," *Prophets, Prophecy, and Prophetic Texts in Second Temple Judaism* [M.H. Floyd and R.D. Haak,

Chapters 25–26: Immediately following these dramatic claims, Ben Sira reverts back to more traditional wisdom teaching, taking up the topics of praiseworthy and loathsome people and good and bad women. In these chapters, he employs five numerical proverbs—25:1, 2, 7; 26:5, 28—several of which introduce longer poems. The topics covered, which are largely practical in nature, are not of as much interest to me as the forms by which Ben Sira frames them. Elsewhere in Israelite literature, numerical proverbs are characteristically articulated in the first-person singular, and in that respect Ben Sira has employed a conventional form.[19] But, more to the point, they are characteristic of both wisdom teaching and prophecy—two prominent examples being the numerical proverbs in Proverbs 30 and in Amos 1 and 2.[20] If we are not sensitive to the use and origin of the form, the transition from chapter 24 to chapter 25 might seem jarring, even inexplicable. Why move from a masterful theological statement about the sages as recipients of heavenly revelation to the much more mundane topics of traditional wisdom? Here the *form* makes the comment. By using a prophetic/sapiential form, Ben Sira reinforces the relationship between revelation and sapiential instruction in the person of the sage, and he emphasizes that even such practical teaching is the product of revelation. He thus confers the authority that he claims for the sage in chapter 24 on a specific body of instruction.

33:16–19: In this famous passage, the sage places himself at the end of a line of predecessors, after whom he "gleans." Yet, apparently much remains from the harvest, since what he gathers at the end of the grape picking fills his wine press. One wonders whether the reference to being "the last to keep vigil" in verse 16a is an allusion to prophetic activity, since both Ezekiel and Habakkuk use a similar metaphor of keeping watch. If so, is he claiming continuity with previous wisdom teachers, with prophets, or with both? In verse 18, Ben Sira reiterates almost verbatim the claim of 24:34 that the sage's labors are for others and not just for himself. Whereas the earlier passage does not mention any

---

eds.; Library of Hebrew Bible/Old Testament Studies 427; London/New York: Clark, 2006] 135–50).

[19] There is also a numerical proverb in 23:16, although that one is in the third person, not the first person.

[20] Ben Sira also uses the form of the prophetic "Woe," but again these are in the third person; see 12:12–14 and 41:8.

specific task, here Ben Sira's labor has a clear referent, his gleaning, the product of which is the instruction that he offers to his students.

34:9–13: In these verses the sage underscores his experience and education. Verses 9–11 present a third-person description of the educated and uneducated in typical wisdom style, and verse 11 focuses on travel that produces "cleverness." Verse 12, then, indicates the sage's own status as an educated person by paralleling the earlier third-person description of the educated. So, "an educated person knows many things, and one with much experience knows what he is talking about" (v. 9). The sage then claims, "I have seen many things in my travels, and I understand much more than I can express" (v. 12); that is, he has exceeded by far the qualifications for being educated. Moreover, this experience has enabled the sage to escape danger—probably an exaggeration that plays on the danger of travel in order to show the depth of the sage's experience.

39:12–13, 32–35: These verses form an inclusio for the hymn in praise of God given in 39:16–31, which follows on the heels of Ben Sira's meditation on the sage. The first two verses introduce the hymn. As in 34:12, the sage claims that he has much to express, but here he compares what he has to say to the full moon, which emphasizes both fullness and illumination. This characterization is similar to another first-person description of the sage's wisdom as being illuminating, 34:32, except there the comparison was to the dawn—presumably highlighting the quality of the sun's bright light. In verse 13, Ben Sira addresses his students as children and direct speech follows, comprised of a series of imperatives, all dependent on the first one, "Listen to me." Thus, in verses 12–15 the sage exploits two separate devices, the voice of the authorial "I" and the adoption of parental authority. The similes that Ben Sira employs in verses 13 and 14 feature the rose and the lily together with the aroma of incense, all of which recall Wisdom's self-description in 24:13–17. The subsequent imperatives—"sing," "bless," "ascribe" and "give thanks"—lead up to the hymn itself, which is presented as "what you shall say in thanksgiving."

Verses 32–35 conclude the hymn. Verse 32 contains the only first-person language in the passage, but it is nonetheless suggestive. The phrase "from the beginning" recalls—and perhaps is intended to allude to—two other passages: 24:9 where Wisdom was present "in the beginning" and 39:20, within the hymn, where the identical phrase speaks of God's transcendence over time. Does use of this phrase connect the sage's understanding and thought with that of heavenly Wisdom and God? Or is it a statement about the sage's inspired insight into creation and God's intentions, particularly in light of the opening verses of the hymn, which refer to creation?[21] If he is indeed implicitly invoking such connections, then his remark in verse 32 about leaving his teaching in writing takes on added significance, since elsewhere wisdom and books/writing are closely related. In 24:23 Wisdom is embodied in a "book," and later in 50:27, the sage puts knowledge, understanding and wisdom in a "book." In this case, to conclude with an appeal to writing might also represent a claim to authority for his teaching, since his book is also in a way the embodiment of wisdom (or Wisdom).

42:15; 43:32: Both in an introduction and a conclusion to the praise of God's creation that leads up to the Praise of the Ancestors, the sage appeals to what he has seen of God's works. He begins with an appeal to personal experience, "I will call to mind the works of the Lord and will declare what I have seen." Thus, what follows in this long poem is presented as the sage's own insight into the wonders of creation. Yet his relating of the things he has seen represents more than his human observations of the natural world. Beyond simple description, the sage often explains the *purpose* of natural phenomena. It is certainly tempting to ask how he knows such things. Given (1) that Ben Sira sees himself as having a sort of prophetic inspiration (24:30–33), (2) that Wisdom will "reveal her secrets" to those who follow her (4:18), and (3) that God reveals the secrets of creation and history (probably via Wisdom; 42:19), it seems likely that the sage's access to heavenly Wisdom, who speaks of herself as traversing God's creation in 24:3–6, has revealed this knowledge to him.[22] At the end of the poem, the sage again appeals to personal observation, but this time he emphasizes that he has seen "but few of God's works" (43:32), an acknowledgment of his position vis-à-vis God.[23]

---

[21] Based on Ben Sira's wide array of comments on creation, Aitken argues "that through studying the creation one can come to know God's secrets." He further compares Sirach to 4QInstruction: "For Ben Sira, as for the author of *Sapiential Work A* [i.e., 4QInstruction], creation and history are the sources for revelation and the understanding of God's plan" (Both quotes, "Apocalyptic Revelation," 190).

[22] See Aitken, "Apocalyptic Revelation," 189–90.

[23] The Greek in this place has the plural "we," but the first-person singular in the Hebrew forms a balanced inclusion with the first-person singular in 42:15 and is to be

50:25–26: These two verses comprise a numerical proverb in the style of Amos 1 and 2.

50:27: This epilogue to the sage's teaching contains a nexus of knowledge, understanding, a book and wisdom. From it we also learn the name of our author (that is, outside of the grandson's prologue to his translation). The wisdom that has poured forth—and note here the revival of the water metaphor so central to claims about the sage's prophet-like inspiration—from the sage's mind has been put into a book. This description is remarkably like that of heavenly Wisdom being embodied in the "book of the covenant," although I imagine that in 50:27 "wisdom" should most likely have a lower case "w." Nevertheless, the implicit comparison between heavenly Wisdom residing in a book and the sage's wisdom being preserved in a book, in my view, represents a claim on the part of the sage for the authoritative status of what he has written, and it reinforces that same claim in 39:32.

Chapter 51: This chapter contains two discreet first-person speeches. The first, 51:1–12, is a psalm of thanksgiving for deliverance from enemies, which compares closely in certain respects with the petitionary prayer for deliverance in chapter 22. The major point is that the author's enemies have used slander and lies against him, looking for a way to destroy him, but God rescued him after he prayed that God not forsake him.[24]

The chapter's second first-person speech, 51:13–25, provides an important clue to discovering the rhetorical function of the first-person sections.[25] Many scholars look at this section as autobiography, but I think that such an assessment underestimates what the poem accomplishes in the book, however much it does or does not tell us about Ben

---

preferred. I also wonder whether the idea that the sage has not seen everything might also go back to the thought he expresses in 3:23, when he says, "[F]or more than you can understand has been shown to you." On this passage, see Chapter 5, "Fear the Lord and Honor the Priest: Ben Sira as Defender of the Jerusalem Priesthood," 114–18. For a different view, see Aitken, "Apocalyptic Revelation," 188–90.

[24] We might also favorably compare this psalm to biblical psalms of this type, but my interest is in the way that the psalm functions internally to the book.

[25] The text of this prayer is different in the Greek, Ms B and 11QPsalms[a]. So, for example, Greek and Ms B have "in prayer" in 51:13, whereas 11QPsalms[a] lacks the phrase. The textual differences among these three witnesses do not affect the larger argument I am making here, however.

Sira himself. In the poem the young sage goes searching for Wisdom. His efforts are erotically tinged, and he is undaunted in his relentless pursuit of her. The first several verses reiterate much of what Ben Sira has advised his students to do in their own searches, and they hark back to a number of earlier passages. He sought wisdom in prayer and went to the temple to ask for her (vv. 13–14; cf. chap. 24), he "delighted in her," "walked on the straight path" and "followed her steps" (v. 15; cf. 4.17–18). As a result, he "made progress in her," prayed to God lamenting his ignorance, and ultimately found her. He gained her and now has her as a possession. Consequently he will praise her.

The poem, then, comprises a summary of and foundation for all the claims that the sage has made for himself throughout the book. It briefly charts the paradigmatic search for Wisdom that results in the sage gaining access to wisdom, achieving, and thus embodying within himself, the ideal that he sets before his students—being filled by Wisdom and transmitting it as prophecy for anyone searching for that same heavenly Wisdom. Here, the sage sets himself up as the ideal to be emulated. If one searches in the manner that the sage has searched and submits to Wisdom's discipline as the sage has, then that student will become the sage who has taken Wisdom as a possession. This poem purports to describe Ben Sira's own experience, but whether it does or not, it offers a powerful motivation for the student not simply to abide by the sage's teaching, but to emulate and then become the sage who produced it. As we will now see, it also forms the basis for the sage's ability to position himself as an ideal type.

THE MEDITATION ON THE SAGE—38:34C–39:11

Ben Sira's well-known description of the trades in 38:24–34b actually forms an introduction to a meditation on the activity of the ideal sage. The section begins, "The wisdom of the sage depends on the opportunity of leisure; only one who has little business can become wise." After his description of the tradespeople, Ben Sira exclaims in verse 34, "How different the one who devotes himself to the study of the law of the Most High!" How different indeed! Most commentators on this passage emphasize the objects of study for the sage—sayings of the famous, parables, proverbs, etc.—but it also provides important evidence for understanding the idea of the inspiration of the sages, particularly with the sage's endowment with a "spirit of understanding," as Leo Perdue has shown.[26] For my purposes, however, I want to draw attention to the sage's activities and the way that they are reflected in other significant passages in the book, especially in the first-person speeches.[27]

Sirach 39:1–3 describes the material with which the sage works:

1 He seeks out the wisdom (σοφία) of all the ancients,
   and is concerned with prophecies (προφητεία);
2 He preserves the sayings of the famous (διήγησιν ἀνδρῶν ὀνομαστῶν)
   and penetrates the subtleties of parables (στροφαῖς παραβολῶν);
3 he seeks out the hidden meanings of proverbs (ἀπόκρυφα παροιμιῶν)
   and is at home with the obscurities of parables (αἰνίγμασι παραβολῶν).

Here we see precisely the kinds of instruction that Ben Sira purveys in his book. Two elements of these verses are particularly important. First, Ben Sira concerns himself with what has come down to him in the tradition from his predecessors. The sage of 33:16 has already noted that he "gleans" from what others have left, but that with the gleanings "I filled my wine press." Second, Ben Sira emphasizes the obscure nature of these materials. Parables and proverbs can be subtle and obscure, and prophecies almost by their very nature have to be decoded.[28]

In 39:4, Ben Sira notes that the ideal sage travels in foreign lands and learns "what is good and evil in the human lot." Of course, the sage speaking in the first person has already made the same point in the short speech of 34:9–13. Verse 5 finds the sage early at prayer petitioning the Most High and asking pardon for sins. Ben Sira has already put such a prayer in the mouth of the sage as a first-person prayer, beseeching God to keep him from sin (22:27–23:6). As a result of his prayer, "if the great Lord is willing," the sage will "be filled with a spirit of understanding." Not everyone, then, receives this spirit, since God must be willing to give it.[29] The reception of the spirit is directly

---

[26] Perdue, "Ben Sira and the Prophets," 138–42.

[27] Perdue also discusses these activities, but he does not draw the lines of connection to these other passages.

[28] The evidence in Ben Sira suggests that he saw prophecy as foretelling the future. In 48:23–25, Isaiah has revealed to him "what was to occur at the end of time" and "hidden things before they happened," and in the prayer of 36:1–22, Ben Sira asks God to "fulfill the prophecies spoken in your name" (v. 20). Perdue argues that Ben Sira's inspiration enabled him to determine "the meaning of these prophecies about the future, including those that had not yet come to pass, due to his divine inspiration" ("Ben Sira and the Prophets," 153). See also Beentjes, "Prophets and Prophecy."

[29] Perdue, "Ben Sira and the Prophets," 140–41 and J.D. Levenson, who argues that Ben Sira's "use of pneumatic language to describe wisdom teaching (Sir 36:9) recalls

parallel to the following colon in which the sage will "*pour forth* words of wisdom." We have encountered this verb several times in the first-person speeches, and it is connected with the prophetic activity of the sage. In verse 6, Ben Sira notes that because God has endued the sage with wisdom and understanding, he will give thanks. Such a prayer of thanksgiving comes directly following this meditation on the sage, introduced by a first-person speech and presented as the very words that should be said.[30] Verse 7 also intimates that the sage will receive inspiration in that "[t]he Lord will direct his counsel and knowledge as he meditates on his mysteries (ἐν τοῖς ἀποκρύφοις αὐτοῦ)."

Finally verses 9–11, with the emphasis on memory, provide a link with the Praise of the Ancestors in chapters 44–50. Leaving behind a good memory is a central theme throughout Sirach, and it constitutes the primary means of achieving some kind of immortality. The sage repeatedly admonishes the proper upbringing of children so that one can have a good memory (see 30:1–6). Evil children bring shame both now and posthumously, and Ben Sira even thinks that no memory is better than having evil children (16:3). But here and in the Praise of the Ancestors, memory and fame are intimately linked. About the ideal sage we read:

> 9   Many will praise his understanding;
>   it will never be blotted out.
>   His memory will not disappear,
>   and his name will live through all generations.
> 10 Nations will speak of his wisdom,
>   and the congregation will proclaim his praise.
> 11 If he lives long, he will leave a name greater than a thousand,
>   and if he goes to rest, it is enough for him.

The ancestors whom Ben Sira singles out in chapters 44–50 have already achieved such praise and memory. Sirach 44:1 even begins, "Let us now sing the praises of famous men." Several verses in the introductory verses to the Praise of the Ancestors share vocabulary with 39:9–11

Psalm 119 and suggests that he regarded his own book as inspired" ("The Sources of Torah: Psalm 119 and the Modes of Revelation in Second Temple Judaism," *Ancient Israelite Religion: Essays in Honor of Frank Moore Cross* [P.D. Miller, Jr., P.D. Hanson, and S.D. McBride, eds.; Philadelphia: Fortress Press, 1987] 559–574, here 568).

[30] Although not a prayer in thanks for wisdom, a prayer of thanksgiving is included at the end of the book, but, as we saw, there it is for deliverance from enemies.

or have sentiments very close to it. So, about the famous ancestors
we read: they were "honored in their generations" (v. 7); their glory
"will never be blotted out" (v. 13); their names "live on generation
after generation" (v. 14); and "the assembly declares their wisdom and
the congregation proclaims their praise" (v. 15). Thus, the ideal sage
who achieves praise and fame and memory should ideally be included
among those famous ancestors whom Ben Sira separates out from the
history of Israel for special praise, and indeed, Ben Sira himself should
be included in that list.

The Sage as Exemplar

Even in this brief review, I think that we can see that the rhetorical force
of the father-son discourse, the first-person speeches and the meditation
on the ideal sage work together to construct the ideal sage as an exemplar for his students. His is not simply an example to be imitated, but
he is someone to be emulated. Furthermore, if we read the first-person
speeches as Ben Sira's deliberate attempt to construct an ideal sage who
serves as an exemplar rather than simply as a report of his first-hand
life experience, several similarities with the pseudepigraphical exemplars
that Najman discusses emerge. First, as in some pseudepigraphical texts,
Ben Sira's sage frames what he teaches as prophecy that is authorized
by a heavenly source. Although the sage's inspiration is not revelation
in an identical sense that we encounter revelation in *Jubilees*, *1 Enoch*
or *4 Ezra*, Ben Sira's sage does claim to have direct access to a source
of wisdom given by God that comes from God's inspiration. Second,
the sage sets himself up as one who must be emulated, identified with,
rather than one whose behavior should be imitated. Another way to put
it might be to ask—if one were simply to behave as Ben Sira advises,
would that be enough in his eyes? My suspicion is that it would not.
The sage's expressed goal is to pursue and court Wisdom, to possess
her. Once the student acquires her, walks in her paths and submits
to her discipline, he will achieve an understanding that enables him
to behave in all the ways that the sage teaches. The ideal sage, then, is
one who embodies Wisdom, and the student also can embody Wisdom
only inasmuch as he regards the sage as the exemplar to be emulated.
Third, the connection between Wisdom and a book (or perhaps more
generally writing) seen several times in Sirach—both with respect to the
"law" and to Ben Sira's own teaching—suggests that the sage understands

himself as producing an authoritative text, in a similar manner as the author of *Jubilees* understood his text to be authoritative.[31]

In certain respects, of course, Ben Sira and books like *Jubilees* or *4 Ezra* could not be more different. He does not experience, nor does he advocate, heavenly journeys or visions; he does not have any developed eschatology such as we encounter in these works. But one of my goals in this paper was to see if the idea of exemplarity helps to provide any new insights into the book. I can say at this stage that on the basis of this initial exercise, the idea has enabled me to understand more clearly some of Ben Sira's rhetorical objectives. If pseudonymous attributions to Moses in *Jubilees* or to Ezra in *4 Ezra* are "semantic enactments of emulation" that claim to find inspiration from the past and that "take utterly seriously the identification" with those figures, then exemplarity functions somewhat differently in Ben Sira. We do not encounter pseudonymous attribution in Sirach, but by deploying the discursive strategies that we have seen above to construct an ideal sage who functions as an exemplary figure, Ben Sira does take "utterly seriously" the idea that his students should identify with an exemplary figure. But as Ben Sira articulates it, that figure is not necessarily someone from the past; it is also Ben Sira who presents himself as an embodiment of the ideal sage. Furthermore, sapiential exemplarity (if we can call it that) locates inspiration, understood both as revealed by God in a prophetesque manner and as developed from the interpretations of the inherited tradition, in the corporate work of the sages as a class of people who produced, transmitted and preserved the Israelite wisdom/literary tradition.[32]

---

[31] See Wright, "*Jubilees*, Sirach, and Sapiential Tradition."
[32] Perdue, "Ben Sira and the Prophets," 133, makes a similar point.

CHAPTER NINE

B. SANHEDRIN 100b AND RABBINIC
KNOWLEDGE OF BEN SIRA

I am grateful to the editors of this volume for the chance to write in celebration of Professor Maurice Gilbert, whose work on the book of Ben Sira has been so influential. Several years ago Prof. Gilbert wrote a programmatic article on Ben Sira in a collection of essays entitled *Jewish Civilization in the Hellenistic-Roman Period*.[1] In this essay, Gilbert posed two questions about the rabbinic citations of the book of Ben Sira. He wrote,

1. The rabbinic quotations from that book generally are not literal. Segal reasons that the rabbis quoted from memory.[2] According to M. R. Lehmann, literalness was not required; the quotations were adapted to suit the later context because the book of Ben Sira was not a biblical book.[3] Which theory should we follow?
2. Were the quotations taken from a complete edition of Ben Sira without any additions? Or did the rabbis quote a florilegium?[4]

In an effort to begin to answer Gilbert's queries I will look in this essay at one important rabbinic text, B. Sanhedrin 100b, which contains both an extended discussion of the acceptability of reading Ben Sira and a number of "quotations" from the book.

The section on Ben Sira in Sanhedrin 100b begins as a commentary on M. Sanhedrin 10:1 where Akiba notes that those who read the "outside books" (ספרים החיצונים) have no share in the world to come. The first section of the talmudic commentary reports that R. Joseph understood Akiba's statement to forbid reading the book of Ben Sira. Abaye asks R. Joseph why this should be so since Ben Sira contains

---

[1] M. Gilbert, "The Book of Ben Sira: Implications for Jewish and Christian Traditions," *Jewish Civilization in the Hellenistic-Roman Period* (S. Talmon, ed.; Philadelphia: Trinity Press International, 1991) 81–91.
[2] M.H. Segal, "The Evolution of the Hebrew Text of Ben Sira," *JQR* 25 (1934–35) 135–36.
[3] M.R. Lehmann, "11QPs^a and Ben Sira," *RevQ* 11 (1983) 242–46.
[4] Gilbert, "The Book of Ben Sira," 85.

many things that the rabbis also say, and he adduces a number of passages as examples. The second section again begins with R. Joseph who says in reply to Abaye's objections, "We may expound to them the good things it contains." Another series of quotations follows. Altogether B. Sanhedrin 100b contains, depending on how one counts, ten different passages that purportedly come from Ben Sira. Each deserves some brief description.

1. "Do not strip the skin [of a fish] even from its ear, lest you spoil it, but roast it [all, the fish with the skin] in the fire and eat it with two loaves."[5] This Aramaic admonishment appears in none of the extant manuscripts of Ben Sira.

2. The second of Abaye's examples comes originally from Sir 42:9–10, a passage about daughters. In both the Masada scroll and Ms B from the Cairo genizah, this passage contains eight cola. The rabbinic quotation, given in Hebrew, contains seven, only six of which parallel the Ben Sira manuscripts. The one colon not found in the manuscripts concerns keeping one's daughter from witchcraft in her old age. In general the outlines of the thought are the same, but the wording and order of the lines differ widely between the rabbinic citation and the manuscripts.[6]

3. "Do not let anxiety enter your heart, for it has slain many a person." This third of Abaye's examples is an admonition in Aramaic that has no direct parallel in Ben Sira, although Segal argues that it "is a combination of several lines in our book."[7] Indeed some of the material from this quotation does occur in somewhat similar contexts in Ben Sira—30:21 "Do not give yourself over to grief"; 30:23c "For grief has killed [many]"; perhaps 14:1b, "Whose heart has not brought grief upon him" (as Segal corrects the Hebrew).[8] The similar content of Prov 12:25 cited immediately after this passage may also have influenced the form of the quotation.

---

[5] The translation here is adapted from I. Epstein, *The Babylonian Talmud* (London: Soncino, 1935).

[6] The Masada scroll and Ms B from the Cairo genizah have some textual variants between them. Although some terms are in common between the rabbinic passage and the manuscripts, the manuscripts are much closer to each other than to the rabbinic text.

[7] Segal, "Evolution," 143.

[8] Ibid., 112.

4. Abaye's fourth example, which is cited in Hebrew, "Keep the multitude from your house, and do not let everyone enter your house," derives from Sir 11:29. The first half of the citation seems to be a summarizing form of the second half, which parallels 11:29a (Ms A) very closely.[9]

5. The last of Abaye's citations is, like the first, given in Aramaic and is nowhere to be found in any Ben Sira text. "A thin-bearded man is very astute; a thick-bearded one is a fool. The one who blows in his glass is not thirsty. He who says, 'With what shall I eat my bread?' Take his bread from him. The one who parts his beard no one can overcome."

6. In reality the first part of the list of examples of the "good things" from Ben Sira that R. Joseph puts forward is actually comprised of five passages in Hebrew on wives and women.

(a) The first is an almost exact quote of Sir 26:3. Only one word in the Talmud differs from Cairo genizah Ms C (Talmud = בחיק, Ms C = ובחלק). The Talmud also agrees with Ms C and the Syriac translation in having the singular "he who fears" rather than the plural of the Greek.

(b) The next section on the evil wife appears to summarize the thought of Sir 25:23–26. One specific part of the citation, the talmudic injunction to divorce such a wife, is not found in the GKI recension of Ben Sira (no Hebrew is extant for these verses), but is found in GKII and the Syriac.

(c) The following sentence reproduces Sir 26:1 almost exactly except that the Talmud has יפה instead of טובה (Ms C) as a description of the good wife.

(d) Next the Talmud cites Sir 9:8a; 9:3b; 9:9a, b; 9:8c. Although the verse order does not agree with Cairo Ms A, the wording of the passages is often very close. Sanhedrin 100b reproduces almost exactly the text of 9:8a, and 9:3b differs substantially only in the verb (Talmud = תלכד, Ms A = תפול). The citation of 9:9a, b is somewhat complicated. The Talmud's אל תט אצל בעלה למסוך עמו יין ושכר is close in form to 9:9a, b in Ms A, עם בעלה אל תטעם וא[ל ת]סב עמו שכור. The Greek translation for this verse, however, is actually an injunction warning against drinking with a married *woman* rather than with her husband (μετὰ ὑπάνδρου γυναικὸς μὴ κάθου τὸ σύνολον). Either the Greek has mistranslated the Hebrew or the Hebrew of Ms A (and the Talmud)

---

[9] For the Hebrew text of Ben Sira I have used P.C. Beentjes, *The Book of Ben Sira in Hebrew* (VTSup 68: Leiden: Brill, 1997).

is corrupt. Perhaps the talmudic form of the verse has influenced the text of Ms A here.[10] The subsequent sentence in the Talmud is a fairly close representation of Ms A for 9:8c. Sanhedrin 100b reads כי בתואר אשה יפיה רבים רבים הושחתו compared with שחתו רבים [.]בעד אשה. The final talmudic clause "and numerous are those killed by her" looks like a summary of the preceding clause which has no close parallel in Ben Sira.

(e) Although a continuation of the section about women, the next several clauses come from Sir 11:29–34, a section that is textually corrupt in Ms A. The first clause, "and many are the blows sustained by peddlers," is a form of Sir 11:29b in Ms A, which itself probably does not reflect the original Ben Sira.[11] The following sentence takes part of 11:32a about sparks kindling embers and applies it to "those who seduce to adultery" rather than to those who enter one's house, the original context in Ben Sira. This sentence seems to end the section treating women.

7. There follows in both the Talmud and Ms A a quotation of Jer 5:27, the talmudic citation probably influencing the development of the manuscript tradition of Ben Sira.[12] Then comes a citation of 11:29a about people entering one's house which is identical to the one offered by Abaye earlier in Sanhedrin 100b.

8. The next section cites Sir 6:6 in a form close to Ms A. The Talmud reads, רבים יהיו דורשי שלומך גלה סודך לאחד מאלף; Ms A has a different word order for colon a and uses the more generic אנשי instead of דורשי. In colon b Ms A reads בעל סודך, not גלה סודך as in the Talmud, and it does not use the preposition before אחד.

9. The Talmud continues with Mic 7:5 and then Prov 27:1b attached to a clause of unknown origin, "Do not worry about tomorrow's trouble." These quotations are apparently also intended to be part of the "good things" in Ben Sira.

10. The end of Sanhedrin 100b begins with a short quotation of Prov 15:15, "All the days of the poor are evil," which is followed (in Hebrew) by "Ben Sira said, So are the nights. The lowest roof is his roof, and on the height of the mountains is his vineyard. The rain of roofs is on his

---

[10] Segal, "Evolution," 137 suggests that such is the case for Ms A at 11:29c, d.

[11] Ibid. and G.H. Box and W.O.E. Oesterley, "Sirach," *Apocrypha and Pseudepigrapha of the Old Testament* (R.H. Charles, ed.; 2 vols.; Oxford: Clarendon, 1913) 1.357.

[12] Segal, "Evolution," 137.

roof and the earth of his vineyard is on other vineyards." None of this has any parallel in any manuscript of Ben Sira.

The citations of Ben Sira contained in Sanhedrin 100b are basically of three different kinds: (1) some represent closely what we find in the manuscripts of the book; (2) some clearly originate among Ben Sira's proverbs, but they are characterized by extensive textual variation, corruptions, displacements of order and context; and (3) some do not appear at all in any Ben Sira manuscript; indeed several biblical passages appear as part of the book's contents. How can this situation be explained? Both Segal's and Lehmann's solutions, as outlined above by Gilbert, begin with the book's non-canonical status as the basis for explanation.

Segal argues that the only explanation of the rabbinic Ben Sira texts that makes sense is that "the Rabbis quoted our book from memory."[13] According to him, since the text of Ben Sira was not canonical scripture, the rabbis took certain freedoms with it that they would not with an authorized text. In the process of homiletical use of the book, the rabbis combined passages with similar ideas from different places in Ben Sira or even with verses from the Bible, and they transmitted these combinations orally. Such combinations got included in anthologies of Ben Sira together with other proverbs, many of which were incorrectly ascribed to Ben Sira, and with "miscellaneous popular and even vulgar saws in Aramaic."[14]

Lehmann argues that different "categories of text transmission" help to explain the situation in places like Sanhedrin 100b. He distinguishes "1) authorized (= Biblical) texts, transmitted in scribal reference texts, 2) authorized texts transmitted in non-scribal reference texts (e.g. in legal, liturgical, homiletic, literary texts), 3) unauthorized (= apocryphal) texts, transmitted in non-scribal texts."[15] For the second of his categories, Lehmann maintains that in such contexts even biblical quotations suffer from changes in vocabulary, grammatical form, conjunctions, etc. The Talmud was not thought of as a "scribal reference text," and thus it belongs to this second category. It utilized biblical texts as adjuncts to legal arguments or in expositional contexts, and the citation of these "authorized texts" did not require the same strictures as did manuscript

---

[13] Ibid., 135.
[14] Ibid., 135–36.
[15] Lehmann, "11QPsª and Ben Sira," 241.

copies of the Bible. "Undoubtedly," Lehmann says, "the verses were often committed to writing from memory; certainly none of the usual safeguards for faithful transmission of an authorized text were used."[16] And, of course, if the biblical texts could be subject to such changes, then one ought to expect far more radical changes in the text of books that were, like Ben Sira, unauthorized.

Both Segal and Lehmann, then, develop their understandings of the rabbinic quotations of Ben Sira from slightly different appeals to a nexus of three notions: its unauthorized status, citations from memory, and less-than-careful textual transmission. I do not think, however, that these three notions alone explain the rabbinic quotations of Ben Sira. In addition to these, the texts raise other issues that need to be considered before we can answer the questions raised by Gilbert.

Whether the rabbis did or did not regard Ben Sira as canonical, it is clear that they cite approvingly from the book in a number of contexts.[17] In Sanhedrin 100b, it is clearly the *book* of Ben Sira that is the subject of discussion.[18] In other places, however, the rabbis cite proverbs from the book as if Ben Sira were himself a rabbinic sage. In Genesis Rabbah 8, the introductory formula has R. Eleazar quoting Sir 3:21–22 in the name of Ben Sira, ר' אלעזר אמר בשם בן סירא. Other texts offer quotations from the book in the name of rabbinic authorities without any attribution to Ben Sira at all. In Shabbath 11a, for instance, a passage originating in Sir 25:13 is attributed to Rab. Any explanation of rabbinic knowledge of Ben Sira must also take into account the variety of introductory formulae.

When we look at the quotations in Sanhedrin 100b, it seems clear that the dispute between R. Joseph and Abaye centers on ספר בן סירא. But what form of the book was it? The most satisfactory answer is the suggestion of Segal that an anthology of the book is in view. But given

---

[16] Ibid., 242.

[17] The literature on the development of the Jewish canon is quite large. For two views, see S.Z. Leimann, *The Canonization of Hebrew Scripture: The Talmudic and Midrashic Evidence* (Transactions of the Connecticut Academy of Sciences 47; Hamden, CT: Hamden Books, 1976) 92–102 and R.T. Beckwith, *The Old Testament Canon of the New Testament Church and Its Background in Early Judaism* (Grand Rapids, MI: Eerdmans, 1985).

[18] Sometimes the book is cited in the same way as scripture. See, as one example, B. Hagigah 13a (citing Sir 3:21–22). B. Baba Kamma 92b has a proverb originally from Sirach cited as כתובים. It is also cited with other scriptural passages. See, for example, Shabbath 153a (with Qoh 9:8), Niddah 16b (with Prov 19:16); Baba Kamma 92b (with Gen 28:9 and Judg 11:3).

the textual forms of the various citations found there, Segal's claim that the rabbis cited from memory is perhaps not nuanced enough. In a number of cases the talmudic form of a passage is very close to the Hebrew manuscripts of Ben Sira. The citations of 6:6, 9:3b, 9:8a, c, 11:29a, and 26:1, 3 all essentially reflect the text of Ben Sira found either in Ms A or in Ms C. Indeed, the form of 26:3 even agrees with Ms C and the Syriac against the Greek in having a singular rather than a plural subject. In 11:29b, the form of the talmudic passage is related to a text of Ben Sira that is itself already corrupt. Even the passage that summarizes Sir 25:26 witnesses a form of the verse found in the expanded form of the book, in this case Syriac and GKII (ms 248).[19] All of these cases imply some relationship of *texts* to one another and thus a direct connection on the part of the rabbis with the text of Ben Sira. Yet even in some of the instances noted directly above, as well as others, like the citations of Sirach 42 on daughters or 11:32a on sparks and embers, the order of verses or the summarizing nature of the passage indicates manipulation of the text beyond straightforward citation. And how should one account for the non-Ben Sira proverbs?

It seems certain that after the Jewish canon was more or less delineated the text of Ben Sira was not handled in the same manner as biblical texts, but Lehmann's solution of carelessness or lack of precision in transmission due to the book's non-canonical status does not explain the situation well enough for earlier centuries. Indeed, the original Hebrew of Joshua ben Sira suffered from the start, especially at the hands of his grandson whose translation evidences at times mistranslation and misreading of the Hebrew.[20] Thus, even before any discussions about the authorized nature of certain books took place among the rabbis, the text of Ben Sira had its problems, and the book came into the hands of the rabbis in a far from pristine state. Additionally, it seems to me that Lehmann's three categories do not really apply to the situation in periods earlier

---

[19] There is no Hebrew extant for this verse. On the expanded form of Ben Sira, see P.W. Skehan and A.A. Di Lella, *The Wisdom of Ben Sira* (AB 39; New York: Doubleday, 1987) 55–82 and C. Kearns, "Ecclesiasticus or the Wisdom of Jesus the Son of Sirach," *A New Catholic Commentary on Holy Scripture* (R.C. Fuller, ed.; London: Nelson, 1969) 547–50. The expanded text can be found in the second Greek recension (GKII), the expanded Hebrew (HTII) found in the Cairo genizah manuscripts, the Old Latin and the Syriac.

[20] Kearns, "Ecclesiasticus," 546–47; Segal, "Evolution," 93–104. On the translation technique of the grandson, see B.G. Wright, *No Small Difference: Sirach's Relationship to Its Hebrew Parent Text* (SBLSCS 26; Atlanta: Scholars Press, 1989).

than the first couple of centuries CE when it is much more difficult to talk about a canon, especially a tripartite canon of scripture in Judaism.[21] But while neither Segal's nor Lehmann's explanations entirely resolve all the difficulties of the rabbinic quotations of Ben Sira, both contribute important elements for a potential solution to the problem.

How then can we adequately account for the passages from Ben Sira given in Sanhedrin 100b and elsewhere in rabbinic literature? One of Gilbert's conclusions given in the article cited in the opening of this paper provides the place to begin. There he makes the following remarks about the various additions to Ben Sira found in the Hebrew, Greek and other versions.

> These facts suggest that the expanded text of Ben Sira grew little by little. We must not imagine only one official second edition, revised and expanded, but rather a long process of expansion. Not being acknowledged as a biblical book in Judaism, the text of the book of Ben Sira could freely incorporate doublets and additions, which were not necessarily transmitted in all manuscripts and all versions. The expanded text of Ben Sira, therefore, is multiform.[22]

The process of textual variation began in Ben Sira very early. As the text was transmitted into the first and second centuries CE, a number of the errors and variants that we see in the quotations from Sanhedrin, such as changes in word order or vocabulary that better suited developing Hebrew language and style, changes like יפה for טובה in describing a wife, could easily have entered the manuscript tradition. Some of these variants, many of which are present in the Hebrew manuscripts of the book from the Cairo genizah, would be more or less deliberate; others undoubtedly would be the result of the kind of laxity in textual transmission proposed by Lehmann. Both Lehmann's and Segal's articles eloquently document this process. Alongside of these kinds of variations, more extensive differences developed. At times alternative versions of significant parts of or even entire cola developed and entered into the manuscript tradition. One need only scan the places where the Hebrew

---

[21] On the problems of the development of a tripartite canon, see J. Barton, *Oracles of God: Perceptions of Ancient Prophecy in Israel after the Exile* (New York: Oxford, 1986).

[22] Gilbert, "The Book of Ben Sira," 88. I have argued in my paper "The Use of the Wisdom of Ben Sira in Rabbinic Literature" (presented in the Israelite and Christian Wisdom Section at the Annual Meetings of the SBL, New Orleans, 1990) that the rabbinic quotations provide evidence for a gradual process of expansion of the text of Ben Sira.

manuscripts of Ben Sira overlap to find numerous examples of this type of variation.[23]

Ben Sira's book certainly seems to have reached such a level of popularity that Jews indeed expounded his proverbs for the good advice they gave and for their benefit for living a life according to the Law. Because of its importance and popularity, the text of Ben Sira's book attracted additional material in the course of its transmission history as the existence of the expanded text shows. The specification in the version of Sir 25:26 in Sanhedrin 100b to "give her [the evil wife] a bill of divorce" (יגרשנה), which is lacking in GKI, may show that the rabbis knew the expanded version.

Some of the proverbs of Ben Sira were undoubtedly more popular than others, and people probably used certain types of material more than others. Proverbs on particular topics—like shame, women or friends—ideally suit popular advice and homiletical contexts. Those who employed such proverbs certainly molded them to specific uses or adapted them to differing circumstances, separated out of their original context, and they would cite many of these proverbs from memory. In addition, anthologies of such popular material were created. In these anthologies, material was rearranged, and I imagine it most likely that in them one would find citations like those in Sanhedrin 100b. If the text of the book of Ben Sira itself was handled carelessly because of its non-canonical status, one can only imagine the liberties taken with the book in the creation of anthologies such as Segal describes.

We find good examples in two places of how Ben Sira was anthologized, both of which involve advice about women. First is the appearance in Sanhedrin 100b of Sir 42:9–10, 25:23–26 and 26:1, 3 on daughters and wives. In these cases the texts range from a close representation of the Hebrew manuscripts (26:1, 3) to considerable variation from them (42:9–10) to summation (25:23–26). In the talmudic passages, the order of the verses also differs from the manuscripts. The second example is Ms C from the Cairo genizah. This manuscript is an anthology of Ben Sira that excerpts a number of topics. The section on wives is comprised of 25:8, 13, 17–24; 26:1–3, 13, 15, 17; 36:27–29. Here the manuscript follows the chapter and verse order of Ben Sira and excerpts the material

---

[23] See, for example, Mss B and Bmg, E at 32:18; Mss B and Masada at 41:6; Mss B and A at 15:14. Some of these verses belong to the expanded text of Ben Sira.

on wives. In other places, however, that manuscript has passages inserted out of order, most likely for use as general topic headings.[24]

Concurrent with the textual development, Joshua Ben Sira himself must have gained a reputation as a great wise person. Such notoriety probably had at least two interrelated results. The first was that he became considered like a rabbinic sage, one who was an expert in the law and who possessed great wisdom. He was subsequently cited as such in rabbinic literature. The second result was that proverbs accumulated around and circulated in his name. Some of these probably never found their way into any complete manuscript of his book, but may well have ended up in the kind of popular anthologies described above and that seem to constitute the ספר בן סירא that was at the center of the dispute between R. Joseph and Abaye in Sanhedrin 100b. These kinds of sayings may have originated in Hebrew or Aramaic. It is interesting in this regard that two of the three major sections of Sanhedrin 100b that are not found in any manuscript of Ben Sira are in Aramaic.

In a similar vein, rabbinic sages probably knew and used some of Ben Sira's more popular adages without any specific attribution, and audiences may have understood the sages to have authored some of them. Such sayings would then be reported as those of rabbinic sages rather than of Ben Sira. Two modern analogies illustrate this process: (1) most Americans know the proverb "A penny saved is a penny earned," but many may have learned it divorced from attribution to its source, Benjamin Franklin in *Poor Richard's Almanac*; (2) because Amos 5:24 is attributed to Martin Luther King, Jr. on his memorial in Atlanta, Georgia, some might think that this biblical verse was actually composed by him.[25]

The ongoing development of the book of Ben Sira was thus a very complicated process. Even if a significant portion of the material that

---

[24] On the rationale for the arrangement of the material in Ms C, see P.C. Beentjes, "Hermeneutics in the Book of Ben Sira. Some Observations on the Hebrew MS. C," *EstBib* 46 (1988) 45–59.

[25] This explanation is a little different from that of Segal ("Evolution," 135) who maintains that the rabbis knew the origin of anonymous citations of Ben Sira. He says that they were simply "favorite sayings of the particular sages." He makes the assertion on the basis of two verses from Proverbs that are ascribed to Samuel the Little in 'Abot 4.19. If the book of Ben Sira were treated so differently from the Bible, as Segal and Lehmann claim, then the explanation for the attribution of these verses to Samuel may be different from that of the attributions of Ben Sira passages to rabbinic sages. Or, perhaps our assumptions about how well the sages knew biblical scripture in all its details overestimate the reality.

was added to Ben Sira had content that was "inserted to give expression to certain religious ideas not (sufficiently) represented in the original"[26] and thus represents a more systematic recension of the book, it seems clear that numerous changes and additions as well as entire proverbs do not display that content and provide evidence of an ongoing and gradual process that continued to shape the book of Ben Sira well into the first several centuries CE. Indeed, Segal even suggests that the talmudic citation of Sir 11:29c, d influenced Ms A found in the Cairo genizah.[27] In brief compass I have tried to show that several complex but interrelated impulses and processes account for the citations of Ben Sira that we see in Sanhedrin 100b and other rabbinic texts. I do not think that they can be reduced either to memory or to carelessness with the text alone. Memory, all manner of textual manipulation, and even invention, played roles in how the book of Ben Sira came to the rabbinic sages. I offer this attempt at some answers to the questions posed above to honor Prof. Gilbert's scholarly career and what will undoubtedly be an influential legacy.

---

[26] Kearns, "Ecclesiasticus," 549. Kearns argues that the expanded text originated with the Essenes. See his unpublished Ph.D. thesis, "The Expanded Text of Ecclesiasticus: its Teaching on the Future Life as a Clue to its Origins" (Rome, the Pontifical Biblical Commission, 1951).

[27] See above note 10.

PART TWO

THE *LETTER OF ARISTEAS* AND THE SEPTUAGINT

CHAPTER TEN

THE JEWISH SCRIPTURES IN GREEK:
THE SEPTUAGINT IN THE CONTEXT OF
ANCIENT TRANSLATION ACTIVITY

I would like to begin at the beginning of biblical translations, at least as far as can be determined, with the Septuagint, that is, the translation of the Pentateuch, the Five Books of Moses. This translation most likely was executed in the early part of the third century BCE in Alexandria, Egypt by Jews who felt the need for the Pentateuch to be rendered into the language of their daily lives. As several scholars, most notably S. Brock, have remarked, the translation of the Five Books of Moses into Greek was a relatively unprecedented undertaking. It was the first translation of the religious books of an oriental ethnic group into Greek.[1]

Those who first translated the Jewish holy books were pioneers in biblical translation, and later biblical translators at times would look to their results for inspiration.[2] But even pioneers may need a paradigm, and scholars have looked in different directions to find possible models that may have influenced the Septuagint translators in their work. In this article I want to look at one model in particular, that of the so-called dragoman or on-the-spot translator who is claimed by some to have been an indispensable participant in mercantile and legal transactions in third-century BCE Alexandria.

E. Bickerman, C. Rabin and S. Brock invoke the figure of the dragoman, partly to explain the often literal translation technique of the Septuagint that results in generally uncomfortable and, at times, barbarous Greek. My focus on the dragoman and the three aforementioned scholars' use of this character is a consequence of a longstanding desire

---

[1] S. Brock, "The Phenomenon of the Septuagint," *OtSt* 7 (1972) 12. See also C. Rabin, "The Translation Process and the Character of the LXX," *Textus* 6 (1968) 20 and E.J. Bickerman, "The Septuagint as a Translation," *Studies in Jewish and Christian History* (E.J. Bickerman, ed.; pt. 1; *AGJU* 9; Leiden: Brill, 1976) 198 (published originally in *PAAJR* 28 [1959] 1–39).

[2] E. Tov, "The Impact of the LXX Translation of the Pentateuch on the Translation of the Other Books," *Melanges Dominique Barthélemy* (P. Cassetti, O. Keel, A. Schenker, eds.; OBO 38; Fribourg: Editions Universitaires/Göttingen: Vandenhoeck & Ruprecht, 1981) 577–92.

to examine for myself the evidence for the existence and ubiquity of
such a person in Alexandrian society. As a graduate student reading
these three scholars, I was not convinced that the evidence cited in their
articles supported the theory built upon it. I joked with fellow students
that an article entitled "The Myth of the Dragoman" was waiting to be
written. This conference provided the opportunity for that paper, ten
years in the wings, to come about.[3]

For Bickerman, the Septuagint translators operated according to
the "traditional art of translation as it was understood in their time."[4]
As one aspect of such a "traditional art," he thinks that in the Jewish
synagogues in Alexandria a dragoman, or ἑρμηνεύς (hermēneus) in
Greek, would have stood next to the lector and translated the biblical
reading into Greek for those gathered. This translator was similar to
the ἑρμηνεύς who, according to Bickerman, was responsible in Ptolemaic Egypt for translating business and government documents. These
translators of necessity "clung to the letter" of their source text, and
thus, would have produced translations whose grammar and syntax
were often less at home in the target language than in the original.[5]
Bickerman makes the image clear. He writes, "To understand the task
and achievement of the 'Seventy', it is necessary to visualize them beside
the professional dragomans, the sole men who at the time exercised the
craft of translation."[6]

Rabin argues that these Alexandrian Jews had neither Jewish nor
Greek models for translation. Although they probably were familiar with
midrashic and targumic activity—and these no doubt played a role—
they were only aware of "isolated principles, but without the attendant
intellectual atmosphere."[7] Greeks, for their part, were more interested
in independent rewriting than in translation. But, according to Rabin,
Alexandrian Jews had in their own social environment a paradigm to
use, "the day-to-day oral translation activity of the commercial and court

---

[3] This paper was originally delivered at the conference "Biblical Translation in Context" held at the Joseph and Rebecca Meyerhoff Center for Jewish Studies. University
of Maryland, College Park, MD, 1998.
[4] Bickerman, "Septuagint," 167.
[5] Ibid., 178.
[6] Ibid., 179.
[7] Rabin, "Translation Process," 21. Rabin is apparently not aware of Bickerman's
article: "As there was no Greek model [for the Septuagint], it is strange that the question
seems never to have arisen from where its originators got the idea" (ibid.). Bickerman
had indeed asked the question nine years earlier.

dragomans with which, as middle-class inhabitants of a large port they must have been familiar."[8] Rabin theorizes that the Jewish community in the third century BCE would not yet have successfully penetrated the Greek educational system, and thus, they would not have had access to the traditions of writing educated Greek. They were literate, but "semi-educated" and as such would have "acquired practical experience through reading legal documents and perhaps fiction."[9] In a variant of Bickerman's scenario, Rabin also notes that the "Targum translator" in the synagogue would have reminded the Jews of the dragoman "standing next to the merchant and speaking after each remark of the latter."[10]

Brock, more than Bickerman and Rabin, looks at the various models that might be claimed for the Septuagint translators. Translation is indeed an ancient practice. Sumerian religious texts were translated into Akkadian, for example. Business documents in the ancient Near East were frequently translated. But Jews in Alexandria almost certainly would not have known these examples. In order to counter Bickerman's support of the traditional picture of the origins of the Septuagint as provided by the *Letter of Aristeas*, that the translation of the Pentateuch was commissioned by Ptolemy II, Brock notes that Alexandrian Jews would have been familiar with the dragoman, "who served as an oral interpreter in legal and commercial transactions," and that they would have been aware of written translations of legal documents.[11] They would not, however, have known religious or literary translations, "since these almost certainly only started to appear at a rather late date."[12]

Responding to the argument that the translation of the Septuagint was part of a general policy of translating oriental law codes, Brock expresses doubts that such a policy existed. But, he argues, even if the policy did exist, the Septuagint is not like other oriental law codes, and it would not have been considered such in antiquity.[13] Finally, Brock rejects the notion that the Pentateuch might have been translated to

---

[8] Ibid.
[9] Ibid., 22.
[10] Ibid., 21 note 79.
[11] Brock, "Phenomenon," 12.
[12] Ibid.
[13] Ibid., 13. A number of scholars, primarily French, have continued to argue that the motivation behind the translation of the Septuagint was its status as a law code. See D. Barthélemy, "Pourquoi la Torah a-t-elle été traduite en grec?" *On Language, Culture, and Religion: In Honor of Eugene A. Nida* (M. Black and W.A. Smalley, eds.; The Hague: Mouton, 1975) 23–41; G. Dorival, M. Harl, O. Munnich, *La Bible Grecque des Septante* (Paris: Cerf/C.N.R.S., 1988) 66–78; J. Mélèze-Modrzejewski, *The Jews of*

communicate the Jewish national history to Greeks. First, he notes, Greeks were not very interested in Jewish history or religion. Second, Manetho and Berossos, an Egyptian and Babylonian who produced national histories, do not stand up as parallels. Their works are not translations; they are what Brock calls "potted national histories, dressed up for Greek consumption."[14]

Brock himself understands the motivation for the translation of the Septuagint as arising out of inner-Jewish needs, not out of Egyptian or Greek responses to the Jewish community. He does not, however, like many scholars, look to Jewish liturgy for this motivation; he suggests that the motivation may be educational. He remarks that "it would seem only likely that the Pentateuch would have played a very similar role in Jewish education to that of Homer in Greek...the Bible—in this case the Pentateuch—was the Homer of the Jews."[15]

In whatever context we try to locate it, the translation of the Hebrew Pentateuch was unparalleled in the Hellenistic world, but the problem of where the translators looked for a model for their work remains. For Bickermann, Rabin and Brock, one must look at the dragoman as the most likely of all the possible "suspects."

So we find ourselves with three arguments concluding that the Septuagint translators had at their disposal a mode of translation that was ubiquitous in their world and one which could hardly have failed to influence them. The ἑρμηνεύς and his manner of translating help to explain the translation technique of the Pentateuch and by extension the origins of the Pentateuch as an Egyptian-Jewish translation. The only difficulty is that when one looks at the evidence cited by Bickerman, Rabin and Brock, there is precious little to see. The supposition that in the Jewish synagogue in Hellenistic Alexandria (and I will not even enter into a discussion of what the "house of prayer" was in third-century BCE Alexandria and how it functioned)[16] there was a person who trans-

---

Egypt from Rameses II to Emperor Hadrian (R. Cornman, trans.; Philadelphia: Jewish Publication Society, 1992) 99–119.

[14] Ibid., 13–14.

[15] Ibid., 16.

[16] On the beginnings of Jewish communal buildings in Egypt, see J.G. Griffiths, "Egypt and the Rise of the Synagogue," and A. Kasher, "Synagogues as 'Houses of Prayer' and 'Holy Places' in the Jewish Communities of Hellenistic and Roman Egypt," *Ancient Synagogues: Historical Analysis and Archaeological Discovery* (D. Urman and P.V.M. Flesher, eds.; 2 vols.; StPB 47; Leiden: Brill, 1995) 1.3–16; 1.205–21.

lated the reading into Greek is just that, a supposition.[17] Rabin's social reconstruction of a "middle-class" of Jews who were semi-educated is without supporting evidence. And when one looks at the evidence cited for the existence of this ubiquitous ἑρμηνεύς, much of it comes from the papyri of the Roman period, a period when translation as an activity explodes in the East with the use not only of Greek and indigenous languages, but now Latin, the language of the regnant imperial power.[18] Yet because the Roman period is so different from the earlier Ptolemaic period, I do not think that one can simply assume that what was true for the second century BCE and later was so in the third century BCE, the time of the Septuagint translators.

Shall we then jettison the notion that there was a figure called a ἑρμηνεύς who may have influenced the way the Septuagint translators did their work, or is there enough evidence in the earlier Greek literature and papyri to justify the claims that Bickerman, Rabin and Brock make? Are we to envision a ubiquitous on-the-spot translator of commercial transactions, a "Targum translator" in the synagogue, or something else? In order to answer these questions, we need all the available evidence before us. So, will the real dragoman please stand up?

CLASSICAL GREEK LITERATURE

In the Greek literature of the fifth to the fourth centuries BCE, the term ἑρμηνεύς, translator or interpreter, seems to indicate a number

---

[17] I mean this for the Ptolemaic period. The evidence adduced for the practice of such targumic translation is invariably from the first few centuries CE, especially from the Mishnah. This evidence is then retrojected back into the Hellenistic period, primarily for two reasons. First, there is an assumption that Alexandrian Jews would not have understood their scriptures in Hebrew, and thus, someone must have translated them into Greek in the same way that we hear about later in the Mishnah. Second, some, such as Paul Kahle, argue that the Septuagint had its origins in such Greek targums. For the textual evidence that speaks of this translation activity, see S. Safrai, "The Synagogue," *The Jewish People in the First Century* (S. Safrai and M. Stern, eds.: CRINT I.2; Philadelphia: Fortress, 1976) 930–31 and E. Schürer, *The History of the Jewish People in the Age of Jesus Christ* (rev. and ed. G. Vermes, F. Millar, M. Goodman; 4 vols.; T & T Clark: Edinburgh, 1986) 2.452–53.

[18] For example, Brock lists the studies of R. Calderini, "De interpretibus quaedam in papyris," *Aegyptus* 33 (1953) and W. Snellmann, *De Interpretibus romanorum* (Leipzig, 1914/1919) to support the claim that the translators of the Septuagint would have known the dragoman ("Phenomenon," 12 note 4). Yet both of these studies primarily rely on material from the Roman period.

of different things.[19] Plato in his writings displays several of them. He uses the term to indicate one who explains the gods or religion as, for example, in the *Republic* 427c where Apollo performs such a function. The name of the god Hermes itself indicates interpretation, and he apparently interprets the gods' actions to humans (*Cratylus* 407e). For Plato a ἑρμηνεύς can be one who explains or exegetes legal matters (*Laws* 907d) or the poets (*Ion* 530c, 534e, 535a).[20]

Although one can find a variety of meanings attested, in Plato and elsewhere in Greek literature a ἑρμηνεύς is someone who explains or exchanges one thing into another, and the most prominent function of this ἑρμηνεύς is to translate one language into another. Plato also attests this meaning in *Philebus* 16a where he speaks of an interpreter being found for a "barbarian." In *Agamemnon* (in and around line 1060), Aeschylus has Clytemnestra say to Cassandra, "But if you fail to understand my words [or meaning], then, instead of speech, make a sign with your barbarian hand." The chorus then chimes in, "It is a translator, and a plain one that the stranger seems to need."

The two Greek authors who contribute most to our understanding of the ἑρμηνεύς especially in the Near East and Egypt, however, are Herodotus and Xenophon, two men who traveled in the East. Unlike the differing usages of the term ἑρμηνεύς in Plato, every case of the word in Herodotus indicates someone who translates from one language into another. The "interpreter" or "translator" appears in some very interesting contexts in the *Histories*. In 2.125.6 Herodotus remarks that he had a guide who could translate for him the Egyptian letters (γραμμάτων Αἰγυπτίων), presumably hieroglyphics, on one of the pyramids. Judging from what Herodotus says later in 2.154.2 and 2.164.1, his ἑρμηνεύς

---

[19] I want to acknowledge the marvelous resources of the Perseus Project at Tufts University. I found their web site (http://www.perseus.tufts.edu) and its searchable database to be indispensable. The site makes available a large number of Greek texts along with the Duke Data Bank of Documentary Papyri, which includes over 500 papyrological publications. The search engine is extremely flexible. Almost all of the references in this paper were taken from results of searching Perseus Project databases. The abbreviations for the editions of the papyri cited in this paper can be conveniently found in J.F. Oates, R.S. Bagnall and W.H. Willis, eds., *Checklist of Editions of Greek Papyri and Ostraca* (2nd ed.; BASPSup 1; Chico, CA: Scholars Press, 1978). The checklist is also published and updated on the World Wide Web. The URL is http://scriptorium. lib.duke.edu/papyrus/texts/clist.html.

[20] The meaning of exegete is also found in a speech of Isaeus (*Ciron* 39) where the orator refers to the "interpreter/exegete" of the sacred law and in Pindar (*Odes* 2.85), who creates the image of arrows "which have a voice for those who know, but for the multitudes require an interpreter."

most likely was a native Egyptian. The first passage reports that Greeks received children from the Egyptians who learned the Greek language and then became interpreters. The passage is worth citing in full.

> To the Ionians and the Carians, who had taken his side, Psammetichus gave, to dwell in, lands that lie opposite to one another; their name is The Camps, and the Nile runs between the two peoples. These places he gave them and awarded them everything he had promised as well. Furthermore, he turned over to them Egyptian children, to learn the Greek language. It is from these who learned the language that the present interpreters in Egypt come (2.154.1–2).[21]

Whether Herodotus's story accurately reflects the history of these interpreters or not, the excerpt cited here may indicate that being an interpreter was an occupation passed down in families, one that was in legend connected to those protological translators from the time of Psammetichus.

Shortly after this passage Herodotus lists what he calls the seven classes of the Egyptians, one of which is the ἑρμηνεύς (2.164). The inclusion of the ἑρμηνεύς in this list, if indeed Herodotus's seven classes were those of Egyptian society, would seem to indicate the existence of the kind of professional class that Bickerman, Rabin and Brock envision. It is not exactly clear, however, what the translators were used for, although I imagine that their jobs were more varied than to escort tourists like Herodotus. Herodotus also knows of the use of translators in business contexts. In this instance it is not Egyptians, but Scythians, who apparently are widely travelled and who do business "through seven interpreters and in seven languages" (4.24).

One aspect of ancient translation about which Herodotus and Xenophon agree is that generals need interpreters. Both of these authors include many stories of military encounters, and it is clear that for the two sides in a war to communicate, interpreters must be brought on any military campaign. Herodotus reports that the Persian king Darius hears the messages of the Greeks through an interpreter (3.38.4). In another story about a Greek exile named Sylosan, the same Darius interrogates him through interpreters (3.140). Xenophon, whose *Anabasis* chronicles the Greek army during a Persian campaign, portrays the interpreter as one who almost always accompanied a general. In *Anabasis* 1.8.12,

---

[21] Translation taken from D. Grene, trans., *The History: Herodotus* (Chicago: University of Chicago, 1987) 199.

for example, the Persian general Cyrus "rode along the line, attended only by Pigres, his interpreter, and three or four others." Interpreters were the obvious people to send as emissaries to the other side. "He [Tiribazos the Persian satrap] rode up to the Greeks with a body of horsemen, and sending forth an interpreter, said that he wished to confer with their commanders" (*An.* 4.4.5). Interpreters could also be helpful with indigenous populations when armies were in foreign territory, as Xenophon indicates in *Anabasis* 4.5.34: "As soon as Cheirosophus and Xenophon had exchanged warm greetings, they together asked the village chief, through their Persian-speaking interpreter, what land this was. He replied that it was Armenia."

PAPYROLOGICAL EVIDENCE
(THIRD TO SECOND CENTURIES BCE)

Quite a bit of papyrological evidence is, in fact, extant testifying to the existence of interpreters or translators in Egypt. Unfortunately almost all of this papyrological evidence comes from well into the Roman period, and thus we simply do not have much information from earlier Ptolemaic times. Of the 129 references to interpretation or translation based on the Greek verb ἑρμηνεύω that I found in the papyri contained in the Duke Data Bank of Documentary Papyri, only nineteen come from the centuries BCE, and only a portion of these can be dated to the Ptolemaic period; nine of them mention a ἑρμηνεύς, and ten contain some form of the verb. Eight of these are in one particular formula. The remaining 110 date from the first century CE and later.[22] Given the very few references in the BCE papyri to the ἑρμηνεύς and his activity, I propose to look at all of them to see what kind of a picture might emerge.

References in the papyri to a ἑρμηνεύς

1) CPR 13.11, 3 (Arsinoite Nome, Krokodilopolis, reign of Ptolemais Euergetis, iii BCE): This papyrus contains a list of people, apparently those who must pay the salt tax. Line 10 and following mention Greeks and Arabs, persons of the village subject to the tax. In the section after line

---

[22] The papyri cited in this section were taken from the Duke Data Bank of Documentary Papyri available on the Perseus Project Web Site. For the URL and papyrological abbreviations, see above, note 19.

30, several kinds of occupations are listed with amounts next to them. Lines 37–39 list brewers (ζυτοποιοί), a ἑρμηνεύς and mat weavers (ψιαθοπλόκοι). What the ἑρμηνεύς does is not evident from the list, but it might be notable that the term is in the singular rather than the plural, like the surrounding terms. Does the singular indicate that there is only one ἑρμηνεύς in the village?

2) P.Cair.Zen 1,59065 (Philadelphia, 257 BCE): This is one of several Zenon papyri that mention a ἑρμηνεύς, in the present case a certain "Apollonius the ἑρμηνεύς" who appears a number of times in third-century BCE papyri. Very little can be derived from this small papyrus. It is a letter from Zenon, although his name does not appear, to his boss Apollonius (not the same person as Apollonius the ἑρμηνεύς). After the greeting Zenon says that "we have sent off the fifty fish (θρίσσας) of Apollonius the ἑρμηνεύς." The papyrus provides no illumination as to what a ἑρμηνεύς does, however.

3) P.Cair.Zen 3.59394 (Philadelphia, iii BCE): This rather long papyrus is a memorandum (ὑπόμνημα) from Zenon to Apollonius his employer. It concerns a large quantity of herd animals, over 6,300, that consists at least of goats, rams, cows and horses. The papyrus also has an accounting of prices paid(?) or perhaps taxes for these animals. The account section of the text is very long, but it includes in line 50 a ἑρμηνεύς in the town of Limnaios. The inclusion of the ἑρμηνεύς here is a bit odd, since none of the towns listed in the surrounding lines have occupations singled out. The only other mention of a specific person is someone identified as an Arab in line 45. Like the two preceding cases, what the ἑρμηνεύς does in the town of Limnaios is not made clear. R. Taubenschlag would have it that instances such as these indicate a state appointment of a translator for a town, but I think that this is reading too much into the evidence.[23]

4) P.Col. 4.63 (Philadelphia, 257 BCE?): This papyrus is an account. It lists a number of service providers, like a Nile boat pilot and the orchard keepers for a garden. Several of the persons are named. Line 7 reads "to Glaukias the ἑρμηνεύς for merchandise, 12 copper drachmas" (Γλαυκίαι ἑρμηνεῖ εἰς ἀγοράσματα χαλ(κοῦ) (δραχμάς) 12). The connection of merchandise with Glaukias the ἑρμηνεύς in this papyrus may give some indication about what he does. In a number of first century CE and later

---

[23] R. Taubenschlag, "The Interpreters in the Papyri," *Charisteria Thaddaeo Sinko* (Warsaw: Sumptibus Societatis Philologae Polonorum, 1951) 361.

papyri, especially those from Karanis, the ἑρμηνεύς is clearly a broker of some sort. Most often in these papyri the ἑρμηνεύς owns the measuring scales in a town and is responsible for measuring out commodities like wheat.[24] Thus, Glaukias as a ἑρμηνεύς might have an economic function. Although this is the only mention of merchandise in the papyrus, if one looks at others mentioned in this account, they, too, either purchase or sell commodities like wheat or "provisions/payments" (ὀψώνιον) for a deity. But even though later papyri give evidence for the ἑρμηνεύς as broker, such a meaning is by no means assured in this case.

5) *P.Ryl. 4.563 (Philadelphia, 250 BCE)*: This papyrus contains a letter from one Pataikion to Zenon. The circumstances necessitating the letter are not given in much detail, but they concern a house that Pataikion has assigned to the possession of one Aristodemus. Pataikion subsequently has heard that the original owner of the house is going to Apollonius, Zenon's boss, to try to make trouble for him. Consequently, Pataikion requests that Zenon take some unspecified action against this trouble-maker. In addition to Zenon, Pataikion has also written to "Apollonius the ἑρμηνεύς" requesting of him that he do "as much damage as possible" to his antagonist.[25] Although what a ἑρμηνεύς does is not mentioned, this particular interpreter seems to be in an important enough position to be able to respond to Pataikion's petition if he were so inclined.

6) *PSI 4.332, 1 (Philadelphia, 257/256 BCE)*: The text of the papyrus is an account (λόγος) from someone named Polemarkos for what looks like two days of expenses. Polemarkos gives the totals for the two days and then the specific expenses incurred. Apparently a good part of his activity took place at a garlic market (τὰ σκόρδα). The first of his expenses was for a ἑρμηνεύς "who acted as a guide at the garlic market" (ἑρμηνεῖ τῶι ὁδηγήσαντι ἐπὶ τὰ σκόρδα). In this instance it is hard to see Polemarkus's interpreter as anything other than someone who translated between Egyptian and Greek.

---

[24] For some examples see BGU 11.2123, 17 (Arsinoite nome, 85 CE); P.Mich. 5.321, ctr, 20 (Tebtunis, 42 CE); P.Mich. 9.567, 15 (Karanis, 91 CE).

[25] The translation is based on that of R. Bagnall and P. Derow, *Greek Historical Documents: The Hellenistic Period* (SBLSBS 16; Chico, CA: Scholars Press, 1981) 125. In their introduction to the text, Bagnall and Derow say that Pataikion has written to "Apollonius' interpreter." If this is the interpreter of Zenon's boss, Apollonius, then, he would be a powerful ally, as Bagnall and Derow state. The text of the papyrus, however, has Ἀπολλωνίωι τῶι ἑρμηνεῖ. Rather than this interpreter being in the employ of Zenon's boss, I am inclined to see this as another person of the same name who is distinguished from Zenon's employer by the epithet, ἑρμηνεύς.

7) PSI 4.409, frA (Philadelphia, iii BCE): The text is a memorandum to a certain Artemidoros from a man called Hinoutos, identified as one who rears calves (μοσχοτρόφος). He also has given an account (λόγος) of the herd to Apollonius (Zenon's boss?). Some of the cows in this herd are "official" cows belonging to Apollonius; others have been set aside for sacrifices; still others are old and useless (πρεσβῦται ἀχρεῖοι). Some others have apparently come from other people including six from Apollonius the ἑρμηνεύς. This is probably the same Apollonius to whom Pataikion wrote about his house problems. But, unfortunately we learn nothing about the function and status of a ἑρμηνεύς.

8) UPZ 2.227, 1 (Thebes, ii/i BCE): This papyrus and the next are almost beyond the chronological boundaries set for this study. I include them in order to give all the papyri that have BCE dates. Here we again meet an Apollonius the ἑρμηνεύς, but not the same Apollonius as before, since this one lived at least a century later. This Apollonius calls himself the ἑρμηνεύς of the Trogodytes.[26] He writes to a banker named Diogenes about a business transaction. He admits to Diogenes that he did have business dealings with him through a bank. The most fascinating feature of this papyrus is that apparently Apollonius did not know how to write Greek. One Ptolemaios son of Ptolemaios apparently wrote the letter. Apollonius asked him to write it "because [Apollonius] affirmed that he did not know letters."[27] It would seem from this letter that if Apollonius's job was translation, he did it orally. Taubenschlag claims that Apollonius was "appointed by the state" and that "he commanded Greek and Ethiopian as well,"[28] but he provides no evidence for these assertions. Apollonius's situation does raise the issue of literacy and fluency in antiquity.[29] Apollonius may well have been fluent in Greek and whatever language the Trogodytes spoke, but if one of the functions of

---

[26] I don't know what to make of this identification of Apollonius. Is he in the employ of the Trogodytes? Is he a Trogodyte who speaks Greek? Taubenschlag, "Interpreters," 361, claims that the Trogodytes were an Ethiopian people who settled in Egypt.

[27] The Greek text of the final part of the letter reads as follows:
ἔγραψεν Πτολεμαῖος Πτολεμα(ίου).
Πτολεμαιεὺς ἡγεμόνος ἔξω τάξεων
ἀξιωθεὶς ὑπ' αὐτοῦ διὰ τὸ φάσκειν
αὐτὸν μὴ εἰδέναι γράμματα.
On the final phrase "he did not know letters" see H.C. Youtie, "Because They Do Not Know Letters," *ZPE* 19 (1975) 101–8.

[28] Taubenschlag, "Interpreters," 361.

[29] On ancient literacy see W.V. Harris, *Ancient Literacy* (Cambridge, MA: Harvard University Press, 1989).

a state translator were to deal with official documents, then Apollonius
was clearly not up to that task.

9) SB 10.10743, 2 (i BCE–i CE): This fragmentary papyrus is an account.
It lists an unnamed ἑρμηνεύς. Two lines after the ἑρμηνεύς a scribe
(γραμματεύς) is mentioned, also with no name. Three lines later a scribe
by the name of Didymus appears. The occurrence of a ἑρμηνεύς in a
context with scribes might indicate the linguistic function of the person,
but unfortunately the papyrus provides no additional information.

TRANSLATED DOCUMENTS FROM THE
SECOND CENTURY BCE AND EARLIER

When one looks for actual translated texts in the earlier period, there are
several to be found. Outside of Egypt the two most cited examples are
the Xanthus stele, dating from about 358 BCE, which was inscribed in
Greek, Lycian and Aramaic and concerns the establishment of a religious
cult.[30] The other is the edicts of the Buddhist king Asoka, discovered in
an inscription in Aramaic and Greek dating to the third century BCE.[31]
Inscriptions such as these, however, are as unlikely to have influenced
the translators of the Septuagint as are the other ancient Near Eastern
examples cited by Brock in his article.

When we look to the Egyptian papyri for translated documents, we
find the same situation that pertained to the evidence for the term
ἑρμηνεύς. The bulk of the examples of bilingual documents or outright translations dates to the Roman period.[32] There are some earlier
examples but not a great many. There are some demotic papyri in the
Zenon collection, and their existence there most likely indicates a need
on Zenon's part to work in both languages. In order to do so he may
have had to employ a ἑρμηνεύς.

1) P.Petr. 2.17, fr 2 (Gurob, 229/228 BCE): In this fragmentary papyrus, the verb διερμηνεύω occurs in the phrase, "inasmuch as we have

---

[30] See J. Teixidor, "The Aramaic Text in the Trilingual Stele from Xanthus," *JNES*
37 (1978) 181–85.
[31] D. Schlumberger et al., "Une bilingue gréco-araméenne d'Asoka," *JA* 246 (1958)
1–48 cited in Brock, "Phenomenon," 15 note 1.
[32] When one looks, for example, at R.A. Pack, *The Greek and Latin Literary Texts
from Greco-Roman Egypt* (2nd ed.; Ann Arbor: University of Michigan, 1965), there are
quite a few translated documents. All date from the first few centuries CE.

expounded/interpreted." It is not clear what the circumstances surrounding this exposition/interpretation were or who the "we" is.

2) *UPZ 2.218, 2 (Thebes, ii/i BCE)*: This papyrus, a letter from one Pchorchonsios, mentions one Imouthes who is apparently a village scribe (κωμογραμματεύς), who has, it seems, translated a document from its original form "in native letters" into Greek. Unfortunately, large segments of this papyrus are reconstructions, including the title of Imouthes and most of the verb rendered "translate" (μεθερμηνεύω). Not too much weight, then, can be placed on this text.

3) *UPZ 2.175a (Thebes, 146 BCE)*: I cite this text as an example of the use of a formula that occurs in a number of other papyri.[33] It is apparent that in some cases contracts or other legal documents were originally written in Egyptian and then translated into Greek. The basic formula reads "a copy of an Egyptian contract translated as well as possible" (UPZ 2.175a has ἀντίγραφ[ον συ]νγραφῆς Αἰγυπτίας μεθηρμηνε[υ] μένης κατὰ δύναμιν). In some other cases the formula specifically says that the translation was "into Greek" (Ἑλληνιστί).

Some scholars understand the differences in the quality of the Greek of numerous contracts as indicating that some were translated and others were not. Taubenschlag, for example, explains these variations in Greek style as the result of documents drawn up in Greek by a ἑρμηνεύς, on the one hand, and documents drawn up in Egyptian and then translated into Greek by the ἑρμηνεύς, on the other.[34] He bases his conclusion on papyri like UPZ 2.175a, which is explicitly said to be a copy of a contract originally drawn up in Egyptian and translated into Greek. Yet even though translation is clearly practiced in some everyday contexts, the variations in style of Greek may also depend on the level of training of the scribe and not necessarily on translation. I think it safer only to consider the text of a papyrus a translation if there is a clear indication in the text, as in the cases included here.

---

[33] The usual verb in the formula is μεθερμηνεύω, but on occasion διερμηνεύω appears. The other BCE examples found in the Duke Data Bank are: BGU 3.1002 (Hermoupolis Magna, 56/55 BCE); CPR 15.1, ctr 1, 18 (Soknopaiou Nesos, 3 BCE); P.Giss. 36, II (Pathyris, 145–116 BCE); PSI 5.549 (Oxyrhynchus, 42/41 BCE); P.Tebt. 1.164 (Tebtunis, 118/117 BCE); P.Tor.Choach. 12 (Thebes, 117 BCE); UPZ 2.177 (Thebes, 136 BCE).

[34] Taubenschlag, "Interpreters," 362.

THE DRAGOMAN AND HIS INFLUENCE ON THE
TRANSLATION OF THE SEPTUAGINT

In the Hellenistic world of the third century BCE, especially in Egypt, the evidence adduced above suggests that translation was an important activity. To a certain degree common sense would argue that point as well. With the confluence of cultures and languages in the early Hellenistic world and the imposition of Greek as an official language of government, one would expect that the need for translation would increase, and depending on the context, such translation could presumably be oral or written. Certain official documentation, such as contracts or other legal documents or tax accounts, almost certainly required Greek; apparently, to comply with that necessity, people sometimes drew up documents in Egyptian and then had them translated. Other documents would have been written in Greek originally, whether or not those commissioning the documents were literate in Greek. Although some texts survive in bilingual form, the two languages do not necessarily have to be translations one of the other or even written by the same person. Oral translation alone might be required in other contexts, such as that of Polemarkos, who, we saw above, apparently needed a translator to guide him through the garlic market. The military translators known to Xenophon and Herodotus acted solely in an oral environment as well.

But what of the existence, place and function of the so-called dragoman in this matrix of contexts where translation was required? Although certain aspects of Bickerman, Rabin and Brock's picture of the "dragoman" appear justified, I do not think that the evidence warrants the image of a dragoman standing next to the merchant translating every sentence in turn. This image seems to me to be influenced more by the assumption that there was a translator in the Alexandrian synagogues who, on the spot, rendered the Hebrew biblical readings into Greek.[35] The realities of translation and its importance in third-century BCE Egyptian society appear more complicated and more unclear. The closest one comes to that picture in the Egyptian papyri discussed above is Polemarkos and his garlic market excursion. The case of Glaukias the ἑρμηνεύς and his merchandise may suggest, as well, that the term

---

[35] Both Bickerman ("Septuagint," 172) and Rabin ("Translation Process," 21 note 79) appeal to this image.

ἑρμηνεύς was not simply used of those who translated languages, but that the ἑρμηνεύς may have served as a broker in the early period as he clearly does later.

Whatever his job description may have been, the ἑρμηνεύς Apollonius who is mentioned in several Zenon papyri seems to have been a fairly important person who was able to affect the fortunes of Pataikion and his dispute about a house. Does this indicate that interpreters or translators were people of status in third-century Egyptian society or simply that this Apollonius had achieved some status? What would the status be of the other Apollonius we have encountered, who apparently, although called a ἑρμηνεύς, was illiterate in Greek?[36]

The pre-Roman period evidence, despite its relative paucity, at the least enables us to see a world in which translation was a necessity and where there existed people who translated professionally. However, I think it also prohibits us from accepting as social reality the vivid images of the dragoman and his ubiquity and influence found in Bickerman, Rabin and Brock.

Can we say whether these ancient translators acted as the model for those Jews who translated their sacred literature into Greek? Although I would love to come to a dramatic and certain conclusion, I do not think we can know for sure. Would the Jewish translators have known about translation activity in their social worlds? The papyri suggest that they most likely did. Would they have looked to government or local ἑρμηνεῖς as the model for their work? Perhaps. But I think when we put aside the speculations about the educational levels of Jews in third-century BCE Alexandria or the picture of a translator at every corner or in every office or involved in every business transaction, it is impossible to say what models the Jewish translators actually used. If the Septuagint is the unique phenomenon that it is claimed to be, then perhaps for those Jews in Alexandria who felt the need to have their scriptures in Greek necessity was indeed the mother of invention. Perhaps no model sufficed, and what they arrived at was a process that essentially followed

---

[36] Harris seems to think that a ἑρμηνεύς would have been a person of relatively high social status. He remarks that from the Ptolemaic period we know of no person of high status who was, or at least who admitted to being, illiterate (*Ancient Literacy*, 142). He actually notes the case of "Apollonius the interpreter of the Trogodytes," but calls the text "a curiosity." His judgment seems to be based on a misreading of the papyrus. Harris calls Apollonius an "interpreter of the Troglodytes," not Trogodytes. The Troglodytes were a race of cave-dwelling people who purportedly lived south of Egypt, and, reading the papyrus this way, Harris is unable to take it seriously.

the parent text, if not word for word, at least syntactical unit by syntactical unit while at the same time enshrining their own hermeneutical understanding of particular texts in the translation. Those who translated the Septuagint were clearly men of great ingenuity, and whatever their model, they transformed the Hebrew Pentateuch into a unique creation that served the needs of Greek-speaking Jews so well that its status in many areas eclipsed that of its Hebrew progenitor.

CHAPTER ELEVEN

עֶבֶד/ΔΟΥΛΟΣ—TERMS AND SOCIAL STATUS IN THE MEETING OF HEBREW BIBLICAL AND HELLENISTIC-ROMAN CULTURE*

Introduction

Although the Jews of the Second Temple Period possessed divinely sanctioned laws that included regulations about servitude and enslavement, of both Hebrews and foreigners, they lived in a world where slavery played a role different from and greater than that of their biblical predecessors. Jews, in Palestine and in the diaspora, were in contact with and subject to systems of slavery that differed in basic respects from the slave system practiced in "biblical times." Whereas the world in which the biblical slavery laws developed was apparently not highly dependent on slaves for its economic well being, the Mediterranean world of the Hellenistic-Roman period clearly was.[1] Further, the legal status of the enslaved individual in biblical law was different from that of Greek and Roman slaves who were considered little more than their owners' chattel. The purpose of this essay is to investigate the extent to which Second Temple Jewish literature uses the language of Hellenistic-Roman slave systems, and thus reflects the socio-cultural realities of slavery in the Hellenistic and Roman Mediterranean rather than those of ancient Israel.

---

* This article is dedicated to the memory of my wife, Ann, who died August 17, 1995 of breast cancer. Although some might find it strange that I would dedicate an article on slavery to her, she was always my greatest encouragement, both as a scholar and as a person. She either heard or read everything that I ever wrote. This is the last piece that will have the benefit of her wisdom and insight.

[1] For detailed treatments of slavery in ancient Israel and the Hebrew Bible, see I. Mendelsohn, *Slavery in the Ancient Near East: A Comparative Study of Slavery in Babylonia, Assyria, Syria and Palestine; From the Middle of the Third Millenium to the End of the First Millenium* (Oxford: Oxford University Press, 1949); R. de Vaux, *Ancient Israel: Its Life and Institutions* (London: Darton, Longman & Todd, 1965); P.V.M. Flesher, *Oxen, Women, or Citizens? Slaves in the System of the Mishnah* (Atlanta: Scholars Press, 1988); and M.A. Dandamayev, "Slavery (ANE)" and "Slavery (OT)," *The Anchor Bible Dictionary* (D.N. Freedman, ed.; New York: Doubleday, 1992) 6.58–62; 6.62–5.

The effects of these systems were probably felt by Jews in a number of ways. First, Jews were part of a social world in which slavery was the norm, and they, for various reasons, were undoubtedly part of the system, both as its beneficiaries and its victims. Many were bought and sold as chattel slaves, or perhaps themselves bought and sold slaves (though probably not Jewish ones).[2] They were certainly the beneficiaries of slave labor, whether they lived in Palestine and utilized, for example, the numerous building projects undertaken by Herod, or in diaspora communities where, for instance, public slaves performed important civic duties. In all areas of the Mediterranean Jews had contact with the products of Greek and Roman slave economies.

Jewish involvement in the social world of Hellenistic-Roman slave systems must have had consequences for the ways Jews used words for slaves, and the use of the two major languages of the Mediterranean in this period, Greek and Latin, must have influenced Jewish thought worlds. In appropriating these languages, Jews took over the Greek and Latin vocabulary for slaves and slavery. It is hard to imagine that the lexical content of the Hebrew עבד was simply dumped into the Greek and Latin vocabulary; the idea was socially conditioned as well.

To a great degree, living in the Hellenistic-Roman Mediterranean and speaking (or, at least understanding) Greek and Latin meant transforming the notion of slavery or servanthood from that of the Hebrew Bible to that of the slave systems characteristic of the Mediterranean social world in the Hellenistic-Roman period. Of course, the most critical place in which such a transformation can be found is in the Jewish-Greek biblical translations, and the lexical choices made by the translators to render עבד have the potential to have a dramatic impact on the "biblical" concept of servanthood. The term δοῦλος, one of the two major translations of עבד in the Jewish-Greek Bible, quite simply communicated to the Greek reader in this period something different from what the word עבד did earlier. This consideration most probably applies not only to those instances in which an actual servant or slave is meant, but also to metaphorical uses of the terminology.

---

[2] There is much evidence in literature, inscriptions and papyri that this was indeed the case. Several examples will be noted below. Biblical law does not recognize a Hebrew having another Hebrew as chattel (see, Flesher, *Oxen, Women, or Citizens?*), and Hebrews were required to try to redeem Hebrews who had been enslaved. Non-Hebrews, however, could be bought as slaves, but even their status seems to have been better than the chattel slaves of Greek and Roman slave systems.

A corollary to this issue is whether and to what extent the different words for slaves in this period retained their older connotations and distinctions or were used generally as synonyms for slaves. The degree to which Jewish literature employed slave terms as they were used in the language in general will tell a great deal about whether Hellenistic Jews adopted not only the vocabulary of slavery but the attendant cultural realities/concepts as well.

In what follows, I will look at both of the foregoing problems, because they are connected in important ways. The recognition that Jews in the Second Temple period were not isolated or insulated from Greek and Roman slave pratices and that they used the vocabulary of slavery consistently with their larger socio-cultural surroundings helps to build a picture of what slave language meant to Jews when they encountered it or used it in their literature. Or, taken from the other direction, although the Hebrew Bible's use of slave language, especially the metaphorical uses of such language, may provide a background for understanding the meaning of slave terms in Jewish-Greek sources, such use is only a partial and incomplete background.

I do not intend a review of slavery as it was practiced in the Hellenistic-Roman world.[3] My task is much more circumscribed than that. Two questions will remain the primary focus of this essay: (1) What was the social experience of Jews with slavery in the Greco-Roman world? and (2) How might that experience affect our understanding of the use of language for slavery in Jewish sources? The major effort here will be descriptive. That is, I want to gather as much of the data together as possible in an attempt to provide a basis for answers to the questions just posed. Although it will be primarily descriptive, this essay, given space limitations, cannot be exhaustive. Consequently, in addressing question 2, I will treat mostly Jewish literature in Greek, and I will concentrate on the two major terms used in the Jewish-Greek scriptures

---

[3] The literature on slavery in the Greco-Roman world is vast. On Greek and Roman slavery in general, see M.I. Finley, *Slavery in Classical Antiquity* (Cambridge: W. Heffer & Sons, 1960); idem, *Classical Slavery* (Totowa, N.J.: Frank Cass & Co., 1987); Y. Garlan, *Slavery in Ancient Greece* (Ithaca: Cornell University Press, 1988); J. Vogt, *Ancient Slavery and the Ideal of Man* (Oxford: Basil Blackwell, 1974); W.L. Westermann, *The Slave Systems of Greek and Roman Antiquity* (Philadelphia: The American Philosophical Society, 1955); T. Wiedemann, *Greek and Roman Slavery* (Baltimore: Johns Hopkins University Press, 1981); R.A. Horsley, "The Slave Systems of Classical Antiquity and Their Relevant Recognition by Modern Scholars," *Slavery in Text and Interpretation* (*Semeia* 83/84; A.D. Callahan, R.A. Horsley, A. Smith, eds.; Atlanta: SBL, 1998) 19–66.

to render the Hebrew עֶבֶד—δοῦλος and παῖς. That the translators of the Septuagint, people working at different times and places, preferred these two Greek terms by a large margin over any other Greek words (and there were many for slavery) indicates their potential importance for getting a handle on the conceptual content of the transformation of Hebrew slave language into Greek.

SLAVERY IN THE HEBREW BIBLE—SUMMARY STATEMENT

Although the Hebrew Bible contains many references to עֲבָדִים, there is actually a limited corpus of laws concerning them. In its basic biblical meaning someone is called עֶבֶד who is in a subservient relationship to another.[4] This relationship does not have to be one of ownership but can apply to a king and his subjects, a god and those who serve him/her, a social superior and inferior. Uses such as that found in 1 Sam 19:4 where Jonathan says, "The king should not sin against his עֶבֶד David," or in Deut 34:5 where Moses is called the "עֶבֶד of the Lord" occur frequently in the Hebrew scriptures. But an עֶבֶד can clearly be in a servile relation to another, and these עֲבָדִים are treated primarily in Exodus 21, Leviticus 25 and Deuteronomy 15.

In ancient Israel the Hebrew עֶבֶד was distinguished from the gentile עֶבֶד. In many respects, the Hebrew עֶבֶד was not really a slave as much as a debt-slave or an indentured servant. A Hebrew could be enslaved/indentured as a result of inability to repay theft (Exod 22:3) or for debt (Lev 25:39?; 2 Kgs 4:1), but the slave/servant worked for six years or until the next jubilee year and then was released (Exod 21:2; Lev 25:40; Deut 15:12). A Hebrew could not be enslaved in perpetuity, unless he voluntarily submitted to permanent slave status.[5] This situation, however, seems to apply to males only, since Exod 21:7–11 says that a daughter

---

[4] For more detailed treatments of slavery in the Hebrew Bible, see D.E. Callender, Jr., "Servants of God(s) and Servants of Kings in Israel and the Ancient Near East," in A.D. Callahan, R.A. Horsley, A. Smith, *Slavery*, 67–82 and the bibliography cited there. The Hebrew עֶבֶד is used for a male slave. Hebrew had no word for female slaves from the same root. The standard words for female slaves are אמה and שביה ("captive").

[5] In this case, Exod 21:5–6 describes a ritual where the person voluntarily submitting to slavery has his ear pierced as a sign that he will serve that master for life. This ritual describes men who have been married and had children while in service to their master. Lev 25:41 says that the Israelite should be released on the jubilee year, "he and his sons with him." The text does not state whether the sons are born before or after the Israelite sells himself into servitude.

who is sold as a slave does not "go out" like a male (probably since she is used as a concubine), but either is redeemed or released (a) if her master is not pleased with her, (b) if he gives her to his son, or (c) if he marries another (or takes anther concubine) and does not continue to provide for her. Deuteronomy 15:12–17, in an apparent revision of the Exodus law, explicitly says that the law applies to the female slave.

The situation of foreign slaves was altogether different. In the case of holding foreigners as slaves, Israelites could, in fact, keep them as they would other chattel. Leviticus 25:46, for instance, allows the Israelite to will them to his heirs. But, the foreign slave is not treated as chattel exclusively. Genesis 17:12–13 requires foreign slaves to be circumcised, and circumcised slaves are permitted to participate in the Passover meal. Circumcised slaves of priests are permitted to eat the priestly rations (Lev 22:11). Thus, the foreign slave is at the same time property and a dependent of the householder.[6]

In ancient Israel (and the ancient Near East generally) (debt-) slaves and (indentured) servants were utilized primarily in small numbers in households, not in mass numbers as laborers who worked large agricultural estates or mines. Occasionally large numbers of foreigners might become available as slaves due to military successes, but this was certainly not a frequent or normal occurrence.[7] Those people who were enslaved in ancient Israel had a social and legal status different from that of the chattel slaves who made up the system practiced later in Hellenistic-Roman times.

JEWS AND SLAVERY IN THE HELLENISTIC-ROMAN WORLD:
GENERAL CONSIDERATIONS

Slavery in ancient Greece and Rome was a complex phenomenon, but in general slaves in the Hellenistic-Roman period were their owners' chattel. The slave owned nothing, generally had no independent legal rights, and was obligated to do as his/her master commanded. Failure to obey meant discipline or punishment as the master saw fit. In a papyrus from 225 CE concerning the sale of a slave-girl named Soteris,

---

[6] For a more detailed discussion, see Flesher, *Oxen, Women, or Citizens?* chapter 1.
[7] On the uses, sale and sources of slaves generally, see de Vaux, *Ancient Israel*, 80–90.

"[Kephalon agrees] that [Apion therefore is master] and has possession and [controls her] and can deal with her in whatever [manner he
chooses]."[8] The slave had no legal family. Anyone to whom the slave
was married by the master belonged to the master, and any children
born to a slave were the property of the master to keep or dispose of
as he/she saw fit.

Some incentives were offered to slaves, however, to make the slave
system work. Masters occasionally allowed families to stay together. They
sometimes set up educated or talented slaves in businesses in which
the slave was permitted to keep some of the proceeds. Such is apparently the case in an Oxyrhynchus papyrus where a brother and sister
who have inherited a slave from their parents are petitioning two local
officials. The slave evidently works independently of his masters but is
refusing to pay them the required monies they think he owes.[9] Slaves
were often allowed to keep a *peculium*, a fund that might eventually be
used to purchase the slave's freedom. And not all slaves lived difficult
lives of backbreaking labor. Some slaves, especially in the Roman imperial households, could be entrusted with significant responsibilities that
resulted in that slave accumulating wealth, social prestige and even slaves
of his/her own. These slaves also experienced a greater independence
from their masters than other slaves.[10]

Enslaved persons were used for a wide variety of tasks at all levels
of society. Large numbers of laborers were used in mines, in manufac-
turing facilities or on large agricultural estates. They were also used in
the household as personal attendants, cooks, bath attendants, etc. As
a result, slaves were quite simply ubiquitous in the Hellenistic-Roman
Mediterranean.

Because of the general ubiquity of slaves, Jews, no doubt, were
familiar with Greek and, subsequently, Roman slave systems from early
on. Jewish contacts with the Hellenistic and Roman west were quite

---

[8] *SB* 14.11277. S.R. Llewelyn, *New Documents Illustrating Early Christianity, vol.
6* (Macquarie University: The Ancient History Documentary Research Centre, 1992)
50–1.

[9] P.Oxy.Hels. 26. G.H.R. Horsley, *New Documents Illustrating Early Christianity vol.
4* (Macquarie University: The Ancient History Documentary Research Centre, 1987)
100–3.

[10] For a good summary of these issues, see D.B. Martin, *Slavery as Salvation: The
Metaphor of Slavery in Pauline Christianity* (New Haven: Yale University Press, 1990)
chapter 1. But cf. O. Patterson, *Slavery and Social Death* (Cambridge, MA: Harvard
University Press, 1982) 182–86, 300–10.

extensive already by the turn of the era.[11] These contacts were affected not only by Greek and Roman military and mercantile traffic in the Near East, but by the general spread of Jewish communities into Egypt, Asia Minor, Greece and Rome. Those living as significant minorities in these diaspora communities would likely have had extensive experience with slavery, both with individual slaves and with its larger institutional forms. In many cases, Jews were among those known to have been slaves. For instance, two inscriptions from Delphi, which date to 163/162 and 158/157 BCE, note the manumission of an unknown Jewish slave and a Jewish slave woman and her two daughters.[12]

Although it is not certain when Jews began to settle in Rome, the greatest population expansion of that diaspora community most likely came about beginning in the first century BCE through the importation of Jews as slaves. Pompey undoubtedly brought back captives, who would be sold as slaves, as part of his triumph. Philo, in the first century CE, remarks that most of the inhabitants of the Jewish community in Rome were brought to Rome as slaves and later were manumitted (*Legatio ad Gaium* 155), and certainly many more slaves were brought to Rome to celebrate Titus's triumph over the Jews in the First Revolt.[13]

Several pieces of evidence demonstrate that Palestine also became acquainted with Hellenistic-Roman slave systems at a fairly early period. The Zenon papyri, which give a detailed view of the relationship between

---

[11] Abundant evidence exists for Jewish communities throughout the Mediterranean world. N.b. Josephus's celebrated citation of Strabo (*Ant.* 14.114–15), who remarks that Jews can be found in every city, and also the report of the speech of Agrippa in *War* 2.398 who says "There is not a people in the world which does not contain a portion of our race." On the contacts between Jews, Greeks and Romans, see M. Hengel, *Judaism and Hellenism* (Philadelphia: Fortress, 1974) and M. Stern, *Studies in the History of Israel in the Second Temple Period* (Jerusalem: Yad Yitzchak ben Zvi, 1992 [Hebrew]). On familiarity of gentiles with Jews, see M. Stern, *Greek and Latin Authors on Jews and Judaism, vols 1–3* (Jerusalem: The Israel Academy of Sciences and Humanities, 1976–84). On the various Jewish communities in Asia Minor, see P. Trebilco, *Jewish Communities in Asia Minor* (SNTSMS 69; Cambridge: Cambridge University Press, 1991).

[12] J.-B. Frey, *Corpus Inscriptionum Iudaicarum* as cited in Hengel, *Judaism and Hellenism*, 42 and E.E. Urbach, "The Laws Regarding Slavery as a Source for Social History of the Period of the Second Temple, the Mishnah and Talmud," *Papers of the Institute of Jewish Studies London* (J.G. Weiss, ed.; Jerusalem: Magnes Press, 1964) 13. On the identification of Jews in epigraphic materials, see R.S. Kraemer, "On the Meaning of the Term 'Jew' in Greco-Roman Inscriptions," *HTR* 81 (1989) 35–53 and idem, "Jewish Tuna and Christian Fish: Identifying Religious Affiliation in Epigraphic Sources," *HTR* 84 (1991) 141–62.

[13] A good summary of these importations can be found in G. Fuks, "Where Have all the Freedmen Gone? On an Anomaly in the Jewish Grave-Inscriptions from Rome," *JJS* 36 (1985) 25–32.

Ptolemaic Egypt and Palestine in the third century BCE, provide perhaps
the best evidence about early Jewish involvement with Hellenistic slave
sytems in Palestine. Slaves were but one commodity in an extensive
trading network between Egypt and Palestine in this period. One text,
CPJ 1, will suffice as an example. This papyrus records the sale of a
seven year old slave girl named Sphragis. She was sold to Zenon by a
man named Nikanor "in the service of Tobias."[14] Several other papyri
testify to Zenon's slave acquisitions in the area.[15] In the period of the
Maccabean revolt, 2 Macc 8:11 notes that the Syrian general Nicanor
sold captured Jews as slaves, apparently to Phoenicians on the seacoast,
in order to make two thousand talents, the amount due to the Seleucid
king as tribute.

These several examples do not exhaust the available evidence. What
they demonstrate is that Jews, in Palestine and in the diaspora, were
well acquainted with Hellenistic-Roman slavery. If they knew the social
reality, they were undoubtedly conversant with the vocabulary of slavery
in these periods. Several Jewish writers, Philo and Josephus for example,
are very familiar with the variegated terminology for slaves. What all
this implies is that when these writers use terms for slaves, whether
general or specific, modern interpreters ought to see the thought world
of this language reflecting that of Hellenistic-Roman chattel slavery, not
what might be termed the indentured servitude more characteristic
of the biblical laws. That is, when Philo and Josephus speak of slaves,
they speak, on the whole, the language of Hellenistic-Roman slavery.
The situation is complicated by the fact that both Philo and Josephus
comment specifically on the biblical laws, and a major question is the
extent to which the terms that they use for biblical slaves reveal their
own attitudes towards slavery. I will try to set out some of those com-
plications below.

THE USE OF SLAVE TERMS IN HELLENISTC GREEK

In contrast to Hebrew, which had one principal word for male servants/
slaves and two for female servants/slaves, Greek had quite a number.

[14] V. Tcherikover and G. Fuks, *Corpus Papyrorum Ioudicarum* (3 vols.; Cambridge:
Harvard University Press, 1957–64) 1.118–20.
[15] See Hengel, *Judaism and Hellenism*, 41, and Urbach, "Laws Regarding Slavery," 13.

Each of these had important distinctions in the classical period, but evidently during the Hellenistic period, the several different terms for slaves began to be used more often as synonyms, the older distinctions being generally abandoned. The place where this synonymity is most noticeable is in the papyri, most of which come from Egypt. In the Hellenistic through the Roman periods the papyri show these Greek words used in identical or similar ways to indicate slaves.[16]

Of all the terms used to designate male slaves, δοῦλος (a general word for slave), παῖς (a less general and more familiar word) and its diminutives, οἰκέτης (a domestic or household slave) and θεράπων (personal attendant) are found in Second-Temple Jewish literature. In addition *koine* Greek often uses the nouns ἀνδράποδον (literally "human footed") and σῶμα ("body"), and the adjective οἰκογενής ("houseborn"). Female slaves are most often designated by παιδίσκη, δούλη, θεράπαινα and κοράσιον (although in the Jewish-Greek biblical translations κοράσιον seems to mean "young girl" rather than "slave").

In the Hellenistic and Roman periods, these words can be found maintaining their usual distinctions with relative frequency, but all can be used of slaves in general and do not have to retain the earlier classical differentiation.[17] In several cases δοῦλος and οἰκέτης or δοῦλος and παῖς are used synonymously,[18] so, for instance, the case of a certain Epagathos, who is called both a δοῦλος and a παιδάριον.[19] Often these different terms may be modified by οἰκογενής or even by each other. A number of papyri, for example, use παιδίσκη δούλη.[20]

Important for the use of these terms in the Greek biblical translations and other Second Temple Jewish literature is J. Modrzejewski's

---

[16] J.G. Gibbs and L. Feldman, "Josephus' Vocabulary for Slavery," *JQR* 76 (1986) 288, and Garlan, *Slavery*, 21, make this claim without documentation. The studies of J.-A. Straus, "La terminologie de l'esclavage dans les papyrus grecs d'époque romaine trouvés en Égypte," *Actes du colloque 1973 sur l'esclavage* (Annales Litteraires de l'Université Besançon, 182; Paris: Les Belles Lettres, 1976) 335–50; idem, "La terminologie grecque de l'esclavage dans les papyrus de l'Égypte lagide et romaine," *Scritti in Onore di Orsolina Montevecchi* (E. Bresciani et al., eds.; Bologna: Editrice Bologna, 1981) 385–91; and C. Spicq, "Le vocabulaire de l'esclavage dans le Nouveau Testament," *RB* 85 (1978) 201–26 set out much of the evidence.

[17] See especially Spicq, "Le vocabulaire," who deals in detail with individual terms.

[18] Straus, "La terminologie de l'esclavage dans les papyrus grecs d'époque romaine," 337, 338.

[19] Ibid., 349.

[20] Ibid., 338, 344 note 40.

point that there appears to be two vocabularies for slaves.[21] One is a juridical/official vocabulary which appears "in public acts, in particular requests that are submitted to authorities."[22] The other is a private/daily vocabulary. It is this private/daily vocabulary where the terms for slaves find their most frequent uses as synonyms. Synonymity is possible largely because in such private/daily use those involved would know the status of the slave in question. In requests made to authorities, a greater specificity might be expected.[23] What we will see below is that both the Greek biblical translations and other Second Temple Jewish works use those terms that appear most frequently in the papyri as synonyms. Those terms that are used most in Modrzejewski's public vocabulary, like ἀνδράποδον, or those that are most ambiguous, like σῶμα, are used very little.

The LXX and the Translation of Terms for Slaves[24]

Of the close to 800 uses of the Hebrew term עֶבֶד in the Jewish scriptures, almost 770 are rendered either by δοῦλος or παῖς.[25] Of the remaining equivalents for this Hebrew word only θεράπων and οἰκέτης amount to

---

[21] In Straus, "La terminologie de l'esclavage dans les papyrus grecs d'époque romaine," 347.

[22] Ibid., 347.

[23] F. Dunant (in Straus, "La terminologie de l'esclavage dans les papyrus grecs d'époque romaine," 347–48) argues that this dual vocabulary might be referring to individuals whose status could be termed half-slaves. Modrzejewski's position, that these people are slaves and that the langauge has to do with the social context, makes better sense to me.

[24] Because of the number of occurrences of all words in the slave/servant word group and the scope of this article, I will restrict the material below to the nouns used for slaves in Hellenistic Jewish literature. These are primarily, but certainly not exclusively, δοῦλος and παῖς.

[25] The statistics will vary depending on which edition of the Jewish-Greek Bible one consults. For detailed treatments of δοῦλος and παῖς in the Bible, see K. Rengstorf, "δοῦλος," *Theological Dictionary of the New Testament, vol. II* (G. Kittel and G. Friedrich, eds.; Grand Rapids, MI: Wm. B. Eerdmans, 1967) 261–80; W. Zimmerli, "παῖς θεοῦ," *Theological Dictionary of the New Testament, vol. V* (G. Kittel and G. Friedrich, eds.; Grand Rapids, MI: Wm. B. Eerdmans, 1967) 654–77; and J. Jeremias, "παῖς θεοῦ in Later Judaism in the Period after the LXX," *Theological Dictionary of the New Testament, vol. V,* 677–717. For a basic overview of some words for servant/slave in the Jewish-Greek scriptures, see R.A. Kraft, *Septuagintal Lexicography* (SBLSCS 1; Missoula, MT: Scholars Press, 1975) 176–78. The words for female slaves are somewhat less problematic because the Hebrew has no word for female slaves derived from the verb עֶבֶד. Thus the Greek δούλη occurs very infrequently. The translators of the Jewish scriptures prefer παιδίσκη when a slave/servant is specifically female.

any significant portion. The number of occurrences of these words are relatively meaningless in themselves, however. Only some summary of how and where they are used gives them any meaning for understanding the conceptual transformation, if there is any, between the Hebrew and Greek languages.

The Pentateuch. The most immediately noticeable feature of the renderings of עֶבֶד in the earliest of the biblical translations is that δοῦλος almost never occurs. Genesis, Exodus and Numbers do not use δοῦλος at all. Leviticus uses it only twice and Deuteronomy only once. W. Zimmerli understands the translators as reserving δοῦλος for "especially severe bondage."[26] But this solution is not entirely satisfactory. The difficulties of determining whether any distinction in meaning is to be made between δοῦλος and παῖς can be seen in the several uses of δοῦλος in the Pentateuch.

Leviticus 25:39–44 concerns two issues: the treatment of the Israelite who, due to impoverishment, sells himself to another Israelite and the buying of foreign slaves. In these verses neither the Hebrew nor the way the Greek translator understood it is altogether clear. Verse 39 says that the Israelite who must sell himself is not to be worked as a slave (לֹא תַעֲבֹד בּוֹ עֲבֹדַת עָבֶד), but as a hired or bound laborer.[27] That Israelite shall be released at the next jubilee year, and he can then return to his family. The reason given in verse 42 is that since the Israelites are God's servants and since he brought them out of Egypt, they should not be sold as slaves are sold (לֹא יִמָּכְרוּ מִמְכֶּרֶת עָבֶד). Verse 44 begins the second issue mentioned above. "As for your male and female slaves (וְעַבְדְּךָ וַאֲמָתְךָ) whom you may have, it is from the nations around you that you may acquire male and female slaves (וְעֶבֶד וְאָמָה)." The servants of the beginning of this verse must be understood as the same as those at the end—non-Israelite slaves who can be bought from the surrounding nations.

How the Greek translator understood this passage is very unclear and for the most part depends on how one thinks he understood who the slaves/servants were in each instance. He translates the end of verse 39

---

[26] Zimmerli, "παῖς θεοῦ," 674.

[27] The term translated "bound laborer" is תּוֹשָׁב, which usually indicates a resident alien. The term is used in parallel with "hired laborer" here and earlier in 25:6. Thus, the terms seem to mean an Israelite who is a hired laborer and a resident alien who hires himself out. See, B. Levine, *The JPS Torah Commentary: Leviticus* (Philadelphia: Jewish Publication Society, 1989) 170–71.

οὐ δουλούσει σοι δουλείαν οἰκέτου (lit. "you shall not enslave them with the slavery of a household servant"). In verse 42 the Israelites are called the οἰκέται of God, so they shall not be sold like an οἰκέτης. In these cases, the translator keeps a consistent rendering of the Hebrew, whether one sees the connotation of the passage as good, bad or neutral. In verse 44, however, the translator begins with the παῖς and παιδίσκη who belong to the Israelites, and he finishes the verse with δοῦλον and δούλην. If the translator construed the beginning of the Hebrew of verse 44 as referring to Israelite slaves, connecting it to what came before, and then understood the end of the verse as referring to non-Israelite slaves, Zimmerli's claim would make sense. If, on the other hand, the translator understood the Hebrew correctly, then παῖς and παιδίσκη are synonyms for δοῦλος and δούλη, and Zimmerli's contention would not appear to hold true. Which is the case is very difficult to tell. Further complicating matters is Deut 32:36 where God's people are not called his οἰκέται but his δοῦλοι.

The other use of δοῦλος in the Pentateuch is Lev 26:13 where God again appeals to his role as deliverer from Egypt, but there is added, "when you were slaves (δοῦλοι)." In this case the context makes it clear that the idea of chattel bondage is meant. The latter part of the verse proclaims that God "broke the bonds of your yoke and made you walk upright." In other places, however, the Israelite bondage in Egypt is looked back on and expressed through the use of οἰκέτης (Deut 5:15, 15:15). In the passages that narrate that bondage, especially Exod 5:15–16, the Israelites, who do not understand why Pharaoh is being so hard on them, call themselves his οἰκέται and παῖδες.[28]

Whatever significance one assigns to it, the translators of the Septuagint show a clear predilection for παῖς as a translation of עבד in all its various uses.[29] Several examples will demonstrate the wide variey of uses to which the Septuagint translators put παῖς. Although παῖς can mean "child" with reference to chronological age and so sometimes can refer to a young slave/servant, it does not often have that meaning in

---

[28] The end of the verse is difficult. The MT of Exod 15:16 reads, "Look how your servants are beaten, and the sin of your people." The LXX has this last clause as a full independent clause that suggests that the Israelites saw themselves as Pharaoh's people. It reads "And look, your servants are whipped/beaten. Therefore you are being unjust to your people."

[29] It is the clear favorite rendering in Genesis. The predominance of θεράπων in Exodus can be attributed to that translator's use of the term to represent the servants/attendants of Pharaoh, a phrase that occurs frequently in the book.

the Septuagint. The slave laws in Exodus 21 use the word to refer to the Hebrew slave who is bought and who serves for six years or until the next jubilee. Even the Hebrew slave who renounces his freedom in order to stay with his wife and children (he clearly is no child himself) and voluntarily consents to stay the slave of his master in perpetuity is called παῖς (21:6). In the Joseph story in Genesis, Joseph is sold as a slave in Egypt to one of Pharaoh's officers. Potiphar's wife calls Joseph a Hebrew παῖς at the same time she is finding him sexually attractive and accusing him of attacking her (Gen 39:17–19). It is this same παῖς who is subsequently put in charge of administering food supplies in all of Egypt.

As has often been noted about עֶבֶד, it is a word that does not have to indicate slave status in the absolute, but subservient status vis-à-vis someone or something else. Frequently, one addressing a king or social superior calls him/herself one's servant. Several places in the Pentateuch exemplify this use. In Gen 19:19, Lot responds to the messengers of God who have told him to flee, "Your servant (παῖς) has found favor before you." Later in Gen 33:5 when Esau and Jacob reconcile, Jacob calls himself Esau's servant (παῖς) as a gesture of humility and reconciliation.

A similar idea is also found in relation to God. In several places in the Pentateuch, people are called servants (עֶבֶד) of Yahweh. Although different Greek servant/slave terms are used to express this relationship, δοῦλος is not one of them.[30] The most frequently used term in this context is θεράπων. Moses, for example, is called a θεράπων of God in several places (see Exod 14:31; Num 11:11, 12:7–8). Deuteronomy, however, generally prefers οἰκέτης to θεράπων; at Moses' death, the Deuteronomist calls Moses a servant of God, rendered οἰκέτης κυρίου by the Greek translator. Yet, in Deut 3:24 Moses calls himself a θεράπων of God. παῖς is not left out of this type of usage, either. In Num 14:24, where God singles out Caleb for believing him, he calls him "my servant (ὁ παῖς μου)."

Not only individuals, but families and the nation of Israel as corporate entities, are called God's servants. Here too, no one Greek term characterizes this relationship. In Gen 50:17, for example, Joseph's brothers ask him to forgive the "crime of the servants (θεραπόντων) of your father." Lev 25:42, 55 both refer to the Israelites as the οἰκέται of God.

---

[30] There is considerable discussion of the servant of Yahweh in Zimmerli, "παῖς θεοῦ" and Jeremias, "παῖς θεοῦ in Later Judaism."

Several instances in particular indicate that the translators may have used these words for slaves/servants as relative synonyms, with only minor distinctions. In the curse of Canaan (Gen 9:25–26), he is to be עֶבֶד עֲבָדִים, translated "the lowest of slaves" by the NRSV, to his brothers, and in verse 26 God blesses Shem and makes Canaan his slave. The Greek translator renders the first phrase παῖς οἰκέτης and the second παῖς, thus making the two terms synonymous for "slave." Later in Gen 44:33, Judah pleads with Joseph to allow Benjamin to return to Canaan with his brothers. In his place Judah offers himself as surety that the brothers will return. "I will remain as a slave (παῖς) instead of the boy, a slave (οἰκέτης) of [my] lord/master," begs Judah.[31] For the translator of Genesis, the two uses of עֶבֶד are synonymous, but he uses two different Greek words. παῖς perhaps connotes a slave in a more general fashion while the following use of οἰκέτης has more specificity regarding the duties of the slave. The words should nonetheless be regarded as virtually synonymous. Finally, in Deuteronomy, where the Greek translator uses οἰκέτης to refer to the status of the Israelites as slaves, Moses is called both an οἰκέτης (34:5) and a θεράπων (3:24) of God.

These data, then, indicate that for the translators of the Pentateuch, the several words for slaves used here δοῦλος, παῖς, οἰκέτης and perhaps θεράπων are roughly synonymous, or at least in some cases interchangeable. Zimmerli's distinction between δοῦλος and the other terms does not hold in my estimation. Yet, the reason that the translators of the Pentateuch generally avoided δοῦλος is not clear to me. Perhaps these translators considered the term derogatory or insulting in a way that the others were not (even though some contexts might lend themselves to insult).

The social realities behind these uses is also difficult to ascertain. In Hellenistic-Roman Egypt were Jewish slaves/indentured servants and non-Jewish slaves both called παῖς and/or οἰκέτης as they are in the Septuagint? On the one hand, those Jews who were enslaved for debt were designated by the same words as foreign slaves, but, on the other hand, the laws in Leviticus, while recognizing the "slave" status of these Jewish servants, also demanded that they be treated as hired workers.[32]

---

[31] These same two words appear in Judah's speech to Joseph in 44:16. In this case παῖς is used as a term of social deference.

[32] Westermann notes that the Jewish community near the Black Sea (ancient Panticapaeum) seemed to have expressed "the traditional Hebrew attitude as it expressed itself in slavery," but that "in the formal and external features both of procedure and

At the very least, the Jewish translators are adapting the language of Hellenistic-Roman slavery to a category of Jewish enslavement which has no ready Hellenistic parallel.

Excursus on the Use of a Jewish Form of Greek

This last point raises the issue of whether the Greek of the Septuagint translators reflects a special Jewish Greek spoken by Jews in this period or whether the Septuagint formed the basis for the development of a special Jewish dialect of *koine*. That is, did Hellenistic Jews speak a language like that found in the biblical translations? A recent article by G.H.R. Horsley has conclusively argued against such a notion.[33]

> The issue of Jewish Greek has been brought clearly into focus by the studies which have appeared in the *New Docs* series. The sample of inscriptions and papyri collected in the four previous volumes provides a tangible weight of evidence which has steadily reinforced the impression that to claim any such cleavage between the *koine* and "Jewish" or "Christian" Greek is quite inapposite. In the present chapter it is intended to show that the erroneous belief in Jewish Greek is dependent on
> (a) the acceptance of over-vague terminology and
> (b) lack of contact with linguistic research, particularly in the area of bilingualism.[34]

Recent linguistic theory has shown that the phenomenon of bilingualism is much more complex than those claiming the existence of a Jewish Greek have recognized. The result is that distinctions must be made regarding bilingualism and the question of fluency in the secondary language, the relative status of the primary and secondary languages, which language is the preferred language (not always the primary language), how a secondary language is learned, and whether the secondary language is read and perhaps understood but not spoken.[35] The presence of Semiticisms in Greek, moreover, cannot bear the weight of an argument for Jewish Greek.[36]

---

of publicity of the event, Greek practices and models were copied almost completely" (*Slave Systems*, 125). He argues this latter point on the evidence of four manumission inscriptions.

[33] Horsley, *New Documents*, 5.5–40. This section contains a good history of the scholarly claims made for such a Jewish Greek.

[34] Ibid., 6.

[35] Ibid., 24–25.

[36] Ibid., 26–37.

Although certain "Semitic features" do find their way into the Greek used by Jews and Christians' it should be regarded as "the expected phenomenon of interference which manifests itself in varying degrees in the speech and writing of bilinguals."[37] Jews may well have spoken with an accent, but accents do not make dialects. What distinguished the Greek spoken by Jews in antiquity from other peoples' Greek was the use of technical terms reflecting the particularities of Jewish culture and religion. It was Jewish customs that marked them, not their Greek.[38]

Joshua, Judges, 1–4 Kingdoms. These translations, with the exception of Joshua, restrict the number of terms rendering עבד to παῖς and δοῦλος.

In Joshua, Moses is at the same time called the παῖς of God (1:7, 13; 9:24; 11:12, 15, 14:7[39] and others) and the θεράπων of God (1:2). Joshua, at his death, is called δοῦλος κυρίου (24:30 [29]).[40] The deceit of the Gibeonites reported in Joshua 9 contains the other major uses of slave language in Joshua. The Gibeonites come pretending to be people from a far away land who want to make a treaty with Joshua. In trying to make the ruse convincing, they twice use language of humility claiming to be Israel's "servants/slaves." In the first instance, 9:8, they call themselves οἰκέται, and in the second, 9:9, they use παῖδες. It is unclear whether the translator intends these terms as synonyms, or whether he wants to convey a more subservient status, foreshadowing what is to come a few verses later, because in 9:23 Joshua curses the Gibeonites for deceiving him and says that they shall always be slaves (δοῦλος), wood cutters and water bearers for the "house of my God." The passage clearly understands being a δοῦλος as an undesirable position in which to be, but it sheds little light on the meanings of the two terms used previously.[41]

---

[37] Ibid., 40.

[38] Ibid.

[39] A. Rahlfs prints παῖς in his text (*Septuaginta: Id est Vetus Testamentum graece iuxta LXX interpretes* [2 vols.; Stuttgart: Würtembergische Bibelanstalt, 1935]); Ms A reads δούλους κυρίου.

[40] In 7:7 the Greek has Joshua call himself παῖς, but there is no extant Hebrew for this phrase in the MT.

[41] Another passage may help a bit here. In 5:14, the commander of the army of the Lord meets Joshua, who falls on his face and calls himself the οἰκέτης of the divine warrior. Here, although the term indicates humility and inferiority, it does not seem to have a negative connotation.

Both δοῦλος and παῖς appear frequently in 1–4 Kingdoms. About their uses in these books, Zimmerli argues that "[o]ne may discern a careful distinction between them. παῖς is used only for the freer servants of the king (soldiers, minister, officials) who by their own choice enter his service…δοῦλος, on the other hand, is used for slavery proper."[42] I confess to being a bit puzzled about this claim, however. A careful look at the use of the two terms in 1 Kgdms 16:14–17:38 illustrates the difficulty of making such a sharp distinction.

In 1 Kgdms 16:14 an evil spirit enters Saul and torments him. In 16:15 he calls his παῖδες who diagnose the spirit. They reply, "Let your servants (δοῦλοι) speak and let them seek for our master a man." Saul then requests that his παῖδες find such a man. In chapter 17, Goliath issues his challenge, that if he defeats an Israelite they will be the slaves of the Philistines and if the Israelite triumphs, the Philistines will be slaves of the Israelites, with the term δοῦλος, clearly indicating enslavement for the vanquished. David then appears on the scene and volunteers to fight the Philistine. He convinces Saul and in his argument uses the term δοῦλος three times (17:32, 34, 38) to describe his relationship to Saul.

In the first passage, the Greek translator actually turns the Hebrew text around a bit. The MT has Saul's servants reply, "Let our lord say to your servants who are before you." The Greek makes the servants, here called δοῦλοι, the subject of the verb, and thus more obviously the same group of servants just called παῖδες. By rearranging the text in this way, the two Greek terms must be synonymous, and thus Zimmerli's distinction breaks down. In chapter 17, the same Greek term is used to indicate the status of the vanquished people, reflecting Zimmerli's idea that δοῦλος is reserved for slavery, but David immediately thereafter calls himself δοῦλος in a passage where he is clearly volunteering to enter the service of the king. So, while it is possible that the distinction that Zimmerli claims for these translations might generally apply, it cannot be maintained throughout. I would see these two terms as having an overlap in meaning with the tendency of δοῦλος to indicate slavery and that of παῖς to refer to voluntary service to the king.

The Later Books. Most of the other books use both δοῦλος and παῖς to render עֶבֶד. Some, like the Minor Prophets and Ecclesiastes, use δοῦλος as the stereotyped rendering of the Hebrew. Most, however, use both

---

[42] Zimmerli, "παῖς θεοῦ," 674.

to some degree. Psalms is a good example here. While Psalms clearly favors δοῦλος (παῖς only appears four times in Psalms), both terms designate a servant/slave of God, δοῦλος many times and παῖς in Ps 85(86):16 and 68(69):18. The same situation can be found in the Greek of Isaiah. The general conclusion one can reach for these translations is that δοῦλος and παῖς have become fairly interchangeable as translations of עבד, and the alternatives found most frequently in the earlier books have now fallen out of use.[43]

The one major exception, of those books for which Hebrew is extant, is the Wisdom of Ben Sira. Ben Sira uses neither of the two major Greek terms, but he renders עבד by οἰκέτης in every instance. In this case, the use of οἰκέτης seems to indicate a foreign slave, who is considered chattel. Sirach 7:20–21 encourages a master not to abuse a faithful slave and not to withhold freedom from an intelligent slave.[44] Later in 33:25–33 on the treatment of slaves, Ben Sira advises a master to work a slave hard because idleness will cause a slave to "seek liberty." Thus, a slave is to have "bread and discipline"; for a wicked slave Ben Sira recommends "racks and tortures." If a slave does not obey, he says, "make his fetters heavy." These do not sound like the recommendations for an Israelite slave who is not to be treated like an οἰκέτης (see above on the Pentateuch), laws Ben Sira certainly knows. The only exception to this trend is in the prayer contained in chapter 36. Verse 22 refers to the Israelites as the οἰκέται of God, a use of the term also found in the Greek translation of the Pentateuch.

Conclusions. The lack of use of δοῦλος in the Pentateuch would appear to be intentional on the part of the translators. The reasons for that avoidance are not so obvious, however. Perhaps the use of this particular term was not thought to be appropriate for slaves who would have been used primarily in the household while other terms would. Yet, as we saw, the few cases of δοῦλος that do occur in the Septuagint proper serve to blur this distinction. The Pentateuch does contain a broader vocabulary for slavery than do the rest of the Greek translations, which tend to restrict their uses to δοῦλος and παῖς, both for actual slaves

---

[43] Except for the translator for Job who prefers θεράπων and the translator of Proverbs who also has a predilection for οἰκέτης.

[44] P.W. Skehan and A.A. Di Lella refer to the law of release of the Hebrew slave after six years. It does not appear from the biblical laws, however, that an Israelite master could withhold that freedom, so my inclination is to understand Ben Sira as speaking of foreign slaves that could be considered chattel and either be freed or kept (*The Wisdom of Ben Sira* [AB 39; New York: Doubleday, 1987] 205).

and in figurative uses.[45] This situation may perhaps be attributed to one specific problem facing the Greek translators of the Pentateuch, namely, that the category of Israelite slave represents an in-between category that does not exist in Hellenistic slave systems. Yet even in these instances the translators did not restrict the use of some terms to Israelite slaves and other terms for foreign slaves, further complicating the problem. Later translations narrow the range of possible terms, but they also eliminate distinctions in the meaning of the terms that they use.

What appears to me to be the case is that the translators were struggling to find ways to represent what was a completely different lexical and social world from theirs. Ancient Israelites had a single term for various forms of servitude. An Israelite enslaved to another Israelite, a foreigner enslaved to an Israelite, a free person voluntarily serving a king, a person expressing social deference to another, a person addressing a God, all are designated by the same term, עֶבֶד. Socially, ancient Israel does not seem to have had a slave-dependent economy. Few persons would have held large numbers of slaves, and most slaves were attendants in a household, in close contact with the master and his family.

This was not the lexical and social world of Jews in the Hellenistic period. Greek was replete with words for slaves. A household slave, a field slave, a houseborn slave, a personal attendant, all had different designations in Greek. And, although conditions varied throughout the Mediterranean, it can probably be said that the economy of the Hellenistic-Roman world was much more dependent on slave labor than anything ancient Israel knew.

The translators of the Hebrew Bible lived in the latter world, and their use of terms for slaves in the Jewish-Greek translations reflects their attempts to transform the monolithic slave/servant language of Hebrew to their own. In doing so, these scholars not only lexically translated, but culturally transformed the biblical language of slavery for those who used the texts after them.

---

[45] It should at least be noted that the Greek translations of the Jewish Bible are not the only places where someone can be a slave to a god. To be a slave of a god is used often in the magical papyri. The extant collections of magical texts, for the most part, post-date these translations, and are of minimal use in evaluating the novelty of this translation choice.

Slave Terms in Josephus

In contrast to the Septuagint, Josephus's usual term for slave is δοῦλος, which almost certainly connotes for him a chattel slave. This is most forcefully demonstrated in speeches attributed to Jewish leaders in the *Jewish War*. To be a δοῦλος is, for Josephus, to lose all of one's freedoms. This is not the limited servitude of the biblical laws. More than once are slaves contrasted to free persons. In Agrippa's speech in *War* 2.356 the δοῦλος is contrasted to the φιλελεύθερος, the lover of freedom. In *Ant.* 3.357 to surrender to the Romans is to become a δοῦλος. Here Josephus is certainly referring to the Roman practice of selling captives of war as slaves. δοῦλοι in Josephus's social world seem to occupy a very low place. In *War* 4.508 when Simon bar Giora frees slaves, Josephus links them with evildoers (πονηροί). He also remarks that Simon's army is made up of slaves and brigands (δούλων...λῃστῶν). In *War* 5.443 he calls Simon son of John and his supporters "slaves and rabble and the bastard outcasts of the nation" (δοῦλοι καὶ συγκλύδες καὶ νόθα τοῦ ἔθνους φθάρματα).

Josephus also utilizes a broader vocabulary of slavery than do the Greek biblical translations. Of the nouns used to designate a slave several appear in common with the Greek Bible, δοῦλος, οἰκέτης, θεράπων and παῖς. In addition, several other Greek words refer to, or may refer to, slaves. The most frequently used are αἰχμάλωτος (referring to war captives) and ἀνδράποδον (which does not occur in the Greek biblical translations).[46] What J.G. Gibbs and L. Feldman conclude from the use of these terms is that Josephus did not distinguish very carefully among his words for slaves, generally using them as rough synonyms.[47] They cite several pieces of evidence, all of which justify this conclusion. Two seem most convincing to me.

First, in a number of cases where parallel passages exist between the *Antiquities* and the *Jewish War*, Josephus changes the term used to designate a slave. For instance, in *War* 1.233, Herod, as part of a ruse, sends a servant (οἰκέτης) ahead on the pretext of preparing a meal. When that same incident is narrated in *Ant.* 14.291, the οἰκέτης is now a θεράπων. In *War* 1.620 when certain informers are produced for Herod,

---

[46] For locations and discussion of other nouns and word groups in Josephus having to do with slavery, see Gibbs and Feldman, "Josephus' Vocabulary."

[47] Ibid., 290. I came upon this article after I had examined the uses of these words in Josephus and had come to the same conclusion.

some come from the οἰκέται of Antipater's mother. The same event in *Ant.* 17.93 finds them called δοῦλοι.[48]

The second point made by Gibbs and Feldman is one on which I want to expand. A good way to ascertain how Josephus uses these terms would be to compare them to places where he treats biblical texts. Gibbs and Feldman look closely at 1–4 Kingdoms.[49] They note at several places that Josephus has apparently substituted δοῦλος, or some form of it, for another word. They further point out that since Josephus probably had some "proto-Lucianic" form of these books that definite conclusions are difficult to make.[50]

One finds a similar trend elsewhere in Josephus where he cites or paraphrases biblical passages. I will examine Josephus's use of penta-teuchal traditions here. At the beginning of *Antiquities* 2, Josephus tells the story of Joseph. Both in places where he adds to the wording of the biblical narrative and in those passages where slave terms occur already, he primarily uses δοῦλος. In the interpretation of the brothers' initial dream, Josephus sees the sheaves of his brothers bowing down to his "like δοῦλοι before their masters." This is a clear expansion of the biblical text, but it represents the language Josephus has chosen for this story. When Joseph is sold in Egypt as a slave and he has his encounter with the libidinous wife of Potiphar, she calls him a wicked δοῦλος, although the Septuagint uses παῖς (also in *Ant.* 2.78). Later, after Joseph sets up Benjamin as a thief, Judah pleads with him to let Benjamin go and to keep him as a slave. Josephus uses δοῦλος here whereas the Greek of Gen 44:33 has οἰκέτης.

In other expansions of the biblical law, Josephus adds slaves (δοῦλοι) to the list of those who are to hear the reading of the Law (see *Ant.* 4.209 and Deut 31:10). Although Deuteronomy 17 and 19 do not specify them, Josephus (*Ant.* 4.219) also says that δοῦλοι cannot be counted

---

[48] These two examples were taken from Gibbs and Feldman. For a more detailed list, see ibid., 288.

[49] A crucial issue for the study of Josephus is whether he used a Greek or Hebrew text of the Bible. Gibbs and Feldman claim that one finds in 1–4 Kingdoms the "strongest evidence that Josephus used a Greek text" ("Josephus' Vocabulary," 297). See H.W. Attridge who concludes his "text of scripture used throughout is a Greek version. Josephus may, in some instances, have consulted a Hebrew or Aramaic *targum*, but the evidence for such Semitic sources, and particularly for the use of *targum*, is slender at best" ("Josephus and His Works," *Jewish Writings of the Second Temple Period* [CRINT 2.II; M.E. Stone, ed.; Philadelphia: Fortress, 1984] 211).

[50] For a complete listing of the comparable Greek biblical passages in Josephus and the conclusion cited here, see Gibbs and Feldman, "Josephus' Vocabulary," 298–99.

as possible witnesses in criminal cases due to the "baseness of their soul" (τὴν τῆς ψυξῆς ἀγένειαν). In the law concerning debt slavery, Exodus 22 does not designate by a noun the Israelite who is sold as a slave. Josephus (*Ant.* 4.272) calls him a δοῦλος. Finally, regarding the law concerning the ox which kills a male or female slave, Exod 21:32 calls the slaves παῖδα...ἢ παιδίσκην; Josephus (*Ant.* 4.282) designates them δοῦλον ἢ θεράπαιναν.

While Josephus uses δοῦλος and οἰκέτης by far and away more times than any other term to designate a slave,[51] the one term that really drops out of use as a primary designator for a slave is παῖς. The lack of this word's use to mean slave is especially striking when one remembers how it often far outnumbered uses of δοῦλος in the Greek biblical translations. Of the over 700 occurrences of παῖς in the works of Josephus only a very few could or do mean slave; the rest refer to children.[52]

In several other cases, παῖς clearly means child in a context where slavery is discussed, and thus the meaning of the term stands in contrast to slave. In *War* 7.334 Eleazar exhorts the people on Masada to commit mass suicide by arguing that such an end is more tolerable than surrender to the Romans. He says, "Let our wives thus die undishonored, our children (παῖδες) unacquainted with slavery (δουλεία)." In *Ant.* 19.129, Josephus gives a list of people who cannot believe that the emperor Gaius could be killed. He includes women, children (παῖδες) and slaves (δοῦλοι). *Antiquities* 12.209 and 217 are probably the most interesting passages of this kind. Hyrcanus, who is several times in this entire section called a boy (παῖς), is sent by his father to Alexandria to honor Ptolemy's newborn child. He buys from a slave dealer 100 παῖδας and 100 virgins (παρθένους) as a gift for Ptolemy. He then presents them to Ptolemy and Cleopatra each carrying a single talent. Even though Hyrcanus buys them from a slave dealer, and they are to be considered slaves, the use of παῖς together with "virgins" indicates that Josephus is interested not in their servile status, but in their ages. These are young boys and girls.[53]

---

[51] αἰχμάλωτος occurs more frequently than either of these, but it does not always refer to a slave, so it is not includeed in this section.

[52] Gibbs and Feldman, "Josephus' Vocabulary," 296, list three cases in *War*, 1.82 (twice) and 1.340. These are paralleled by passages in *Ant.* 13.314 and 315 where the same term is used. Of the ten places cited in *Antiquities*, three are parallel to the passages just noted. The two occurrences of the term in *Ant.* 12.209 and 12.217 listed by them as denoting slaves, probably mean simply "boys."

[53] *Contra* Gibbs and Feldman, "Josephus' Vocabulary," 296.

Conclusion. This brief discussion confirms the general conclusion reached by Gibbs and Feldman. Josephus has a varied vocabulary for slaves and generally uses the terms without making hard distinctions between them. Although a few uses of παῖς mean "slave," the term means "child" in the vast majority of its occurrences in Josephus's writings. In this, Josephus is certainly different from the Greek biblical translations which use παῖς often to designate a slave.

Slave Terms in Philo of Alexandria

Given the large corpus of Philo's writings, one might expect terms for slaves to occur fairly often; they do. His vocabulary for slaves is even more widely varied than the Greek Bible's or Josephus's. The main words that Philo utilizes, however, are the same ones on which Josephus relies: δοῦλος, οἰκέτης, θεράπων and sometimes παῖς. Philo speaks about actual slaves and slavery, but since his agenda is frequently philosophical, he also employs slave language in philosophical arguments, and thus it serves metaphorically.

His most common philosophical use of slave language is in the relationship of a person to his/her desires or emotions. For Philo, as for many Hellenistic philosophers, one can be enslaved to one's desires, passions, emotions or appetites. To be a slave (for Philo, primarily δοῦλος) of these desires is to lose one's freedom completely and to be "owned" and controlled by those desires. The result is that such people cannot exercise reason.[54] Philo contrasts slavery, in good Greek fashion, with freedom. Sometimes he does this for actual situations, but other times the slave/free contrast is metaphorical, especially when he speaks about the nature of human beings. Thus, one can be a slave in the body; that is, someone may own/control a person's physical self, but that person may still be truly free. Philo's clearest explication of this idea in the tractate *Every Good Man is Free (Prob.).*[55] Physical slavery, Philo argues, is often simply dependent on bad luck, and "anyone who thinks that people put up for sale by kidnappers thereby become slaves goes utterly

---

[54] This theme is frequent in Philo. See for example, *Opif.* 167; *Leg.* 3.156, 3.194; *Spec.* 4.91, 113; *Prob.* 11, 159. Several of these kinds of passages are Philo's allegories of biblical stories to achieve philosophical purposes.

[55] Philo does treat this issue in other places as well. See, for example, *Spec.* 2.69, where he argues that no person is by nature a slave or *Abr.* 251 in which Sarah's slave Hagar is described as outwardly a slave, but inwardly free.

astray from the truth" (37). And, Philo continues, just as a lion may be captured, but not tamed, still less can a wise man be a slave (40). He concludes a long argument by saying, "Consequently none of the good is a slave (δοῦλος), but all are free. By the same line of argument it will appear that the fool is a slave (δοῦλος)" (50–51).

In other clearly metaphorical contexts Philo speaks of the states-man as the slave (δοῦλος) of the people, an image evidently drawn on deliberately by orators (*Ios.* 35, 67, 76). In *Abr.* 45 Philo reveals his own undertanding of social order when he argues, in a discussion about the Flood, that if human beings were destroyed "none of the inferior kinds would be left, since they were made for humanity's needs, as slaves in a sense, meant to obey their masters' orders."

In the course of these discussions, as well as others, Philo reveals his own social understanding of the place and function of slaves, and though he certainly is aware of the biblical laws (as we will see below), his own social attitude towards slaves seems much more conditioned by the practices he sees around him. Slaves occupy the lower rungs of the social order. He makes this clear in *Decal.* 166: "Parents belong to the superior class (τῇ κρείττονι...τάξει) in which belong elders, rulers, benefactors and masters, while children (παῖδες)[56] belong in the lower (τῇ καταδεεστέρᾳ) in which belong juniors, subjects, receivers of ben-efits and slaves (δοῦλοι)." In his discussion of how virtuous people are not usually honored, Philo says that they do not enjoy the privileges of subject peoples "or even slaves (δούλων)" (*Det.* 34). Although Philo says, and probably believes, that no good person is a slave, in *Spec.* 2.123 his aristocratic sensibilities surface in a discussion of the fact that the biblical law allows the buying of foreign slaves. He says that there are two reasons for this allowance. "[F]irst, that a distinction should be made between fellow-countrymen and aliens; secondly that the most indispensible possession, domestic service (θεράποντας), should not be excluded from his [God's] commonwealth. For the course of life con-tains a vast number of circumstances which demand the ministration of slaves (τὰς ἐκ δούλων ὑπηρεσίας)." He recognizes that slaves can be and were beaten (*Opific.* 85; *Leg.* 3.200), that people can be forcibly enslaved (*Somn.* 2.136), that "bad" slaves take advantage of the kind-ness of a master and act as if they had not been slaves (*Somn.* 2.294), and that even though enslaved, sometimes slaves can be entrusted with

---

[56] See below on the use of παῖς in Philo.

great responsibility and can purchase, lend or pursue other relatively free activities (*Prob.* 35). In general then, the way that Philo describes the position and use of slaves in his writings seems consonant with their place and use in Hellenistic-Roman slave systems.

The terms that Philo uses when speaking of slaves also represent the usual Greek spectrum of terms for enslaved persons. While δοῦλος occurs most often, several other terms appear to be used synonymously with it. One of the best texts in which to see these terms being used without distinction is in *Spec.* 2.65f. where Philo is discussing the Sabbath law. He is quick to note that the law not only requires free persons to rest, but also servants and animals. In the course of his explanation of the reasons for this requirement, he says that masters must get used to working for themseves without the attendance of their οἰκέται, and that these οἰκέται should interpret this Sabbath rest as a taste of freedom. He then recapulates this notion using both οἰκέτης and δοῦλος in the same sentence as synonyms. He then moves on to animals, who are also given a Sabbath rest, because "[f]or servants (θεράποντες) are free by nature, no man being naturally a slave (δοῦλος), but the unreasoning animals are intended to be ready for the use and service of men and therefore rank as slaves (δούλων)." Not only does this passage reveal Philo's attitude toward slaves, it also shows the relative ease with which he can substitute one slave word for another. In another place in *Special Laws* (1.126), Philo comments on the right of priestly slaves to partake of priestly food. In this case Philo refers to the houseborn slave (οἰκογένης) and the bought slave (ἀργυρώνητος). The subsequent discussion contains δοῦλος, οἰκέτης and θεράπων, all meaning slaves, although οἰκέτης probably has here the narrower meaning of domestic slave.

While the previous examples show that Philo could use certain slave words interchangeably, his writings also reveal that παῖς is a special case as it was in Josephus. As in Josephus, παῖς for Philo seems to have the primary meaning of "child." Only a few times does it unequivocally mean "slave." Several passages have παῖς and slave words together where παῖς clearly indicates a child. In *Det.* 13–14 Philo addresses the plausibility of the Joseph narrative. Why, he says, would a father who has slaves and attendants (οἰκετῶν ἢ ὑπηρετῶν) send out his son to find out about his other children (τῶν ἄλλων παίδων)? In *Fug.* 3, he gives reasons that people might flee others, including "children (παῖδες) their parents and slaves (οἰκέται) their masters." Finally, the passage mentioned above from *Decal.* 166, where slaves and children occupy the lower classes of society, has the two words in the same context.

The most interesting aspect of Philo's use of παῖς is that when it means "slave" he is almost always using the term in dependence on the Greek biblical translations. On the one hand, in sections on the slavery laws from the Bible, he often has δοῦλος where the biblical translations have some other term, frequently παῖς. In several different places Philo treats the slave laws from Exodus 21, Leviticus 25 and Deuteronomy 15. His treatment of the laws that distinguish between an Israelite and foreign slave is potentially very revealing. In *Spec.* 2.79ff. Philo cites Deut 15:12 and speaks about the importance of the text using the word "brother" of the debt servant. He further recognizes the biblical injunction to treat that "brother" as a hired laborer rather than as a slave. He then says, "For people in this position, though we find them called slaves (δούλους), are in reality laborers who undertake the service just to procure themselves the necessities of life." The biblical text does not call these people δοῦλοι; Deuteronomy does not use the word slave, and Exodus says, "If you buy a Hebrew παῖδα." Does Philo's remark indicate that in his social context the biblical word is not used for these debt slaves, but that the usual Greek word δοῦλος is? That would appear to be the implication here. The apparent change from παῖς to δοῦλος may indicate that the use of these words by Jews follows contemporary Hellenistic Greek usage in which παῖς is found less and less with the meaning "slave."[57] Several other passages have δοῦλος instead of παῖς: *Leg.* 3.198 (Exod 21:5) on the debt slave who chooses to remain a slave (LXX = παῖς, Philo = δοῦλος), *Sobr.* 51 a citation of Gen 9:26–27, the curse of Canaan (LXX = παῖς, οἰκέτης, παῖς, Philo = παῖς, οἰκέτης, δοῦλος),[58] *Ios.* 228 (Gen 44:33) in which Judah asks to be a slave in return for Benjamin's freedom (LXX = παῖς, Philo = δοῦλος), *Spec.* 3.145 (Exod 21:32) concerning the killing of a slave by an ox (LXX = παῖς, Philo = δοῦλος), *Virt.* 124 (Deut 23:16) on the runaway slave (LXX = παῖς, Philo = δοῦλος).

In other instances where the Greek Bible uses παῖς to mean "slave," Philo retains it and its meaning. In some cases Philo cites the text

---

[57] The diminutives of παῖς are used frequently, however. A similar discussion occurs a bit later in 2.122–123. In this case the person who is bought (ἀργυρώνητος) is not a δοῦλος by nature.

[58] In this case the citation is very close and the question arises as to whether Philo may have a variant Greek text of Genesis that uses δοῦλος.

directly, and in others he paraphrases, but retains παῖς rather than changing it. In *Det.* 30–31 (see also *Cong.* 111) Philo allegorizes the story of Isaac and Rebecca in Genesis 24. Abraham has sent a servant (παῖς in both Genesis and Philo) to find a wife for Isaac. The servant finds Rebecca, and as Isaac approaches, she asks the servant who it is that is coming. The servant replies, "It is my master," a clear indication of the servile status of the παῖς. In a citation of Gen 26:32 (see *Plant.* 78 and *Somn.* 1.38), Isaac's παῖδες report to him about wells they have dug. Philo simply reproduces the word used in the Septuagint, here clearly referring to slaves. In one of the two uses of παῖς in the curse of Canaan, Philo retains the παῖς found in the Septuagint (see above). He cites Num 31:49–50 in *Ebr.* 114 in which Moses' officers (called παῖδες in the Greek Bible and in Philo) report to him.

There are other instances where it seems as if Philo is deliberately playing on the lexical ambiguity of παῖς. In a passage on the value of wisdom (*Cherub.* 71–73), he quotes Exod 21:5–6 on the indentured servant who chooses to remain a slave, this time retaining the παῖς of the Septuagint. He draws the conclusion that the mind that has heard lofty and wise words and rejects them is "a παῖς in very truth and wholly childish (νηπίου)." Here παῖς might as well mean "boy" as "slave." Philo apparently wants the lexical ambiguity at work. Another very interesting passage is *Cong.* 154 in which Philo is treating Gen 16:6 where Sarah sends Hagar away. The Greek Genesis calls Hagar παιδίσκη, and about this title Philo comments, "Indeed in calling her παιδίσκη he [Abraham] makes a double admission, that she is a slave and that she is childish, for the name suits both of these. At the same time the words involve necessarily and absolutely the acknowledgment of the opposites of these two, of the full grown as opposed to the child, of the mistress as opposed to the slave." In this passage Philo not only understands, but intentionally plays upon the duality and ambiguity of παῖς words used for slaves.

Some of this ambiguity may be present in one specialized use of slave language in Philo, the servant/slave of God. To be a slave of God (the Jewish God, that is) is not a bad thing, but is valued positively by Philo. His language of slavery to God is varied, like his other uses of slave terms. Sometimes this service can be described using δοῦλος language. In *Det.* 56, Philo speaks of loving God by which "we mean some such service as slaves (δοῦλοι) render to their masters." Philo also deals with God's concern for the world in *Mut.* 46. He concludes, "Shall we then his slaves (δοῦλοι) follow our Master with profoundest awe and reverence for Him Who is the Cause, yet not forgetting the calls of our common humanity." The slave of God designated by θεράπων is also frequent in Philo and the word is used synonymously with δοῦλος in *Her.* 6 where Philo is interested in speaking with God.[59] A slave, Philo argues, properly speaks to his master when his words and actions are all for the master's benefit. Thus, "when else should the slave (δοῦλος) of God open his mouth freely to Him who is the ruler and master both of himself and of the All..., when he feels more joy at being the servant (θεράπων) of God than if he had been king of the human race."

As with the more usual uses of παῖς, its lexical ambiguity extends to figurative uses as child/slave of God. It is apparent from the examples given above that Philo does play on that ambiguity. One passage, *Conf.* 147, shows how that problem extends to figurative uses of παῖς. Philo cites Gen 42:11 according to the Septuagint, "We are all sons (υἱοί) of one man." He then continues, "For if we have not yet become fit to be thought children (παῖδες) of God yet we may be [children] of his invisible image, the most holy word." Here παῖς almost certainly means "children," but what impact does such use have on other places, like *Abr.* 132 where Philo discusses the singularity of God? He cites Gen 18:3: "Sir, if indeed I have found favor with you, do not pass your παῖς by." Is it child or slave/servant, especially since these ambiguities seem to be present when Philo quotes or uses a biblical passage that has παῖς as the central term?

Conclusion. The uses to which Philo puts nouns for slaves, then, are similar to those found in Josephus and, to a degree, in the Greek biblical translations. δοῦλος, οἰκέτης and θεράπων are used mostly as synonyms. Occasionally, οἰκέτης may be used to indicate a household servant particularly, but certainly not in every case. παῖς in Philo's writings has a clear lexical ambiguity on which Philo plays. Yet, most of Philo's uses of παῖς to mean "slave" come in contexts where he is dealing with biblical passages in which the word has that meaning already. In other places, Philo would seem to prefer some other word. This general synonymity would put Philo, like Josephus and the Greek Bible, in agreement with the uses of the terms in other contemporary Hellenistic literature.

---

[59] For instances of θεράπων θεοῦ, see *Det.* 62; *Fug.* 67; *Spec.* 1.242 (of priests). That θεράπων is also a normal word for slave in Philo's vocabulary is evident from many places.

Slave Terms in the Apocrypha and Pseudepigrapha

The situation in the Apocrypha (except Ben Sira which I discussed above) and the Pseudepigrapha that are extant in Greek is not too much different from what was the case for the biblical translations, Josephus and Philo. The usual slave terms seem to refer to chattel slaves when actual slaves are the referent. What is somewhat surprising is the frequency with which παῖς means "servant/slave" in addition to its meaning of "child." One might not expect this given Josephus's and Philo's apparent lack of interest in this meaning of the word. The use in the Apocrypha and Pseudepigrapha may perhaps be attributed to the frequent occurrence of the word in the Jewish-Greek scriptures with the meaning of slave/servant. The best example of this kind of usage is in the *Testament of Abraham* 7:8 where παῖς refers to Isaac and means "child/son," but later in 15:5 at the end of Abraham's life his servants (δοῦλοι) gather around him. In 15:6 these servants are called παῖδες. In 20:7 where the scene is reprised, δοῦλος is the term used. In 17:18 and 18:3, 9 Death kills a large number of Abraham's slaves, called παῖδες.[60] παῖς also is used to mean "slave" in passages in *Testaments of the Twelve Patriarchs, Joseph and Asenath,*[61] *The Letter of Aristeas,* Judith, and 1 Maccabees.[62]

The title "servant of God" appears a number of times in these works with both παῖς and δοῦλος, sometimes in the same work. In the *Testament of Levi*, for example, the Aramaic Prayer of Levi, extant in Greek in Mount Athos ms e and in Aramaic in 4QAramaic Levi, has עֶבֶד in relation to God twice in the text and once as a fairly certain reconstruction. The Greek uses δοῦλος once and παῖς two times, apparently as synonyms.[63] In *Paraleipomena Ieremiou* 6:19 Baruch is called the δοῦλος of God and in 6:24 Jeremiah is God's παῖς—both apparently meaning "servant/slave."[64] *Psalms of Solomon* may witness a distinction between the two Greek words. παῖς is used twice, in 12:6 and 17:21. In each case Israel is being singled out as the servant of God. The three cases

---

[60] These passages are in the A recension. The B recension does not use δοῦλος.

[61] Primarily as the servants of Pharaoh. The same Greek is used of Pharaoh's servants in the biblical translations.

[62] 1 Macc 3:41 is the only place I have encountered where παῖς seems to refer to war captives being sold as slaves.

[63] For the text of the prayer in 4QAramaic Levi and the Mount Athos manuscript, see M.E. Stone and J.C. Greenfield, "The Prayer of Levi," *JBL* 112 (1993) 247–66.

[64] For the text see R.A. Kraft and A.-E. Purinton, *Paraleipomena Ieremiou* (SBLTT 1, Pseudepigrapha 1; Missoula, MT: Society of Biblical Literature, 1975).

of δοῦλος, 2:37, 10:4 and 18:12, are used in an indefinite plural to refer
to God's slaves. Israel is the παῖς of God; individuals are his δοῦλοι.[65]
All the uses of servant of God in 1–2 Maccabees use δοῦλος.

The one work in which the use of παῖς of God shows some ambiguity
is Wisdom of Solomon. The book does use δοῦλος, and the speaker in
9:5 calls himself God's δοῦλος, "the son (υἱός) of your serving girl, a man
who is weak and short-lived with little understanding of judgment and
laws." Wisdom 18.11 speaks about the killing of the Egyptian firstborn
and remarks that the slave (δοῦλος) was killed along with the master.
Both uses of δοῦλος designate a chattel slave, one in relation to God.

The occurrences of παῖς, where the meaning is clear, serve to illuminate those places where the meaning is not. In 8:19, the speaker remarks
that as a child (παῖς) he was "naturally gifted," that he had "entered into
an undefiled body." The three occurrences of παῖς in chapter 12 all seem
to mean "child/children." Wisdom 12:3–11 deals with the sins of the
Canaanites and the giving of the land to the Israelites. The author singles
out the original people of the land as those who sacrificed their children
(τέκνων). He returns to this theme in verse 6, referring to "parents who
murder helpless lives." As a result, God gave the "land most precious"
to him to the Israelites, a "worthy colony of the παίδων of God." In
the context, "children" of God seems to me to make the best sense.[66]
Wisdom 12:20–21 continues the theme with "For if you punished...the
enemies of your παίδων...with what strictness have you judged your
υἱούς." The use of υἱός and παῖς in parallel suggest that παίδων means
"children" here. Finally in verses 24–25 the Egyptians, who worshipped
animals and were deceived like "foolish infants (νηπίων)," are judged
by God as "children (παισίν) with no reason." The parallelism makes
the meaning clear. The context of 18:9–10, the killing of the Egyptian
children, makes the use of παῖς in the phrase "holy παῖδες" clearly
mean children.

That leaves 2:13, 9:4 and 19:6. Wisdom 2:13 refers to an individual
against whom the ungodly conspire. This righteous man calls himself
"παῖδα κυρίου." Both 9:4 and 19:6 refer to the people of God with the
plural παῖδες. Since the other plural uses of παῖς mean children, these
probably do as well. Wisdom 2:13, as the only use of the phrase παῖς

[65] Text is taken from Rahlfs, *Septuaginta*.
[66] The NRSV translates "servants," but D. Winston has "children" (*The Wisdom of Solomon* [AB 43; New York: Doubleday, 1979]).

of God in the singular in this book, is more uncertain, but should also probably be rendered "child."

Conclusion. Generally in the Apocrypha and Pseudepigrapha slave terms do not seem to have any clear cut distinctions in use, even in their religious contexts. This situation is not very different from the other Jewish literature of the Second Temple period discussed above. The terms seem largely interchangeable. With the exception of Wisdom of Solomon, where παῖς of God should be translated "child/children of God," the uses of παῖς with reference to God probably mean "servant/ slave," especially in these places where it occurs together with δοῦλος.

CONCLUDING REMARKS

I think the evidence surveyed above warrants the general conclusion that Jewish writers in the Second Temple period are using words for slaves as they know them to be used in their contemporary socio-cultural environment, that is, that the main terms for slaves can be roughly synonymous even though in individual uses some distinction of function might be intended. I want to emphasize at the beginning of this concluding section that this seems to me to be the best way to construe the use of these terms. On the other hand, several issues stand out as deserving special attention here.

First, Philo and Josephus demonstrate an intimate knowledge of Hellenistic-Roman slave systems. Many passages in their writings point to this fact. Philo certainly can be read in such a way that it appears as if he not only knows about slaves, but that he has personal interactions with slaves and masters; perhaps he even owned slaves. In addition, Philo's own attitudes towards slaves and slavery surface throughout his works, attitudes that reveal an acceptance on his part of the necessity and place of slaves in society. Josephus, as well, knows these systems from his involvement in the First Jewish Revolt and from his later relocation to Rome. Both of these authors' uses of slave terms would then seem quite consonant with the social realities that they experienced. Something of this may be what prompts both of these men to use the general word for slave, δοῦλος, instead of the more ambiguous παῖς in several places where they discuss biblical passages that contain the latter term.[67] Like the papyri from this period and later, παῖς itself is

---

[67] Realizing, however, that they may have had texts that vary from what is now known as the Septuagint, and that they do not do this in every case.

not used a great deal for slaves, although its diminutives are, both in the papyri and in Philo and Josephus.

The glaring absence of δοῦλος from the Greek Pentateuch remains somewhat of a mystery. The possible reasons that I adduced above for its absence, particularly the idea that the terms other than δοῦλος connote a greater familiarity between slave and master, represent informed speculation, but may be a different way of articulating what Zimmerli was trying to suggest and yet still account for the ambiguity inherent in the several cases of δοῦλος that do occur. δοῦλος, of course, appears with great frequency in the later translations where all the major terms for slaves serve broadly as synonyms. Thus, the Jewish translations of the Bible witness the same process evidenced in the *koine* of the period, the increasing interchangeability of these terms for slaves.

When one looks to the metaphorical uses of the words for slaves, most of them can be seen in other Hellenistic literature. The use of these terms in the language of political subjection is not unique to Jews, and certainly Philo's utilization of this language to speak about domination by human appetites and desires draws on Hellenistic philosophy as does his notion that the wise person can never be a slave.

The one use that would seem to be drawn specifically from Jewish sources, the Bible in particular, is the notion of the "slave of God." Although the Greek term for slave can be any of those I have looked at in this essay, to be a "slave of God" is a good thing. Further, it does not seem to have ready sources in Hellenistic literature.[68] One other place where such an idea is prevalent is in the Greek magical papyri. One finds numerous examples like that in *PGM* XIII.637 where the supplicant says to Sarapis, "I am your slave and petitioner and the one who hymns your name."[69] Unfortunately, most of these papyri date from well after the first century CE, and, as a methodological point, such use may have come to these magical texts via Jewish or Christian sources. It would seem, then, that this idea is unique to Jews, an idea that they

---

[68] See, S.S. Bartchy, "Slavery (NT)," *Anchor Bible Dictionary*, 6.65–73. The more specific question of exactly what this term means is not the focus of this essay, but is, of course, critical for understanding its uses in Christian literature (see, for example, Jeremias, "παῖς θεοῦ in Later Judaism").

[69] For the Greek text, see K. Preisendanz, *Papyri Graecae Magicae: Die griechischen Zauberpapyri* (Berlin: Teubner, 1928). For English translations of the Greek Magical Papyri, see H.D. Betz, *The Greek Magical Papyri in Translation* (Chicago: University of Chicago Press, 1986).

drew from their scriptural traditions and their self conception as a nation of people who are "servants of God," as opposed to servants of human rulers.

CHAPTER TWELVE

ACCESS TO THE SOURCE: CICERO, BEN SIRA, THE SEPTUAGINT AND THEIR AUDIENCES

This study is an initial exploration into some issues that I hope will eventually become a more extensive project examining the social functions and contexts of translation in the ancient Mediterranean world. As such it is somewhat experimental and represents an early attempt at thinking about some problems connected with translation in antiquity.[1] In what follows I will examine three different examples of ancient translation and ask some questions about how the relationships between translation, source text and anticipated readership operate in each one. As I have begun my work, what I have discovered, both to my delight and to my chagrin, is the wealth of recent material that constitutes a field of study now known as "Translation Studies." Although this field initially developed out of the grand nineteenth century philological tradition and more recently out of linguistic theory and is concerned for the most part with modern translation theory, a number of studies have attempted to examine the history of translation in the West. Even in these, however, the emphasis is primarily on theory and how it has developed.[2] Because of their primary focus on translation in the West, the origins of which many attribute to Roman philhellenism, these studies most frequently begin with the Latin translations of Greek works, with perhaps a nod here and there to the Jews who translated their

---

[1] I presented an earlier form of this paper at "From Hellenistic Judaism to Christian Hellenism: International Colloquium," March 26–28, 2001, Institute for Advanced Studies, Jerusalem, Israel.

[2] See, for example, E. Jacobsen, *Translation: A Traditional Craft* (Copenhagen: Gyldendalske Boghandel-Nordisk Forlag, 1958); L. Kelly, *The True Interpreter* (New York: St. Martin's, 1979); M. Ballard, *De Cicéron à Benjamin: Traducteurs, traductions, réflexions* (Paris: Presses Universitaires de Lille, 1995); J. Delisle and J. Woodsworth, *Les Traducteurs dans l'Histoire* (Ottawa: Les Presses de l'Université d'Ottawa, 1995). A number of sourcebooks have also appeared that collect primary sources on translation in the West. See A. Lefevere, *Translation/History/Culture: A Sourcebook* (London: Routledge, 1992) and D. Robinson, *Western Translation Theory from Herodotus to Nietzsche* (Manchester: St. Jerome Publishing, 1997).

Hebrew Bible into Greek.[3] But those translators who, like Cicero, write about and reflect on translation receive the greatest amount of attention and are often credited with initiating real translation in the West. This is especially true of Cicero, since his remarks on doing translation come closest in antiquity to one modern ideal of translation, dynamic equivalence.

This scholarly attention given to translation from Cicero onwards and the relative inattention paid to translations made before the late Hellenistic period are the result of several factors. First, there appears to be, at least in the scholarly literature, a mutual lack of awareness of work on translation between scholars in classics, a field very central to much work in Translation Studies, and scholars of ancient religion. This circumstance can be attributed partially to the tensions manifested in the nineteenth century between Christian missionizing activity and its attendant enterprise of Bible translation and the progressively more secular definition of academic life where classics loomed so large.[4] One need only scan the footnotes of work on the Septuagint, for example, to see that studies by classicists on translation are cited infrequently. The classicists, for their part, many of whom do not know Hebrew, cite work on translations like the Jewish-Greek scriptures almost as infrequently. Second, translation theory in the West has explicitly relied on and reacted to what Latin writers like Cicero and Jerome say about the act of translation. They provide a precedent and foundation for theory. Even translation of the Hebrew Bible can fall under the umbrella of Western translation theory, since Jerome and Augustine wrote about translating the Bible from Hebrew. Third, the traditional importance of Latin particularly and Greek secondarily in Western education in the eighteenth through the early twentieth centuries has granted these languages and their classical authors a prestige not accorded other writers. The high status occupied by the classical Latin and Greek writers ultimately means that scholars who work in Translation Studies

---

[3] Recent work in Translation Studies has begun to move away from being centered on the West, especially as theoretical movements such as deconstruction and post-colonial theory have had an impact. Yet my own reading in the field indicates a deeply rooted indebtedness to the field of classics, which has played a significant role in the studies that I have used in this paper.

[4] For a discussion of translation and translation theory in the nineteenth century, see N.J. Girardot, *The Victorian Translation of China: James Legge's Oriental Pilgrimage* (Los Angeles, Berkeley & London: University of California Press, 2002) chap. 6, "Translator Legge: Closing the Confucian Canon, 1882–1885."

are probably much more comfortable with the classical discussions of translation and the translations produced by these writers than they are with other ancient translations like the Septuagint.

As I have spent more time reading works in Translation Studies, I have become convinced that this field of study has the potential to contribute greatly to our ability to understand translations like the Septuagint. I also think that the converse is true, that scholars who have spent much of their careers working on texts like the Septuagint have something to contribute to the field of Translation Studies. This paper represents my initial steps in the direction of engaging the insights of these disciplines that in my experience have been too isolated from each other.[5]

The immediate impetus for this study came from a remark made by S. Bassnett-McGuire in her slim but influential volume entitled *Translation Studies*.[6] On page 44 she says,

> But there is also an additional dimension to the Roman concept of enrichment through translation, i.e. the preeminence of Greek as the language of culture and the ability of educated Romans to read the texts in the SL [source language]. When these factors are taken into account, then the position of both the translator and the reader alters. The Roman reader was generally able to consider the translation as a metatext in relation to the original. The translated text was read *through* the source text, in contrast to the way a monolingual reader can only approach the SL text through the TL [target language] version. For Roman translators, the task of transferring a text from language to language could be perceived as an exercise in comparative stylistics, since they were freed from the exigencies of having to 'make known' either the form or the content *per se*, and consequently did not need to subordinate themselves to the frame of the original. The good translator, therefore, presupposed the reader's acquaintance with the SL text and was bound by that knowledge, for any assessment of his skill as translator would be based on the creative use he was able to make of his model.

Essentially, then, if the translator could rely on his readership having knowledge of the source language, then he would not need to be bound by any formal representation of the source text since his readership had the ability to read the source text itself. Translation under these

---

[5] By this I do not mean to imply that I am alone in this enterprise. Recent work, for example, by A. Pietersma at the University of Toronto and one of his graduate students, C. Boyd-Taylor, also utilizes literature from classics and translation theorists with great profit.

[6] London: Methuen, 1980.

conditions does not need to act as a vehicle for bringing the reader to
the source language; the reader already has the requisite knowledge.
The translator's "creative use" of the source text, then, eventuates in
what we might call a free translation. The formal aspects of the source
language are subordinated to the needs of the translator in the target
language. For someone like Cicero, translation of this sort could serve
several different purposes including being a virtuoso display of his own
rhetorical skills and mastery of Latin.

This kind of translation, which assumes and even depends on the
reader's knowledge of the source language, stands in direct contrast to
translations like the Septuagint and Sirach.[7] These translations have a
much closer relationship with the formal aspects of their source language, Hebrew. In Sirach, the author's grandson, who translated the
book, wrote a prologue in good literary *koine* Greek that accompanies
the translation. Yet, when we compare the prologue to the translation
of the Hebrew, the character of the Greek changes dramatically. Ben
Sira's grandson reproduces in many instances idiomatic Hebrew in
Greek dress and often formally represents in his translation aspects of
the Hebrew, such as the word order. For its part, the Septuagint can be
characterized in much the same way. It mimics in Greek many formal
aspects of its Hebrew source text, which results in a translation that has
at times been called everything from awkward to stilted to simply bad.
If Ciceronian translation is a result of the audience's knowledge of the
Greek source language, does the fairly close, formal representation of
the Hebrew source in the Septuagint and Sirach indicate a monolingual
audience who must be provided entrée into the source language? If so,
why would such access to the source language be important for these
translators?

The three examples selected for this paper provide different contexts
in which we can investigate the relationships among translation, source
language and audience. These three provide varying degrees of information about their attitudes to translating. Cicero writes a fair amount
about translation; Sirach has a prologue where the grandson reflects on
the translator's task and his own reasons for making the translation; the
origins of the Septuagint and its translators' approaches to the work are

---

[7] In this paper my focus is on the Septuagint in its more restricted and, most Septuagint scholars would argue, more proper sense—the translation of the Pentateuch
accomplished in Alexandria somewhere in the early third century BCE.

obscure and still very much an object of scholarly debate. The social and cultural worlds of these translators are very different, and we know them with varying degrees of detail and certainty. Furthermore, the translators assume different relationships to the texts they are translating and the languages into which they render their source texts.

Cicero

Marcus Tullius Cicero (106–43 BCE) may have been Rome's greatest orator. While there is no need here to rehearse Cicero's turbulent life and career, I only note that he had an education thoroughly grounded in things Greek, and he, as all Romans of his social class, went to Greece for a period to study philosophy and oratory. He is regarded by many modern scholars as the first translation theorist, and whether he was that or not, his influence on subsequent translators, like Jerome, is undeniable. His comments on translation are probably cited in studies of translation in the West more often than any other writer's. I, like so many others, have to begin with him.

Cicero comments on translation in a number of places, but the *locus classicus* is his discussion in *De optimo genere oratorum*, a short treatise that appeared in 46 BCE sometime between his *Brutus* and the *Orator*.[8] It was intended as an introduction to translations of Demosthenes's *On the Crown* and Aeschines's *Against Ctesiphon*, orations considered by many to be the epitome of Greek oratory, which they delivered against each other.[9] In this treatise Cicero extols Demosthenes as the greatest of orators and encourages imitation of him as one of the keys to becoming a great orator. His comments on translation begin with his motivations for making a translation of the great Attic antagonists. He says in *De optimo* 14,

> But since there was a complete misapprehension as to the nature of their style of oratory, I thought it my duty to undertake a task which will be useful to students, though not necessarily for myself. That is to say I translated the most famous orations of the two most eloquent Attic orators, Aeschines and Demosthenes, orations which they delivered against

---

[8] H.M. Hubbell, *Cicero: De inventione, De optimo genere oratorum, Topica* (LCL; Cambridge, MA: Harvard University Press, 1949) 349.

[9] The two translations are not extant, and Hubbell in his introduction to this treatise in the Loeb Classical Library series maintains that Cicero most likely never made them (p. 350).

each other. And I did not translate them as an interpreter, but as an orator (*nec converti ut interpres, sed ut orator*), keeping the same ideas and the forms, or as one might say, the "figures" of thought, but in language that conforms to our usage. And in doing so I did not hold it necessary to render word for word but I preserved the general style and force of the language (*In quibus non verbum pro verbo necesse habui reddere, sed genus omne verborum vimque servavi*). For I did not think I ought to count them out to the reader like coins, but to pay them by weight as it were. The result of my labor will be that our Romans will know what to demand from those who claim to be Atticists and to what rule of speech, as it were, they are to be held.[10]

A bit later in section 18 Cicero anticipates objections to his translations.

Two sorts of objections can be raised to this undertaking of mine. The first is, "It is better in the original Greek." One might ask this critic whether they themselves can produce anything better in Latin. The second is, "Why should I read this translation of yours, rather than the Greek original?" But at the same time they accept the Andria, the Synephebi, and likewise the Andromache or the Antiope or the Epigoni in Latin. Why their aversion to speeches translated from the Greek when they have none to translations of poetry?

These sections provide some telling insights into Cicero's approach to translation, at least of the Attic orators, and its function in Roman culture.

First, Cicero seems to be holding up his translation as a model of what Quintilian would later call *aemulatio*. In his *De institutione oratoria* x.v.4 Quintilian says, "And I do not mean by 'translation' mere paraphrase but struggle and rivalry over the same sense" (*Neque ego paraphrasin esse interpretationem tantum volo, sed circa eosdem sensus certamen atque aemulationem*). In this approach to translation, the translator "is setting up a relationship between himself and the author of the original, with the two languages, source and target, as mediators."[11] This relationship is not one between translator and text, but one between two people.

This is certainly how Cicero sees his intended translations of Demosthenes and Aeschines. These two Greeks are "models for our imitation (*ad imitandum*)" (*De optimo* 13). But Cicero, by translating in the manner he describes, does more than imitate; he appropriates and even

---

[10] Translations of Cicero's *De optimo* come from Hubbell, *Cicero*.
[11] Kelly, *True Interpreter*, 42.

successfully rivals (in Quintilian's sense) these Greek orators. L. Kelly articulates it this way, "It was not a given work that was imitated, but the art of *aemulatio* consisted in bending the techniques of another author to one's own subject and language."[12] Cicero, of course, was not the first to see Greek literature as an ideal for Roman emulation and appropriation. Some, like Fabius Pictor, wrote treatises in Greek. Others, like Gnaeus Naevius (270–201 BCE) who composed tragedies on Greek subjects, or Plautus (254–184 BCE) and Terence (190–159 BCE) who utilized Greek works, sometimes borrowing from them and occasionally directly translating them, wrote Latin works based on Greek using Greek models in periods much earlier than Cicero.[13]

But the *aemulatio* of these earlier Roman writers was not exercised in the service of translation as we find it here in Cicero. Elsewhere Cicero like his predecessors certainly writes using Greek models without translating them. Yet even Cicero's *translations* must be seen as literary (re)creations that attempt to do for Latin what Demosthenes and Aeschines did for Attic Greek. Cicero's motivation seems to be a desire to clear up the "misapprehension" of other Romans about what Attic style is by producing it in Latin. He does not translate in order to provide his audience with entrée into the speeches of Demosthenes and Aeschines as much as he translates to show how it is done in Latin. His concern is with his own language and good rhetorical style in Latin, not the source language and text *per se*. If there is any doubt about this, he clears it up when he responds to his fictive critics who say that the Greek is better than the translation, "One might ask this critic whether they themselves can produce anything better in Latin."

A second important factor for understanding Cicero's approach to translation is his expectation that his audience would be able to read the Greek originals for themselves were they so inclined. Roman education by Cicero's time had long been modeled after that of Greece. In fact, the first known translation from Greek to Latin was that of Homer's *Odyssey* made by Livius Andronicus (latter third of the third century BCE), who was a Greek taken to Rome as a slave and who served as a *paedagogus* in his master's home. The familiar figure of the *paedagogus* was most often a Greek slave entrusted with the education of his master's children.[14]

---

[12] Ibid.

[13] Ballard, *De Cicéron à Benjamin*, 39.

[14] The classic treatment of education in the ancient world is H.I. Marrou, *A History of Education in Antiquity* (G. Lamb, transl.; London: Sheed and Ward, 1956). For Rome,

Due to such pervasive influence of Greek education in Rome, H. Marrou can claim that "from the time of Horace onwards an educated Roman was proficient in the two languages, Greek and Latin."[15]

Cicero's thorough immersion in Greek is apparent in all that he writes, and as Marrou notes, "One feels that he thought in Greek and that he was writing to men like himself, who could appreciate his subtleties."[16] Whether Marrou overestimates the situation or not, there seems little question that Cicero's audience would have been able to read the Greek writers he translates. Even allowing for some degree of rhetorical flourish in Cicero's anticipatory responses to his critics in *De optimo*, they only make sense if Cicero's audience was of a sort that could and might well make such objections to his enterprise.

Thus, Cicero's translations seem intended to be a kind of virtuoso exercise that have a "gee whiz" quality about them, as a colleague of mine puts it.[17] It was a way for Cicero to show off his mastery of Latin, to demonstrate the proper way to emulate in Latin the best oratorical style, which as Cicero says is that of Demosthenes and Aeschines. As I noted above, his translations were about Latin, not about Greek, and given his responses in *De optimo* 18 he expects that his critics could easily consult the Greek themselves. By comparing the Greek original with the Latin translation, they could see how complete Cicero's command of Latin (and Greek, for that matter) was. In fact, it may be that the success of his translations of the Attic orators depended on such comparison.

These first two issues lead to a third, that is, the fidelity of Cicero's translations to their originals. Kelly notes that for the greater part of the history of Western translation, fidelity was equated with a formal equivalence with the original, a wooden representation of the form of the original text. This notion originates with Horace's famous admonition in his *Ars poetica* 133, where he equates faithfulness with literalness. "Do not render word for word as a faithful translator," he says. Fidelity, however, according to Kelly, is not about formal equivalence; it is about the translator's commitment, which is shaped by the authority structure

---

see especially Part III, chaps. II–III. See also S.F. Bonner, *Education in Ancient Rome* (Berkeley: University of California Press, 1977).

[15] Marrou, *History of Education*, 255.

[16] Ibid., 259.

[17] I want to thank C.R. Phillips of the History Department here at Lehigh for his responses to a number of questions I had about Cicero in particular and Latin translation in general. This section is much indebted to him.

he/she adopts in relation to the source text.[18] He argues that the translator can assume one of two types of authority structures, which he calls "personal" and "positional."

> Within personal authority structures, one takes responsible autonomy and retains power of decision, while positional structures impose formal patterns of obligation. Commitment, then, based on a personal authority structure, gives rise to translation behaviours akin to an elaborated sociolinguistic code: the translator's approach to text is multidimensional, author or reader-centered and subjective. Where, however, the translator sees the relation between him and the text as positional, the approach is that of restricted sociolinguistic code: unidimensional, text- and object-centered and objective. Thus, depending on the type of authority his text exercises over the translator, fidelity will mean either collaboration or servitude.[19]

Whereas both types of authority structures assume a communicative purpose, the goals and methods of translation that result from adopting one structure or the other can vary dramatically.

If we look at Cicero through the lens of Kelly's two types of authority structures, his is clearly a personal authority, characterized by those aspects outlined by Kelly above. I would articulate the problem a bit differently from Kelly by saying that personal authority structures may also be characterized less by a relationship to text or language, but by relationship with the author of the original. It seems to me that the Roman ideal of *aemulatio* would necessarily produce in the translator a personal authority structure. It would result in a translation whose communicative goal is more akin to what we now call dynamic equivalence rather than formal equivalence. In Cicero's translations his stance of personal authority with its elaborated code means that he is concerned to *say* what Demosthenes and Aeschines *say* and to do it in a manner that they might do it. Moreover, his overall approach to translation certainly appears to fit Kelly's characterization of personal authority as author- and reader-centered and subjective.

But we might also ask *why* it is that Cicero can assume such a stance vis-à-vis the Greek originals. Certainly Cicero's personal concern for the Latin language and literature in Latin would suggest that he would

---

[18] Kelly, *True Interpreter*, 205–6.
[19] Ibid., 206–7. Kelly's analysis of the two authority structures here depends on the work of B. Bernstein in "Social Class, Language and Socialisation," *Language and Social Context* (P.P. Giglioli, ed.; New York: Penguin, 1972) 157–78 (cited in Kelly, 252 note 1).

adopt a personal authority structure in translation. That this is in large part his interest emerges in his introduction to *De finibus bonorum et malorum*. Here, as in *De optimo*, Cicero feels obligated to defend what he is about to write, in this case a treatise on ethics in which he treats several Greek systems. Part of this defense is similar to that in *De optimo*. He says in 1.ii,

> A more difficult task therefore is to deal with the objection of those who profess a contempt for Latin writings as such. What astonishes me first of all about them is this—why should they dislike their native language for serious and important subjects, when they are quite willing to read Latin plays translated word for word from the Greek? Who has such a hatred, one might say, for the very name of Roman, as to despise and reject the *Medea* of Ennius or the *Antiope* of Pacuvius, and give as his reason that though he enjoys the corresponding plays of Euripedes he cannot endure books written in Latin? "What," he cries, "am I to read *The Young Comrades* of Caecilius, or Terence's *Maid of Andros* [*Andria*] when I might be reading the same two comedies of Menander?" With this sort of person I disagree so strongly that, admitting the *Electra* of Sophocles to be a masterpiece, I yet think Atilius' poor translation of it worth my while to read...For to be entirely unversed in our own poets argues either the extreme of mental inactivity or else a refinement of taste carried to the point of caprice. To my mind no one can be styled a well-read man who does not know our native literature.[20]

For Cicero, Latin treatments of Greek subjects, like the plays of Caecilius and Terence are not simply rehashes of the Greek plays, but legitimately original works of Latin literature that any educated person should read. As a result, I see only a very thin line of differentiation between Terence's *Andria*, which Cicero understands as a version of the play of Menander, and what Cicero expects his translations of Demosthenes and Aeschines to be.

But Cicero's authority structure is not only conditioned, it seems to me, by his personal attitude toward texts, but also to a degree by his social and cultural context and his presumed audience. Cicero inherited a long tradition of Roman philhellenism. Not only had Roman writers imitated Greek literature and its subjects, but Greek teachers and lecturers were widely popular in Rome for many years before Cicero.[21] It would seem strange if Cicero had not seen these traditional ideas of

---

[20] Translation by H. Rackham, *De finibus bonorum et malorum* (LCL; New York: Macmillan, 1914).
[21] See Marrou, *History of Education*, Part III, chap. II.

imitation and appropriation as important operative principles for his translations. In addition, even though Cicero had imbibed Greek language and culture more thoroughly than many of his contemporaries, he clearly intended his translations for those like him who could read Greek. He probably expected that his audience *would* compare his translations with the originals.

Thus, it was Cicero's own approach to Greek language and literature combined with his expectation that his audience would be able to read the originals that allowed him to adopt a personal authority structure in his translations. Cicero was not some rogue philhellene; he was part of a larger social structure that itself was immersed in Greek things. Consequently, he did not have to try to find a way to give his audience access to the source text or language. This kind of access would have been little more than a surface access, and for his audience unnecessary. In his translations he was providing *real* access to the *real* source.

The Wisdom of Ben Sira[22]

When we turn to a translation like the Greek of the Wisdom of Ben Sira (also called Sirach or Ecclesiasticus), we are at a distinct disadvantage in comparison with Cicero. We can get a handle on Cicero because he speaks at length about translation; he outlines both his reasons for doing it and his approach to the process. But Cicero is the exception, not the rule, for ancient translations. Most translations, even the most important ones like the Septuagint, which I will treat in the next section, provide no explicit information on who the translators were and what their approach to the enterprise was. So even a modest statement about translation, like that contained in the translator's Prologue to the Greek of Ben Sira, is welcome.

The Wisdom of Ben Sira is a Jewish wisdom book produced in Hebrew by a sage who lived in Jerusalem somewhere in the latter part of the third and the early decades of the second centuries BCE. The book's Greek translator claims to be the author's grandson; he calls the author ὁ πάππος μου Ἰησοῦς, "my grandfather Jesus." The usual date given for

---

[22] A revised version of this section appeared independently as "Why a Prologue? Ben Sira's Grandson and His Translation," *Emanuel: Studies in Hebrew Bible, Septuagint and Dead Sea Scrolls in Honor of Emanuel Tov* (S.M. Paul et al., eds.; VTSup 94; Leiden: Brill, 2003) 633–44.

the translation is somewhere shortly after the death of Ptolemy VII Euergetes II in 117 BCE.[23]

Three issues provide possible insight into the questions I am concerned with in this paper. First, the grandson makes some remarks about his reasons for making the translation and the audience for whom he intended it. Second, in the prologue he reflects briefly on the process of translation, although his reflections may not make matters as clear as we might like. Third, the fact that the grandson is able to write good koine Greek in the prologue but resorts to an often wooden Greek translationese for the actual translation reveals something of his ability as a translator and/or his expectations of what constitutes translation. Unfortunately, however, most commentators on Sirach do not pay a lot of attention to the prologue for what it says about ancient translation. They, of course, take account of the evidence it provides for the date of the Hebrew of the book, and they note the implications of the grandson's reference to "the Law, the Prophets and the rest of the books" for discussion about the development of the canon. They also usually note the grandson's *apologia* about the relationship between the Hebrew original and the Greek translation, especially as it bears on the possibility of trying to recover the original Hebrew of the book. Thus, they look to the prologue primarily as a source of information for investigating the Hebrew original and not for its value in understanding the Greek version as an example of ancient translation activity. Even scholars who are interested in the history and theory of translation give little notice to Ben Sira's grandson. Whereas they often refer to the legend of the Septuagint and list it in collections of texts about translation, they almost never include the prologue to Ben Sira.[24] I am not sure why this is, but a careful reading of the grandson's statements in the prologue provides fascinating insight into his translation.

Perhaps the first question we ought to ask is why the grandson decided to translate his grandfather's book into Greek. The answer to it actually helps us arrive at an understanding of who his audience was. The

---

[23] See the argument in P.W. Skehan and A.A. Di Lella, *The Wisdom of Ben Sira* (AB 39; New York: Doubleday, 1987) 8–9. The argument for Ben Sira's early second century *floruit* is founded on the date of the grandson's migration to Egypt in the "thirty-eighth year of Euergetes" (about 132 BCE), Ben Sira's description of the high priest Simon in chapter 50, usually thought to be Simon II, and the complete absence of any awareness of the events in Jerusalem during the reign of Antiochus IV.

[24] The two collections that I have used, that of Robinson and Lefevere, do not include or refer to the grandson's prologue.

grandson begins his prologue by noting that "Many and great things have been given to us through the Law, the Prophets, and the others that followed them, for which reason it is necessary to commend Israel for education and wisdom" (1–2).[25] But the grandson recognizes that those truths contained in the great books of Israel must be mediated to others. He says in the next clause, "whereas it is necessary that not only those who read (ἀναγινώσκοντας) them gain understanding, but also that those who love learning be capable of service to outsiders (τοῖς ἐκτός), both when they speak and when they write" (4–6).[26] Here the grandson emphasizes that those who know these books and the truths transmitted through them must be "of service" to those who do not have them. His grandfather, Jesus, was one of those who was useful in this way because, beyond devoting himself to the study of "the Law, the Prophets and the other ancestral books" and acquiring his own expertise in them, he "was led to compose something pertaining to education and wisdom, in order that lovers of learning, when they come under their sway, might gain much more in living by the law" (7–14). Ben Sira's audience, then, was comprised of Jews to whom he might communicate the insights that he had acquired through his study of the Jewish scriptures.

Apparently, the grandson perceives his own audience to be like his grandfather's, in his case Jews whom he encountered in Egypt who could benefit from his grandfather's wisdom and instruction in the Jewish Law. The idea for the translation seems to have been sparked by the grandson's encounter with similar kinds of instruction that he found upon his arrival in Egypt. He says that after coming to Egypt and having "stayed a while, when I had discovered an exemplar (ἀφόμοιον) of no little education" (28–29). The Greek word ἀφόμοιον probably here indicates that he found actual manuscript copies of works of instruction similar to his grandfather's.[27] Thus, the occasion for the translation

---

[25] I cite the prologue by the line numbers given in J. Ziegler's critical edition of Ben Sira, *Septuaginta: Vetus Testamentum Graecum Auctoritate Academiae Litterarum Gottingensis editum vol. XII, 2: Sapientia Iesu Filii Sirach* (Göttingen: Vandenhoeck & Ruprecht, 1965).

[26] In each case in this clause the object "them" has to be supplied in English because none is explicit in Greek. The question might be raised concerning what the unstated object of these phrases is. The "them" could refer to the books of "the Law, the Prophets, and the others" or to the "wisdom and instruction of Israel." For the purposes of the argument here the exact object intended by the grandson is not crucial.

[27] Here I follow Ziegler's critical text. A number of manuscripts have the reading ἀφόρμην, indicating that the grandson had access to instruction, without necessarily seeing copies of manuscripts.

seems to have been the desire to add his grandfather's instruction and wisdom to that already available to Greek-speaking Jews in Egypt who otherwise would not have access to his grandfather's Hebrew original. He makes a more explicit reference to his audience toward the end of the prologue when he says that he lost a lot of sleep making the translation for "those living abroad (ἐν τῇ παροικίᾳ), if they wish to become learned, preparing their character to live by the law" (34–36). In the light of these considerations, I would conclude that the grandson intended his translation for an Egyptian Jewish readership that did not know Hebrew.

The Greek of the prologue shows that Ben Sira's grandson could write in what P.W. Skehan and A.A. Di Lella call "carefully crafted prose, employing the grammar and syntax of literary *koine* Greek." His text is constructed using "three fairly elegant periodic sentences."[28] The first and third of these sentences provided the evidence for asking about the motivation and the audience of the translation. In the second sentence the grandson expresses the frustration of many translators over the centuries in the form of a short *apologia* for his work. Since the sentence is both important for our understanding of the grandson's translation and difficult in some ways to interpret, I give it in full here in the form I have translated it for the New English Translation of the Septuagint.[29]

> You are invited, therefore, to a reading with goodwill and attention and to exercise forbearance in cases where we may be thought to be insipid with regard to some expressions, that have been the object of great care in rendering; for what was originally expressed in Hebrew does not have the same force when it is in fact rendered in another language. And not only in this case, but also in the case of the Law itself and the Prophets and the rest of the books the difference is not small when these are expressed in their own language (15–26).[30]

---

[28] Skehan and Di Lella, *Wisdom of Ben Sira*, 132.

[29] The New English Translation of the Septuagint (NETS) is a complete English translation of the Jewish-Greek Scriptures being undertaken by the International Organization for Septuagint and Cognate Studies. For the initial NETS publication, see A. Pietersma, *A New English Translation of the Septuagint and Other Greek Translations Traditionally Included Under That Title: The Psalms* (New York: Oxford, 2000) [The entire corpus is now available in A. Pietersma and B.G. Wright, *A New English Translation of the Septuagint and Other Greek Translations Traditionally Included Under That Title* (New York: Oxford, 2007)].

[30] My first attempts at translating these lines, and what I originally published in this article, was: "You are invited, therefore, to give a reading with goodwill and attention

Scholars frequently understand this statement to be about fidelity to the Hebrew original. In this reading of the passage, the grandson is attempting to head off the criticism that his Greek in many cases does not faithfully render the Hebrew. He responds by saying that as a matter of method it is very difficult to render Hebrew into Greek. But if the potential critic is not willing to believe him on this score, he attempts to deflect the criticism by citing evidence beyond his own translation that the Law, the Prophets and the other books also suffer from this same deficiency—a claim that could be construed as critical of the Jewish-Greek scriptures.

Another way of understanding the passage would be to interpret it as a purely rhetorical disclaimer that aims to head off any criticism of the work. To argue that the grandson is simply resorting to a rhetorical *apologia* makes little sense to me, however. Given what he says about the importance of those truths found in the Jewish scriptures for those who love learning and who wish to live a life according to the Law, I find it surprising that as a matter of rhetorical protection of his own translation he would invent a criticism that the Greek version of the scriptures itself is somehow deficient. Why would he level a criticism at precisely the version of the Jewish scriptures used by his reading audience? In fact, I do not think that this passage constitutes a criticism of the Jewish-Greek scriptures at all.

Although these readings of the prologue are plausible, in view of the constituency for whom the grandson claims he is translating, I want to suggest an alternative reading of this section. The three key phrases in it that require some explanation are: (1) "in cases where we may be thought insipid with regard to some expressions" (20); (2) "for what was originally expressed in Hebrew does not have the same force when it is in fact rendered in another language" (21–22); (3) "but also in the case of the Law and the Prophets and the rest of the books the difference is not small when these are expressed in their own language" (23–26).

I think that the grandson's expression of nervousness is quite genuine. He does expect possible criticism of his work. But if his expected reader-

---

and to have forbearance for those things where we may seem to lack ability in certain phrases, despite having labored diligently in the translation. For those things originally in Hebrew do not have the same force when rendered in another language; and not only these things, but also the Law itself and the Prophets and the rest of the books are not a little different when expressed in the originals." I have updated the text here to reflect what my final NETS translation has. The interpretive points I am making, however, are not affected.

ship consists of Greek-speaking Jews, how would they be in a position to know whether he was being faithful to his original or not? Cicero could assume his audience was able to read the Greek on which his Latin translations were based; Ben Sira's grandson apparently could not make a similar assumption about his audience's knowledge of Hebrew. I imagine that there may have been Jewish scholars in the community who knew Hebrew and who could level such criticism, but why would such people worry about the translation of a wisdom book like Ben Sira's? The grandson is not claiming that what he has translated is in any way divine revelation that might conceivably warrant scrutiny of the translation for "faithfulness," whatever that might mean in such a case. He says explicitly that he hopes his grandfather's wisdom would "gain much more in living by the law." There is no evidence in this introduction to his translation that the grandson is attempting to address any sort of dispute about what it meant to live according to the Law.

I suspect that the primary clue to the grandson's anxiety rests not in the presumed difference between the Hebrew original and the Greek translation, but in the difference between the quality of the Greek of the prologue and the Greek of his translation. The prologue, as we saw above, is written in fairly good, literary Greek. The Greek of the translation, on the other hand, is written in a more or less stilted translationese that is often at pains to represent the form of the Hebrew very closely.[31] One of the criticisms that could be leveled at the grandson, and one of which he might indeed be wary, is that the Greek of his translation is not very good. And, in fact, it is not, especially if it is measured against the kind of Greek he uses in the prologue. His response to this possible criticism, his appeal to the Jewish scriptures, then would make eminent sense. The type of Greek (and translation approach) used for his translation is not very different from the Greek of the Law, the Prophets and the other books. In the context of this reading of the prologue, the grandson's reference to the Jewish-Greek scriptures would not have to be construed as a negative evaluation of them, but rather as a comparison with them.[32]

An examination of the key Greek terms used in the three passages cited above can sustain my reading of the prologue. In the first (#1

---

[31] On the Greek translation of Ben Sira, see my *No Small Difference: Sirach's Relationship to its Hebrew Parent Text* (SBLSCS 26; Atlanta: Scholars Press, 1989).

[32] Skehan and Di Lella claim that the grandson is here "criticizing freely not only his translation but also the LXX" (*Wisdom of Ben Sira*, 134).

above), the issue seems to be the grandson's perceived inability "with regard to some expressions" (τισὶν τῶν λέξεων). He uses the verbs δοκῶμεν…ἀδυναμεῖν to express what some might see as a weakness of his translation. Liddell-Scott-Jones lists the *verb* ἀδυναμέω, "to be incapable," as only occurring in the prologue to Sirach.[33] The much more common noun form of the root indicates generally "inability" or "incapacity." The ambiguous "some expressions" stands as the object of the infinitive. But are these "some expressions" in Greek or Hebrew? The qualifying participial phrase κατὰ τὴν ἑρμηνείαν πεφιλοπονημένων, "that have been the object of great care in rendering" provides the key for my interpretation. The Greek ἑρμηνεία indicates an "interpretation" or "explanation," what I translate "render," especially of thoughts by words; it can also refer to an expression. The use of "interpretation/explanation," "rendering," or perhaps even "expression," appears to place the focus of the clause on phrases in Greek, rather than in Hebrew. The grandson in this passage seems to be asking the reader to forgive any perceived inability of his *in the way he writes Greek*.

The second key term, ἰσοδυναμεῖ, is the verb of the second crucial clause (#2 above). The grandson remarks that "what was originally expressed in Hebrew does not have the same force when it is in fact rendered in another language." The verb appears very infrequently in Greek, and it means "to have equal force or power." This term creates so much difficulty in this passage because its semantic range not only indicates equivalence of force or strength, but also equivalence generally, and even equivalence of meaning. But does the term have to refer to equivalence of meaning here as so many commentators have understood it? If we keep in mind that the grandson's audience is made up of people who most likely do not know Hebrew and that the grandson has just addressed any perceived inability on his part in writing Greek, then I think that he is saying that due to the translation *process* what is originally in Hebrew does not have the same *rhetorical power or force* in Greek, not that things in Hebrew do not have the same *meaning* when translated into another language.[34] And, in fact, that the Greek of the

---

[33] They list only two other occurrences: one in Simplicius (6th century CE) and one in P.Lond. 2.361 (1st century CE). H.G. Liddell, R. Scott, H.S. Jones, eds. *A Greek-English Lexicon* (Ninth ed.; Oxford: Clarendon, 1940).

[34] The verb is often taken this way, however. See most recently, for example, J.F.A. Sawyer, *Sacred Languages and Sacred Texts* (London/New York: Routledge, 1999) 79, who translates the beginning of this second sentence, "Please read carefully and with good will; excuse me where I have got the meaning wrong despite my efforts to translate.

translation does not have much rhetorical force is apparent throughout his work. This interpretation falls well within the viable semantic range of the verb ἰσοδυναμεῖ, and this interpretation is consistent with the social context that the prologue seems to establish for the translation. So, we do not have to understand this passage as an expression of the grandson's anxiety about fidelity to the meaning of the Hebrew, but we can read it as a statement addressed to an audience that is about to read his work of his frustration with a translation process that seems inevitably to produce inelegant Greek.

The third key term (#3 above) is embedded in the clause that immediately follows the grandson's statement about the difference in rhetorical force between the Hebrew original and the Greek, and its meaning in this clause is dependent on the meaning of ἰσοδυναμεῖ in the preceding clause. The translator says, "And (δέ) not only in this case, but also in the Law itself and the Prophets and the rest of the books the difference is not small (οὐ μικρὰν ἔχει τὴν διαφοράν) when these are expressed in their own language." While the use of δέ establishes a close grammatical relationship with the prior clause, the neuter plural "these things" refers to the "what was expressed originally in Hebrew" about which the grandson just spoke. So when the grandson claims that even the translation of the Jewish scriptures "are not a little different," what exactly is that difference? If we read the clause without considering (1) what the prologue indicates about the grandson's intended audience generally and (2) what immediately precedes it in particular, we might conclude that the grandson is speaking in this clause about differences of meaning between the source text and its translation. If, however, the clause is read within these two contexts, as I have articulated them, then the grandson seems to be saying in this clause that the same difference in the rhetorical force or power between the Hebrew original and the Greek that might be thought by some to characterize his translation also characterizes the Jewish-Greek scriptures. Here again, my reading of the prologue finds the grandson concerned with the Greek of his own translation and its deficiencies as a Greek text, not as a translation that is deficient with regard to its source text.

When translated into another language, words do not have the same meaning as they have in Hebrew." Kelly (*True Interpreter*, 214) also seems to understand the passage in this manner, although his translation does not make it so explicit.

So, if in the prologue the grandson is making an *apologia* for the Greek of his translation, the obvious question arises—why did he translate that way? He clearly could write good literary Greek. Why not render his grandfather's Hebrew into the same sort of Greek that he used to introduce his translation? To utilize Kelly's two stances of authority outlined above in the section on Cicero, the grandson clearly adopts a positional authority vis-à-vis his source text. The translation certainly can be described as largely unidimensional, text-centered and objective. Or, to use Kelly's terms, the grandson does not collaborate with the text; he serves it. But in the same way as such a characterization was not sufficient to understand Cicero, it does not completely suffice here either. Given the grandson's obvious abilities to compose good, rhetorically pleasing *koine* Greek, why should he assume a positional authority towards his source text? Part of my answer to this question takes into account what the grandson tells us in the prologue; the other part is somewhat speculative.

The grandson tells us that his motivation for translating his grandfather's book was to make it available to those "living abroad" who wanted to live their lives according to the Law. He apparently came to this decision after going to Egypt and encountering "an exemplar of no little education." He then determined that he ought to "bring some speed and industry to the translating of this tome." This much we know. The evidence of the prologue, however, also suggests that the grandson is no experienced translator. He apparently made an *ad hoc* decision to translate his grandfather's book for those Greek-speaking Jews whom he met in Egypt who he thought could benefit from its wisdom and instruction. But making the decision to translate would only have been the first step. Where would he learn how to translate? How would he go about it? It seems to me that he comes close to telling us. He refers to "the Law and the Prophets and the other books" three separate times (1–2, 7–10, 24–25). As we saw above he compares the Greek of his translation to that of the Jewish-Greek scriptures. My guess is that he adopted for his own work the same authority structure that he saw in those translations. The books of the LXX also utilize a kind of translationese that seems to have formal representation of the Hebrew as one of its primary objectives. As he cast about for a way to approach his recently formulated project, he came upon a readily available model, one the Jewish community was already using and with which it was familiar. If the character of his Greek translation is like that of the Jewish-Greek scriptures, as he himself points out, that might not be accidental.

The result is, of course, that what Ben Sira's grandson produced was a fairly literal translation. But can we say about this literal product what many who discuss translation say about literal translations—that it is intended to bring the original to the reader, to give the reader access to the source language/text?[35] The reading that I have given the prologue in this section suggests that the grandson was not troubled by some sense that he might not have rendered his Hebrew original with fidelity. His frustration with the translation process seems based in his awareness that the resultant Greek was not very elegant. What is interesting is that it does not seem to have occurred to him that he could translate any other way. My reading also suggests that the grandson was not somehow as a matter of method trying to give his readers access to the Hebrew of his grandfather. The ultimate literalness of his work may well be an unintended consequence of the grandson's decision to translate his grandfather's wisdom.

THE SEPTUAGINT

In contrast to Ben Sira and certainly to Cicero, we know very little with certainty about the origins of the Septuagint. We know nothing specific about any of the translators, and no first-hand testimony about the origins of the translation exists. Several versions of an origination legend circulated among Jews and Christians in antiquity, however. The oldest is contained in a Jewish work usually called *The Letter of Aristeas to Philocrates*.[36] *Aristeas* claims that at the request of the Egyptian king Ptolemy Philadelphus seventy-two Jewish translators were brought to Alexandria from Jerusalem to render the Jewish Law into Greek for the king's library. The translators labored for seventy-two days, each day working and then comparing the product of their labors in order to arrive at the finished translation. Upon its completion, Demetrius, the

---

[35] In addition to the studies of translation listed above, see S. Brock, "Translation in Antiquity," *Alta* (II) 8 (1969) 99.

[36] For translation and commentary on *Aristeas*, see the classic treatment given by M. Hadas, *Aristeas to Philocrates* (Philadelphia: Dropsie College, 1951) who uses H.St.J. Thackeray's Greek text. See also A. Pelletier, *Lettre d'Aristée à Philocrate* (SC 89; Paris: Cerf, 1962). A convenient English translation is that of R.J.H. Shutt in J.H. Charlesworth, ed., *The Old Testament Pseudepigrapha* (Vol. 2; Garden City, NY: Doubleday, 1985).

king's librarian, read the translation to the assembled Jewish community whose leaders confirmed its accuracy and who proclaimed that no
revisions to the translation should be made. This story wound its way
through early Jewish and Christian writers all the while taking on more
miraculous elements, as for example in Philo, *The Life of Moses* 2.25–44
who says, "[T]hey [the translators] became as it were possessed, and,
under inspiration, wrote, not each several scribe something different,
but the same word for word, as though dictated to each by an invisible
prompter" (37).[37] Philo envisions not translation by committee, as does
Aristeas, but translation by divine inspiration.

In general most scholars doubt the historical veracity of *Aristeas*'s
version of the events, although some conclusions about the translation
can be derived from *Aristeas*'s account. The bottom line is that Jewish
translators most likely executed the translation in Alexandria sometime
in the first part of the third century BCE for use by other Jews.[38] In
what context the translation originated is another matter altogether.
The general character of the Greek of the Septuagint conforms to what
can be described as a literal approach to the source text that intends
to reflect to a great degree the formal aspects of the Hebrew original.
Sometimes the resultant Greek is quite adequate, if pedestrian; at other
times it can be downright nonsensical. Different scholars have theorized
that such a translation could have derived from a variety of needs, all of
which, it is claimed, would have produced the literal, often Hebraistic,
renderings characteristic of the Septuagint. The three contexts most
frequently suggested are: liturgical—Jews who no longer understood
Hebrew needed to hear the Law in their own language, a sort of Greek
targum;[39] pedagogical—the Greek arose as a sort of interlinear pony to

---

[37] Translation taken from F.H. Colson, *Philo VI* (LCL; Cambridge, MA: Harvard
University Press, 1935).
[38] For more detail on what *Aristeas* tells us about the Septuagint, see S. Jellicoe,
The Septuagint and Modern Study (Oxford: Clarendon, 1968) 55–6 and more recently
N. Fernández Marcos, *The Septuagint in Context: An Introduction to the Greek Versions
of the Bible* (Leiden: Brill, 2000) and M. Silva and K. Jobes, *Invitation to the Septuagint*
(Grand Rapids: Eerdmans, 2000).
[39] See, especially, H.St.J. Thackeray, *The Septuagint and Jewish Worship: A Study in
Origins* (London: Oxford University Press, 1923).

the Hebrew in school contexts;[40] legal—the translation was motivated by a general Egyptian policy of rendering oriental law codes into Greek.[41]

It is precisely the obscure nature of the translation's origins that creates difficulties when one tries to answer the questions I have posed in this paper. Scholars who write on translation are often tempted to accept the *Aristeas* legend or even one of the later versions of it. Kelly, for instance, cites the Septuagint as an example of a translation where the translators worked in subjection to their original. In support of this notion, he says the following, utilizing Philo's account of the Septuagint's origins:

> For, according to their concepts of divine inspiration, the texts were the direct creation of God, who had taken over the faculties of the human author. As the word of God, the Old Testament was an objective historical account expressed in the most adequate way. Therefore, as Philo Iudaeus puts it in his life of Moses, Scripture translation was akin to that of science: there is a 'wording which corresponds with the matter', and is therefore the only one adequate.[42]

Kelly understands the essentially literal character of the Septuagint to result from the translators' regard for their text as sacred scripture. Literalness in translation is a function of their attempt to render a sacred text.[43] Yet, *Aristeas*, most likely Philo's main source for the legend, does not articulate the work of the translators in this way. About the translation process the author simply says that the Jewish translators did their work and compared their results in order to accomplish the task. After the completion of the translation the Jewish leaders confirmed the translation's accuracy. In §§314–316 where the author describes previous attempts at translation of the Hebrew scriptures, the point is to show that *this* translation, the Septuagint, had divine sanction. It does not provide evidence for why it was translated as it was. In the quote above, Kelly essentially confuses Philo's embellished form of the legend with the translators' own motivations and approach to the source text.

---

[40] Most recently suggested by A. Pietersma in his paper "A New Paradigm for Addressing Old Questions: The Relevance of the Interlinear Model for the Study of the Septuagint" where he extends the work of S. Brock. See below and note 44 on Pietersma's paper.

[41] See, for example, D. Barthélemy, "Pourquoi la Torah a-t-elle été traduite en grec?" *On Language, Culture, and Religion: In Honor of Eugene A. Nida* (M. Black and W.A. Smalley, eds.; The Hague: Mouton, 1975) 23–41.

[42] Kelly, *True Interpreter*, 69.

[43] Many scholars of the Septuagint also make this argument. See, for instance, H.M. Orlinsky, "The Septuagint as Holy Writ and the Philosophy of the Translators," *HUCA* 46 (1975) 89–114.

In fact, how one understands the social, cultural and linguistic circumstances of the translation will go a long way toward determining what one concludes about the translators' motivations. A. Pietersma, in a recent paper in which he attempts to articulate what he calls the "interlinear" model of the Septuagint's translation, presents one view that leads in a direction away from the idea that the translators rendered their Hebrew literally because they were translating Holy Scripture. In "A New Paradigm for Addressing Old Questions: The Relevance of the Interlinear Model for the Study of the Septuagint," Pietersma's analysis of the linguistic character of the Septuagint leads him to suggest that the Septuagint may have originated in the context of Jewish education, not as an independent, self-standing translation intended to replace the Hebrew, but as an interlinear "crib."[44]

Pietersma argues that modern theories of the origins of the Septuagint assume the claim inherent in *Aristeas*'s account that the Septuagint was intended to function as an independent text that would replace the Hebrew original. He maintains that such an assumption does not sufficiently account for the "Hebraic dimension of the LXX." Utilizing G. Toury's notion of linguistic interference in translations,[45] he argues concerning the Septuagint that "for some essential linguistic information, the parent text needs to be consulted, since the text as we have it cannot stand on its own feet." In other words, the translation is at times unintelligible and cannot be understood apart from its Hebrew original. In fact, scholars of the Septuagint resort in practice to the interlinear model; they often feel compelled to look to the Hebrew for the necessary linguistic information that makes sense out of the Greek. It is this periodic inability of the Septuagint to stand on its own that creates the problems Pietersma tries to resolve.

By "interlinear" Pietersma intends to say that the Septuagint is two-dimensional; it has both horizontal and vertical dimensions. In the horizontal dimension "morphemes are knit together into syntactic units to convey information"; in the vertical, "the parent text forms

---

[44] Pietersma presented this paper at two recent conferences concerned with Septuagint Studies, and the interlinear paradigm underlies the New English Translation of the Septuagint Project, which he and I co-edited. It appeared in *Bible and Computer: The Stellenbosch AIBI-6 Conference. Proceedings of the Association Internationale Bible et Informatique "From Alpha to Byte." University of Stellenbosch 17–21 July 2000* (J. Cook, ed.; Leiden: Brill, 2002) 337–64.

[45] G. Toury, *Descriptive Translational Studies and Beyond* (Benjamins Translation Library 4; Amsterdam: John Benjamins, 1995).

the *de facto* context for units of meaning, and as a result of excessive one-for-one dependence on the source text the receptor text may be rendered disjointed or worse." Pietersma ultimately finds the most congenial social context for a translation that originates in this manner in the Jewish school, and he argues that what we know about Hellenistic schools shows that texts were treated precisely in such an "interlinear" manner as he has described.[46]

He concludes by arguing for a four-stage development of the Septuagint. First, the Hebrew text serves as the sole authority. Second, the Hebrew is translated into Greek, which is supposed to act as a crib for the study of the Hebrew. Third, the Greek text later achieves a status independent of its Hebrew original. Fourth, debates ensue over which text, Hebrew or Greek, should be viewed as authoritative.

In this paradigm, the translators' stance of positional authority toward their Hebrew text (to use the language I have utilized for both Cicero and Ben Sira) is not only clear, but fully explicable. The translation has the unidimensional and object-centered character that Kelly describes for translations that adopt a positional authority vis-à-vis the source text. The Septuagint translators were indeed intending to bring the original Hebrew to the reader. In fact, Pietersma's interlinear model as an explanatory paradigm requires this idea as a basic motivation for the translation of the Septuagint.

Furthermore, this paradigm also provides some explanation of why the translators adopted this approach to translation, and it accounts well for "the Septuagint's aspect of unintelligibility as well as for its intelligibility," to use Pietersma's words. And most crucially for the purposes of my argument in this paper, one of the implications of using this paradigm to consider the origins of the Septuagint is that there exists no inherent reason to claim that the sacredness of the text has anything to do with the translators' motivation. The Greek translation may have acted as a crib for study of the Jewish scriptures in the Jewish school, just as *koine* Greek translations served the same function for study of Homer in the Hellenistic school. Pietersma puts it this way:

> Furthermore, though Egyptian Jews may well have believed that the biblical text was essentially a legal document and may have regarded it as verbally inspired, neither can be inferred from the nature of the text as we have it or from its origin. What its school origin does allow us to infer is that what Homer was to the Greeks, the Hebrew Bible was to the

---

[46] Pietersma uses the example of an interlinear *koine* "translation" of Homer.

Jews. Both were clearly regarded as texts to be studied in schools, texts that were normative for the community.[47]

In Pietersma's paradigm, literalness, a positional authority, bringing the reader to the original—however one might want to describe the Septuagint and its relation to its source text—does not necessarily arise out of the translators' belief that the original is a verbally inspired, sacred text.

Later, when the Septuagint does become established as an independent text whose reading and use was divorced from its Hebrew original, the idea of divine inspiration indeed becomes very germane. As Pietersma notes, after the Greek text achieves a status independent from its source text, debate centered on the relative authority of the Hebrew and Greek texts, and a number of subsequent revisions of the Greek attempted to bring it into greater conformity with the Hebrew text of the Bible, which was changing and developing independently. S. Brock attributes these revisions to the growing conviction that the Hebrew language should be thought of as the sole medium of authority and revelation. He says, "Such an attitude to the unique role of Hebrew as the language of divine revelation effectively ruled out the possibility that a biblical translation could legitimately enjoy any authority at all independently of the Hebrew original."[48] In a sense, then, with the revisions to the Septuagint we come somewhat full circle. A text that Pietersma argues was born in close contact with its Hebrew original grew up to become independent of its parent and later revisers of the Greek attempted to regain that initial intimacy.[49]

So, by almost any assessment of the origins of the Septuagint, it appears that its translators did try to provide their readership access to the source text via their Greek translation. Why that was so important to them is not so clear. The social context that one envisions for the Septuagint's origins will form the basis for determining what motivated this particular approach to the Hebrew text of the Bible. To the degree that we lack a clear originating context for the Septuagint, we will struggle

---

[47] Pietersma, "New Paradigm," 360.
[48] S. Brock, "To Revise or Not to Revise: Attitudes to Jewish Biblical Translation," *Septuagint, Scrolls and Cognate Writings* (G.F. Brooke and B. Lindars, eds.; SBLSCS 33; Atlanta: Scholars Press, 1992) 321.
[49] Of course, the issue is not entirely that simple. The Hebrew text of the Bible was itself developing in this period and in many cases was not the same as the Hebrew text used by the translators. As a generalization, however, the above holds true.

to ascertain why the translators took the approach that they did; one
that seemed to become the norm for translation as time went on.

Conclusions

What then can we conclude about the relationships among translation,
source text and audience in these three different examples of ancient
translation? Certainly about Cicero we can say quite a bit. The kind
of literary translation that Cicero advocated seems at least to a good
degree a function of the abilities of his audience. Cicero is able to adopt
his personal authority stance toward the text for several reasons. As an
orator he has a professional kinship with the authors he translates, and
even more than that, one certainly senses that Cicero feels a kind of
intimacy with those he renders into Latin. But his relationship with his
audience also conditions the relationship between him and his Greek
original; he can translate the way he does because his readers can read
these authors for themselves. For Cicero, however, we have a lot of
evidence—his own testimony as well as the wealth of data about Roman
translation of things Greek. I wonder whether we would say the same
sorts of things if there were not as much evidence available.

   In the case of Ben Sira matters are much less clear. The prologue to
the translation contains evidence that suggests that Ben Sira's grandson
translated his grandfather's book of wisdom on an *ad hoc* basis, not as
part of some carefully preplanned translation project. He may well have
thought a fair amount about what it meant to undertake such a task, but
I think that those places where the grandson is often understood to be
defending the potentially problematic relationship between his Hebrew
original and the Greek translation turn out in actuality to concern the
possibility that his readership might think his Greek to be inadequate.
If his admission that he is aware that his Greek might be thought
inadequate did not do the trick, he adds that it is of similar quality to
that of the translation of the Bible. His comments to his prospective
reading audience indicate that he believed such a result to be part of the
nature of the translation process. In fact, he may well have developed
his approach to translating by observing how the biblical translators
accomplished their task.[50] One does get the feeling, however, that the

---

[50] The grandson does not, however, depend on the Jewish-Greek scriptures for the
details of his own work. See Wright, *No Small Difference*, chap. 3.

grandson never read any translation of the caliber and style that Cicero would later advocate. As a result, the grandson in his prologue appears at first glance to be reflecting on the difficulty of rendering Hebrew into Greek because the two languages are so different, but I think in the end he really reveals something of his own apprehensions about the reception of his work due to the inelegant Greek of the product, an inelegance he sees as unavoidable.

The Septuagint, on the other hand, turns out to be a good example of a translation whose translators self-consciously adopted a positional authority stance vis-à-vis their Hebrew texts. There seems little doubt that the approach they took to their translations was intentionally worked out. What is so hard to figure out with the Septuagint is why they utilized this approach. Any attempt to resolve this problem depends on how one understands the original social context of the Septuagint, itself still something of a conundrum. The social and linguistic context in which one places the translation determines to a great extent who the reading audience was and what motivated the translation. It does indeed appear that the Alexandrian Jewish translators were endeavoring to give their readers some access to the source language—but what readers and for what reason?

The three examples of ancient Greek-to-Latin and Hebrew-to-Greek translations that I have considered in this paper demonstrate that studying them alongside each other and asking questions about the relationships to be found in them among translation, source text and reading audience can be very fruitful, especially as those questions are framed by some insights from translation theory. In these three cases, there seems to be some correlation between literal translation and the translator's desire to provide access to the source language for the reader. The question of the anticipated readership, inasmuch as the audience provides clues to the translation's social and linguistic context, would appear to be an important focus of inquiry. Why translators adopt a particular stance of authority towards their source texts has the potential to reveal much about the motivation for any particular translation. And while I have learned much about these ancient translators from these self-described first steps, it is apparent that there are many other questions that could be asked and much more yet to discover about ancient translators and their work.

CHAPTER THIRTEEN

THE *LETTER OF ARISTEAS* AND THE RECEPTION HISTORY OF THE SEPTUAGINT

My argument in this paper originated in two separate places: conversations about the methodological foundation for the New English Translation of the Septuagint (NETS) and the proposed NETS Commentary Series, which will complement the NETS translations (Society of Biblical Literature Commentary on the Septuagint [SBLCS]), and some preliminary thinking about the *Letter of Aristeas* on which I am beginning to write a commentary.[1] As I see it, the essential problem is this: many scholars, either explicitly or implicitly, no matter what they say about the historical and/or propagandistic value of the work, accept the basic notion promulgated by Pseudo-Aristeas that the LXX was originally intended to serve as an independent and self-standing replacement for the Hebrew text rendered by it. As we will see, at almost every point Pseudo-Aristeas argues that the translators (as commissioned by their Ptolemaic patron) produced an exemplary work of Greek philosophy and literature, highly acceptable (to use the language of translation theorist, G. Toury) in its target culture, and that the Jewish community of Alexandria adopted the LXX as its sacred scriptures.

Yet, as scholars pursue a solution to the major problems connected with the LXX and its origins, we must place one basic fact at the center of the stage—the LXX is a translation, not a work originally composed in Greek.[2] This realization matters, and matters a great deal. C. Boyd-Taylor aptly articulates why.

> Quite simply, a translated text never represents a straightforward instance of performance in the target language. Translations deviate from the conventions governing well-formed texts and this fact has both linguistic and

[1] I extend thanks to S. Fraade for his kind invitation to present an early version of this paper at Yale University. The questions and conversation there caused me to make a number of significant revisions to the argument. I am also grateful to A. Pietersma and C. Boyd-Taylor, who read an earlier version of the paper and who, as always, pushed me on a number of important points.

[2] By "Septuagint," I mean the Pentateuch, most likely translated in the third century BCE in Alexandria.

socio-cultural implications. The practices of reading brought to bear on a translation, the expectations of its readership, the uses to which it is put, will vary systematically from those proper to non-translational texts.[3]

That is, the LXX was intended to occupy a specific sociocultural niche for the Jews of Alexandria, and its textual expression, social location, uses and transmission are all conditioned by the fact that it is a translated text. What seems necessary, then, as a means of approaching the problem I have in mind, and what we scholars of the LXX rarely seem to employ, is a theory of translation that will provide an adequate explanatory framework for addressing the central questions we ask about this important translation.[4]

The importance of seeing the LXX as a translation and the concurrent need for some theoretical framework in which to discuss it was nowhere more obvious than in the beginning stages of the NETS project. The editors and the committee charged with creating the policies for translating the LXX into English had to reckon constantly with the fact that we were translating a translation, and one that had a close relationship to its Semitic parent text at that. One theoretical approach to the enterprise of translation that has proved very productive for the way that we look at the Septuagint is the work of the Israeli translation theorist, G. Toury, as set out most recently in his book, *Descriptive Translation Studies and Beyond* (DTS).[5] Fundamentally, Toury argues that

> the position and function of translations (as entities) and of translating (as a kind of activity) in a prospective target culture, the form a translation would have (and hence the relationships which would tie it to its original), and the strategies resorted to during its generation do not constitute a series of unconnected facts.[6]

---

[3] C. Boyd-Taylor, "In a Mirror, Dimly: Reading the Septuagint as a Document of its Times," *Septuagint Research: Issues and Challenges in the Study of the Greek Jewish Scriptures* (W. Kraus and R.G. Wooden, eds.; SBLSCS 53; Atlanta: SBL, 2006) 16–7.

[4] See A. Pietersma, "A New Paradigm for Addressing Old Questions: The Relevance of the Interlinear Model for the Study of the Septuagint," *Bible and Computer: The Stellenbosch AIBI-6 Conference. Proceedings of the Association Internationale Bible et Informatique "From Alpha to Byte." University of Stellenbosch 17–21 July 2000* (J. Cook, ed.; Leiden: Brill, 2002) 340 citing J.Z. Smith, *Drudgery Divine* (Chicago: University of Chicago Press, 1990) 79.

[5] G. Toury, *Descriptive Translation Studies and Beyond* (Benjamins Translation Library 4; Amsterdam: John Benjamins, 1995).

[6] Ibid., 24.

The interconnected nature of these "facts" gives rise to the claim that all translations originate within a particular cultural environment and they "are designed to meet certain needs of, and/or occupy certain 'slots' in it."[7] In short, translations need to be thought of first and foremost as facts of their target cultures.

According to Toury, not only are a translation's function/position, its textual-linguistic makeup (what Toury calls "product") and the strategies employed by the translator (called "process" by Toury) interconnected, they exert specific influences in a particular direction. As Toury describes this threefold series of relationships, he argues that the intended position of any translation in its target culture exerts a determining influence on its surface realization or textual-linguistic makeup. Further, this surface realization establishes the parameters and strategies that a translator can use in the execution of that translation.[8] He diagrams this series of relationships as follows:

The (prospective) systemic position and function of a translation
↓   determines
its appropriate surface realization
(= textual-linguistic makeup), and
↓   governs
the strategies whereby a target text (or parts thereof)
is derived from its original, and hence the
relationships which hold them together[9]

Figure 1. *Toury's Relations between function (position), product and process*

Since Toury's categories are inextricably linked in such a way that each informs the other, presumably, what we know about one or two of these elements should provide some indications of the nature of the other(s). This inter-connectedness of function, product and process has potential significance for the study of the LXX, since we actually do know quite a bit about the textual-linguistic makeup of the translations and the strategies employed by the translators, while we are still relatively in the dark about the translation's origins. To put it in Toury's language of function-product-process, knowing something of the product and process of the LXX should enable us to derive some conclusions about the intended function of the translation in the target culture. That intended function might provide clues as to the origins of the translation.

---

[7] Ibid., 12.
[8] Ibid.
[9] Ibid., 13.

While the terms "function" or "position" might lead us to think that Toury has in mind the *Sitz im Leben* of a translation, he appears to mean something else.[10] For a translation like the LXX we really cannot know what the translators intended to do with it once it existed in Greek. By function/position, Toury means cultural location. The "slots" within the target cultural environment more appropriately have to do with the value of a text within that target culture. When he speaks of function/position, Toury is interested in the systemic value of the translation, which is structural and which can perhaps best be expressed in oppositions such as literary/non-literary, central/peripheral, prestigious/non-prestigious, monolingual/bilingual.[11] In any function-oriented analysis of a translation, these oppositions, to which we could probably add others, will provide indicators of a translation's intended function.

Translators, by dint of the fact that they must work in two language systems and thus with two differing sets of linguistic norms, are faced with decisions about which norms to follow. A translator could subject him/herself to the norms of the source text or to the norms of the target culture. This "basic choice" between the source norms or target norms, which a translator can make at the macro and/or micro levels, Toury calls an initial norm.[12] Some translations "tend to subscribe to the norms of the source text, and through them also to the norms of the source language and culture." Such translations "may well entail certain incompatibilities with target norms and practices, especially those lying beyond the mere linguistic ones."[13] Translations can also work in the other direction, adopting the norms of the target system. In these cases, the translators pursue different agendas. Toury characterizes the pursuit of these differing translational agendas with the terms adequacy and acceptability. "Thus," he writes, "whereas adherence to the source norms determines a translation's adequacy as compared to the source text, subscription to norms originating in the target culture determines

---

[10] Ibid., 12. I am indebted in this short section to several e-mail exchanges with A. Pietersma and C. Boyd-Taylor in which we tried to sort out a bit what Toury was getting at in his discussion of function.

[11] This list of oppositions comes from a private communication from C. Boyd-Taylor. It should be pointed out here that Toury's theoretical approach is rooted in Polysystem theory, which itself is a development within structuralism and (Russian) formalism. See also S. Fraade, "Locating Targum in the Textual Polysystem of Rabbinic Pedagogy," *BIOSCS* 39 (2006) 69–90.

[12] Toury, *Descriptive Translation Studies*, 56.

[13] Ibid.

its acceptability."[14] Adherence to source (adequacy) or target (acceptability) norms bears initially on any evaluation of the textual-linguistic makeup of a translation, but, as Toury notes, the norms pursued are not strictly linguistic. They are also more broadly cultural. In that sense, any assessment of the degree to which the translator pursued adequacy or acceptability would seem to provide potential evidence for the intended function/position of a translation.

One of the important and productive consequences of the theoretical insights advocated by Toury is that they can provide a framework within which to ask historical questions about translations, since translation is a social behavior and translations, as he argues, are facts of target cultures. As the large quantity of scholarly literature on the LXX will attest, the matter of its origins remains a vexed and largely unanswered question. Since we possess no first-hand testimony from those connected with the production of the LXX, we are left, it seems to me, with two sorts of evidence upon which to draw: (1) the claims of the earliest "account" of the translation's origins, the *Letter of Aristeas* (external evidence), which conveys a great deal of information about what Pseudo-Aristeas envisioned the function of the LXX to be,[15] and (2) the evidence of the textual-linguistic makeup of the LXX itself (internal evidence). In what follows, I employ aspects of Toury's theoretical framework in order to discover what the *Letter of Aristeas* says about the intended function of the LXX and, since Toury's model posits a connection between intended function and textual-linguistic makeup, to see if Pseudo-Aristeas's construction comports with the evidence derived from the translations themselves.

THE SEPTUAGINT IN THE *LETTER OF ARISTEAS*

This early Jewish text stands at the center of any discussion of the translation of the LXX. In general scholars agree that the *Letter of Aristeas* is pseudonymous, the product of a Jewish author and not the

---

[14] Ibid., 56–7. Important to note at this juncture is that acceptability is relative to the norms of literary composition in the target culture. Toury is not talking about the relative acceptability of a text *qua* translation.

[15] For the purposes of my argument, it is immaterial whether Aristobulus is earlier or later than *Aristeas*. Aristobulus mentions Demetrius of Phalerum as the instigator of the translation as *Aristeas* does. The relationship of these authors and their possible sources for the tradition about Demetrius are still open questions.

creation of its putative author, "Aristeas," a Greek courtier of Ptolemy II
Philadelphus (hence the designation of the author as Pseudo-Aristeas);
is not a contemporary account that chronicles the making of the translation, but one made a significant time after it, probably sometime in
the mid-second century BCE; and reflects the Jewish author's interests
and concerns in his own time, not the concerns of third-century BCE
Judaism. Significant scholarly disagreement remains about the author's
motivations for writing the book. Possible motivations are: a response
to some contemporary crisis, a polemic targeting the emergence of rival
translations, or certain problems of Hellenism and Judaism. Whatever
the author's motivation, and despite the fact that only a small portion of
the book actually describes the process and acceptance of the translation,
Aristeas is occupied throughout with the rendering of the Torah into
Greek. For starters, this task frames the entire work. The translation is
the reason for the deputation to the high priest Eleazar (§§1–3),[16] and
the book culminates with the acceptance of the translation by the Jewish community and the approbation of the king (§§308–21). The four
major digressions (the description of the gifts [§§51–83]; the journey
to Jerusalem [§§83–120]; Eleazar's apology for the Law [§§128–71];
the symposia [§§187–300]) all contribute to the overall purpose of the
book, "to transform the translation of the Law into a 'major event,'" that
is, to articulate a myth of origins for the LXX.[17] Of these four digressions, the section describing the series of symposia given by the king in
honor of the Jewish translators bears most directly on Pseudo-Aristeas's
construction of the nature of the LXX, since it demonstrates how the
translators' proficiency in Greek philosophy and Jewish piety outstrips
the Alexandrian philosophers' and why they are qualified to undertake
this momentous task in the life of the Jewish people.

Even though scholarly opinion holds that *Aristeas* is not a contemporary historical account of the production of the LXX, scholars often
assume that the letter supplies important evidence for the origins and
character of the translation. Yet, if we examine carefully just what
Pseudo-Aristeas claims for the LXX as a translation of the Hebrew Torah
we find that the central (and apologetic) goal is to portray the LXX as

---

[16] For the Greek text of *Aristeas*, see A. Pelletier, *Lettre d'Aristée à Philocrate* (SC
89; Paris: Cerf, 1962).
[17] S. Honigman, *The Septuagint and Homeric Scholarship* (London/New York: Routledge, 2003) 32. For arguments about the purpose of *Aristeas*, see also Chapter 14,
"Translation as Scripture: The Septuagint in Aristeas and Philo," 304–9.

genealogically a translation deriving prestige and authority from its source text. At the same time, however, the author constructs the LXX as genetically an independent entity, of great literary and philosophical quality, highly acceptable, occupying a prestigious slot in the target culture. Pseudo-Aristeas effectively ignores, however, the actual, and observable, relationship between the Hebrew and the Greek.[18] If we look back at Toury's arguments, his model posits that function/position governs the textual-linguistic makeup of a translation and that the translators' position (the initial norm) on adequacy/acceptability reveals which cultural norms are being followed. *Aristeas*'s story of LXX origins does not account for the disconnect between its claim of the LXX's function/position as a highly acceptable, prestigious and independent work of literature and the results of textual-linguistic analysis of the translations themselves.[19]

Pseudo-Aristeas's story begins when King Ptolemy charges his librarian, Demetrius of Phalerum, with gathering together "if possible, all the books of the world" (§9). Demetrius purchases and transcribes as many as he can, but missing from the collection is the Jewish Law, which, Demetrius tells the king, "should be given a place in your library, for their [the Jews'] legislation is most philosophical and flawless (διὰ τὸ καὶ φιλοσοφωτέραν εἶναι καὶ ἀκέραιον τὴν νομοθεσίαν ταύτην), inasmuch as it is divine" (§31). The reason for the absence of such a prestigious text, Demetrius notes, is that "translation/interpretation (ἑρμηνείας) is required." The *raison d'être* for the translation, then, was to occupy a place in the royal library alongside all the other books that Demetrius had acquired. The claims made about the Jewish Law and the intention to have it in the library indicate that from its inception, the translation was supposed to be read and used independently of the Hebrew. The king's copies would be accorded high cultural status, and the expectation was that the accomplished translation would itself be highly acceptable to the target culture. That is, it would be a work of high literature (a point to which I will return). That Pseudo-Aristeas credits the Hellenistic king with initiating the translation emphasizes both its independence from the Hebrew, since its users would have been Greek speakers who presumably would not have been able to read the

---

[18] For the language of genetics, I am indebted to A. Pietersma, "LXX and DTS: A New Archimedean Point for Septuagint Studies?" *BIOSCS* 39 (2006) 1–11.

[19] See below pp. 288–90 for studies that have characterized the nature of Septuagintal Greek.

original, and its prestige, since from the beginning the translation was connected with royal patronage.

The vocabulary of translation/interpretation employed throughout the book furthers this twofold agenda of independence and prestige. The term ἑρμηνεία, which can mean "interpretation" as well as "translation," occurs often along with the verb ἑρμηνεύω and its roughly synonymous compounds μεθερμηνεύω and διερμηνεύω. While they probably mean "to translate" (cf. especially §§15, 38–39) for the most part, and terms for translation routinely appear in contexts with words for transcription and copying (§§9, 15, 19, 307, 309), the built-in lexical ambiguity in these terms actually works in the author's favor, and he probably even plays intentionally on that ambiguity.[20] Indeed, we might expect as much from Pseudo-Aristeas. On the one hand, the connotation of translation explicitly connects the Greek version as a representation of its genealogically famous parent, and in §§32 and 310, Pseudo-Aristeas makes clear that the rendering was "accurate." On the other hand, the language of interpretation establishes the LXX as an independent entity, able to stand on its own without dependence on the parent text. Thus, Pseudo-Aristeas lexically wants to have it both ways. The LXX shares the prestige and divine quality of the Hebrew Law through its genealogical, that is translational, relationship, but at the same time it can take its own place in the king's library as an independent work of Greek literature. The language of interpretation/translation that Pseudo-Aristeas employs provides an important initial indication that the LXX is culturally prestigious and therefore highly acceptable in the target culture.

In order to execute the task of translating the Hebrew Law, Demetrius dispatches a deputation to Eleazar, the high priest of the Jews, seeking "elders who have led exemplary lives and are expert in their own law and are able to translate" (§§32, 39). He should send these men to Alexandria where they will execute the translation. From the beginning, it is clear that they will be engaged in a cooperative effort to achieve "accuracy in the translation" (τὸ κατὰ τὴν ἑρμηνείαν ἀκριβές). Once accomplished Ptolemy intends to "place it conspicuously, worthy of the subject and of your [Eleazar's] benevolence." The translators carry with them manuscripts on which the Law is written in Hebrew script

---

[20] For a good discussion of this terminology, see Honigman, *The Septuagint and Homeric Scholarship*, 44–9 and H. Gzella, *Lebenzeit und Ewigheit: Studien zur Eschatologie und Anthropologie des Septuaginta-Psalters* (Berlin: Philo, 2002) 13–39.

in golden characters. Upon their arrival, the Gentile king acknowledges the divine nature of the Hebrew. "When they had uncovered the rolls and unrolled the parchments, the king paused for a considerable space, and after bowing deeply some seven times, he said, 'I thank you, good sirs, and him that sent you even more, but most of all I thank God whose holy words these are'" (§177). These manuscripts vouchsafe the authenticity of copies of the Hebrew Law, especially in light of Demetrius's earlier statement in §30 that the Law "has been transcribed rather carelessly and not as is proper."[21] That the translation was made from these divinely impressive and carefully transcribed manuscripts argues powerfully for its own verisimilitude and sanctity.

Before the translation can be executed, the king fêtes the translators in a series of symposia, which serve to highlight the characteristics of these formidable men. Through a series of questions that the king proposes, each of the translators demonstrates a keen grasp of Greek philosophy. Their answers outstrip those of the court philosophers because they additionally make the Jewish God the basis for their arguments. They are eloquent, learned/cultured (πεπαιδευμένοις, §321) and virtuous (cf. §§200, 235, 293–96). The work's portrayal of the translators presents them as men who are well versed in both Greek philosophy and the Hebrew Law. They draw their superior answers to the king's questions from their divine legislation—God is at the center of all their responses.

If we recall the lexical ambiguity of the translation/interpretation vocabulary that Pseudo-Aristeas employs with respect to the translation itself, this same ambiguity surrounds what these men do. That is, they are interpreters in addition to being translators. They do more than render into Greek what is in Hebrew; they are divinely led authors who also endow their product with their superior philosophical qualities and exemplary learning. Pseudo-Aristeas's descriptions of the qualities that these men possess and of the symposia in which they participate help support the claim that the LXX, the result of their efforts, is an outstanding example of philosophical literature, indeed even better than Greek

---

[21] P. Kahle argued that this section referred to earlier translations of the Law into Greek, but the interest of this passage is in the Hebrew text (*The Cairo Geniza* [2nd ed.; Oxford: Blackwell, 1953] 212–13). It thus almost certainly refers to Hebrew manuscripts. The key term in the passage is the verb σεσήμανται, here translated "transcribed." The verb has been variously translated by a variety of English verbs, including "edit," "copy," "transmit," or "write." For a discussion of the meaning of the verb, see Honigman, *Septuagint and Homeric Scholarship*, 48–9.

philosophy. Additionally, as S. Honigman argues, the translators engage in activities that Pseudo-Aristeas intentionally modeled after those of the Alexandrian grammarians, and their scholarly activity assures the literary quality of their product.[22] They read, interpret and then translate this most philosophical and flawless of texts, providing a work of the same quality for their Ptolemaic patron. Pseudo-Aristeas's emphasis on the accuracy (κατὰ πᾶν ἠκριβωμένως) of the translation, the piety with which it was executed (ὁσίως διηρμήνευται), how well it was done (καλῶς ἔχον ἐστίν), and that it needs no revision or alteration, all reassert the exemplary philosophical, and hence literary quality of the work (§310). We find pictured in *Aristeas* cultured men producing a text of high culture for a cultured elite. According to Pseudo-Aristeas's vision of the LXX's creation, these translators were perfectly capable of employing the norms of the target language and culture when producing their translation. In such claims, we see yet again the assertion of the high prestige and thus high acceptability of the LXX in the target culture as envisioned in *Aristeas*.

Later in §§303–307, Demetrius assists with finding an appropriate place for the translators to work, and they ultimately settle on the island of Pharos. The Jewish scholars operate by translating and then comparing their work, harmonizing their differences, which Demetrius puts into writing. Every day before beginning to work, they appear before the king, wash their hands and pray. When asked by Aristeas about the purpose of this washing, the translators tell him that in this way they demonstrate that they have done no evil. Pseudo-Aristeas continues to show that these men are indeed the learned and pious scholars that Ptolemy had sought from the beginning, and they ultimately produce a perfect translation.

As far as *Aristeas* is concerned, the translation also acts as an independent replacement for the Hebrew Torah within the Jewish community of Alexandria, which in §§308–11 not only affirms the accuracy of the translation, but also binds itself to the LXX as divinely-inspired scripture. In these paragraphs, the central claim is "to accord the Septuagint version of the Torah the same sanctity and authority long held by the Hebrew original—in a word to certify the 'divine' origin of the

---

[22] Honigman, *Septuagint and Homeric Scholarship*, 47–9.

Septuagint."[23] Establishing the translation as scripture places it on an equal status with its Hebrew original, and thus the LXX can stand in its place. Pseudo-Aristeas accomplishes this goal by framing the creation and acceptance of this Greek translation in similar language to the reception of the Hebrew Torah by Israel. H.M. Orlinsky argues that the public reading of the Septuagint accompanied by the consent of the people closely resembles Exod 24:3–7, where Moses reads the Law and afterward the people consent to follow it. Orlinsky concludes that the phrase "to read aloud to the people" followed by some expression of consent "describes the biblical procedure in designating a document as official and binding, in other words, as divinely inspired, as Sacred Scripture."[24] After the people approve of the translation, the Jewish priests and elders command that it cannot be altered or revised in any fashion, and a curse should fall on anyone who might do so. Deuteronomy 4:1–2 employs the same tactic with respect to the laws commanded by God.[25] *Aristeas* 312–317, which describes the unsuccessful attempts by Theopompus and Theodectes to translate portions of the Law, reinforces the assertion made here that only this version deserves the approbation accorded it by the entire Jewish community. The punishment experienced by these two Gentiles for their presumably arrogant actions demonstrates that only the LXX can be regarded as authoritative scripture.[26]

The confirmation scene in §§303–307 is actually the third of three scenes that Honigman dubs the "Exodus paradigm" and that demonstrate that *Aristeas* has as a central thematic concern the elevation of the LXX to scriptural status.

> This paradigm equates the story of the translated Law, the LXX, with the story of the original Hebrew Law, the Torah. Equating their stories is, implicitly, a way of equating the status of both texts. By the end of [the] *B[ook of] Ar[isteas]*, the LXX has been turned into the text of the Alexandrian Jews who, in turn, stand for the whole people of Israel.[27]

The first of the three "Exodus paradigm" scenes is Ptolemy's liberation of the Jewish slaves. According to §§12–14, the Jews were imported as slaves under oppression. At Aristeas's behest, Ptolemy frees them while

---

[23] H.M. Orlinsky, "The Septuagint as Holy Writ and the Philosophy of the Translators," *HUCA* 46 (1975) 94.
[24] Ibid. See also the reading of the Law in Ezra/Nehemiah.
[25] Ibid., 95.
[26] Ibid., 98–103.
[27] Honigman, *Septuagint and Homeric Scholarship*, 53.

at the same time lavishing gifts upon them. The one element of this story that, of course, does not comport with Exodus is that Ptolemy is not forced to free the Jews against his will; he does so out of his great benevolence. Honigman explains, however,

> In the Bible, the Jews escape from Egypt not only to material freedom, but also to be given the Law on Mount Sinai, before they are finally led into the Promised Land. Ptolemy's benevolence means that there is now no need to flee. The Law can and will be received in Alexandria. *B.Ar.* is the story of a non-Exodus.[28]

The second "Exodus paradigm" scene is the selection of the 72 elders in Jerusalem. This scene prepares for the final scene of confirmation of the translators' work, the giving of the Law. These elders, explicitly said to be from each of the 12 tribes, parallel the elders who ascended Mount Sinai with Moses to receive the Law (Exodus 24).[29]

Honigman also emphasizes that Pseudo-Aristeas does more than appeal to Hebrew scripture in order to establish the LXX's scriptural status. The author employs the language and ideology of Homeric scholarship in Alexandria to certify that the manuscripts of the Law acquired by the king were the most reliable form of the text. They had been transcribed carefully and reliably, unlike the other forms of the text that Demetrius knew; they were authentic and authoritative. Such authoritative copies provide the basis for establishing that the LXX was sacred scripture. She writes,

> By informing his account with this paradigm [of Alexandrian Homeric scholarship] *B.Ar.*'s author was, first and foremost, interested in convincing his readers that translation of the LXX was the best possible one, primarily because it was based on the most authentic original. Establishing the quality of the translation was an indispensable prerequisite before he could establish the claim that really mattered for him and which was to be conveyed by the secondary theme of the central narrative: that the LXX was a sacred text. Sacredness implies first of all flawless quality. He presented this quality in the form that was most natural both for him and his well-educated Alexandrian readers, namely, the Alexandrian ideology related to the recovering of original texts by textual emendation as practiced by the grammarians subsidized by the Ptolemaic dynasty.[30]

---

[28] Ibid., 56.
[29] Ibid., 58.
[30] Ibid., 48.

While the gist of Honigman's argument here is on target, perhaps the emphasis needs some revision. Honigman suggests that *Aristeas* focuses on authenticity and that Pseudo-Aristeas uses the language of Alexandrian scholarship to make that point. But in *Aristeas*, while the results of Homeric scholarship and textual emendation might contribute to claims of authenticity, the arrival of the Hebrew parchments inscribed in gold brought (and presumably used) by the translators would seem to certify that. The quality of the translation is certainly crucial, and it derives from its genealogical relationship with these Hebrew manuscripts, and from the piety, learning and culture (if not divine inspiration) of the translators themselves.[31] What Honigman correctly senses here, I think, is that the pedigree of the Greek, inasmuch as it is based on an authentic Hebrew text, contributes to Pseudo-Aristeas's claim of the high prestige of the resulting translation and its sanctity. Pseudo-Aristeas, of course, does not appeal to the relation between the source text and the target text, as Philo will do later, because to do so would undercut his picture of the translation as a highly acceptable instance of Greek literature.

To sum up, at each point in *Aristeas*'s narrative, the author makes a concerted effort to make three essential claims for the intended function of the Greek translation of the Pentateuch that we can organize around the kind of function-oriented analysis outlined above. First, according to *Aristeas*, the LXX is intended from the beginning to stand alone as a replacement for the Hebrew Law. As an independent text, Pseudo-Aristeas clearly envisions the LXX operating in a monolingual environment in which its readers ought to be able to engage it as a Greek text just as they would any other Greek text.

Second, to describe the LXX as a stand-alone text does only partial justice to what *Aristeas* presents. Not only can the LXX stand on its own, it is a work of high literature wholly sufficient to itself that can match up to and even exceed other Greek philosophical works. The strategies that Pseudo-Aristeas pursues emphasize that the Hebrew Law on which the LXX is based is philosophical and flawless, and the translators/interpreters who produced the LXX are capable and learned philosophers who can interpret and translate their flawless original.

---

[31] The language of this paragraph suggests that Honigman recognizes the genealogical connection. In another place in her book she emphasizes that the theme of piety is important to *Aristeas* and helps to make the case that the LXX is now sacred scripture. See ibid., 58–63.

For *Aristeas*, what characterizes the Hebrew Law *mutatis mutandis* will also characterize the LXX. As far as Pseudo-Aristeas is concerned, the translators have worked almost exclusively in the norms of the target language and culture, and he portrays the LXX as a Greek literary work, highly acceptable to what he presents as the LXX's target culture—the cultural elite of Hellenistic Alexandria.

Third, the LXX constitutes the sacred scripture of the Jewish people, and it holds a status equal to the Hebrew Law given to Moses on Sinai. It is, in effect, a new revelation of the Law transmitted through the work of the Jewish translators. While the *modus operandi* of the translators in which they compare the results of their work and arrive at an agreed upon translation does not bear the stamp of divine inspiration (unlike in Philo of Alexandria, whose story more heavily highlights divine activity in the translation process), Pseudo-Aristeas does note that the 72 scholars completed their work in 72 days "as if this coincidence had been the result of some design" (οἰονεὶ κατὰ πρόθεσίν τινα τοῦ τοιούτου γεγενημένου, §307). The author certainly intimates that the deity had something to do with the LXX's production. Here again what applies to the Hebrew original extends to the translation—in this case the centrality and prestige of being sacred scripture.

Near the end of the book, the king's reaction to hearing the translation read encapsulates these last two themes of high literary and philosophical quality and scriptural status. He first marvels "exceedingly at the intellect of the lawgiver" and then asks why it is that none of the poets or historians had mentioned "such enormous achievements." Demetrius responds that the reason is that the Law "is holy and has come into being through God." He then cites the abortive attempts by Theopompus and Theodectes to include the Jewish Law in their work. The king responds by showing reverential deference to the books. "When the king heard the account of these things from Demetrius, as I have said before, he bowed deeply and gave orders that great care be taken of the books and that they be watched over reverently" (§317). This reverential reaction mirrors his initial attitude to the Hebrew manuscripts when they arrive with the translators (§177, see above).

THE CONSTITUTIVE CHARACTER OF THE SEPTUAGINT

We have seen how the *Letter of Aristeas* constructs the intended function of the LXX, but what about the LXX itself? If *Aristeas* communicates the LXX's actual intended function/position, then DTS would lead us to expect to find evidence of it embedded or reflected somehow in the LXX's textual-linguistic makeup. If it is not, then that disparity requires some explanation. What we discover when we look at the LXX is that at every point its textual-linguistic makeup contradicts what *Aristeas* would have us expect.

If there is one general agreement among scholars who have studied the LXX over the last two centuries, it is that the Greek of the LXX does not represent good literary Greek. Scholars have characterized Septuagintal Greek in a variety of fashions, but generally they note its frequent Hebraisms, its pedestrian character, its transliterations and its occasional impenetrability. Descriptions range from that of F.C. Conybeare and St.G. Stock, who note that LXX Greek is often "hardly Greek at all, but rather Hebrew in disguise,"[32] to R.R. Ottley who remarks on the "flat, bald surface of the Greek."[33] Even J.W. Wevers, who insists that "the product of the Alexandrian translators was throughout sensible," can remark about the LXX of Numbers that this dictum is "hard put to the test in [Numbers]; in a few cases I have been forced to admit that I was uncertain as to what [Numbers] was trying to say."[34]

The Greek of the LXX often contains, for example, a fairly high degree of stereotyping of lexical items, word order that follows the Hebrew, odd to sometimes non-Greek syntactical features like unidiomatic uses of prepositions. The frequent occurrence of these features does not suggest that the translators produced throughout nonsensical Greek, however. Much, even most, of the Greek of the LXX is adequate and understandable, but it certainly does not generally rise to a level that one might characterize as literary.[35]

---

[32] F.C. Conybeare and St.G. Stock, *Grammar of Septuagint Greek* (Boston: Ginn, 1905; repr. *With Selected Readings, Vocabularies, and Updated Indexes*, Peabody, MA: Hendrickson, 1995) 21.

[33] Cited in Pietersma, "A New Paradigm," 341.

[34] J.W. Wevers, *Notes on the Greek Text of Numbers* (SBLSCS 46; Atlanta: Scholars Press, 1998) x.

[35] Yet, to characterize the translations that we find in the LXX as often quite literal, even at times isomorphic, does not imply that they are free of the translators' exegesis of their source texts. Often, though, that exegesis is constrained by the translators' basic isomorphic or metaphrastic approach to the source text. C. Boyd-Taylor uses the term "metaphrasis," which "captures the isomorphic verbal relationship between the translation and its *Vorlage*" ("A Place in the Sun: The Interpretive Significance of LXX-Psalm 18:5c," *BIOSCS* 31 [1998] 75 note 8).

Additionally as Pietersma notes, even if we were to ignore an entire range of LXX translation phenomena, such as transliterations, purely mechanical translations or unidiomatic uses of prepositions and other "structure words," we would still be faced with a Greek whose most prominent Hebraism "consists in the excessive use of and 'the special prominence given to certain correct, though unidiomatic, modes of speech, because they happen to coincide with Hebrew idioms.'"[36] This phenomenon, what Toury calls interference, consists of the transference to the target text of "phenomena pertaining to the makeup of the source text," and Toury argues that all translations experience it.[37] However it might be articulated, across the board in the history of scholarship on the LXX, the consensus has been that we consistently see interference in the LXX, that it occurs with great frequency, and that it is one phenomenon that connects the translation to its source text.[38]

This all-too-brief and general assessment of the Greek of the LXX suffices for my purposes to highlight the contrast with what the *Letter of Aristeas* says about the translation. The nature of the LXX's Greek enables us to conclude that the translation is not and apparently was not intended to be a literary translation, despite the fact that Pseudo-Aristeas says that it was supposed to be one. Here I adopt Toury's definition of literary translation, which

> involves the imposition of 'conformity conditions' beyond the linguistic and/or general-textual ones, namely, to models and norms which are deemed literary at the target end. It thus yields more or less well-formed texts from the point of view of the *literary* requirements of the recipient culture, at various possible costs in terms of reconstructions of the source text."[39]

Producing a literary translation will of necessity involve suppressing certain features of the source text and perhaps reshuffling some while adding others.[40] Perhaps another way to put it is to say that the character of LXX Greek suggests that the translators, when confronted with

---

[36] Pietersma, "A New Paradigm," 343, citing H.St.J. Thackeray.

[37] Toury, *Descriptive Translation Studies*, 275. Interference is manifested as either negative transfer, "deviations from normal, codified practice of the target system," or, what Pietersma describes here, positive transfer, the propensity to select and employ features of the source text that also exist in the target system.

[38] For a detailed explanation of the consequences of these observations for questions of the LXX and its origins, see Pietersma, "A New Paradigm."

[39] Toury, *Descriptive Translation Studies*, 171.

[40] Ibid.

Toury's initial norm, pursued adequacy rather than acceptability—quite the opposite of what Pseudo-Aristeas claims. In short, the LXX is not the great work of literature that Pseudo-Aristeas envisioned.

The LXX's textual-linguistic makeup also does not support Pseudo-Aristeas's contention that it was intended to act as a substitution or replacement for its Hebrew original and to function in a monolingual environment. In fact, just the reverse appears to be the case; the textual-linguistic makeup of the LXX suggests that it was intended to have a close relationship with its Hebrew *Vorlage*. The overall literal, and frequently isomorphic, technique of the LXX translators functions in such a way as to bring the original to the reader rather than the reader to the original.[41] That is, the LXX was meant from its inception to act as a gateway to lead the reader back to the Hebrew original, which was the more presitigious text of the two. The LXX translators faced a basic translational choice (Toury's initial norm). They could subject themselves either to the norms of their source text (adequacy) or to those of the target text (acceptability).

L. Kelly, working from a somewhat different methodological approach from Toury, sees the translator faced with a similar basic choice. Kelly articulates this choice as one of competing authority structures in relation to the source text, which he calls "personal" and "positional."[42] Within personal authority structures, one takes responsible autonomy and retains power of decision, while positional structures impose formal patterns of obligation. Commitment, then, based on a personal authority structure, gives rise to translation behaviours akin to an elaborated sociolinguistic code: the translator's approach to text is multidimensional, author- or reader-centered and subjective. Where, however, the translator sees the relation between her/him and the text as positional, the approach is that of restricted sociolinguistic code: unidimensional, text- and object-centered and objective. Thus, depending on the type of authority her/his text exercises over the translator, fidelity will mean either collaboration or servitude.[43]

---

[41] S. Brock, "The Phenomenon of the Septuagint," *OtSt* 17 (1972) 17.

[42] L. Kelly, *True Interpreter* (New York: St. Martin's Press, 1979) 206–7. Kelly's analysis of the two authority structures here depends on the work of B. Bernstein in "Social Class, Language and Socialisation," *Language and Social Context* (P.P. Giglioli, ed.; New York: Penguin, 1972) 157–78 (cited in Kelly, 252 note 1). For an application of Kelly's categories to other ancient translations, see Chapter 12, "Access to the Source: Cicero, Ben Sira, the Septuagint and Their Audiences."

[43] Kelly, *True Interpreter*, 206–7.

The LXX translators adopted a positional stance (or à la Toury made the fundamental decision to pursue adequacy), and as a result, the translation has the unidimensional and object-centered qualities that Kelly sees as characteristic of a positional authority stance. In the case of the LXX, servitude generally wins the day. Almost certainly, it seems to me, such a positional stance has at the least as a consequence, at most as the motivation, of bringing the original text to the reader, and it is difficult in this respect to see how the LXX could be intended to act as an independent replacement for the Hebrew.

Whether the textual-linguistic makeup of the LXX indicates anything about its authoritative or scriptural status poses a thorny problem. While one of Pseudo-Aristeas's central agendas is to certify the LXX as sacred scripture, what the textual-linguistic makeup of the LXX reveals about the translator's approach to Toury's initial norm may provide some insight. Even if the translators understood themselves to be *translating* a sacred text, I certainly do not think that there is any inherent reason to claim that the desire to *produce* a sacred text was part of the intended function for the translation. The translators' process and final product in which they subject themselves to the norms of the source text (Toury), adopt a positional stance toward the original text (to use Kelly's language), or bring the reader to the original (Brock, Pietersma) implicitly recognize the more privileged status of the original. That is, the translation does not supplant or rival the prestige of the original, but it was intended to act as a way of accessing it. Thus, whereas Pseudo-Aristeas presents the LXX as the equal of the Hebrew, these considerations suggest a less prestigious status for the translation when placed alongside the Hebrew original. These considerations justify Pietersma's comments about the relationship between *Aristeas* and the textual-linguistic makeup of the LXX when he writes:

> But to regard Aristeas's depiction as reflective of the constitutive character of the text itself and thus to elevate it to the status of explanatory model for its linguistic makeup, and hence its exegetical dimension, cannot be accepted. Rather than being rooted in the text, the paradigm built of Aristeas is nothing more than a superimposition upon the text as produced.[44]

---

[44] A. Pietersma, "A New English Translation of the Septuagint and a Commentary to Follow," *TLZ* 129 (2004) 1012.

ARISTEAS: A WITNESS TO THE RECEPTION HISTORY OF THE SEPTUAGINT[45]

How then should we make sense of the obvious disconnect between *Aristeas*'s construction of the intended function/position of the LXX and the actual textual-linguistic makeup of the translation? The most likely conclusion is that the picture offered by the *Letter of Aristeas* does not, indeed it cannot, provide any indication of what the original intended function of the LXX was. We can only try to discover the intended position of the LXX from the internal evidence we derive from the translation itself. If *Aristeas*, then, has no evidentiary value for getting at the intended function of the LXX, what is the purpose of the fiction that Pseudo-Aristeas (or his sources) creates? P. Kahle, I would suggest, actually pointed to the answer in his comments about *Aristeas* in *The Cairo Geniza*. Kahle thought that *Aristeas* was not even concerned with the "original" LXX at all, but with a revised version that was being touted as superior to other versions. He argued in part that the LXX could not be the subject of *Aristeas* because "[n]obody makes propaganda for something a hundred years old. Propaganda is made for something contemporary. We can be sure that the translation had just been made when the letter of propaganda was written."[46] Kahle was trying to drive a wedge between *Aristeas*'s account and the origins of the translation of the Pentateuch in order to construct his larger argument about the LXX's beginnings. Kahle was right about *Aristeas* in a way, I think, but we do not have to accept his larger reconstruction of the nature of LXX origins in order to argue that *Aristeas* has nothing to do with the actual production of the translation or with its original intended function.

Toury offers a caveat about the relationships between position-product-process. "[T]ranslations which retain their status as facts of the target culture may nevertheless change their position over time."[47] In these cases the actual function/position of the translation will differ from its initial one, obscuring the original relationship between position and product. I think that this is exactly what happened with the LXX, and this changed function necessitated the kind of claims that

---

[45] Much of this section originates in Chapter 14 "Translation as Scripture."
[46] Kahle, *Cairo Geniza*, 211.
[47] Toury, *Descriptive Translation Studies*, 30.

Pseudo-Aristeas makes about it. The LXX gradually lost its dependent relationship with the Hebrew, and those who read it began to regard it in the manner that we see reflected in *Aristeas*, as an independent free-standing replacement for the Hebrew. While the textual-linguistic makeup of the translation did not change, it was no longer moored to the Hebrew, which was its initial and primary context. At the point of its inception, the LXX was meant to serve as the gateway to the Hebrew, a way of bringing the reader to the original, but the Hebrew scriptures remained the major focal point. The Hebrew was regarded as authoritative, and the translators certainly regarded it as sacred. The Greek provided the Alexandrian Jewish community the means of accessing its scripture. As readers later encountered the LXX separated from its original mooring, its status perhaps became something of a problem due to the inelegant, pedestrian and sometimes-obscure nature of its Greek, but almost certainly the relative authority of the translation, now severed from its parent, presented a fundamental problem. In fact, in the prologue to the Greek of Ben Sira, we see the author's grandson worrying about just this sort of problem in his own translation.[48] The linguistic relationship between the two texts, Hebrew and Greek, had been severed, which raised the crucial problem of what relationship the two texts continued to have, if any, as individual and independent repositories of the divine will. How authoritative was the LXX by itself?

We know how it all turned out in the end because Pseudo-Aristeas tells us. The LXX came to be regarded as sacred scripture. But somewhere along the road to the LXX's becoming scripture someone had to offer a justification for accepting it as a prestigious, central and sacred text. Pseudo-Aristeas presents precisely that kind of justification. And here is where Kahle was wrong, even though his impulse was correct. If the LXX's intended function was dependent on the Hebrew, if it was less prestigious than the original and non-literary, for example, then however old it was when it began to be read as a replacement for the Hebrew and as a literary and authoritative text, someone did have to make propaganda for it. Propaganda would have been essential, and Pseudo-Aristeas provides that propaganda. *Aristeas* does not contain any genuine reflection of the original intended function of the LXX; it

---

[48] See my "Why a Prologue? Ben Sira's Grandson and His Greek Translation," *Emanuel: Studies in Hebrew Bible, Septuagint and Dead Sea Scrolls in Honor of Emanuel Tov* (S.M. Paul et al., eds.; VTSup 94; Leiden: Brill, 2003) 633–44.

legitimizes what the LXX had become by the middle part of the second century BCE. In other words, *Aristeas* offers us a foundation myth of origins for the LXX's transformed function/position as an independent, scriptural authority.

The story in *Aristeas* of the translation of the LXX, then, belongs to the reception history of the LXX, and it has little to no evidentiary relevance for the question of the origins of the translation. Those origins remain clouded, but because *Aristeas* contains the oldest "account" of the making of the translation, it exerts a seductive power on those investigating the circumstances in which the LXX originated. However much we might be tempted to adopt its viewpoint, *Aristeas* testifies to a place in the process of transmission of the LXX at which the translation had become independent and scriptural. In the end, however, we must search for the intended function of the LXX not in the external sources, but in the place where Toury's model predicts it will be found, in the textual-linguistic makeup of the third-century BCE translation itself.[49]

---

[49] Toury speaks of the use of what he calls "extratextual" sources for reconstructing translational norms (*Descriptive Translation Studies*, 65–7). The products of translation, the translations themselves, are the "*primary* products of norm-governed instances of behaviour, and can therefore be taken as immediate representations thereof" (p. 65). About extratextual sources, he writes, "Normative pronouncements, by contrast, are merely *by*-products of the existence and activity of norms. Like any attempt to formulate a norm, they are partial and biased, and should therefore be treated with every possible circumspection; all the more so since—emanating as they do from interested parties—they are likely to lean toward propaganda and persuasion" (p. 65).

CHAPTER FOURTEEN

TRANSLATION AS SCRIPTURE: THE SEPTUAGINT IN *ARISTEAS* AND PHILO

THE INTERLINEAR MODEL OF THE SEPTUAGINT

At the beginning of the work on the New English Translation of the Septuagint (NETS), those involved in preparing the foundations for the project had to reckon with the problems of translating into English, not an original work in the Greek language, but a Greek *translation* of a Hebrew (and Aramaic) original. The Septuagint presented quite a few difficulties in this respect, not the least of which was the frequency of what one might call infelicitous translations that ranged from awkward Greek to nonsensical Greek in some cases. The principles of translation ultimately adopted by NETS require the translators to "seek to reflect the meaning of the Greek text in accordance with the ancient translator's perceived intent and as occasioned by the ancient translator's linguistic approach, even when this policy may result in an unidiomatic (though grammatical) English rendering."[1] Such an approach to translating a translation stems from the realization that the Septuagint, as a translation, has a particular relationship to its Hebrew original. The introduction to the first fascicle of NETS, Albert Pietersma's translation of Psalms, puts it this way:

> While it is obvious that the so-called Septuagint *in time* achieved its independence from its Semitic parent and that it *at some stage* shed its subservience to its source, it is equally true that it was at its inception a Greek *translation* of a Hebrew (or Aramaic) *original*. That is to say, the Greek had a dependent and subservient linguistic relationship to its Semitic parent. More particularly, for the vast majority of Septuagint books this linguistic relationship can best be conceptualized as a Greek inter-linear translation of a Hebrew original within a Hebrew-Greek diglot.... Looked at from a different perspective, NETS is presupposing a Greek translation which aimed at bringing the reader to the Hebrew original rather than

---

[1] A. Pietersma, *Translation Manual for "A New English Translation of the Septuagint"* *(NETS)* (Ada: Uncial Books, 1996) 9.

bringing the Hebrew original to the reader. Consequently, the Greek's subservience to the Hebrew may be seen as part of its aim.[2]

The reasons for the preceding claims lie at the heart of what Pietersma would later develop more fully as the "interlinear paradigm of Septuagint Studies."[3] This approach to the Septuagint utilizes the work of G. Toury, who argues in his book *Descriptive Translation Studies and Beyond* that "translations are facts of target cultures: on occasions facts of a special status, sometimes even constituting identifiable subsystems of their own, but of the target culture in any event." Since any translation is fundamentally rooted in its target culture, "the [prospective] position (or function) of a translation within a recipient culture (or a particular section thereof) should be regarded as a strong governing factor of the very makeup of the product, in terms of underlying models, linguistic representation, or both." In other words, the textual-linguistic makeup of a translation provides strong indications of its intended position in the target culture.[4]

Toury describes a three-fold series of relationships operative in any translation, which he labels position/function-process-product. The intended position or function of any translation in its target culture exerts a determining influence on its textual-linguistic make-up. Recognizing that every translation originates in a specific cultural milieu and meets particular needs in the recipient culture, Toury writes, "[T]ranslators may be said to operate first and foremost in the interest of the culture into which they are translating, however they conceive of that interest."[5] Further, the "surface realization" of the translation, its textual-linguistic makeup, establishes the parameters for the individual translation strategies employed by the translator.[6] Toury diagrams

---

[2] See now A. Pietersma and B.G. Wright, "To the Reader of NETS," *A New English Translation of the Septuagint, and the Other Greek Translations Traditionally Included under that Title* (New York: Oxford University Press, 2007) xiv.

[3] A. Pietersma, "A New Paradigm for Addressing Old Questions: the Relevance of the Interlinear Model for the Study of the Septuagint," *Bible and Computer: The Stellenbosch AIBI-6 Conference; Proceedings of the Association Internationale Bible et Informatique 'From Alpha to Byte'; University of Stellenbosch 17–21 July, 2000* (J. Cook, ed.; Leiden: Brill, 2002) 337–64.

[4] G. Toury, *Descriptive Translation Studies and Beyond* (Benjamins Translation Library 4; Amsterdam: John Benjamins, 1995). The quotes are from pp. 29 and 12, respectively.

[5] Ibid., 12.

[6] Ibid.

the relationships among the three characteristics in the following manner:

> The (prospective) systemic position and function of a translation
> ↓   determines
> its appropriate surface realization
> (= textual-linguistic makeup)
> ↓   governs
> the strategies whereby a target text (or parts thereof)
> is derived from its original, and hence the
> relationships which hold them together[7]

Figure 1. *Toury's Relations between function (position), product and process*

When we approach one particular set of translations, the Septuagint,[8] Toury's analysis holds out tremendous promise for understanding several dilemmas that this Greek corpus presents to scholars. Pietersma applies Toury's insights to the Septuagint in a seminal paper entitled "A New Paradigm for Addressing Old Questions: The Relevance of the Interlinear Model to the Septuagint." There Pietersma has argued that the Septuagint's textual-linguistic nature (Toury's "product"), one in which many aspects of the Greek text are unintelligible without resort to the Hebrew original (and indeed he notes that the Greek often "cannot stand on its own feet"), indicates that the linguistic relationship of the Greek to the Hebrew was originally one of subservience and dependence. That is, the Greek translation was intended from the first to be used in concert with the Hebrew. This relationship Pietersma characterizes by the term "interlinear." Such a description does not mean, in Pietersma's words, "that every linguistic item in Greek can only be understood by reference to the parent text, or that the translation has an isomorphic relationship to its source, but that the Greek text *qua* text has a dimension of unintelligibility."[9] Pietersma contends, then, that only a relationship of dependence of the translation on its source text can account both for the Septuagint's intelligibility *and* for its unintelligibility at the same time. To use Toury's language from the diagram above, the textual-linguistic makeup/surface realization of the Greek that we find in the Septuagint suggests an intentionally close relationship, indeed a dependent one, of

---

[7] Ibid., 13.
[8] I use the term "Septuagint" in this paper in the more restrictive sense of the term— the translation of the Pentateuch into Greek, probably in the early third-century BCE.
[9] Pietersma, "A New Paradigm," 350.

the Greek translation on its Hebrew original. The translators developed the particular translation strategies utilized in rendering the Hebrew into Greek in order to achieve the textual-linguistic makeup they deemed necessary. The intended "function" of the Septuagint in the cultural environment of the translators (the hotly debated question of the origins of the Septuagint) was the factor that determined the appropriate textual-linguistic makeup or surface realization.

These three relationships constitute the basic information out of which we might reconstruct the social location of the Septuagint, what Toury calls "contextualization." He writes, "In an almost tautological way it could be said that, in the final analysis, a translation is a fact of whatever target sector it is found to be a fact of, i.e. that (sub)system which proves to be best equipped to account for it: function, product and underlying process."[10] Of all the various social locations that have been proposed for the Septuagint, Pietersma suggests that the most satisfactory place for a translation with its particular textual-linguistic makeup would be the school, where the subservient and dependent Greek translation would function for students as a kind of crib to the Hebrew.

NETS, then, relies on Pietersma's interlinear paradigm for essentially three reasons:

> First, this paradigm best explains the "translationese" aspect of Septua-gintal Greek with its strict, and often rigid quantitative equivalence to the Hebrew. As Conybeare and Stock (and others) noted nearly a century ago, Septuagintal Greek is often "hardly Greek at all, but rather Hebrew in disguise," especially in its syntax. Secondly, the interlinear paradigm of Septuagint origins makes it legitimate for the NETS translator to draw on the Hebrew parent text as an arbiter of meaning, when appropriate. Differently put, the interlinear paradigm recognizes that unintelligibility of the Greek text *qua Greek text* is one of its inherent characteristics. Thirdly, and perhaps paradoxically, the interlinear paradigm safeguards the Greekness of the Septuagint by emphasizing that its linguistic strangeness, rather than reflecting a form of the living language at serious odds with its Hellenistic environment, was made to serve a pedagogical purpose.[11]

These comments only provide the general contours of Toury's theoretical analysis and Pietersma's development of the interlinear paradigm. While the interlinear paradigm undergirds the ongoing work of the NETS project, it also offers the potential for new insights into some

---

[10] Toury, *Descriptive Translation Studies*, 29.
[11] Pietersma and Wright, "To the Reader of NETS," xiv–xv.

other questions about the Septuagint and related issues that might not at first blush be so obvious. Here we turn to the *Letter of Aristeas* and to Philo of Alexandria.

The *Letter of Aristeas* and Septuagint Origins

At the heart of any discussion about the origins of the Septuagint lies the *Letter of Aristeas*. This early Jewish text represents the earliest account of the translation of the Septuagint.[12] It is not necessary to review the complicated history of scholarship on the *Letter of Aristeas* here; it suffices to say that scholars generally agree that the work (1) is pseudonymous, written by a Jew reflecting Jewish concerns, not by "Aristeas," a Greek member of Ptolemy's court,[13] (2) is not a contemporary account, but one written a significant time after the actual translation was made,[14] and (3) reflects interests contemporary with the Jewish writer of the work, not those of the third century BCE. Scholars have suggested a number of motivations for the writing of the *Letter of Aristeas*, among them a response to some contemporary crisis, a polemic targeting the emergence of rival translations to the Alexandrian Septuagint, the problems of Hellenism and Judaism. Whatever its original purpose, and despite the fact that only a small portion of the letter actually describes the translation process, the *Letter of Aristeas* is occupied throughout with the rendering of the Hebrew Torah into Greek. Indeed, this task frames the entire work, since it is said to be central to Aristeas's deputation to Eleazar the Jewish High Priest (§§1–3).

Despite the general scholarly consensus that the *Letter of Aristeas* is not a contemporary account and that it does not accurately describe

---

[12] The Jewish writer Aristobulus (ca. 160 BCE), mentioned by Eusebius in his *Preparatio Evangelica* 13.12.2, apparently also knew the story of the translation of the Septuagint. Depending on what date one assigns to the *Letter of Aristeas*, Aristobulus might be earlier. Aristobulus's notice, however, is very attenuated and reflects nothing like the fuller "account" given by Ps.-Aristeas.

[13] Since scholars do not think that the author of the books was the Gentile courtier Aristeas, I refer to him as Ps.-Aristeas.

[14] Dates assigned to the book range from the mid-third century BCE down to the first century CE. A date sometime in the second century BCE seems most probable. For the various possibilities, see especially R.J.H. Shutt, "Letter of Aristeas," *Old Testament Pseudepigrapha* (J.H. Charlesworth, ed.; 2 vols.; Garden City: Doubleday, 1985) 2.8–9; M. Hadas, *Aristeas to Philocrates (Letter of Aristeas)* (Philadelphia: Dropsie College, 1951) 9–17; A. Pelletier, *Lettre d'Aristée à Philocrate* (SC 89; Paris: Cerf, 1962) 57–8; S. Jellicoe, *The Septuagint and Modern Study* (Oxford: Clarendon, 1968) 47–9.

the actual events surrounding the translation of the Septuagint, scholars continue to use the letter as foundational evidence for reconstructing the origins of that translation. Some make minimal use of the letter together with other external evidence to derive a date for the production of the translation—usually the early part of the third century BCE. Others want to take more seriously the claim of the letter that the Greek transla-tion of the Jewish Law had official Ptolemaic sanction. Most scholars, however, accept as true, whether implicitly or explicitly, Ps.-Aristeas's assumption that the Septuagint was intended to be a free-standing and independent replacement for the Hebrew Pentateuch, and acceptance of Ps.-Aristeas's claim often appears as one of the major building blocks of scholarly theories about the original purpose of the Septuagint.

Almost all scholars accept that the Septuagint was a Jewish transla-tion undertaken in response to Jewish needs. They may disagree over what those needs were, but in each case, the requirements of the Jewish community for a translation of its scriptures almost always assumes that the community had to have a translation that would function indepen-dently of its Hebrew original. Several examples illustrate this point. The proposal that the Septuagint was made for liturgical purposes assumes that the Jews of Alexandria had lost the ability to use Hebrew, and so a Greek translation became necessary as a stand-in for the Hebrew scriptures during Jewish worship.[15] Any proposal that operates under the assumption that the Septuagint was made for official government purposes necessarily has to claim that the Septuagint was meant to substitute for the Hebrew. This is true, for instance, of the suggestion that the translation was motivated by an official Egyptian policy of rendering oriental law codes into Greek.[16]

Several scholars have suggested the school as the place where the Septuagint may have originated. Sebastian Brock's work is especially noteworthy in this regard. His analysis of the Septuagint has convinced him that the textual-linguistic nature of the translation indicates that it tries to bring the reader to the original, not the original to the reader,

---

[15] This theory was championed by H.St.J. Thackeray, *The Septuagint and Jewish Wor-ship: A Study in Origins* (2nd ed.; Schweich Lectures of the British Academy; London: Humphrey Milford, 1923).

[16] See D. Barthélemy, "Pourquoi la Torah a-t-elle été traduite en grec?" *On Language, Culture and Religion: In Honor of Eugene A. Nida* (M. Black and W.A. Smalley, eds.; Approaches to Semiotics 56; The Hague: Mouton, 1974) 23–41; J. Mélèze-Modrzejewski, *The Jews of Egypt from Rameses II to Emperor Hadrian* (Philadelphia: Jewish Publica-tion Society, 1995) 99–119.

and he points specifically to the school as a possible location for the Septuagint's origins. Yet even he, despite these conclusions, stops short of arguing for such an originating context.[17] Pietersma speculates that one contributing reason for Brock's reluctance to argue for an educational context might be that

> [I]n spite of Brock's observation that literal texts aim to bring the reader to the text, and thus play a patently subservient role vis-à-vis the source text, he nevertheless believes that both as to its original function and as to its later role the Septuagint was a free-standing text that took the place of the original, precisely as the *Letter of Aristeas* maintains, and thus is in continuity with modern mainstream translations of the Bible.[18]

If, however, the *Letter of Aristeas* was indeed composed many years after the translation of the Septuagint and if Pietersma's interlinear paradigm has any explanatory force when applied to the Septuagint, why should scholars give such credence to Ps.-Aristeas's account as a legitimate explanation of the Septuagint's origins? In short, if we accept what the interlinear paradigm pushes us to conclude about the nature of the Septuagint *as a translation*—that the Greek text is subservient to and dependent on the Hebrew—then the picture offered by the *Letter of Aristeas* does not, indeed cannot, accurately reflect the origins of the Septuagint. In fact, Toury's work and Pietersma's use of it with respect to the textual-linguistic nature of the Septuagint provide a lens through which to look at the function of the legend of Septuagint origins offered in the *Letter of Aristeas*. Although Pietersma applies the interlinear paradigm to certain observations about the nature of the Septuagint as a translation, as he himself argues, it has important implications for attempts to answer questions about the Septuagint's origins. Toury's three-relationship model provides an analytical tool for understanding some basic characteristics of translations—perhaps most significantly in the present context that the textual-linguistic character of the Septuagint must have a role to play in discussions of the intended function of the translation. Simply put, the textual-linguistic nature of the Septuagint makes it difficult to think that it was originally intended to function as an independent replacement for the Hebrew. Because the *Letter of Aristeas* is the earliest and most complete "account" of the Septuagint's origins, however, and because practically every scholarly reconstruction

---

[17] S. Brock, "The Phenomenon of the Septuagint," *OtSt* 17 (1972) 11–36.
[18] Pietersma, "A New Paradigm," 346.

of the Septuagint's origins utilizes the *Letter of Aristeas*, not only do we need to ask if the letter's version of the events is relevant, we must also try to account for it if it is not.

Thus, if Pietersma is correct about the notion of interlinearity and his subsequent suggestions about the pedagogical origins of the Septuagint make sense, then the *Letter of Aristeas* has no evidentiary value for explaining the origins of the Septuagint. If the *Letter of Aristeas* does not provide the evidence scholars often claim it does, how then can we make sense of the letter and its contents? The answer to this question must satisfy objections like the one made by Paul Kahle, who thought that the *Letter of Aristeas* was not even concerned with the Septuagint, but with a revised version of the Septuagint that was being accorded authority over other versions. He argued that the Alexandrian translation could not be the subject of the *Letter of Aristeas* partly because "[n]obody makes propaganda for something a hundred years old. Propaganda is made for something contemporary. We can be sure that the translation had just been made when the letter of propaganda was written."[19] Even for Kahle, the version in the *Letter of Aristeas* and its perceived centrality for explaining Septuagint origins demanded explanation. In my estimation, however, we do not need to resort to Kahle's assessment of the *Letter of Aristeas*. It is possible to explain its story of the translation of the Septuagint even while, at the same time, rejecting its usefulness as an account of how the Septuagint actually came to be.

If the Septuagint's origins were in subservience to and dependence on its Hebrew source, then it becomes patently clear that the function of the Septuagint did shift over time from that original dependence to independence—it ultimately did function as a replacement for the Hebrew. Of course, the intended function/position of a translation can change over time without experiencing any modification of its textual-linguistic makeup. In such cases one then observes a surface realization that becomes out of sync with the later function/position of the translation. Toury notes, "[T]ranslations which retain their status as facts of the target culture may nevertheless change their position over time."[20] I would contend that this is precisely what happened with the Septuagint. It gradually lost its close relationship to the Hebrew from

---

[19] P. Kahle, *The Cairo Geniza* (2nd ed.; Oxford: Basil Blackwell, 1959) 211. Kahle's larger argument, that there was no "original" Septuagint, but various competing translations, has largely been rejected by scholars as unconvincing.

[20] Toury, *Descriptive Translation Studies*, 30.

which it was translated, and its users began to regard it in the manner that Ps.-Aristeas does, as an independent, free-standing replacement for the Hebrew. It retained its unintelligible features, but they were no longer moored to the Hebrew, which had given them at least a measure of intelligibility. In its beginnings the Septuagint was intended to serve as a point of entry to the Hebrew, a way of bringing the original to the reader as Brock says, but the Hebrew continued to remain the main focus of interest. The Hebrew original was the text regarded as authoritative, with the Greek translation being a means of accessing it. As readers encountered the Septuagint separated from its original moorings, its status must have become somewhat of a problem. The linguistic relationship between the two texts may have been severed, but a crucial issue must have been what relationship they continued to have, if any, as individual and separate repositories of divinely sanctioned Jewish law and practice. How authoritative was the Septuagint on its own?

We know the end of the process, of course. The Septuagint came to be regarded by many Jews as authoritative, divinely inspired scripture. But somewhere along the line someone had to offer a justification for regarding the Septuagint in this way; the *Letter of Aristeas* provides precisely that kind of justification. And here is where I believe Kahle, in the statement I quoted above, is wrong. If the Septuagint's origins were indeed characterized by subservience to and dependence on the Hebrew, then, however old it was when it began to be used as an independent and authoritative text, someone *did* have to make propaganda for it, and that is exactly what the *Letter of Aristeas* does. Rather than an accurate reflection of the origins of the Septuagint, I think it more probable that the *Letter of Aristeas* presents us with a foundational myth of origins for the Septuagint's transformed position/function as an independent, scriptural authority.

Despite the long symposium section in the middle of the book, Ps.-Aristeas's primary concern is the translation of the Jewish law. One of the ways that Ps.-Aristeas creates a myth of origins intended to legitimate the Septuagint's independence from the Hebrew and its authoritative status is to claim that it was never intended to relate to the Hebrew in the first place. One can read the claim that the undertaking was commissioned by the Ptolmaic king as a primary feature of the myth of the Septuagint's original independence. It is difficult to know if the legend of official Ptolemaic sanction is the author's own creation or if it represents use of a preexisting tradition that the author inherited. The Jewish philosopher Aristobulus, like Ps.-Aristeas, connects the translation with the Ptolemaic court, and he makes the same error as Ps.-Aristeas, connecting Demetrius of Phalerum with Ptolemy Philadelphus rather than Ptolemy I Soter.[21] It is not clear if Ps.-Aristeas knew Aristobulus, if it was the other way around, or if both drew on an independent tradition. Whatever the case, if the Septuagint actually arose out of the needs of the Jewish community as most scholars think, why does the earliest form of the legend attribute its genesis to Gentile rulers? One thing such a claim accomplishes is to distinguish the translation from its Hebrew parent text *from its very inception*. The initial motivation reported by the *Letter of Aristeas*, that a translation of the Hebrew sacred books must be included in the royal library, leaves no doubt for the reader that the Septuagint, as a translation, had always been intended to replace the Hebrew. The later scene in §§308–11 in which the Jewish community hears and accepts the translation reinforces that it replaces the Hebrew, even for the Jews of Alexandria.

As a translation that was meant to function independently of its source, the accuracy of the translation concerned the author of the *Letter of Aristeas*, who takes pains to make the point that both the Hebrew manuscripts used for the translation as well as the translation itself were completely accurate. According to §30, the Hebrew books were missing from the king's library because "they have been transcribed somewhat carelessly and not as they should be."[22] When the translators travel to Alexandria, they arrive "with the fine skins on which the Law had been written in letters of gold in Jewish characters; the parchment had been excellently worked, and the joining together of the letters was imperceptible" (§176). The king inquires about the scrolls and then does obeisance to them "about seven times" (§177). The fine execution of the scrolls and the king's reaction to seeing them confirms their complete accuracy and sanctity. Here are copies, to

---

[21] Scholars debate Aristobulus' dates, but A.Y. Collins places him in the middle of the second century BCE, roughly contemporary with the most probable time of the composition of the *Letter of Aristeas* ("Aristobulus," in Charlesworth, *Old Testament Pseudepigrapha*, 2.832.3).

[22] Kahle argued that this verse referred to earlier translations of the Law into Greek, but the interest of the passage is in the Hebrew text, and thus probably refers to Hebrew manuscripts. The key to this passage is the verb σεσήμανται, here translated "transcribed." Almost all commentators note the difficulty of the passage. The verb has been variously translated as "edited," "copied," "transmitted," or "written." See E. Tov, "The Septuagint," *Mikra: Text, Translation, Reading, and Interpretation of the Hebrew Bible in Ancient Judaism and Early Christianity* (M.J. Mulder, ed.; CRINT 2.1; Assen: Van Gorcum, 1988) 166–7.

rephrase §30, that "are transcribed completely accurately and as they should be." Ps.-Aristeas also emphasizes that the translation made from these scrolls is just as accurate as the original. After the completion of the translation, Demetrius assembles the Jewish people and reads it aloud. The Jewish leaders affirm that the translation "has been made rightly and reverently, and in every respect accurately" (§310). This use of the language of accuracy for both the original and translation serves to place the Septuagint on a par with its Hebrew source. Ps.-Aristeas wants us to know that each of the two texts possesses its own authority guaranteed by its accuracy.

In addition, the claims made about the translators themselves, that they were men of skill in the Law, who led exemplary lives and were of mature experience (§32), further vouchsafe the accuracy of the Septuagint as a perfectly reliable version of the Jewish Law. Each day before they begin translating, they wash their hands in the sea and pray to God. Ps.-Aristeas explains that these practices show that these men had done no evil, "for all activity takes place through the hands; thus they nobly and piously refer everything to righteousness and truth" (§306). Translation, conducted in writing, constitutes an activity of the hands, and here the *Letter of Aristeas* implies that the piety and rectitude of the translators extends to their product, the Greek translation of the Law.

Unlike later versions of the legend, the *Letter of Aristeas* is decidedly unmiraculous.[23] In fact, the translators work in a very sensible manner. They reach agreement by comparing the versions that they produce. The result is one version agreed upon by all these pious men. Demetrius himself copies the final version of their work (§302). The only explicit hint that the deity might be guiding the process comes in §307 where Ps.-Aristeas claims that the seventy-two translators finished their work in seventy-two days "just as if such a result was achieved by some deliberate design."

When speaking of the Septuagint, however, it is Ps.-Aristeas who works with a deliberate design. The emphasis on accuracy contributes to a larger and more central claim, "to accord the Septuagint version of the Torah the same sanctity and authority long held by the Hebrew

---

[23] For the sources of the later versions of the legend, see Jellicoe, *Septuagint and Modern Study*, 38–47 and G. Dorival, M. Harl, O. Munnich, *La Bible Grecque des Septante: Du Judaisme Hellénistique au Christianisme Ancien* (Initiations au Christianisme Ancien; Paris: Cerf, 1988) 45–50.

original—in a word to certify the 'divine' origin of the Septuagint."[24]
Ps.-Aristeas accomplishes this aim in part by framing the creation and
acceptance of the Septuagint in the same language as the making and
acceptance of the Hebrew Torah. H.M. Orlinsky notes, for example, that
the reading of the translation followed by the consent of the people in
§§308–11 closely resembles Exod 24:3–7 where Moses reads the Law
to the people who then consent to follow it. He maintains that the
phrase "to read aloud to the people" followed by some expression of
consent "describes the biblical procedure in designating a document
as official and binding, in other words, as divinely inspired, as Sacred
Scripture."[25] After the people's consent, the Jewish priests and elders
command that no one should alter this version in any way, and they
curse anyone who might try. Deuteronomy 4:1–2 employs the same
tactic with respect to the Hebrew laws commanded by God.[26] Paragraphs 312–17, which describe the abortive attempts by Theopompus
and Theodectus to translate sections of the Jewish Law, reinforce Ps.-
Aristeas's assertion that only *this* translation was made from accurate
copies of the law by upright men who produced a completely accurate
version and thus only *this* version deserves the approbation given to it
by the Jewish elders and priests and the Jewish people as a whole. God's
punishment of these two Gentile figures for their presumably arrogant
actions demonstrates that only the version that Ps.-Aristeas describes
can be authoritative scripture.[27]

   In the light of the close original relationship between the Septuagint
and the Hebrew Torah, what Ps.-Aristeas tells us about is not original
function, but reception history. The Septuagint's textual-linguistic
makeup points to its intended original function, one in which the
Greek was dependent on rather than a replacement for the Hebrew.
One might also conclude that such a relationship between the Greek
and the Hebrew meant that the Greek translation was most likely not at
first considered authoritative scripture, but instead it provided a means
of gaining access to the Hebrew scriptures.[28] The *Letter of Aristeas* offers

---

[24] H.M. Orlinsky, "The Septuagint As Holy Writ and the Philosophy of the Translators," *HUCA* 46 (1975) 94.
   [25] Ibid.
   [26] Ibid., 95.
   [27] These examples make the point. For additional argumentation, see ibid.,
98–103.
   [28] See the section on the Septuagint in Chapter 12, "Access to the Source: Cicero,
Ben Sira, The Septuagint and Their Audiences" and in Pietersma, "A New Paradigm
for Addressing Old Questions."

a justification, a myth of origins, for what the Septuagint had become by the author's time, and it had become two things that it probably was not in the beginning: independent and scriptural. The *Letter of Aristeas* testifies to a place in the process at which the Septuagint had acquired these two characteristics. It does not, unfortunately, provide evidence for the precise circumstances in which the Septuagint made the transition from dependence to independence and from access point to scripture. What seems clear is that somewhere between the early third century BCE and the composition of the *Letter of Aristeas* the Septuagint, warts and all, struck out on its own.

PHILO OF ALEXANDRIA AND THE SEPTUAGINT

By the first century, when Philo was writing in Alexandria, the Septuagint had long since acquired the status of an independent, scriptural authority. The actual origins of the translation were shrouded in the mists of time and tradition, even for one who wrote in the city of the Septuagint's genesis. But the myth that had its first complete articulation in the *Letter of Aristeas* was alive, well and developing. In *Moses* 2.25–44 Philo reports on the translation of the Mosaic Law into Greek. He tells essentially the same story as the *Letter of Aristeas*, but with some interesting subtractions and additions. Scholars remain divided about whether Philo knew the *Letter of Aristeas* or whether he had inherited the same tradition. Much of what Philo lacks from the version in the *Letter of Aristeas* can be attributed to his own interests, and the answer to the question of Philo's possible dependence on the *Letter of Aristeas* is not what concerns me here. Several developments in the story, whether Philo created them or whether he obtained them through Alexandrian tradition, indicate that the myth that the *Letter of Aristeas* had offered was sufficient for Philo's purposes, and it served particular aims for him.

For Philo, like the *Letter of Aristeas*, the Septuagint began its existence as an independent replacement for the Hebrew, commissioned by Ptolemy Philadelphus. Whereas Ps.-Aristeas grounds the motivation for the translation in the need for inclusion of the Jewish sacred books in the king's library, in Philo the translation of the Mosaic Law was made so that it would be available for the benefit of all human beings, not just the Jews. Philo writes, "In ancient times the laws were written in the Chaldean tongue, and remained in that form (καὶ μέχρι πολλοῦ διέμειναν ἐν ὁμοίῳ) for many years, without any change in language, so

long as they had not yet revealed their beauty to the rest of humankind"
(2.26).[29] The fame and knowledge of the Jewish Laws spread among non-
Jews, and Ptolemy, "having conceived an ardent affection for our Laws,"
decided to have the Law translated into Greek. Y. Amir has argued that
Philo's use of the term *form* (ὅμοιος) rather than *language* when he refers
to translation into Greek implies that "now that the law of Moses can
reveal its beauty to all humankind in the garment of the Greek language,
the Hebrew is of no importance."[30] While I am not convinced that this
statement can bear the evidentiary weight that Amir assigns it, he does
hit on an important theme in Philo's legend of the Septuagint, its form,
or I think more properly, its linguistic nature.

When Philo describes the work of the translators, we find several
fascinating developments from what we saw in the *Letter of Aristeas*, all
of which look to me like an *apologia* for the specific linguistic form of
the Septuagint rather than a more general argument for the scriptural
status of the translation, which Philo certainly assumed. While Philo's
story lacks the public reading of the translation and its acceptance by
the Jewish people (which as we saw served the purpose for the *Letter of
Aristeas* of establishing the translation's status as scripture), his version
retains the claim of the importance of not changing anything, but it is
relocated and reconfigured. Philo describes the translators' task this way,
"Reflecting how great an undertaking it was to make a full version of
the laws given by the Voice of God, where they could not add or take
away or transfer anything, but [they] must keep the original form and
shape (ἀλλὰ τὴν ἐξ ἀρχῆς ἰδέαν καὶ τὸν τύπον αὐτῶν διαφυλάττοντας),
they proceeded to look for the most open and unoccupied spot in the
neighborhood outside the city" (2.34). Philo's major concern is not for
the inviolability of the text of the completed translation as was the case
for the *Letter of Aristeas*, but that the translation cannot alter in any way
its Hebrew source, in either nature or shape. The two must be an exact
match, and this is the crucial point of Philo's version of the story.

In order to meet this challenge, the translators discover the island
of Pharos as the best available place; they stretch the Hebrew books up
toward heaven and pray that God might keep them from failing (2.36).
And sure enough, when they actually begin to work on the translation,

---

[29] Translations come from F.H. Colson, *Philo VI* (LCL; Cambridge: Harvard University Press, 1935).
[30] Y. Amir, "Authority and Interpretation of Scripture in the Writings of Philo," in
Mulder, *Mikra*, 443.

"they became, as it were, possessed, and, under inspiration, wrote, not each several scribe something different, but the same word for word, as though dictated to each by an invisible prompter" (τὰ δ᾽ αὐτὰ πάντες ὀνόματα καὶ ῥήματα, ὥσπερ ὑποβολέως ἑκάστοις ἀοράτως ἐνηχοῦντος) (2.37). Philo reports no translation by committee *à la* the *Letter of Aristeas*; God answered the translators' prayers by taking the matter out of their hands. In effect, God accomplished the translation using the translators as writing instruments.

Philo follows up this version of the events with another justification for the Septuagint's textual-linguistic character. He claims that, even though every language, but especially Greek, allows great flexibility in the possible ways to express things, such is not the case with the Septuagint. He insists that for the Septuagint by contrast:

> [T]he Greek words used corresponded literally with the Chaldean, exactly suited to the things they indicated. For, just as in geometry and logic, so it seems to me, the sense indicated does not admit of variety of expression which remains unchanged in its original form, so these writers, as it clearly appears, arrived at a wording which corresponded with the matter, and alone, or better than any other, would bring out clearly what was meant. The clearest proof of this is that, if Chaldeans have learned Greek or Greeks Chaldean, and read both versions, the Chaldean and the translation, they regard them with awe and reverence as sisters, or rather one and the same, both in matter and words, and speak of the authors not as translators but as prophets and priests of the mysteries, whose sincerity and singleness of thought has enabled them to go hand in hand with the purest of spirits, the spirit of Moses (2.38–41).

This long paragraph strikes me as somewhat Shakespearean—Philo protests a bit too much. But why does he feel compelled to defend the Septuagint in this way? Although I cannot really claim that much evidence could be marshaled to give a definitive answer, a couple of possibilities strike me as at least suggestive. First, Philo, given his own abilities and Greek education, must be cognizant of the problematic textual-linguistic nature of the Septuagint. Even though he probably could not make a comparison with the Hebrew on his own, his description of the translation process and its resultant form offer a justification for the actual state of affairs as he knows them. Perhaps he did even rely on those who knew both Greek and Hebrew for this information.[31]

---

[31] The issue of Philo's knowledge of Hebrew has been widely debated. For a cogent argument against Philo's knowledge of Hebrew that invokes the same passages used in

Philo himself, however, engages an interlinear text divorced from its interlinear partner, and he may well be uncomfortable with what he has. He thus goes to great lengths to reinforce the claim that the *form* as well as the content is part of the divine sanction accorded this translation; indeed it is part of the Septuagint's inspired nature. For someone who was skilled at writing Greek and who explicitly recognizes the rhetorical possibilities of the language, the Greek of the Septuagint must have been something of an embarrassment for which he had to account. He does so by arguing that the translation does not add to, subtract from or alter anything in its source, and that is the way God intended it.

Secondly, Philo appeals to those who know both languages (as he apparently did not)—they would testify that the two translations are not just related, but in fact are "one and the same, both in matter and words" (ὡς μίαν καὶ τὴν αὐτὴν ἔν τε τοῖς πράγμασι καὶ τοῖς ὀςνόμασι). Such complete correlation with the original demonstrates for Philo that the translators were more than simply pious men who rendered one language, Hebrew, into another, Greek, but they were actually "prophets and priests of the mysteries" who possessed the same pure spirit that Moses had. Here Philo utilizes the language of prophecy and oracle, language he uses elsewhere for Moses and the Mosaic Law.[32] This claim establishes that the translation, in form and content, is just as inspired as the original, since God worked through the translators in the same way as God had through prophets and priests.

Several possible explanations can account for this emphasis in Philo's version of the legend of the Septuagint in *Moses*. The least likely, I think, is that Philo is responding to criticisms of the Septuagint that its close correspondence to its Hebrew source somehow detracts from its status as a scriptural text.[33] Philo turns the issue on its head and claims that precisely this close relationship of form and content makes the Septuagint what it is. The Septuagint's textual-linguistic character is not a drawback, but quite the opposite, a proof of its divine origins. The ability to establish such a claim would be especially crucial for someone

---

this section of my paper, see D. Gooding, "Philo's Bible in the *De Gigantibus* and the *Quod Deus sit Immutabilis*," *Two Treatises of Philo of Alexandria: A Commentary on De Gigantibus and Quod Deus Sit Immutabilis* (D. Winston and J.M. Dillon, eds.; BJS 25; Chico, CA: Scholars Press, 1983) 119–22. See also S. Sandmel, *Philo of Alexandria: An Introduction* (New York: Oxford University Press, 1979) chap. 9.

[32] Amir, "Authority and Interpretation," 443.

[33] Sandmel speculates, however, that Philo's account was a response to unknown people who were critical of the Septuagint (*Philo of Alexandria*, 52).

like Philo, in the first instance because the Septuagint constituted his sacred scripture and in the second because Philo's own hermeneutical enterprise revolved so directly around the *exact* words used in those scriptures. Since Philo most likely did not know Hebrew, he could not on his own consult it and compare it to the Greek. He thus had to resort to the purported testimonials of those who could. For Philo, the Jewish scriptures embodied in the Septuagint are the key to disclosing the activity and will of God in the world. In his allegorical interpretations he takes seriously each and every word and why it occurs where it does. Philo's hermeneutical approach to the Jewish scriptures only works if the Greek can be claimed to be inspired like the Hebrew and if it bears such a close resemblance to the Hebrew original.[34] He works hard in his report of the story to establish both of these claims.

Philo's primary goal, then, is not like that of the *Letter of Aristeas*, which offers a myth of origins that establishes the independence and sanctity of the Septuagint. Philo does not need to establish the translation's scriptural status; that is undoubtedly beyond question for him. In order for Philo to pursue his exegetical methods, he must go an additional step and argue that the form of the Septuagint constitutes an indispensable part of its claim to being scripture. I cannot say if this argument is part of some theological conflict to which Philo was responding, although I think it possible. Philo's repeated insistence on the inspired nature of the textual-linguistic *form* of the Septuagint leads me to conclude that at the least he *has* to make the case in order to build a solid theological foundation for the kind of scriptural exegesis in which he is engaged.

Conclusion

The accounts of the translation of the Septuagint in the *Letter of Aristeas* and Philo have traditionally occupied an important place in scholarly reconstructions of its origins. The interlinear paradigm, however, suggests that both versions have more to tell us about the fate of the Septuagint in times contemporary with those writers rather than with the

---

[34] For similar conclusions, see Amir, "Authority and Interpretation," 440–4; Sandmel, *Philo of Alexandria*, 52; R. Williamson, *Jews in the Hellenistic World: Philo* (Cambridge Commentaries on Writings of the Jewish and Christian World, 200 BC to AD 200 1.2; Cambridge: Cambridge University Press, 1989) 168–9.

translation's beginnings. What the interlinear paradigm requires is that to understand the nature of the Septuagint, its original function and the social location of its origins, we are thrown back upon the translation itself with all the attendant difficulties that presents.

CHAPTER FIFTEEN

THREE JEWISH RITUAL PRACTICES IN *ARISTEAS* §§158–160*

In the *Letter of Aristeas to Philocrates* §§128–71, the Jewish high priest, Eleazar, who speaks to the deputation sent from Ptolemy II to Jerusalem in order to fetch the scholars who would translate the Law into Greek, presents an *apologia* for Judaism, primarily organized around a criticism of Gentile idol worship and an allegorical interpretation of the Jewish food laws.[1] Included in this rather long section, Ps.-Aristeas describes in §§158–60 three Jewish ritual practices: the wearing of fringes on clothes, the placing of mezuzot on doors and gates and the binding of phylacteries (tefillin) on the hands. Through the consistent deployment of similar vocabulary, Ps.-Aristeas specifically connects these practices to one of the major themes of the larger *apologia*, that the statutes and commandments in the Jewish law, particularly the food laws, have been "set out allegorically" (τροπολογῶν ἐκτέθειται), and thus they function as "signs" (παράσημον), "symbols" (σημεῖον) and "reminders" (μνεία) for the Jews that the Law contains deeper spiritual truths about the will of God.

While almost all commentators note that *Aristeas* §§158–60 refers to these Jewish ritual practices, we know little about them in the centuries before the rabbis regulated their form and contents, even in light of the discoveries in the Judean desert, among which a number of textile fragments with fringes, thirty fragments of phylacteries and fragments of seven mezuzot were found.[2] In fact, outside of the biblical commands,

---

* I am grateful to the editors for the opportunity to contribute to a volume honoring Betsy Halpern-Amaru, who has been a friend and colleague for lo these many years.

[1] Although *Aristeas to Philocrates* is not really a letter by the canons of ancient letter writing, the title has become conventional in modern scholarly parlance, and I use it here. I also distinguish between the title of the book and the author by referring to the author as Pseudo-Aristeas, especially since almost unanimously, scholars recognize that a Ptolemaic courtier named Aristeas was not the author of this work. The usual date given to *Aristeas* is somewhere in the middle of the second century BCE.

[2] For the textiles, see G.M. Crowfoot, "The Linen Textiles" (DJD 1; Oxford: Clarendon Press, 1955) 18–38. The phylacteries come from Qumran (Phylactery A–U), Wadi Muraba'at (Mur 4) and Nahal Se'elim; (XHev/Se 5 A, B). The mezuzot are from Qumran (Mezuzah A–G). See L.H. Schiffman, "Phylacteries and Mezuzot," *Encyclopedia*

Aristeas is the first Jewish text to mention that Jews actually performed these biblical rituals. The passage is worth citing in full at the outset:

> §158 For also with food and drink, he has commanded those who have offered first fruits to avail themselves of them right away. And indeed also he has given us a symbolic reminder on our clothes, just as also on doors and gates he has prescribed that we set up the sayings (τὰ λόγια) to serve as a reminder of God. §159 And also he has commanded us expressly to fasten the sign upon our hands, showing clearly that every activity must be accomplished with righteousness, keeping in mind our own constitution, and above all the fear of God. §160 And he has also commanded that when sleeping and rising we study God's provisions, not only in word, but also in judgment, observing their own movement and impression when sleeping and waking, that there is a certain divine and incomprehensible interchange between them.[3]

Beyond listing the specific biblical passages alluded to in this section, commentators say very little about the description of these practices in *Aristeas*. Yet, these paragraphs raise a number of interesting questions about them. Can we tell from these paragraphs what Jews actually did? Do the texts and artifacts from Qumran shed any light on understanding what is in *Aristeas*? How should we translate the rather ambiguous Greek phrase τὰ λόγια? Since the Judean desert finds have shown that there was a developing corpus of texts that would have been copied in phylacteries and mezuzot, does this Greek phrase indicate that Ps.-Aristeas is aware of specific texts used in phylacteries and mezuzot? What is the relationship between *Aristeas* and the Jewish-Greek scriptural texts?

"HE HAS GIVEN US A SYMBOLIC REMINDER ON OUR CLOTHES"

Ps.-Aristeas mentions the first of the three practices in §158 in a short notice. In the cases of food and drink, they are to be consumed immediately after offering them. This statement presumably clarifies the preceding sentence in §157 about calling to mind "the ruling and preserving nature of God." Apparently, the immediate consumption of

---

   [3] The Greek of these paragraphs is sometimes obscure, especially the transition from first-person plural to third-person plural in §160. The translation is my own prepared for an upcoming commentary on *Aristeas*.

the sacrificed items constitutes a reminder of God's nature to the one eating.[4]

Then follows the enigmatic statement that God "has given us a symbolic reminder on our clothes" (καὶ μὴν καὶ ἐκ τῶν περιβολαίων παράσημον ἡμῖν μνείας δέδωκεν). This reference cannot be to phylacteries, since Ps.-Aristeas explicitly discusses them in §159. M. Hadas gives the most reasonable interpretation of the clause arguing that the author is referring the "fringes" or "tassels" that according to Num 15:38–9 and Deut 22:12 Israelites were to wear on their clothes.[5] Indeed Ps.-Aristeas connects the fringes with the Law in a manner similar to the Numbers passage. Along with τὰ λόγια, whose mention comes later in the same sentence, the fringes in *Aristeas* serve as a "reminder of God" (πρὸς τὸ μνείαν εἶναι θεοῦ). In Numbers God addresses Moses and says, "Speak to the Israelites, and tell them to make fringes on the corners of their garments throughout their generations and to put a blue cord on the fringe at each corner. You have the fringe so that, when you see it, you will *remember* (μνησθήσεσθε) all the commandments of the Lord and do them, and not follow the lust of your own heart and your own eyes." The command in Deuteronomy, by contrast, does not contain any notion of remembrance of the Law; it simply enjoins tassels "on the four corners of the cloak with which you cover yourself." Even though the mention of the fringes in *Aristeas* is not a citation of Num 15:38–9—it does not even share its major vocabulary items—it is difficult to think that the author does not have in mind the command in the form we find it in Numbers.

"ON DOORS AND GATES HE HAS PRESCRIBED THAT WE SET UP THE SAYINGS"

As part of the same sentence in which he alludes to the tassels on Jewish garments, Ps.-Aristeas mentions mezuzot, which, he says, Jews fasten "on doors and gates" (ἐπὶ τῶν πυλῶν καὶ θυρῶν). Certainly Ps.-Aristeas has in mind the obligations placed upon Israel that we

---

[4] The Greek word for offering sacrifice is ἀπαρξαμένους, which can indicate the offering of firstlings or first fruits. If that is the case, Ps.-Aristeas could be referring to the eating of the firstlings of the flocks commanded in Deut 15:19–23. M. Hadas understands the term more generally and translates "after first having offered a portion as sacrifice" (*Aristeas to Philocrates* [Philadelphia: Dropsie College, 1951] 163).

[5] Hadas, *Aristeas*, 162.

find in Deut 6:4–9 and 11:13–21 in which God commands that "these words of mine" (MT דברים האלה [6:6], דברי אלה [11:18]; LXX τὰ ῥήματα ταῦτα in both places) be placed as a sign on the hand, on the forehead and on doorposts and gates (see below on phylacteries). Unlike its description of the tassels, the text of *Aristeas* bears at least some minimal resemblance to the command in Deuteronomy. The LXX of both Deut 6:9 and 11:20 has the commandment concerning mezuzot in identical language—καὶ γράψετε αὐτὰ ἐπὶ τὰς φλιὰς τῶν οἰκιῶν ὑμῶν καὶ τῶν πυλῶν ὑμῶν. With Deuteronomy, *Aristeas* shares part of the prepositional phrase indicating where the "words" should be placed—ἐπὶ τῶν πυλῶν, "upon the gates." Instead of Deuteronomy's "doorposts of your houses" (τὰς φλιὰς τῶν οἰκιῶν ὑμῶν), *Aristeas* has the much more streamlined "doors" (θυρῶν) which, in fact, is actually a different location from the Deuteronomic one. The command in Deuteronomy enjoins the Israelites to "write" the "words" (αὐτά in v. 9 with ῥήματα in v. 6 as the antecedent), but the command in *Aristeas* makes the form of the obligation to "place" (τίθεναι) "the sayings." Although we might see the command to set up mezuzot in *Aristeas* as a closer reflection of the LXX, the differences between *Aristeas* and the Greek biblical text remain substantial.[6]

One critical interpretive problem with this paragraph is the meaning, and hence translation, of the phrase τὰ λόγια, a much more ambiguous reference than the LXX's unambiguous τὰ ῥήματα, "words." Modern scholars have understood the phrase in *Aristeas* in different ways. Hadas renders it "the chapters," as if Ps.-Aristeas was referring to a clearly delineated group of texts that he knows should be included in mezuzot.[7] R.J.H. Shutt translates it as "Words," apparently understanding the phrase to refer to the Jewish Law more generally. In this he seems to follow A. Pelletier who translates "les divines <<Paroles>>."[8] As part of a larger word group, Ps.-Aristeas employs both the noun λόγος and the verb λογίζομαι extensively in the book. In *Aristeas* the noun has a range

---

[6] In his translation, Hadas places language that reflects the LXX in capital letters, but my analysis of §§158–60 makes me wonder the extent to which these phrases could be classified as quotations. Some of the language, like "on the gates" for example, might simply be a serendipitous overlapping of language that parallels the biblical texts only accidentally.

[7] Hadas, *Aristeas*, 163.

[8] R.J.H. Shutt, *Old Testament Pseudepigrapha* (J.H. Charlesworth, ed.; 2 vols.; Garden City, NY: Doubleday, 1985) 2.23; A. Pelletier, *Lettre d'Aristée à Philocrate* (SC 89; Paris: Cerf, 1962) 177.

of meanings including "word," "argument," "speech" and "reason." The verb usually means "to use or to apply reason." Despite the frequency of these words throughout the work, they do not provide much help in determining the meaning of τὰ λόγια in §158. We do find the noun λόγιον in two other places in *Aristeas*, however, §§97 and 177, and both bear directly on how scholars have understood the noun in the passage on mezuzot.

Paragraphs 96–9 comprise a short section on the vestments of the Jewish high priest Eleazar. The entire section reflects the vocabulary of LXX Exodus 28 and 29, which describe the priestly garments. Among these is the "breastpiece of judgment" (NRSV)—חשן משפט in the MT and τὸ λόγιον τῶν κρίσεων in the LXX—translated "oracles of judgments" in the New English Translation of the Septuagint (NETS).[9] The LXX translator clearly understood this article of high priestly clothing to be connected with oracles, especially since Aaron's breastpiece contained the Urim and Thummin or sacred lots by which he divined God's will (see, for example, Num 27:21). The translator thus selected the Greek λόγιον to render the Hebrew חשן. This meaning is consistent with the way the word is used in classical writers like Herodotus who uses it in the plural to refer to oracles.[10] The appearance of this term in *Aristeas* for the high priest's breastpiece probably derives ultimately from the Greek translation of Exodus, even though some textual confusion has crept into the LXX during the process of its transmission.[11]

Perhaps somewhat surprisingly, Ps.-Aristeas does not seem concerned about any connection between Eleazar's λόγιον and any high priestly

---

[9] For NETS, see A. Pietersma and B.G. Wright, *A New English Translation of the Septuagint and the Other Greek Translations Traditionally Included Under That Title* (New York: Oxford University Press, 2007).

[10] Hadas, *Aristeas*, 138. H.G. Liddell, R. Scott, H.S. Jones, eds. *A Greek-English Lexicon* (Ninth ed.; Oxford: Clarendon, 1940); see under λόγιον.

[11] A number of LXX manuscripts have the Greek term λογεῖον in place of λόγιον in Exodus. The first word means "a place for speaking, especially a term in Attic theater," whereas the second indicates an "oracle or utterance." J.W. Wevers in his Göttingen edition of Exodus has λόγιον in his main text (*Septuaginta: Vetus Testamentum Graecum Auctoritate Academiae Scientiarum Gottingensis editum II.1: Exodus* [Göttingen: Vandenhoeck & Ruprecht, 1991]), and P. Walters (Katz) has made a compelling case that the translator of Exodus would have used λόγιον and that λογεῖον represents an ittacistic variant despite the fact that it is a separate Greek word (*The Text of the Septuagint: Its Corruptions and Their Emendations* [Cambridge: Cambridge University Press, 1973] 283–84). Philo and Josephus, who both refer to this object as λόγιον, provide additional evidence that the Hebrew חשן was rendered by λόγιον in the Jewish-Greek scriptures. See Philo, *Leg.* 3.126, 132 and *Fug.* 185; Josephus, *Ant.* 3.167, 217.

oracular activity, even though that is the main idea of the biblical passage. For Ps.-Aristeas the entire spectacle of Eleazar dressed in his priestly outfit "produces awe and distraction, so that one might think that he had gone out of this world into another. And I insist that any person who comes near to the sight of those things that I have previously recounted will come into amazement and indescribable wonder, turning his mind to the sacred construction of each thing" (§99). In this light, how then ought we to translate the word λόγιον in this passage? Certainly, the evidence from the LXX and Ps.-Aristeas's usage of the term consistently with the LXX suggests that the English "oracle" is the most appropriate translation for the word when used to refer to this article of high priestly clothing.[12]

Although Ps.-Aristeas employs the term λόγιον in §97, it occurs in the singular denoting an article of clothing. The use of the plural τὰ λόγια in §177 matches much more closely the way the phrase appears in §158. After Eleazar sends the translators to Alexandria, the king receives them, but he is most interested in the manuscripts that they have brought with them. When the Jewish translators unpack and unroll the scrolls, the king "pausing for a long time and doing obeisance about seven times, said, 'I thank you, O men, and even more the one who sent you, but mostly the God whose sayings/utterances (τὰ λόγια) these are.'" In this instance, the Greek phrase almost certainly refers to the entirety of the Jewish law written on the scrolls brought by the prospective translators.

Several occurrences of the term λόγιον in the LXX, Second Temple Jewish literature and the New Testament help us to understand its use in *Aristeas*. In the LXX of Num 24:16, at the beginning of his second prophecy, Balaam refers to himself as one who hears λόγια θεοῦ, "oracles of God." (The identical phrase occurs in 24:4 as well.) In its context, the term almost certainly has its more classical sense of prophetic oracle, and it does not denote any scriptural tradition, especially since it comes from a non-Israelite prophet who "hears" (ἀκούων) them. In Deut 33:9–10, the translator appears to have used the plural λόγια to refer to the scriptures. In Moses' blessing of Levi, the MT has "for they observed your word (אמרתך) and kept your covenant. They teach Jacob your ordinances and Israel your law." The LXX translator rendered the

---

[12] Hadas gives this English as the translation (*Aristeas*, 138).

singular אמרתך by the plural λόγια, and given the parallel context, which contains the terms "covenant," "ordinances" and "law," the plural might well have significance and could refer somehow to some scriptural or authoritative sayings. Since 33:10 refers to ordinances and law, the plural λόγια used together with "covenant" (διαθήκη) could identify the corpus of divine sayings that contains the ordinances and laws. A similar situation obtains in Psalms, which has more than 20 occurrences of the word. Two, however, illustrate the possibilities in Psalms. In 19(18):14 the Psalmist says, "Let the words (אמרי) of my mouth…be pleasing unto you." The translator renders אמרי with λόγια, here certainly "sayings" or "utterances" in English. In Ps 119(118):148 the second line of the Hebrew verse reads, "that I may meditate on your promise (אמרתך)." The entire phrase in the Greek is τοῦ μελετᾶν τὰ λόγιά σου, "in order to mediate on your λόγια." The Greek verb μελετάω translates שיח, which is not the usual rendering in Psalms. The usual translation, even within this Psalm is ἀδολεσχέω (see vv. 15, 23, 48, 78 where one meditates on "ordinances" and "commandments"). The conclusion here is that, at the very least, the translator understands τὰ λόγιά σου as something that can be studied. Elsewhere, in Ps 1:2 the same verb appears as a translation of הגה and has the object "law" (νόμος). Whether there is an intertextual relationship within the corpus of Psalms going on here is difficult to know, but the parallel idea in Greek, that one can study the Law and the "sayings," lends support to understanding the latter term as referring to scripture in some form.

Philo uses the word in two places, *On Rewards and Punishments* 1 and *On the Contemplative Life* 25. In both cases, the word refers to Jewish scripture, but it clearly has the meaning of prophetic oracle. Philo begins *On Rewards and Punishments* by saying, "The oracles (λογίων) delivered through the prophet (προφήτου) Moses are of three kinds."[13] Moses here takes on the role of prophet, not lawgiver as in *Aristeas*, even though these three kinds of oracles—"the creation of the world," "history" and "legislation"—undoubtedly refer to the Pentateuch. In a similar vein, when Philo describes the houses of the Therapeutae in *On the Contemplative Life* 25, he says, "They take nothing into it [their house], either food or drink or any other thing necessary for the needs of the body, but laws (νόμους) and oracles (λόγια) delivered through

---

[13] Translations of Philo are taken from those of F.H. Colson, *Philo* (LCL; 10 vols.; Cambridge: Harvard University Press, 1956–1962).

the mouth of prophets, and psalms (ὕμνους), and anything else which fosters and perfects knowledge and piety." Again, even though he does not indicate that all these spiritual resources are from Moses and that laws are different from oracles, the word λόγια has to indicate prophetic oracles in this case.

Josephus's use of the term in *Jewish War* 6.311 is a bit more ambiguous, but probably it refers to the Jewish scriptures as having within them prophetic oracles. Commenting on the fact that due to "folly and calamities of their own choosing" Jews were responsible for their own destruction, he writes, "Thus the Jews after the demolition of the Antonia, reduced the temple to a square, although they had it recorded in their own oracles (λογίοις) that the city and sanctuary would be taken when the temple should become four-square."[14] Whatever source Josephus had in mind here, the plural of λόγιον seems to indicate the collective Jewish scriptures, which contained this prophetic oracle. Thus, both Philo and Josephus emphasize the predictive, oracular character of the word λόγιον, a meaning consonant with its classical usages, but with the clear intention that these oracles either comprise the Jewish scriptures (Philo) or are contained within the Jewish scriptures (Philo and Josephus).

In Rom 3:2, Paul writes about the advantages of the Jews. "First of all," he notes, "they have been entrusted with the oracles of God" (πρῶτον μὲν ὅτι ἐπιστεύθησαν τὰ λόγια τοῦ θεοῦ). Paul does not elaborate on the meaning of the phrase "oracles of God," but given the context in which he uses it—he speaks of the unfaithfulness of some Jews in verse 3—he more than likely intends the entire corpus of the Jewish scriptures.[15] The same holds true for Heb 5:12. The author of Hebrews upbraids his readers. They should be teachers themselves, but they still need to be taught "some of the first principles of the sayings/utterances of God" (τινὰ τὰ στοιχεῖα τῆς ἀρχῆς τῶν λογίων τοῦ θεοῦ). In this case, the "utterances" probably refer to the Jewish scriptures, especially as they are the repository of divine revelation.[16] The NRSV translates the phrase in Hebrews as "word of God," understanding τὰ λόγια as a reference

---

[14] Translation from H.St.J. Thackeray, *Josephus IV–VII* (LCL; Cambridge, MA: Harvard University Press, 1928).

[15] On τὰ λόγια τοῦ θεοῦ in this passage as a reference to the entire Old Testament, see J.A. Fitzmyer, *Romans* (AB 33; New York: Doubleday, 1992) 326.

[16] See H.W. Attridge, *The Epistle to the Hebrews* (Hermeneia; Philadelphia: Fortress, 1989) 159.

to the collective Jewish scriptures. In both of these cases, τὰ λόγια is accompanied by the genitive τοῦ θεοῦ, which qualifies who made the utterances. The same thing happens in *Aristeas* §177 with the relative οὗτινος that introduces the clause and whose antecedent is God.

The term also appears without any genitive complement in Acts 7:38, part of Stephen's speech before his death. As he gives a rehearsal of Israelite history, he speaks about the Israelite rejection of Moses. "This is the Moses," he says, "who said to the Israelites, 'God will raise up a prophet for you from your own people as he raised me up.'" This Moses was with an angel who spoke to him at Sinai and "he received living oracles (λόγια ζῶντα) to give to us." Connected as they are with Stephen's injunction of the "prophet like Moses" (Deut 18:15), the "living oracles" seem to play a double role. They comprise the Law that God gave to Moses on Sinai, but they also serve as prophetic predictions of the coming of Jesus, who is that prophet like Moses. In this passage, we see as in Philo, for example, a clear connection between the Law and prediction, that is, the oracular origination of the Jewish Law.

In all the cases in the New Testament, the plural τὰ λόγια suggests an understanding of the Jewish scriptures as those things that God had spoken, but also perhaps as oracular predictions of the coming of Christ. While this divine speech ultimately ended up in writing and was transmitted in some relatively fixed form, God initially gave the scriptures as divine utterances, acts of divine speech. Thus, τὰ λόγια, which walks the semantic line of both speech and prediction, is seen as the most descriptive way to refer to them.

Returning to §158, it appears most appropriate to translate τὰ λόγια as "the sayings" or "utterances" or perhaps, although I think it less likely, "oracles," in line with the use of the term in §177 and in the LXX and the New Testament (and probably Philo and Josephus). The evidence of §158 suggests that Ps.-Aristeas also understood the Jewish Law to originate as acts of divine speech—in this sense they are oracular—even though he consistently attributes the origination of the law to Moses, the lawgiver. Interestingly, nowhere in *Aristeas* does the author talk explicitly of God giving the Law to Moses orally at Sinai in the form of divine utterances. The closest he comes is in §139 when he says that Moses was "prepared by God for knowledge of all things" (ὑπὸ θεοῦ κατασκευασμένος εἰς ἐπίγνωσιν τῶν ἁπάτων). Ps.-Aristeas does not display any real interest in the potential predictive aspect of the term. The designation of the high priest's breastpiece as τὸ λόγιον seems to me to be simply conventional by the time of *Aristeas*, and for Ps.-Aristeas it is devoid of any oracular function.[17] Thus, either "utterances" or "sayings" makes the most sense to me as a translation of τὰ λόγια in §158.

Another facet of the problem is what exactly the author of *Aristeas* understood the content of τὰ λόγια to be. Almost certainly in §177 the phrase refers to the entire Jewish Law, and Pelletier in his *Sources chrétiennes* edition of *Aristeas* understands it the same way in §158 when he comments, "C'est le plus ancien exemple de τὰ λόγια pour designer l'ensemble de la Loi."[18] But can this really be the intended content of the mezuzot referred to in §158? Ps.-Aristeas must have known, if he was indeed familiar with the practice of placing mezuzot on doorposts and gates, that these small boxes did not contain the entire Law. In later rabbinic tradition Deut 6:4–9 and 11:13–21, which provide the warrant for the use of mezuzot, always appear as required texts. As we will also see with the phylacteries, the finds from Qumran have provided much additional information about the use of mezuzot in the Second Temple period, including what texts they might contain. The mezuzot from Qumran often include additional texts to those on the rabbinic list, especially Exod 20:1–14, Deut 6:6–18 and the Ten Commandments.[19] It seems unlikely that Ps.-Aristeas simply is referring to the Ten Commandments in §158, since they are not called λόγια in the Greek Pentateuch, but λόγοι in LXX Exodus (20:1) and ῥήματα in Deuteronomy (5:22).

So what does the phrase τὰ λόγια refer to in *Aristeas* §158—the collective Jewish Law or some smaller collection of texts? Several considerations provide a basis for some informed speculation about the answer to that question. First, I do think that Ps.-Aristeas is familiar with the practice of Jews affixing mezuzot to their doors and gates.

---

[17] In the *Testament of Levi*, Levi's investment as a priest involves a "breastplate of understanding" (λόγιον συνέσεως). The phrase differs from the Septuagint's τὸ λόγιον τῶν κρίσεων. The translation above is from H.W. Hollander and M. de Jonge, *The Testaments of the Twelve Patriarchs: A Commentary* (SVTP 8; Leiden: Brill, 1985) 151. They comment that the phrase is reminiscent of the high priest's breastplate in Exodus 28 and that the "term 'understanding' may refer to the ability of the priests to interpret God's will and predict the future by means of the Urim and Tummim kept in the breastplate (one should note that λόγιον [also] means 'oracle')."

[18] Pelletier, *Lettre d'Aristée*, 177 note 5.

[19] See, Schiffman, "Phylacteries and Mezuzot," 677 and J.T. Milik, "Mezuzot A–G (149–55)" (DJD 6; Oxford: Clarendon, 1977) 80–5.

Aristeas does not demonstrate a clear enough relationship with the LXX to argue that the author directly depends on the biblical text for his description of the mezuzot. If he was interested in reflecting directly the text of the LXX, we would expect closer conformity with the LXX than we find, not only in the wording of the descriptions in *Aristeas*, but also in the manner that Jews employ mezuzot. So, for example, one might reasonably expect Ps.-Aristeas to agree more exactly with the LXX about where the mezuzot are placed—on the doorposts rather than on the doors themselves.

If we assume for the moment that Ps.-Aristeas actually does know about these things first hand, I find it hard to believe that τὰ λόγια in §158 signifies the entire Law. The author had to know better. But is he familiar with a collection of standard texts that should appear in mezuzot? The evidence from Qumran suggests that whoever made the ritual objects found there drew on a relatively well-defined corpus of texts, even if it was not always identical to the corpus approved by the rabbis later on. Indeed, this fascinating question is what initially drew me to this passage. Unfortunately, the evidence in *Aristeas* does not allow us to draw any conclusions about this problem. My suspicion is that the Qumran evidence is relevant only inasmuch as there was probably a "short list" of texts, but which texts got copied into phylacteries and mezuzot might have varied from place to place. There is no reason to assume that the practice at Qumran would have been the same as that in Alexandria.

"HE HAS COMMANDED US EXPRESSLY TO FASTEN THE SIGN UPON OUR HANDS"

Unlike his reference to the fringes and even the mezuzot, Ps.-Aristeas more unambiguously reflects the biblical warrant for the use of phylacteries or tefillin. The text of *Aristeas* reads, "καὶ ἐπὶ τῶν χειρῶν δὲ διαρρήδην τὸ σημεῖον κελεύει περιῆφθαι" ("And also he has commanded us expressly to fasten the sign upon our hands"). *Aristeas* shares some of the vocabulary of the command in the Septuagint, even if it is not a close citation of it. The LXX contains four places where God commands Israelites to wear phylacteries. Deuteronomy 6:8 and 11:18 both report the requirement to bind God's commandments on the hands and forehead. In Deut 6:8 we read, καὶ ἀφάψεις αὐτὰ εἰς σημεῖον ἐπὶ τῆς χειρός σου ("And bind [sg.] them as a sign on your [sg.] hand"), whereas 11:18, the parallel commandment, differs slightly, καὶ ἀφάψετε αὐτὰ εἰς σημεῖον ἐπὶ τῆς χειρὸς ὑμῶν ("and you [pl.] shall bind [pl.] them as a sign upon your [pl.] hand").

The second two passages, Exod 13:9 and 16, do not mention explicitly what is to be on the hands and forehead, nor do they use the verb "to bind."[20] The injunction, however, as we see when we compare the Deuteronomy passage, seems to assume the same practice—placing something on the hands and the forehead as a sign. The commands in Exodus differ from each other in small but important details. Both 13:9 and 16 are the culmination of separate discussions of the divine injunction to "Consecrate to me every firstborn, first-produced, opening every womb among the sons of Israel, from human being to animal." Exodus 13:9 follows immediately after the institution of the Feast of Unleavened Bread and the command to tell one's son, "For this reason the Lord God acted for me when I was going out of Egypt." The verse itself reads, καὶ ἔσται σοι σημεῖον ἐπὶ τῆς χειρός σου καὶ μνημόσυνον πρὸ ὀφθαλμῶν σου, ὅπως ἂν γένηται ὁ νόμος κυρίου ἐν τῷ στόματι σου ("And it will be a sign for you upon your [sg.] hand and a memorial before your [sg.] eyes, in order that the Law of the Lord might be in your [sg.] mouth" [NETS]). The second command comes several verses after the first. Again, the son asks about the meaning of redeeming of the firstborn. After the father's reply, which notes the divine act of killing the firstborn of Egypt and the redemption of the firstborn, the text continues, "καὶ ἔσται εἰς σημεῖον ἐπὶ τῆς χειρός σου καὶ ἀσάλευτον πρὸ ὀφθαλμῶν σου. ἐν γὰρ χειρὶ κραταιᾷ ἐξήγαγέν σε κύριος ἐξ Αἰγύπτου ("And it shall be for a sign on your [sg.] hand and immovable before your [sg.] eyes. For with a mighty hand the Lord brought you out of Egypt" [NETS]).

Aristeas shares with LXX of Exodus and Deuteronomy the noun σημεῖον but employs the plural of χείρ rather than the singular of both Exodus and Deuteronomy; it has the compound verb instead of the simplex in Deuteronomy. (Exodus has no verb either for binding or for writing.) Furthermore the word order of Ps.-Aristeas's allusion to the biblical commands differs from the text of LXX in both Exodus and Deuteronomy. Ps.-Aristeas places the prepositional phrase "on the hands" in front of the verb, which in *Aristeas* is an infinitive comple-

---

[20] I am grateful to Shani Berrin of the Hebrew University of Jerusalem for drawing my attention to this passage.

ment to the main verb κελεύει. In one intriguing way, *Aristeas* echoes the form of the commandment given in Exod 13:9. As I noted above, the entirety of Eleazar's *apologia* is dominated by words having to do with signifying and remembering. Both of these ideas find expression in Exodus.[21] The command will be a "*sign* upon your hand and a *memorial* before your eyes." Although no word for remembering occurs in *Aristeas* in direct connection with the practice of using phylacteries, the theme of calling to mind the Law or remembering it permeates the entirety of Eleazar's speech, including two mentions of reminding right at the end of §158.

The greatest difference between *Aristeas* and the biblical injunctions, of course, is Ps.-Aristeas's omission of the second part of the biblical command—to bind the Law on the forehead in addition to the hands. If Ps.-Aristeas were directly dependent on the LXX of Exodus and/or Deuteronomy, then this citation might work as shorthand for the entire commandment. Nothing in *Aristeas* unambiguously indicates that such is the case, however. Perhaps this passage describes the practice as Ps.-Aristeas knew it. Uncertainty remains, however, whether Ps.-Aristeas intended only the binding of the phylactery on the hands or whether he meant to include the binding on the forehead as well. Even if no specific practice lies behind this report, the text in *Aristeas* raises important questions about the relationship between texts and their transmissions as well as the way that these traditions were understood in particular Jewish contexts and communities.

In §159, Ps.-Aristeas states that the commandment is to fasten "the sign upon the hands"—that is, unlike the commands in Deuteronomy where God's words are the object of the binding or in Exodus where there is no binding mentioned, in *Aristeas* τό σημεῖον is the object of the verb. Ps.-Aristeas makes no mention of texts being contained in the phylacteries. As the passage is worded, apparently the phylacteries themselves, not the texts placed in them, are the reminder that one's actions must be accomplished with righteousness.[22] The reference to the practice using the essential vocabulary of both Exodus and Deuteronomy might

---

[21] In Deuteronomy one teaches, observes, talks about the commandments, but neither Deuteronomy 6 nor Deuteronomy 11 enjoins remembering.

[22] Hadas translates the beginning of §159 as "And he has expressly bidden us to 'bind *them* [emphasis mine] for a sign upon the hands'" (*Aristeas*, p. 163). The grammar of the sentence, however, provides no warrant for an unexpressed *them* as the object of the binding. I think that the LXX of Deuteronomy has influenced Hadas here. The grammar of *Aristeas* indicates that τὸ σημεῖον is the object.

indicate that Ps.-Aristeas understood that at least these passages should be contained in the phylactery, but such a suggestion really amounts to little more than speculation. In the phylacteries from Qumran, the four passages that the rabbis later standardized appear—Exod 13:1–10, 13:11–16, Deut 6:4–9, 11:13–21—along with some additional and longer passages, especially Deut 5:1–6:9, 10:12–11:21, Exod 12:43–13:16, Deut 32 (in one case).[23] Yet for Ps.-Aristeas, whatever text(s) might be contained in the phylactery seems of little consequence when compared to the symbolic value of the object itself.

In the very next paragraph, §160, Ps.-Aristeas does cite at least part of LXX Deuteronomy exactly. Deuteronomy 6:7 enjoins the Israelites to "recite (προβιβάσεις) them (i.e., the commandments) to your children and talk (λαλήσεις) about them at home and when you are away and when you lie down and when you rise (κοιταζομένους καὶ διανισταμένους)." Ps.-Aristeas reproduces these last two participles precisely in these forms. Yet, he claims that the obligation is to study or meditate on (μελετᾶν) the commandments rather than to "recite" them or "talk" about them. Although there is no clear evidence that Ps.-Aristeas is familiar with Greek translations of the Hebrew scriptures other than the Pentateuch, it might be of more than passing interest that the verb μελετάω occurs in LXX Ps 1:2 as what the righteous person does with the law—καὶ ἐν τῷ νόμῳ αὐτοῦ μελετήσει ἡμέρας καὶ νυκτός ("And in his law he will meditate day and night"). Yet, whether or not Ps.-Aristeas knows an actual translation of Psalms, the use of μελετάω in this passage might well point to an intertextual interplay that results in the interpretations of the Mosaic commandments that we see in *Aristeas* generally.

The object of μελετάω in this paragraph is also of some interest. According to *Aristeas* one is to study the κατασκευάς, "provisions," when one lies down or rises up. The noun κατασκευή and the verb

    [23] S.W. Crawford, *Rewriting Scripture in Second Temple Times* (Grand Rapids, MI: Eerdmans, 2008). I am grateful to the author for making a prepublication version of one chapter available to me. Since Ps.-Aristeas does not say which passages get included in phylacteries, I am not concerned here with the forms of the text and whether they are sectarian or not. For these issues, see Schiffman, "Phylacteries and Mezuzot," 2.676; G. Vermes, "Pre-mishnaic Worship and the Phylacteries from the Dead Sea," *VT* 9 (1959) 65–72; E. Eshel, "4QDeut[n]—A Text That Has Undergone Harmonistic Editing," *HUCA* 62 (1991) 117–53; G.J. Brooke, "Deuteronomy 5–6 in the Phylacteries from Qumran Cave 4," *Emanuel: Studies in Hebrew Bible, Septuagint, and Dead Sea Scrolls in Honor of Emanuel Tov* (S.M. Paul et al., eds.; VTSup 94; Leiden: Brill, 2003) 57–70.

κατασκευάζω occur with relative frequency as all-purpose words in *Aristeas*, and they have a range of meanings, usually "prepare" or "construct." So, for example, in §2 a "pure disposition of mind" is "fashioned/prepared" (κατασκευάζεται). In §17, Aristeas prays that God would "dispose/prepare (κατασκευάσαι) the mind" of the king to grant his request for the release of the Jewish slaves. Paragraph 76 refers to the "construction" (κατασκευήν) of the bowls sent by the king to the high priest Eleazar. In §160, these "provisions" most likely refer to the Mosaic Law, which enables the Jew to judge properly and to observe the "divine and incomprehensible interchange" between waking and sleeping. In this case, Ps.-Aristeas apparently is referring to the entire corpus of commandments that God has provided for the Jews. Yet, the repetition of κελεύει δέ, "and he commanded," in both §159 and §160 probably indicates that Ps.-Aristeas thought of the two paragraphs as separate divine commands, even though they are linked together in Deuteronomy. The meaning of κατασκευάς, then, in §160 would appear to have no bearing on how we understand §159, especially regarding the identity of specific texts contained in the phylacteries.

"He has commanded"—*Aristeas* and the Sources of Jewish Ritual Practice

When I initially began to look at the three paragraphs under investigation in this article, I was attracted by the question of whether the phrase τὰ λόγια gave any indication that Ps.-Aristeas was aware of a specific corpus of texts that would have been included either in mezuzot or phylacteries. No clear answer to that question emerges from the discussions above. The question that does emerge more forcefully is how the descriptions of these ritual practices relate to the biblical passages from which they most likely derived. Certainly Ps.-Aristeas has a notion of scripture. As we looked at the meaning of τὰ λόγια in §158, we saw that the likelihood is that he understood the Jewish scriptural tradition as comprised of acts of divine speech which were given in written form by the lawgiver, Moses. This conclusion finds some additional confirmation in §155, where Ps.-Aristeas, commenting on the relationship between memory and Jewish food laws about cud-chewing animals, offers a passage from what he calls scripture (γραφή). Yet, even here he connects a term for writing with an act of divine speech: διὸ παρακελεύεται καὶ διὰ τῆς γραφῆς ὁ λέγων οὕτως ("Therefore he also exhorts us through the scripture, when he says...").[24]

In the paragraphs before us, however, the references in *Aristeas* are far from what could be called citations. Indeed, we find similar circumstances elsewhere in the work. Perhaps the best places to look for comparison are the descriptions of the high priest's garments and of the table prepared by the king as a gift for the Jewish Temple. In his description of the high priest's garments (§§96–9), Ps.-Aristeas does know the names of the major pieces of high priestly clothing and their decoration. So, for example, he reports that the χιτῶν has golden bells and pomegranates on its hem. He also says that the priest wears a κίδαρις and a μίτρα on his head. Yet, despite what scholars see as allusions to almost the entirety of Exodus 28, only a select few words or short phrases appear in both the biblical passage and in *Aristeas*. The same holds true of the description of the table for the Temple. Almost the entire description (§§51–72) differs completely from the text of the LXX, with only a few phrases matching the language of the Greek Bible. Two examples will suffice here to illustrate the situation. In §57, the measurements of the table are give as δύο γὰρ πήχεων τὸ μῆκος πήχεος δὲ τὸ εὖρος, τὸ δὲ ὕψος πήχεος καὶ ἡμίσους συνετέλουν ("So they fashioned [it] two cubits in length and a cubit in width and a cubit and a half in height").[25] These measurements match the language of Exodus almost exactly, except for the last phrase, which Exodus has as ἡμίσους τὸ ὕψος. Immediately following this clause, *Aristeas*'s description turns to the materials used to construct the table. *Aristeas* agrees with the LXX and Josephus against the MT when it reports that that the table was made "of pure gold" (χρυσίου δοκίμου). Even here, however, where *Aristeas* agrees with the LXX's description of the table, the text differs from the exact wording of the LXX. Whereas *Aristeas* uses the adjective δοκίμου, the LXX modifies the noun with καθαροῦ.[26]

The range of examples cited above in §§57, 96–9 and 158–60 are typical of *Aristeas*, and they suggest that even though we do not find

---

[24] The quotation, however, does not come from any one place, but looks like a combination and adaptation of Deut 7:18 and 10:21.

[25] The phrase πήχεος δὲ τὸ εὖρος does not appear in manuscripts of *Aristeas*, but in the estimation of most scholars, it has dropped out accidentally in the process of transmission and does belong in the text. See, Pelletier, *Lettre d'Aristée*, 134.

[26] While the two adjectives can be translated roughly as synonyms here, the manuscript tradition of Exodus does not contain δοκίμου anywhere as a variant of καθαροῦ.

direct citation of the Greek Jewish scriptures, Ps.-Aristeas probably knew them. These examples also point to larger concerns in *Aristeas*. Recently two scholars have argued that the story of the Exodus plays an important and central role in shaping the narrative in *Aristeas*. S. Honigman has identified three scenes that she calls the "Exodus paradigm"—the freeing of the Jewish slaves, the selection of the 72 translators, and the community reception of the translation—by which Ps.-Aristeas claims scriptural status for the Greek translation of the Law.[27] Going much farther than Honigman, A. Kovelman contends that *Aristeas* "includes all the major contents of the Exodus, from Egyptian enslavement of the Jews to the gift of Torah on Mount Sinai, from the construction of the tabernacle to the banquets of the elders. What looks like digression on the surface is the real essence inside."[28] Whether one agrees with Honigman or Kovelman on how influential the Exodus is in *Aristeas*, it clearly frames a number of important features of the story, even if Ps.-Aristeas does not appear interested in citing the biblical form of the narrative directly.

Thus, when talking about the relationship of *Aristeas* to the LXX, two basic questions seem to confront the interpreter. First, how do we understand the role of this "big picture" in which the Exodus story seems so critical to the way that Ps.-Aristeas composed his narrative? Second, to what degree can we speak of Ps.-Aristeas being dependent on the text of the LXX for individual passages or sections?

Despite the fact that Ps.-Aristeas portrays the LXX as a *text*, indeed *an authoritative text derived from an authoritative text*, he also appears heavily invested in the oral nature of the Jewish scriptures as acts of divine speech. This portrayal of scripture (γραφή) as originating or grounded in divine speech might provide some entrée into thinking about the bigger picture. Writing about ancient texts and scribal education, D.M. Carr, in his recent book *Writing on the Tablet of the Heart*, argues:

> The fundamental idea is the following: as we look at how key texts like the Bible and other classic literature functioned in ancient cultures, what was primary was not how such texts were inscribed on clay, parchment, or papyri. Rather what was truly crucial was how those written media were part of a cultural project of incising key cultural-religious traditions—word

---

[27] S. Honigman, *The Septuagint and Homeric Scholarship* (London/New York: Routledge, 2003).

[28] A. Kovelman, *Between Alexandria and Jerusalem: The Dynamic of Jewish and Hellenistic Culture* (Brill Reference Library of Judaism 21; Leiden: Brill, 2005) 131.

for word—*on people's minds*...Scribal recollection of early traditions was assured partly through teaching students to read and reproduce written copies of the key traditions. Nevertheless the aim of the educational process was ultimately the scribe's memorization of the cultural tradition and cultivation of his (or occasionally her) ability to perform it.[29]

For Carr, in antiquity there was a complex and sophisticated interplay between orality and literacy even in cultures where literacy and textuality were widespread. Despite the traditional attempt to identify dependence on a written text, *Aristeas* might well testify to the importance of the text inscribed on the heart of the scribe, that is, the text's author, who in his work "performs" the biblical text by embedding it as the foundation and frame of his story of the translation of the Mosaic Law and thereby, by his mastery of the text, manipulates and shapes it in the performance. In Carr's estimation, we should not necessarily look to *Aristeas* to reproduce the exact text of the LXX, even though the work's author almost certainly knew it. In fact, his ability to manipulate the LXX within the context of his own work testifies to his mastery of the biblical text. Might we see in his performance reflections of the LXX text in *Aristeas*? Of course we might, and indeed we should probably expect them. The ancient scribe who learned and performed the text was not necessarily or even primarily interested in a reproduction of the text within another work, even if he had indeed memorized and mastered the text he now performed.

The work of H. Najman offers a slightly different, but not necessarily an unrelated, lens through which we might view this set of issues, particularly the way that *Aristeas* treats the Mosaic Law. Najman identifies in Jewish antiquity what she calls a Mosaic Discourse, a discourse tied to a founder, which, beginning with the biblical book of Deuteronomy, ascribes an expanded role to Moses and recognizes an authoritative law that comes to be known as the Torah of Moses.[30] Najman writes about Mosaic Discourse:

> The idea of a discourse tied to a founder provides, I want to suggest, a helpful way to think about the developing conceptions of the Mosaic Law and figure of Moses. On this understanding of a discourse tied to a founder, to rework an earlier text is to update, interpret and develop the

---

[29] D.M. Carr, *Writing on the Tablet of the Heart: Origins of Scripture and Literature* (New York: Oxford, 2005) 8–9.

[30] H. Najman, *Seconding Sinai: The Development of Mosaic Discourse in Second Temple Judaism* (JSJSup 77; Leiden: Brill, 2003).

content of that text in a way that one claims to be an authentic expression of the law already accepted as authoritatively Mosaic. Thus, when what *we* might call a "new" law—perhaps even what we might regard as a significant "amendment" of older law—is characterized as the Law of Moses, this is not to imply that it is to be found within the actual words of an historical individual called Moses. It is rather to say that the implementation of the law in question would enable Israel to return to the authentic teaching associated with the prophetic status of Moses.[31]

She further argues that a participant in Mosaic Discourse incorporates a number of specific features: (1) a text that expands or reworks older Mosaic traditions "claims for itself the authority that already attaches to those traditions;" (2) "[t]he new text ascribes to itself the status of Torah;" (3) "[t]he new text is said to be a re-presentation of the revelation at Sinai;" (4) "the new text is said to be associated with, or produced by, the founding figure, Moses."[32] While Ps.-Aristeas does not make these claims about his own narrative, he does make them about the Septuagint. So, in the case of Eleazar's *apologia*, and more broadly his claims about the LXX, one could claim that *Aristeas* is a participant in Mosaic Discourse.

What I find especially helpful in Najman's work is the notion of the development of a discourse tied to a founder, which shifts our focus from the particular textual details of agreement or disagreement between *Aristeas* and the LXX to the manner in which Ps.-Aristeas employs what he understands to be Mosaic Law in the service of his larger aims. Thus, through Eleazar's *apologia* for the Law, one of Ps.-Aristeas's concerns is to identify those things that distinguish Jews from Gentiles—they do not worship idols and they follow a set of divinely given laws, most visibly having to do with food—while at the same time he argues that Jewish values are consistent with and even superior to those of the dominant Hellenistic culture, since these laws are intended to remind Jews of their moral obligations to God.

So, even as we note in *Aristeas* §§158–60 the similarities with and differences from the biblical text concerning the ritual practices of the fringes, mezuzot and phylacteries, we are reminded that our conception of what a biblical text is and how it ought to be used probably differs from that of *Aristeas*'s author. These paragraphs fit into larger agendas

---

[31] Ibid., 13.
[32] Ibid., 16–7.

being played out in *Aristeas*—for example, the scriptural status of the Septuagint and the relationship of Jews to Hellenistic culture.

Nevertheless as scholars try to understand Jewish ritual practice in the Second Temple period, these three paragraphs in the *Letter of Aristeas* will continue to constitute primary evidence for Jewish observance of aspects of Mosaic legislation. Combined with the evidence of the phylacteries and mezuzot from Qumran, the evidence from *Aristeas* helps us to fill in a few more of the details.

INDEX OF PASSAGES

HEBREW BIBLE

Apocrypha

<h2 style="text-align:center">EARLY JEWISH LITERATURE</h2>

CLASSICAL LITERATURE

INDEX OF SUBJECTS